# MAMMOTH BOOK OF FUN & GAMES

Here are 500 pages chock full of alfabits, quizzes, parlor tricks, pencil games, dice games, word games, crosswords, puzzles, jokes, across-tics, threezies, and many other kinds of entertainment for the whole family.

This is a book to be indulged in for months, with material for every kind of mood. And all of it is first-rate and challenging.

# MAMMOTH
## BOOK OF
## FUN & GAMES

*Richard B. Manchester*

HART PUBLISHING COMPANY, INC.
NEW YORK CITY

COPYRIGHT © 1977, HART PUBLISHING COMPANY, INC.
NEW YORK, NEW YORK 10012

ISBN NO. 08055-0301-3
LIBRARY OF CONGRESS CATALOG CARD NO. 76-44993

MANUFACTURED IN THE UNITED STATES OF AMERICA

**4**

# CONTENTS

6

# MAMMOTH BOOK
# OF FUN & GAMES

# EAT, DRINK, AND BE MERRY

On this and the following page, you will find 52 expressions, phrases, and song or story titles. Each of these contains the name of some food or drink. How many goodies can you fill in?

A score of 33 is just peachy; 42 is a whale of a score; and 47 or more puts you at the top of the heap.

*Answers on page 464*

1. The _____ is as high as an elephant's eye

2. _____ of human kindness

3. Yes, we have no _____

4. The queen of hearts, she ate some _____

5. _____ hill

6. _____ house of the August moon

7. Of _____ and kings

8. You can catch more flies with _____ than with _____

9. _____ in the straw

10. _____ are jumpin' and the cotton is high

11. _____ and roses

12. Slower than _____

13. _____'s Peak

14. Partridge in a _____ tree

15. In the shade of the old _____ tree

16. Mrs. Murphy's _____

17. _____ barrel polka

18. Don't put all your _____ in one basket

19. That won't cut the _____

20. _____ of the crop

21. _____ 'n' _____ 'n' everything nice

22. What's your _____?

23. Eating his Christmas _____

24. To _____ in your own juice

25. Life is just a bowl of _____

26. Jack and the _____ stalk

27. _____ tree, very pretty

28. Red as a _____

29. _____ drum

30. To work for _____

31. The princess and the _____

32. Under the spreading _____ tree

33. The _____ of wrath

34. _____ boats are comin'

35. He stuck in his thumb and pulled out a _____

36. Georgia _____

37. _____ Little

38. You're the cream in my _____

39. A jug of _____, a loaf of _____, and thou

40. The moon is made of green _____

41. Big rock _____ mountain

42. Sermons and _____ the day after

43. One _____, two _____

44. _____ actor

45. Pease _____ hot

46. _____ house

47. Candy is dandy, but _____ is quicker

48. _____ to you

49. I don't care a _____ about that

50. _____ blossom special

51. Bringing home the _____

52. The proof is in the _____

# IT'S THE LITTLE THINGS
# THAT COUNT

Below, you will find 50 familiar expressions, each containing the word LITTLE. Fill in the blanks with the appropriate word or phrase which completes the expression.

A score of 30 is fair; 35, good; 40, excellent; and 45 is just dandy.

*Answers on page 464*

1. Little Miss _____

2. Try a little _____

3. In my little corner of _____

4. A little bit of _____

5. Little things mean _____

6. Hush, little baby, don't _____

7. It only _____ for a little while

8. A little learning is a _____

9. Where oh where has my little _____ gone

10. Little Annie _____

11. It's just a little street where old _____ meet

12. I'm called little _____

13. Every little movement has a meaning all _____

14. Say a little _____ for me

15. Daddy's little _____

16. Those little white _____

17. Suffer little _____ to come unto me

18. Little Big _____

19. Mighty oaks from little _____ grow

20. My little brown _____

21. And a little child shall _____ them

22. There was little girl and she had a little ⎯⎯⎯⎯⎯⎯⎯⎯⎯⎯

23. O little town of ⎯⎯⎯⎯⎯⎯⎯⎯⎯⎯

24. Little strokes fell great ⎯⎯⎯⎯⎯⎯⎯⎯⎯⎯

25. Little ⎯⎯⎯⎯⎯⎯⎯⎯⎯⎯ have big ears

26. Little old ⎯⎯⎯⎯⎯⎯⎯⎯⎯⎯

27. Mary had a little ⎯⎯⎯⎯⎯⎯⎯⎯⎯⎯

28. Little boys are made of ⎯⎯⎯⎯⎯⎯ and ⎯⎯⎯⎯⎯⎯

29. The fog comes on little ⎯⎯⎯⎯⎯⎯⎯⎯⎯⎯

30. Thank heaven for little ⎯⎯⎯⎯⎯⎯⎯⎯⎯⎯

31. When he is worst, he is little better than a ⎯⎯⎯⎯⎯⎯⎯⎯⎯⎯

32. Little boats should keep ⎯⎯⎯⎯⎯⎯⎯⎯⎯⎯

33. Little Boy Blue, come blow ⎯⎯⎯⎯⎯⎯⎯⎯⎯⎯

34. Little ⎯⎯⎯⎯⎯⎯⎯⎯⎯⎯ sat in a corner

35. Little ⎯⎯⎯⎯⎯⎯⎯⎯⎯⎯, who made thee?

36. A little ⎯⎯⎯⎯⎯⎯⎯⎯⎯⎯ and soon hot

37. Men who ⎯⎯⎯⎯⎯⎯⎯⎯⎯⎯ much say little

38. The little old lady from ⎯⎯⎯⎯⎯⎯⎯⎯⎯⎯

39. Little ⎯⎯⎯⎯⎯⎯⎯⎯⎯⎯ has lost her sheep

40. He is always a ⎯⎯⎯⎯⎯⎯⎯⎯⎯⎯ who cannot live on little

41. Little ⎯⎯⎯⎯⎯⎯⎯⎯⎯⎯ on the Prairie

42. Little goody ⎯⎯⎯⎯⎯⎯⎯⎯⎯⎯

43. The little ⎯⎯⎯⎯⎯⎯⎯⎯⎯⎯ that could

44. A little ⎯⎯⎯⎯⎯⎯⎯⎯⎯⎯ told me

45. Big fish in a little ⎯⎯⎯⎯⎯⎯⎯⎯⎯⎯

46. Ye of little ⎯⎯⎯⎯⎯⎯⎯⎯⎯⎯

47. Little ⎯⎯⎯⎯⎯⎯⎯⎯⎯⎯ Annie

48. A Little Night ⎯⎯⎯⎯⎯⎯⎯⎯⎯⎯

49. My Little ⎯⎯⎯⎯⎯⎯⎯⎯⎯⎯

50. God's Little ⎯⎯⎯⎯⎯⎯⎯⎯⎯⎯

# AROUND THE HOUSE

Below, you will find 24 familiar expressions. Complete each one by filling in the blank with the name of a household item; for example, sweep the dirt under the *rug*.

A score of 12 is passing; 18 is good; 22, superb.

*Answers on page 464*

1. Old _____'s got me

2. A new _____ sweeps clean

3. You turned the _____ on me

4. Skeleton in the _____

5. All alone by the _____

6. Home on the _____

7. Everything but the _____

8. _____, Iowa

9. Polly, put the _____ on

10. Little _____ have big ears

11. _____, _____, on the wall

12. Out of the _____ and into the fire

13. Blue-_____ special

14. Rub-a-dub-dub, three men in a _____

15. Heavenly _____ of night are falling

16. _____ of Vital Statistics

17. The _____ ran away with the spoon

18. Strike while the _____ is hot

19. Oil for the _____ of China

20. Ring down the _____

21. Life is just a _____ of cherries

22. April _____

23. Lay your head upon my _____

24. The _____ was bare

# FANFARE

Below, you will find 20 words, phrases, or expressions. Each one of these should suggest to you an expression which contains the word FAN. The dashes correspond to the letters that are missing. For example, *whimsical* or *capricious* is FAN ciful.

If you get 11 right, you're doing fine; 14 is excellent; and 17 is an outstanding score.

*Answers on page 464*

1.  FAN _ _ _ _ _                    Lively Spanish dance

2.  FAN _ _ _ _ _ _                  Without amorous attachment

3.  _ _ _ _ _ FAN _                  Jack London novel

4.  FAN _ _ _ _  _ _ _ _             Noted Boston building

5.  FAN  _ _ _ _                     Letters sent to public figures

6.  _ _ FAN _                        Newborn baby

7.  FAN _ _  _ _ _ _                 John Cleland novel

8.  _ _ _ _ _  _ _ _  _ _ _ _ _ _
        FAN _ _ _ _ _ _             Dance

9.  FAN _ _ _ _                      Imagination; hallucination

10. FAN _ _ _ _                      Exhibiting excessive enthusiasm

11. FAN _ _  _ _ _ _ _               Well-known comedienne and singer of yesteryear

12. _ _ FAN _ _ _                    Foot soldiers

13. FAN- _ _ _                       Chinese gambling game

14. FAN  _ _ _  _ _ _ _ _            Incite

15. _ _ _ FAN _                      Secular; impure; irreverent

16. FAN _ _  _ _ _                   Showy fellow; skillful boxer

17. FAN _ _ _ _ _                    Disney movie

18. FAN _ _ _ _                      Girl in *Les Miserables*

19. FAN _ _ _ _ _ _
        _ _ _ _ _ _                  Science fiction movie of 1960's

20. FAN _ _ _ _                      Chair style

# BODY ENGLISH

Below, you will find 24 familiar expressions or titles. Complete each one by filling in the blank with the name of a part of the body; for example, you go to my *head*.

A score of 16 is run-of-the-mill; 20 is good; and 23 is superb.

*Answers on page 464*

1. All _____ on deck

2. The _____ of Darkness

3. Rings on her _____, bells on her _____

4. I've got you under my _____

5. Mine _____ have seen the glory

6. By the skin of our _____

7. Little pitchers have big _____

8. _____ and bacon

9. _____ of clay

10. Keep your _____ up

11. A well-turned _____

12. Stick your _____ out

13. _____ grease

14. Was this the _____ that launched a thousand ships?

15. _____ in cheek

16. A lump in the _____

17. Rule of _____

18. Pot _____ stove

19. Fallen _____

20. _____ Diamond

21. The long _____ of the law

22. Community _____

23. The golden _____

24. Put your head on my _____

# THE NIGHT GAME

Below, you will find 21 words, phrases, and expressions. Each should suggest an expression which contains the word NIGHT. For example, *a frightening dream is a* NIGHT *mare.*

A score of 12 is average; 15 is quite good; and 18 is outstanding.

*Answers on page 464*

1.  Shady; irresponsible; transitory    _____
2.  1967 film starring Rod Steiger and Sidney Poitier    _____
3.  Garment designed for wear in bed    _____
4.  The activity of after-dark pleasure seekers    _____
5.  Cole Porter song from *Gay Divorcée*    _____
6.  English nurse known as "The Lady with the Lamp"    _____
7.  Beatle film and album    _____
8.  Stopover; single performance    _____
9.  Eugene O'Neill play    _____
10. Shakespeare comedy featuring Sir Toby Belch    _____
11. F. Scott Fitzgerald novel    _____
12. Famous Rembrandt painting    _____
13. Restaurant open after dark, with music and dancing    _____
14. Popular Yuletide poem    _____
15. Refreshment taken at bedtime    _____
16. Shakespeare comedy featuring Puck    _____
17. Tennessee Williams play    _____
18. Musical by Stephen Sondheim    _____
19. Belladonna    _____
20. The tales of Scheherazade    _____
21. Narrative poem by Longfellow    _____

# HORSING AROUND

Below, you will find 15 words, phrases, and expressions. Each should suggest an expression which contains the word HORSE. For example, *to beat with a strap* is to HORSE whip.

A score of 9 is not bad; 11 is above average; and 14 is dandy.

*Answers on page 465*

1. 1932 Marx Brothers' movie, set in an American college         _____

2. Trade offered by Richard III at Bosworth Field; famous quote from Shakespeare's *Richard III*, V, iv, 7         _____

3. National symbol of the Saxons; a popular brand of Scotch         _____

4. A different matter; something of a different nature         _____

5. Derisive response to early automobile riders         _____

6. Reprimand advising one not to question favors         _____

7. 1969 movie about dance marathons during the Depression, starring Jane Fonda         _____

8. Gymnastics apparatus used for vaulting         _____

9. Mask; pretense; in politics, a candidate put forward to split the opposition         _____

10. Person undertaking arduous labor         _____

11. Flying insect         _____

12. Nut producing tree; reddish-yellow color         _____

13. An unknown; in politics, a candidate unexpectedly nominated         _____

14. Colossal figure used by the ancient Greeks as a strategem of war         _____

15. Instinctive, practical judgment         _____

# THE CAT GAME

Below, you will find 18 words, phrases, and expressions. Each should suggest an expression which contains the word CAT. For example, *a tragic event or disaster* is a CAT astrophe.

A score of 12 is okay; 14 is good; and 16 is super.

*Answers on page 465*

1. Short story by Edgar Allan Poe   _____

2. Finger game played with string   _____

3. Given to malicious gossip; slyly spiteful   _____

4. American suffragist   _____

5. Whip for chastisement of youngsters   _____

6. Underground cemetery; tombs of Christian martyrs in Rome   _____

7. Mechanical device used to hurl rocks, arrows, spears, etc. as weapons   _____

8. The best; the epitome   _____

9. Unable to speak; taciturn   _____

10. Prosperous businessman   _____

11. Play by Tennessee Williams; movie starring Elizabeth Taylor and Paul Newman   _____

12. Old European coin   _____

13. List; complete enumeration of items   _____

14. State of total inactivity brought on by mental disorder, characterized by blank stare   _____

15. Derisive cry, usually directed at a performer   _____

16. Tell a secret; reveal a confidence   _____

17. Mountain area of New York State   _____

18. Character in *Alice in Wonderland* known for his wide grin   _____

# TAKE IT TO HEART

Below, you will find 23 words, phrases, and expressions. Each should suggest an expression which contains the word HEART. For example, *sincerely or genuinely* is whole HEART edly.

A score of 13 is fair; 16 is above average; and 20 is superlative.

*Answers on page 465*

1.  Vital center or driving impulse     _____

2.  Area of decisive importance     _____

3.  Anguish; sorrow     _____

4.  Pleasantly moving or stirring     _____

5.  Novel by Nathaniel West     _____

6.  Area in front of a fireplace     _____

7.  The deepest emotions or affections     _____

8.  Sincere, frank discussion     _____

9.  Causing intense grief, anguish, or pain _____

10. To commit to memory     _____

11. Tony Bennett recording     _____

12. Profoundly felt; earnest     _____

13. Edgar Allan Poe short story     _____

14. Cloying expressions of endearment     _____

15. Generous and kindly     _____

16. Beatle recording     _____

17. Discourage; depress     _____

18. To envy or regret deeply     _____

19. Darling; lover     _____

20. Movie starring Alan Arkin     _____

21. Callous; unsympathetic     _____

22. Graham Green novel     _____

23. Ailment caused by excess stomach acid     _____

# MOONGAZING

Below, you will find 23 words, phrases, and expressions. Each should suggest an expression which contains the word MOON. For example, *a vacation by newlyweds* is a honeyMOON.

A score of 12 is fair; 16 is superior; and 20 is stupendous.

*Answers on page 465*

1.  Movie starring Betty Grable     _____

2.  Well-known Beethoven work     _____

3.  Song by Henry Mancini     _____

4.  Comic strip character     _____

5.  Henry Hudson's ship     _____

6.  Song by Rogers and Hart     _____

7.  Very infrequently     _____

8.  Chinese pastry     _____

9.  Illegally distilled corn whiskey     _____

10. Movie starring Marlon Brando     _____

11. Ray of a certain night light     _____

12. Hold two jobs at once     _____

13. September celestial phenomenon     _____

14. Play by Eugene O'Neill     _____

15. Aimless reverie; vacuous contemplation     _____

16. Detective novel by Wilkie Collins     _____

17. Novel by Somerset Maugham     _____

18. Novel by Jules Verne     _____

19. Song by Glenn Miller     _____

20. Fancied celestial figure of a face     _____

21. Walt Disney movie     _____

22. Movie starring Ryan O'Neal; song of the 1930's     _____

23. Bossa nova hit of the 1960's     _____

# NO HOLDS BARRED

Below, you will find 21 expressions or definitions. Each one of these should suggest a word or phrase which contains the word BAR. For example, *a man who serves drinks* is a BARtender.

A score of 11 is average; 14 is excellent; and 17 is extraordinary.

*Answers on page 465*

1. Star of *Funny Girl*             _____

2. Primitive; savage; uncivilized   _____

3. Bonnie and Clyde's gang were known by this name   _____

4. Outdoor cooking   _____

5. One who cuts hair   _____

6. Drug taken to induce sleep   _____

7. Well-known English financial institution   _____

8. Professional poet or singer   _____

9. Voracious giant fish of southern waters   _____

10. Grain used for feeding stock; a cereal   _____

11. Woman who serves drinks   _____

12. Without exception   _____

13. To begin on a journey   _____

14. Robber released by Pontius Pilate instead of Jesus   _____

15. To discomfit or disconcert   _____

16. Block of chocolate, sometimes with nuts   _____

17. Round bulging wooden vessel; cask   _____

18. Female founder of the Red Cross   _____

19. Iron or steel tool used as a pry   _____

20. Eject from the lawyers' association   _____

21. Governmental edict prohibiting departure or entry of certain ships at ports   _____

# A RUN FOR YOUR MONEY

Below, you will find 19 expressions or definitions. Each one of these should suggest a word or phrase which contains the word RUN. For example, *a person who comes in second in a contest* is a RUNNer-up.

A score of 10 is fine; 13 is superior; and 16 is exceptional.

*Answers on page 465*

1.  Person who leaves home and disappears      _____

2.  Site of initial Civil War battle      _____

3.  A try-out      _____

4.  Eventually; in the course of time      _____

5.  Film directed by and starring Woody Allen      _____

6.  Tired; worn out      _____

7.  To campaign for election      _____

8.  To meet unexpectedly      _____

9.  Ordinary; average      _____

10. To go through an ordeal at many hands; Indian physical trial      _____

11. A light motorboat      _____

12. Expression advising someone to escape from mortal danger as swiftly as possible      _____

13. Have a fever      _____

14. Slang expression meaning to show marked superiority over      _____

15. To come to an end of; to exhaust      _____

16. Level strip on which airplanes land      _____

17. A late breakfast; combination of first meal and mid-day meal      _____

18. Author of "guys and dolls" stories      _____

19. Predecessor or precursor      _____

# THE GAME OF MAN

Below, you will find 36 words, phrases, or expressions. Each should suggest an expression or word which contains the word MAN. For example, *a raving lunatic* is a MANiac.

A score of 20 is okay; 25 is pretty good; and 30 is super.

*Answers on page 466*

1. Most important of New York's five boroughs _____

2. An aperture in the pavement through which workmen enter _____

3. Rudyard Kipling story recently made into a film starring Michael Caine and Sean Connery _____

4. A large West African baboon _____

5. To have fingernails trimmed and polished _____

6. 1960's novel by Claude Brown _____

7. A facing of stone, wood, or marble above the fireplace _____

8. Food miraculously provided for the Israelites in the desert _____

9. Human beings as a species _____

10. 1960's film about Thomas More's conflict with King Henry VIII _____

11. Public official under the Chinese empire _____

12. Stringed musical instrument similar to a lute _____

13. Author of *The Magic Mountain* and *Death in Venice* _____

14. Required; obligatory _____

15. Richard Condon novel (1974) about a victim of brainwashing _____

16. Supervisor of a construction crew _____

17. Constituents' wishes expressed through an election _____

18. Title of Rudyard Kipling poem (1892) _____

19. Public declaration of policy or opinion _____

20. Speech in which Abraham Lincoln freed the slaves _____

21. Metallic element used in making glass, paint, medicine _____

22. Handcuffs _____

23. Director or administrator _____

24. Spanish veil or scarf worn by women _____

25. Short story by Edward Everett Hale _____

26. Small explanatory book or pamphlet _____

27. Unprinted book or paper, typed or handwritten _____

28. Factory owner or one who produces goods _____

29. Poem by Edwin Markham _____

30. Historical novel of the 18th century by Sir Walter Scott _____

31. Birthplace of Virgil in Italy _____

32. Hit song from Gershwin's *Porgy and Bess* _____

33. Waste products of animals; also fertilizer _____

34. Clothing model in store windows _____

35. Large industrial city in Lancashire, England _____

36. Use someone skillfully to one's own advantage _____

# DOUBLE TROUBLE

Double trouble words are paired words which rhyme or sound similar to each other when pronounced, or are even identical.

Below you will find 15 definitions for such words, with a blank supplied for each letter of the correct answer. For example, *to be indecisive* is to <u>s</u> <u>h</u> <u>i</u> <u>l</u> <u>l</u> <u>y</u> - <u>s</u> <u>h</u> <u>a</u> <u>l</u> <u>l</u> <u>y</u>.

How many of these words can you find? A score of 8 is good; 10 is even better; and 12 words marks you as a whiz kid.

*Answers on page 466*

1. A delicate morsel of food     <u>T</u> _ _ <u>B</u> _ _
2. A griddle cake     <u>S</u> _ _ _ <u>J</u> _ _ _
3. The sound made by a ringing bell     <u>D</u> _ _ _    <u>D</u> _ _ _
4. Short and pudgy     <u>R</u> _ _ _    <u>P</u> _ _ _
5. To make designs on fabric in many colors     <u>T</u> _ _ - <u>D</u> _ _
6. Receptacle for hitch-hiker's belongings     <u>B</u> _ _ _    <u>P</u> _ _ _
7. Upside-down     <u>T</u> _ _ _ _ - <u>T</u> _ _ _ _
8. Uproar and turmoil     <u>H</u> _ _ _ _ - <u>B</u> _ _ _ _
9. Indian term meaning conference or meeting     <u>P</u> _ _ - <u>W</u> _ _ _
10. Native Hawaiian dance     <u>H</u> _ _ _ - <u>H</u> _ _ _
11. Plank for children's play     <u>S</u> _ _ - <u>S</u> _ _
12. To retrace your steps     <u>B</u> _ _ _ <u>T</u> _ _ _ _
13. To waste time; delay; trifle     <u>D</u> _ _ _ _ - <u>D</u> _ _ _ _
14. The metallic ringing sounds of Hades     <u>H</u> _ _ _ _'   <u>B</u> _ _ _ _
15. An equal division     <u>E</u> _ _ _    <u>S</u> _ _ _ _ _

# THE PEN GAME

Below you will find 19 words, phrases, or expressions. Each should suggest an expression or word which contains the word PEN. For example, *a roof-top apartment* is a PENthouse.

A score of 10 is fair; 13 is above average; and 16 is outstanding.

*Answers on page 466*

1. A strip of land, surrounded on three sides by water  _____

2. Ulysses' faithful wife  _____

3. Intestinal organ frequently the site of an inflammation.  _____

4. Public amusement area featuring coin-operated games  _____

5. In a thoughtful mood  _____

6. Imminent; about to occur  _____

7. The last but one of a series  _____

8. Seaport in southwest Florida  _____

9. To pierce or perforate  _____

10. To begin; not closed  _____

11. Mideastern state; home of the Liberty Bell  _____

12. A strong liking or fondness for something  _____

13. Extreme poverty  _____

14. Condensed summary; short collection  _____

15. Swinging part of a grandfather clock  _____

16. A frugal, stingy person  _____

17. Island off the coast of northwest Malaya  _____

18. Emotion held to the breaking point  _____

19. To develop; to reach maturity  _____

# HOMONYMS

Homonyms are words which sound alike, but which have different meanings and are spelled differently; for example, the words *deer* and *dear*.

Below, you will find 36 sentences, each containing a blank line representing a missing word. The blank line is followed by a word in parentheses. The word supplied and the missing word sound alike, but are spelled differently. Fill in the correct homonyms in the space provided.

A score of 20 is good; 28 is grand; and 32 is superduper.

*Answers on page 466*

1. He was considered a prophet and _____ (sear) when his book was published.

2. That was his _____ (forth) touchdown this season.

3. Every girl dreams of a handsome escort, her own _____ (bow).

4. The new school will be on that wooded _____ (sight).

5. Her ring contains a three- _____ (carrot) diamond.

6. The minister had written a moving _____ (him).

7. My favorite _____ (whether) comes in Indian Summer.

8. There was a short _____ (paws) while he collected his thoughts.

9. After a while, she began to sense she had over- _____ (staid) her welcome.

10. Every woman loves a _____ (complement).

11. The astronaut's _____ (dissent) was smooth.

12. Every day she _____ (past) the house where she was born.

13. During the King's _____ (rain), many new laws were propagated.

14. That's where our _____ (knew) house will be.

15. The countess was _____ (feign) to put on her glasses.

16. Queen Elizabeth is often seen wearing a _____ (rough).

17. After backbreaking labor, his whole body felt _____ (soar).

18. He was required to have his parents' _____ (ascent).

19. All that glitters is not _____ (guilt).

20. The student from France liked to wear a blue _____ (bask) beret.

21. The mother ran out to _____ (shoe) the flies away from her baby.

22. My sister mistook the cries of the Koala _____ (bare) for the cries of her own infant.

23. Her child had been born with a _____ (call).

24. Seeing the car on the wrong side of the road, she hit the _____ (break).

25. He crossed the _____ (plane) on horseback.

26. In many countries, people wait in _____ (cues) for buses.

27. Every day, his wife waited eagerly for the _____ (male).

28. The old woman was in the _____ (throws) of despair.

29. She loved to shop at _____ (sails).

30. The fawn seemed to sense the danger and ran after the _____ (row).

31. Everyone could hear him _____ (grown) as he slowly picked himself up off of the floor.

32. That went over like a _____ (led) balloon.

33. The wind _____ (blue) in from the east.

34. His son insisted he had to have a calculator to get the proper _____ (some).

35. He _____ (least) the apartment to them for one year.

36. The ship was docked along the _____ (peer).

# CLASSROOM BONERS

The original "Classroom Boner" (or as the British say, "Schoolboy Howler") probably dates back to the day that some dumb pupil first touched quill to parchment. Today, these blunders continue to pour forth in great numbers; there seems to be no end to the droll twists students can unintentionally give to the simplest facts.

There is scarcely a teacher in the land who has failed to collect choice specimens of this artless art. What follows is a collection of some of the most priceless student errors ever penned. Each one is an authentic blunder, not a made-up wisecrack—as the utter absurdity of these gems will readily demonstrate.

To collect fumes of sulphur, hold a deacon over a flame in a test tube.

Although the patient had never been fatally ill before, he woke up dead.

The invention of the steamboat caused a network of rivers to spring up.

If one angle of a triangle is more than 90 degrees the triangle is obscene.

Germany is an industrial country because the poor have nothing to do so they make lots and lots of factories.

A polygon with seven sides is called a hooligan.

A triangle inside a circle is called a circumcised triangle.

Zanzibar is noted for its monkeys. The British Governor lives there.

What's a myth?
> *A myth's a female moth.*

Rural life is found mostly in the country.

A cascade is a drink like lemonade that is made in a cask.

Chaucer was a great English poet who wrote many poems and verses and
sometimes wrote literature.

The best way to eat cream cheese and lox is with a beagle.

A martyr is a pile of wood set on fire with a man on top.

Napoleon had three children, not one of whom lived to maternity.

The natives of the Midi, France, were the first to wear middy skirts.

Carton was doing something he had never done before—dying for someone else.

A horse divided against itself cannot stand.

The Pilgrim Fathers were Adam and Eve.

The Trojans rode a wooden horse that said, "Beware the Greeks, asking for lifts."

A psalmist is one who tells fortunes by reading hands.

Joseph Haydn had a lot of will power; he died in 1809 and is still dead.

An executive is the man who puts murderers to death.

One of the most popular fugues was the one between the Hatfields and the McCoys.

Mata Hari means suicide in Japanese.

Robert Louis Stevenson got married and went on his honeymoon. It was then he wrote *Travels with a Donkey*.

The Constitution of the United States was adopted to secure domestic hostility.

Cyanide is so poisonous that one drop of it on a dog's tongue will kill the strongest man.

Faith is that quality which enables us to believe what we know to be untrue.

Chopin had many fast friends. Among the fastest was Miss Sand.

Bach was the most famous composer in the world and so was Handel.

Paganini was a famous fiddler. He fiddled with many of the greatest singers in Europe.

Before a man could become a monk he had to have his tonsils cut.

The government of Athens was democratic because the people made the laws with their own hands.

The government of England is a limited mockery.

A octopus is a person who hopes for the best.

☖

Algebraical symbols are used when you do not know what you are talking about.

☖

When you breathe you inspire. When you do not breathe you expire.

☖

Peter Minuit invented a very popular dance in the Colonial times.

☖

Autobiography is a history of motor cars.

☖

The Bourbons were a French family that used to make whisky.

The general direction of the Alps is up.

☖

Horace Greeley was the worst defeated candidate ever elected.

☖

To pick up courage, he whistled in the dark. After he thus buoyed himself up, he felt like a boy—no longer a child.

☖

A glacier is a man who goes along the street with glass in his hand and puts it in windows.

☖

Burlesque is a kind of take-off.

☖

Shakespeare wrote tragedies, comedies, and errors.

When there are no fresh vegetables you can always get canned.

The difference between a king and a president is that a king is the son of his father, but a president isn't.

Owing to slackness of demand there was a great slut on the market.

A virgin forest is a forest in which the hand of man has never set foot.

A bibliomaniac is a person who reads the Bible incessantly from cover to cover.

Unleavened bread is bread made without any ingredients.

There were no wars in Greece, as the mountains were so high they couldn't climb over to see what their neighbors were doing.

Hansom was a very good looking cab driver.

The people of Uganda don't wear much clothing; they dress like statues.

In many states, murderers are put to death by electrolysis.

Acrimony is what a man gives his divorced wife.

Chivalry is the attitude of a man toward a strange woman.

In Christianity a man can only have one wife. This is called monotony.

To be a good nurse you must be absolutely sterile.

A Shintoist is an original dancer who shakes his shins and his toes.

The Indian squabs carry porpoises on their backs.

What would you do in the case of a man bleeding from a wound in the head?
*I would put a tourniquet around his neck.*

Magna Carta provided that no free man should be hanged twice for the same offense.

Geometry teaches us to bisex angels.

What is the chief cause of divorce?
   *Marriage.*

Herrings go about the sea in shawls.

Emphasis in reading is putting more distress in one place than another.

Illegal parking is staying longer than you should in a place where you are
   not allowed to stay at all.

The benefit of longitude and latitude is that when a man is drowning he can
   call out what latitude and longitude he is in and we can find him.

Homer was not written by Homer but by another man of that name.

A morality play is a play in which the characters are goblins, ghosts, virgins,
   and other supernatural creatures.

Armadillo is the Spanish navy which defeated the Duke of Wellington.

Two popular ancient sports were Antony and Cleopatra.

# HOW TO SOLVE FOUR-LETTER ALFABITS

The idea is to try to form as many words as you can out of the letters which compose the given title.

The answers are governed by the following rules:

1. Words must be composed of four-letter roots. Pluralized three-letter words such as CATS, DOTS, etc., and inflected verb forms such as GOES, SITS, etc., are barred.

2. Only one form or tense of a word may be used—either ABLE or UNABLE, POSE or POSED, BOTTLE or BOTTLES, KEEP or KEEPER, WORTH or WORTHY, etc. In other words, you may use either the noun form or the verb form, either the noun form or the adjective form, but not both.

3. Foreign, obsolete or archaic words are taboo. Reformed spellings are out.

# DANDELIONS

There are at least 36 words, each of four letters or more, that can be made out of the letters in the word DANDELIONS.

If you can fill in the spaces with at least 17 words, that's good; 22 is unquestionably better; 26 is top-notch; and 30 wins you a trophy!

*Answers on page 466*

1. _____
2. _____
3. _____
4. _____
5. _____
6. _____
7. _____
8. _____
9. _____
10. _____
11. _____
12. _____

13. _____
14. _____
15. _____
16. _____
17. _____
18. _____
19. _____
20. _____
21. _____
22. _____
23. _____
24. _____

25. _____
26. _____
27. _____
28. _____
29. _____
30. _____
31. _____
32. _____
33. _____
34. _____
35. _____
36. _____

# GENEALOGY

There are at least 10 words, each of four or more letters, that can be made out of the letters in the word GENEALOGY. How many can you find? List them below.

If you fill in the 10 spaces with 6 words, you're doing just fine; 8 words puts you right on top.

*Answers on page 466*

1. _____   4. _____   8. _____
2. _____   5. _____   9. _____
3. _____   6. _____   10. _____
                     7. _____

# GINGER ALE

There are at least 57 words, each of four letters or more, that can be made out of the letters in the words GINGER ALE.

Finding 33 words means you're really good at this game; 40 indicates exceptional ability; and 48 or more is astonishing.

*Answers on page 466*

1. _____   20. _____   39. _____
2. _____   21. _____   40. _____
3. _____   22. _____   41. _____
4. _____   23. _____   42. _____
5. _____   24. _____   43. _____
6. _____   25. _____   44. _____
7. _____   26. _____   45. _____
8. _____   27. _____   46. _____
9. _____   28. _____   47. _____
10. _____   29. _____   48. _____
11. _____   30. _____   49. _____
12. _____   31. _____   50. _____
13. _____   32. _____   51. _____
14. _____   33. _____   52. _____
15. _____   34. _____   53. _____
16. _____   35. _____   54. _____
17. _____   36. _____   55. _____
18. _____   37. _____   56. _____
19. _____   38. _____   57. _____

41

# SHEEPISHLY

There are at least 15 words, each of four letters or more, that can be made out of the letters in the word SHEEPISHLY.

If you can find 8, that's great; 10 is terrific; and 12 or more is super-duper!

*Answers on page 467*

1. _____     6. _____     11. _____
2. _____     7. _____     12. _____
3. _____     8. _____     13. _____
4. _____     9. _____     14. _____
5. _____    10. _____     15. _____

# IMPLAUSIBLE

There are at least 56 words, each of four letters or more, that can be made out of the letters in the word IMPLAUSIBLE.

If you can fill in the spaces below with at least 35, that's nice; 40 words is nifty; 45 words is first-rate; and 50 words gets you a blue ribbon.

*Answers on page 467*

1. _____     20. _____     38. _____
2. _____     21. _____     39. _____
3. _____     22. _____     40. _____
4. _____     23. _____     41. _____
5. _____     24. _____     42. _____
6. _____     25. _____     43. _____
7. _____     26. _____     44. _____
8. _____     27. _____     45. _____
9. _____     28. _____     46. _____
10. _____    29. _____     47. _____
11. _____    30. _____     48. _____
12. _____    31. _____     49. _____
13. _____    32. _____     50. _____
14. _____    33. _____     51. _____
15. _____    34. _____     52. _____
16. _____    35. _____     53. _____
17. _____    36. _____     54. _____
18. _____    37. _____     55. _____
19. _____                          56. _____

(DIRECTIONS FOR SOLVING FOUR-LETTER ALFABITS ARE ON PAGE 40)

# SINGULARLY

There are at least 35 words, each of four or more letters, that can be made out of the letters in the word SINGULARLY. How many can you find? List them below.

If you fill in the spaces with 20 words, you're mighty clever; 25 words is a grand score; and 30 words puts you at the top of the heap!

*Answers on page 467*

| | | |
|---|---|---|
| 1. _____ | 13. _____ | 24. _____ |
| 2. _____ | 14. _____ | 25. _____ |
| 3. _____ | 15. _____ | 26. _____ |
| 4. _____ | 16. _____ | 27. _____ |
| 5. _____ | 17. _____ | 28. _____ |
| 6. _____ | 18. _____ | 29. _____ |
| 7. _____ | 19. _____ | 30. _____ |
| 8. _____ | 20. _____ | 31. _____ |
| 9. _____ | 21. _____ | 32. _____ |
| 10. _____ | 22. _____ | 33. _____ |
| 11. _____ | 23. _____ | 34. _____ |
| 12. _____ | | 35. _____ |

# MARGARINE

There are at least 28 words, each of four letters or more, that can be made out of the letters in the word MARGARINE.

A score of 14 is good; 18 means you're really on the ball; and 22 words shows exceptional ability.

*Answers on page 467*

| | | |
|---|---|---|
| 1. _____ | 10. _____ | 20. _____ |
| 2. _____ | 11. _____ | 21. _____ |
| 3. _____ | 12. _____ | 22. _____ |
| 4. _____ | 13. _____ | 23. _____ |
| 5. _____ | 14. _____ | 24. _____ |
| 6. _____ | 15. _____ | 25. _____ |
| 7. _____ | 16. _____ | 26. _____ |
| 8. _____ | 17. _____ | 27. _____ |
| 9. _____ | 18. _____ | 28. _____ |
| | 19. _____ | |

(DIRECTIONS FOR SOLVING FOUR-LETTER ALFABITS ARE ON PAGE 40)

# PUNCTILIOUS

There are at least 38 words, each of four letters or more, that can be made out of the letters in the word PUNCTILIOUS.

If you can find 22, that's fairly good; 27 is excellent; and 32 words is simply colossal.

*Answers on page 467*

| | | |
|---|---|---|
| 1. _____ | 14. _____ | 26. _____ |
| 2. _____ | 15. _____ | 27. _____ |
| 3. _____ | 16. _____ | 28. _____ |
| 4. _____ | 17. _____ | 29. _____ |
| 5. _____ | 18. _____ | 30. _____ |
| 6. _____ | 19. _____ | 31. _____ |
| 7. _____ | 20. _____ | 32. _____ |
| 8. _____ | 21. _____ | 33. _____ |
| 9. _____ | 22. _____ | 34. _____ |
| 10. _____ | 23. _____ | 35. _____ |
| 11. _____ | 24. _____ | 36. _____ |
| 12. _____ | 25. _____ | 37. _____ |
| 13. _____ | | 38. _____ |

# STATUTORY

There are at least 31 words, each of four or more letters, that can be made out of the letters in the word STATUTORY.

If you can find 20 words, you're wonderful; 24 words means you're incredible; and 28 words is simply colossal.

*Answers on page 467*

| | | |
|---|---|---|
| 1. _____ | 11. _____ | 22. _____ |
| 2. _____ | 12. _____ | 23. _____ |
| 3. _____ | 13. _____ | 24. _____ |
| 4. _____ | 14. _____ | 25. _____ |
| 5. _____ | 15. _____ | 26. _____ |
| 6. _____ | 16. _____ | 27. _____ |
| 7. _____ | 17. _____ | 28. _____ |
| 8. _____ | 18. _____ | 29. _____ |
| 9. _____ | 19. _____ | 30. _____ |
| 10. _____ | 20. _____ | 31. _____ |
| | 21. _____ | |

(DIRECTIONS FOR SOLVING FOUR-LETTER ALFABITS ARE ON PAGE 40)

# NOTHINGNESS

There are at least 56 words, each of four letters or more, that can be made out of the letters in the word NOTHINGNESS.

    If you can fill in the spaces with at least 35, that's good; 40 is a very good showing; 45 indicates exceptional ability; and 50 puts you in the league with the real pros. Congratulations!

*Answers on page 467*

| | | |
|---|---|---|
| 1. _____ | 20. _____ | 38. _____ |
| 2. _____ | 21. _____ | 39. _____ |
| 3. _____ | 22. _____ | 40. _____ |
| 4. _____ | 23. _____ | 41. _____ |
| 5. _____ | 24. _____ | 42. _____ |
| 6. _____ | 25. _____ | 43. _____ |
| 7. _____ | 26. _____ | 44. _____ |
| 8. _____ | 27. _____ | 45. _____ |
| 9. _____ | 28. _____ | 46. _____ |
| 10. _____ | 29. _____ | 47. _____ |
| 11. _____ | 30. _____ | 48. _____ |
| 12. _____ | 31. _____ | 49. _____ |
| 13. _____ | 32. _____ | 50. _____ |
| 14. _____ | 33. _____ | 51. _____ |
| 15. _____ | 34. _____ | 52. _____ |
| 16. _____ | 35. _____ | 53. _____ |
| 17. _____ | 36. _____ | 54. _____ |
| 18. _____ | 37. _____ | 55. _____ |
| 19. _____ | | 56. _____ |

# EUPHONIOUS

There are at least 17 words, each of four letters or more, that can be made out of the letters in the word EUPHONIOUS.

    A score of 10 is pretty good; 12 is even better; and 14 is really terrific.

*Answers on page 468*

| | | |
|---|---|---|
| 1. _____ | 7. _____ | 12. _____ |
| 2. _____ | 8. _____ | 13. _____ |
| 3. _____ | 9. _____ | 14. _____ |
| 4. _____ | 10. _____ | 15. _____ |
| 5. _____ | 11. _____ | 16. _____ |
| 6. _____ | | 17. _____ |

(DIRECTIONS FOR SOLVING FOUR-LETTER ALFABITS ARE ON PAGE 40)

# CAPRICIOUS

There are at least 22 words, each of four letters or more, that can be made out of the letters in the word CAPRICIOUS.

If you can fill in the spaces below with at least 12 words, that's good; 15 is excellent; and 18 rates you a gold star.

*Answers on page 468*

1. _____
2. _____
3. _____
4. _____
5. _____
6. _____
7. _____

8. _____
9. _____
10. _____
11. _____
12. _____
13. _____
14. _____
15. _____

16. _____
17. _____
18. _____
19. _____
20. _____
21. _____
22. _____


# STOPPAGE

There are at least 26 words, each of four letters or more, that can be made out of the letters in the word STOPPAGE.

If you can find 16, that's great; 19 is terrific; and 22 is super-duper!

*Answers on page 468*

1. _____
2. _____
3. _____
4. _____
5. _____
6. _____
7. _____
8. _____
9. _____

10. _____
11. _____
12. _____
13. _____
14. _____
15. _____
16. _____
17. _____

18. _____
19. _____
20. _____
21. _____
22. _____
23. _____
24. _____
25. _____
26. _____

(DIRECTIONS FOR SOLVING FOUR-LETTER ALFABITS ARE ON PAGE 40)

# I'LL GUESS YOUR AGE

You can tell anyone in your audience his exact age and the date of his birth. All you need is a pencil and piece of paper.

Have a friend write down on the paper the month in which he was born, in number form (for example, January would be 1; July would be 7). Next to the number, your subject should be asked to write down the date of the month in which he was born. These two numbers should now make one complete number; for example June 3rd would be 63; January 26th would be 126; and December 6th would also be 126.

Now have your friend perform the following simple operations:

(a) Multiply the key number by 2.
(b) Add the number 5 to the result.
(c) Multiply the sum by 50.
(d) Then add his age.

When the above operations are completed, ask your subject to tell you the final number reached. As soon as you know the final number, you can tell him the exact date and year of his birth. All you need to do is subtract the number 250 from the number given you by your friend.

For example, let's suppose your subject's birthday is August 14th, and that he is 25 years old. He would write down the number 814. This number he would multiply by 2, which results in 1628. To this he would add five, reaching the sum of 1633, which he would then multiply by 50, making 81650. Finally, he would add his age, 25, to this number. The result would be 81,675.

When your subject tells you this number, you immediately subtract 250 from it, which you can probably do in your head. The number that remains, 81425, is your answer. The last two digits in the number give you his age, and the remaining numbers represent the day and month of his birth.

To find the exact year of his birth, simply subtract his age (in this case 25) from the present year.

In some cases, however, there will be *two* possible answers to the question of the subject's month and day of birth. If the code number you reach has five digits, and if the first two of them are either 11 or 12, you will not be able to tell for certain whether his birthday is in November (if it's 11), December (if it's 12), or January. For example, if the code number is 12725, you can be sure that the subject is 25 years old, but you cannot tell if his birthday is December 7th, or January 27th.

When this happens, there is nothing you can do but take a good, hard look at your subject, and try to guess. At least you have a 50-50 chance of being right!

# EXTRA-SENSORY PERCEPTION

Using just a pencil and a piece of paper, you read minds.

Ask someone in your audience to think of a number, but not to tell you what it is. When he has chosen his number, tell him to take the following steps: (1) double it; (2) add 12; (3) divide the result by 4; (4) subtract half the original number.

For example, if he has picked the number 9, he will double it to obtain 18. When he adds 12, he gets 30; when he divides by 4, he gets 7½. Finally, when he subtracts half of the original 9, or 4½, he is left with 3.

$$9 \times 2 = 18$$
$$18 + 12 = 30$$
$$30 \div 4 = 7\tfrac{1}{2}$$
$$7\tfrac{1}{2} - 4\tfrac{1}{2} = 3$$

How would you know that the answer is 3 if you don't know what number your friend chose? It's simple. The key is the number you told him to add—in this case, 12. Any number could be substituted for 12; all you have to do is divide the key number by 4, and you will obtain the correct answer.

For instance, if you substituted the number 20 for the number 12, your answer would be 5, because 20 divided by 4 equals 5.

If your friend had chosen 9, he would have doubled it to get 18; then added 20 to get 38; then divided by 4, obtaining 9½; and finally subtracted 4½, or half of 9, to get 5.

It works for any number at all.

♔

# SPECIAL DIGIT

All you need for this amusing trick is a pencil and a piece of paper. Write down the numbers 12345679 on the paper. In this sequence, notice that you have omitted the digit 8.

Ask a friend to pick out one of the numbers you have written down. Multiply that number by 9. The answer you reach is your key figure.

Next, multiply the original number—12345679—by your key figure. For example, if your friend has chosen the number 6, ask him to multiply 6 times 9, to reach 54, and to multiply 12345679 by 54. He'll have sixes plenty!

This trick will work for any of the eight numbers you have written down.

♔

# YOU KNOW THE TELEPHONE BOOK BY HEART

Demonstrate to your friends that you know the telephone book by heart. All you need is a telephone book, a pencil, and a piece of paper. Here's how:

Give your friend the pencil and a piece of paper. Tell him to think of any three-digit number, and write it down. He is not to tell you the number.

Then have him reverse the digits, and subtract the smaller number from the larger one. For example, if the number he chooses is 349, the reversed number would be 943. He would then subtract 349 from 943, to obtain 594.

Now instruct him to take the result of his subtraction, and reverse the digits of that number. He now has two three-digit numbers, which you then tell him to add together. In our example, your friend would reverse the digits in 594, obtaining 495. He would add them together to get 1089.

The key to this trick is the number 1089. The instructions you gave your friend are based on a mathematical formula, and the result of these operations, if they are performed correctly, will always equal the number 1089. That is your secret.

When your friend has reached the answer to his addition problem, tell him to take the last two digits in his answer, and turn to that page in the telephone book. Now tell him to take the *first* two digits in his answer, and count down that number of lines from the top of the first column on the page. When his finger has stopped on a particular name, you amaze him by telling him what name it is.

How was this done? Well, since the final result of all that artithmetic will always be 1089, you can find out beforehand which name is the tenth name in the first column on page 89. Just remember that name, and when the time comes, you will be ready with the correct answer.

Since the name will always be the same no matter how many times you do the trick, you obviously cannot perform this trick more than once to the same audience.

# MAGIC LIST

All you need for this trick is a piece of paper and a pencil.

| A | B | C | D | E |
|---|---|---|---|---|
| 2 | 1 | 16 | 8 | 4 |
| 27 | 5 | 24 | 9 | 23 |
| 14 | 17 | 28 | 30 | 20 |
| 15 | 11 | 17 | 10 | 7 |
| 18 | 9 | 30 | 27 | 12 |
| 10 | 21 | 21 | 14 | 15 |
| 22 | 3 | 18 | 26 | 6 |
| 7 | 29 | 22 | 28 | 30 |
| 19 | 19 | 23 | 13 | 5 |
| 26 | 7 | 19 | 11 | 21 |
| 23 | 15 | 26 | 29 | 14 |
| 6 | 5 | 27 | 24 | 22 |
| 3 | 23 | 25 | 12 | 13 |
| 11 | 13 | 20 | 15 | 29 |
| 30 | 27 | 29 | 25 | 28 |

Show a friend this magic list and ask him to secretly select any number from 1 to 30. Of course, he should not tell you what the selected number is.

Now, he looks through the list to find where his number appears. Then have him tell you which columns his number is in.

Once he gives you this information, you can promptly tell him what number he chose.

All you do is add the numbers at the top of the columns he has listed. The sum of those numbers will be the correct answer.

For example, suppose your friend tells you that his number appears in Columns A, D, and E. You add the numbers at the head of those columns, or 2, 8, and 4, to get the sum of 14. And sure enough, the only number which appears in those three columns and nowhere else in 14.

The magic list works every time with any number from 1 to 30.

# GUESS THE SECRET WORD

Prove you can correctly pick the word your friend secretly picked out of a book. The only materials needed are a book, a pencil, and a piece of paper.

Hand a book to your friend, or let him pick one. Ask him to select a page from the book, then choose a line from any of the first nine lines of that page. Next he must pick one word from any of the first nine words on the line he has chosen, and write that word down on the piece of paper. He must not show you what the word is.

Now you direct him to carry out the following operations:

1) Multiply the number of the page by 2.

2) Multiply this result by 5.

3) Add 20.

4) Add the number of the line on which the selected word is located.

5) Add 5.

6) Multiply by 10.

7) Add a number equal to the position of the word in that line.

For example, if your friend has chosen the eighth word on the ninth line of page 561, he will multiply 561 by 2 and get 1,122, then multiply 1,122 by 5 to get 5,610. To this he will add 20, getting 5,630, to which he will add 9, making 5,639. Now he adds 5, getting 5,644. He then multiplies 5,644 by 10, which equals 56,440, and adds 8 to the result, making 56,448 altogether.

When your friend has finished making his calculations, ask him to give you his final number. This is your key number.

How will the key number help you to find out what page, line, and word your friend has chosen from the book? By the use of a simple mathematical formula.

Simply subtract the number 250 from whatever your key figure is. The resulting number will tell you all you need to know.

For instance, if we use the same example, the key figure 56,448 has been given to you by your friend. If you subtract 250 from 56,448, your answer will be 56,198.

Separate 56,198 as follows: 561—9—8.

As you can see, the last number is the place where the word comes on the line; the number to the left is the number of the line when counted down from the top of the page; and the remaining digits form the page number.

You will find that this formula always works if the calculations are done correctly.

# THE EXTRAORDINARY NUMBER 9

Here are some of the unusual stunts that can be performed with that wonderful number 9:

If you add 1,2,3,4,5,6,7,8,9, together, you get 45—and 4 + 5 = 9.

☗

If you multiply any number by the number 9, the digits that make up the answer will *always add up to 9*:

$$9 \times 2 = 18 \text{ and } 1 + 8 = 9$$
$$9 \times 3 = 27 \text{ and } 2 + 7 = 9$$
$$9 \times 4 = 36 \text{ and } 3 + 6 = 9$$
$$9 \times 5 = 45 \text{ and } 4 + 5 = 9$$
$$9 \times 6 = 54 \text{ and } 5 + 4 = 9$$
$$9 \times 7 = 63 \text{ and } 6 + 3 = 9$$
$$9 \times 8 = 72 \text{ and } 7 + 2 = 9$$
$$9 \times 9 = 81 \text{ and } 8 + 1 = 9$$

Even if you use numbers of more than one digit, the digits in your result will always equal 9:

$$9 \times 78 = 702 \text{ and } 7 + 0 + 2 = 9$$
$$9 \times 568 = 5022 \text{ and } 5 + 2 + 2 = 9$$
$$9 \times 183 = 1647 \text{ and } 1 + 6 + 4 + 7 = 18, \text{ then } 1 + 8 = 9!$$

☗

Take any number, for example, 785. Now reverse the digits in the number, making it 587. You will find that if you subtract the smaller number from the larger number, you always get a number that is divisible by 9.

| | 785 |
|---|---|
| Minus | 587 |
| Equals | 198 |

Take any number, for example ..................... 4,325
Add the digits. They add up to ..................... 14
Subtract, and you get ........................... 4,311

You will find that your results will *always be divisible by the number 9!*

♔

Here are some more beauties:

$$987654321 \times 9 = 8888888889$$
$$987654321 \times 18 = 17777777778$$
$$987654321 \times 27 = 26666666667$$
$$987654321 \times 36 = 35555555556$$
$$987654321 \times 45 = 44444444445$$
$$987654321 \times 54 = 53333333334$$
$$987654321 \times 63 = 62222222223$$
$$987654321 \times 72 = 71111111112$$
$$987654321 \times 81 = 80000000001$$

$$1 \times 9 + 2 = 11$$
$$12 \times 9 + 3 = 111$$
$$123 \times 9 + 4 = 1111$$
$$1234 \times 9 + 5 = 11111$$
$$12345 \times 9 + 6 = 111111$$
$$123456 \times 9 + 7 = 1111111$$
$$1234567 \times 9 + 8 = 11111111$$
$$12345678 \times 9 + 9 = 111111111$$
$$123456789 \times 9 + 10 = 1111111111$$

Now look at the almost magical results you get when you multiply the numbers below.

$$1 \times 8 + 1 = 9$$
$$12 \times 8 + 2 = 98$$
$$123 \times 8 + 3 = 987$$
$$1234 \times 8 + 4 = 9876$$
$$12345 \times 8 + 5 = 98765$$
$$123456 \times 8 + 6 = 987654$$
$$1234567 \times 8 + 7 = 9876543$$
$$12345678 \times 8 + 8 = 98765432$$
$$123456789 \times 8 + 9 = 987654321$$

# FUNNY ADS

*From an Indianapolis paper:*
Now you can buy six different products to protect your car from your Mobil dealer.

☗

*From a Long Island paper:*
For Sale—Large crystal vase by lady slightly cracked.

☗

*Personal in the La Marque, Texas Times:*
Unemployed diamonds for sale at big discount. New four-diamond wedding ring. Slightly used seven-diamond engagement ring. Bought in burst of enthusiasm for $550, sentimental value gone, will sacrifice for $250.

☗

*From the Help Wanted column in a Baltimore paper:*
Would you lie to sell real estate? If so, call for an appointment to see us today. We will train.

☗

*From the Long Beach, Cal. Tri-Shopper:*
Jointer-Plane—used once to cut off thumb. Will sell cheap.

☗

*From the Clifton Forge, Va. Daily Review:*
Save regularly in our bank. You'll never reget it.

☗

*In the merchandise columns of the Philadelphia Inquirer:*
Tombstone slightly used. Sell cheap. Weil's Curiosity Shop.

☗

*From a Dayton paper:*
Now on the market—a Norelco shaver for women with three heads.

☗

*From the Bargain Hunter:*
Before you put your baby on the floor, clean it with a Power carpet sweeper.

☗

*From the Sumner, Ia. Gazette:*
For Sale: 1974 Chevy Nova in first clash condition.

*From the Abilene Gazette:*
   For Rent or Sale: Six room house in shady neighborhood.

*From the Abilene, Tex. Reporter-News:*
   $10 reward for south side apartment. Large enough to keep young wife from going home to mother. Small enough to keep mother from coming here.

*Personal in a New York paper:*
   Young man who gets paid on Monday and is broke by Wednesday would like to exchange small loans with a young man who gets paid on Wednesday and is broke by Monday.

*From an advertising circular for a sporting goods store:*
   Special on golf clubs for good players with movable heads.

*In the personal columns of a rural weekly:*
   Anyone found near my chicken house at night will be found there next morning.

*In Shears, the journal of the box-making industry:*
   Situation Wanted—by young woman 21 years of age. Unusual experience includes three years Necking and Stripping. Address Dept. 0-2, Shears.

*From a Missouri paper:*
   Wanted—Men, women and children to sit in slightly used pews on Sunday morning.

**55**

*From the Grand Rapids Press:*

Gelding—spirited but gentle. Ideal for teen-ager. For sale by parents whose daughter has discovered boys are more interesting than horses.

*Classified ad in the New York Herald Tribune:*

Man wanted to work in dynamite factory; must be willing to travel.

*From the Atlanta Journal:*

Wanted—A mahogany living room table, by a lady with Heppelwhite legs.

*From the Charleston Chronicle:*

Help Wanted, part-time. Smart young man to help butcher. Must be able to cut, wrap, and serve customers.

*From a Parsons, Pa. paper:*

Easter Matinee—Saturday Morning 10:30 a.m. Every child laying an egg in the door man's hand will be admitted free.

*From the Hartford Times:*

Front room, suitable for two ladies, use of kitchen or two gentlemen.

*From the Birmingham Age-Herald:*

Wanted—Farm mule. Must be reasonable.

*From a Burns, Oregon paper:*

Why go elsewhere to be cheated when you can come here?

*From the Washington Post:*
Sale: Oak dining room tables, seating 14 people with round legs, and 12 people with square legs.

☗

*From the Help Wanted column of the Long Island Press:*
Housekeeper, sleep in, must be fond of cooking children and housecleaning.

☗

*From a Jamesville, Iowa paper:*
Get rid of aunts. T—does the job in 24 hours. 25¢ per bottle.

☗

*From a Chatham, Ontario paper:*
Special foul dinner, 45¢.

☗

*From an El Paso paper:*
Widows made to order. Send us your specifications.

☗

*From a New York paper:*
Sheer stockings—Designed for dressy wear, but so serviceable that lots of women wear nothing else.

☗

*From a Montesan, Wash. paper:*
For sale—A full blooded cow, giving three gallons milk, two tons of hay, a lot of chickens and a cookstove.

☗

*From a Willimantic, Conn. paper:*
Wanted—A strong horse to do the work of a country minister.

☗

*From The New York Times:*
Situation wanted—Houseworker, plain crook, reliable.

☗

*From a Jacksonville paper:*
Man, honest, will take anything.

# TEST YOUR SPATIAL REASONING

Spatial discrimination of one sort or another is universally accepted by psychologists as a vital element in various mechanical, scientific, and artistic aptitudes. The important question is not whether spaces and forms can be perceived, but whether they can be used as the raw material of reasoning.

This test requires detection of differences and likenesses in shape and size. The test consists of three parts; each has a time limit. Follow the directions carefully.

*Answers on page 468*

## PART ONE

DIRECTIONS: On the blank line next to each object, write the number of surfaces that object has. For example:

A. __10__

The object above has one top surface, three bottom surfaces, four outer side surfaces, and two inner side surfaces—or 10 surfaces in all.

TIME LIMIT: 1 MINUTE

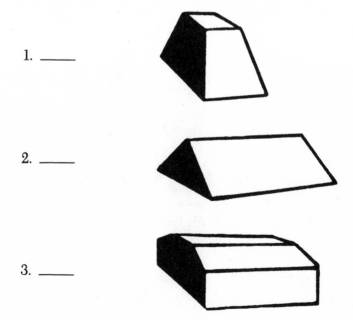

1. _____

2. _____

3. _____

4. ____

5. ____

6. ____

7. ____

8. ____

9. ____

10. ____

# PART TWO

DIRECTIONS: Examine each pair of dice. If, judging from the dots, the first die of the pair can be turned into the position of the second, circle *Yes*. If not, circle *No*. Do not guess. It is better in this test to leave the answer blank than to answer incorrectly.

TIME LIMIT: 2 MINUTES

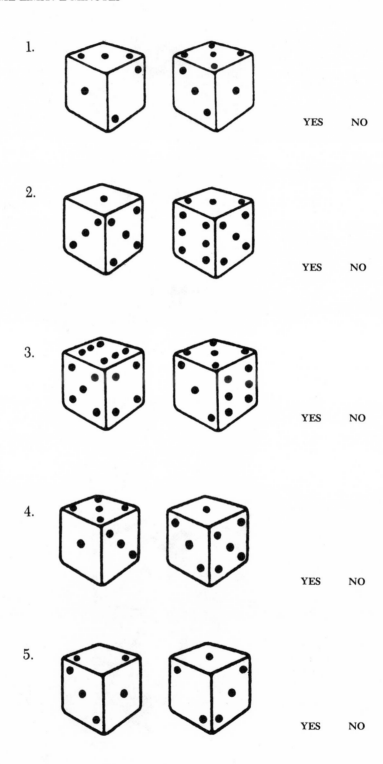

1.  YES    NO

2.  YES    NO

3.  YES    NO

4.  YES    NO

5.  YES    NO

# PART THREE

DIRECTIONS: In each row, the first drawing represents a solid object. If another drawing in that row shows the same object in a different position, circle the number under that drawing. If no drawing in the row shows the first object, do nothing.

TIME LIMIT: 1 MINUTE

A.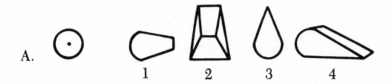

B.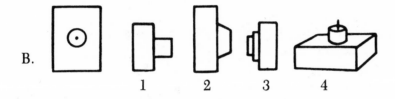

C.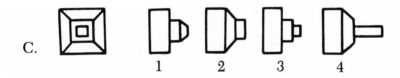

D.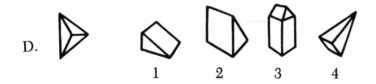

E.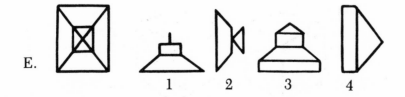

**61**

# ARE YOU THOROUGH?

Genius has sometimes been defined as "an infinite capacity for taking pains." Many an otherwise gifted person falls short of real brilliance because he or she lacks thoroughness. And less endowed folks sometimes come through with surprising successes because the tasks they do perform, they perform thoroughly.

This test will help you measure your ability to follow instructions closely, and to pay meticulous attention to detail. The test consists of two parts. Each has a time limit, but accuracy is more important than speed in this test.

*Answers on page 468*

## PART ONE

DIRECTIONS: The questions on this page refer to the figure on the opposite page. Carefully count the dots in the designated areas, and write your answers on the lines which precede each question.

TIME LIMIT: 3 MINUTES

*How many dots are there:*

_____ 1. In the square, but not in the triangle, circle, or rectangle?

_____ 2. In the circle, but not in the triangle, square, or rectangle?

_____ 3. In the triangle, but not in the circle, square, or rectangle?

_____ 4. In the rectangle, but not in the triangle, circle, or square?

_____ 5. Common to the triangle and circle, but not in the rectangle or square?

_____ 6. Common to the square and triangle, but not in the rectangle or circle?

_____ 7. Common to the square and circle, but not in the triangle or rectangle?

_____ 8. Common to the square and rectangle, but not in the circle or triangle?

_____ 9. Common to the triangle and rectangle, but not in the circle?

_____ 10. Common to the circle, square, triangle, and rectangle?

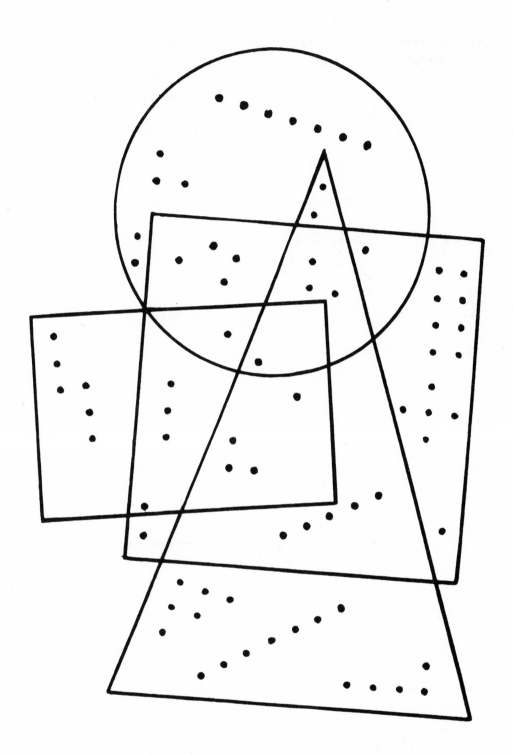

**63**

# PART TWO

DIRECTIONS: The questions on this page refer to the figures below. Write your answers on the lines which precede each question.
TIME LIMIT: 3 MINUTES

*What is the sum of the figures:*

_____ 1. In the square, but not in the circle or rectangle?

_____ 2. In the square, but not in the triangle?

_____ 3. In either the rectangle or the circle, but not in the triangle?

_____ 4. In the square, but not in the triangle, circle, or rectangle?

_____ 5. In the circle, minus the sum of the figures in the triangle?

_____ 6. Common to the square, triangle, and circle?

_____ 7. In the rectangle, but not in the square?

_____ 8. Common to the square, rectangle, and circle?

_____ 9. In the circle, but not in the triangle or rectangle?

_____ 10. Common to the rectangle, triangle, and square?

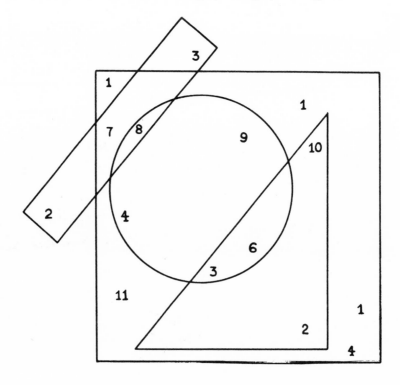

# TEST YOUR LOGIC NO.1

Each question below is self-explanatory. Write your answer on the line which precedes the question. Do not spend too much time on any one question; skip the difficult questions and return to them later if you have the time.

TIME LIMIT: 25 MINUTES

*Answers on page 468*

_____ 1. DIAMOND is to GRIDIRON as BASEBALL is to:
    (1) basketball  (2) rink  (3) football  (4) arena  (5) links

_____ 2. 20 men dig 40 holes in 60 days, so 10 men can dig 10 holes in how many days?

_____ 3. How many letters in this series come just before an odd number and just after a number larger than 6?
    Z, 1, 9, A, 4, B, 3, 14, 19, C, 8, 9, B, 5, D, 12, E, 17

_____ 4. Suppose Milwaukee leads the league and Pittsburgh is fifth, while St. Louis is midway between them. If Chicago is ahead of Pittsburgh and Cincinnati is immediately behind St. Louis, which city is in second place?
    (1) Cincinnati  (2) Pittsburgh  (3) Chicago
    (4) St. Louis  (5) Milwaukee

_____ 5. One series below is in opposite order to the other, except for a certain number. Write the number.
    1, 2, 3 . . .  1, 3, 2 . . .

_____ 6. COMPREHENSIBLE advice is:
    (1) bad  (2) comprehensive  (3) understandable
    (4) good advice  (5) reprehensible

_____ 7. In this group, which word does not belong?
    (1) the  (2) this  (3) an  (4) it  (5) a

_____ 8. Which of these words comes closest in meaning to IS?
    (1) to be  (2) are  (3) lives  (4) exists  (5) accrusticates

_____ 9. A CHASSEUR is a:
    (1) soldier  (2) torso  (3) detective  (4) vase

_____ 10. BLEAK is to BLACK as LEAK is to:
    (1) white  (2) back  (3) leak  (4) lack  (5) water

_____ 11. ADAMANT is the opposite of:
(1) dull  (2) unlike Adam  (3) yielding  (4) stubborn

_____ 12. Half a waiter's earnings, and a dollar besides, come from tips. If he earns 15 dollars, how many dollars come from tips?

_____ 13. Which of these words most nearly corresponds in meaning to OPULENT?
(1) exposed  (2) precious stone  (3) wealthy  (4) exposed at one end  (5) weeping

_____ 14. If a train is running 3 minutes late and losing 3 seconds per minute, how many more minutes will it take for the train to be running an hour late?

_____ 15. Which of these words most nearly corresponds in meaning to DELETE?
(1) permit  (2) erase  (3) rent  (4) tasty  (5) neat

_____ 16. Girls always have:
(1) sweethearts  (2) clothes  (3) giggles  (4) hair  (5) figures

_____ 17. A train running 30 miles per hour is in front of a train running 50 miles per hour. How many miles apart are the trains, if it will take 15 minutes for the faster train to catch the slower one?

_____ 18. PIQUE is most similar in meaning to:
(1) choice  (2) decoration  (3) elf  (4) resentment  (5) sorrow

_____ 19. A train completes half a trip at 30 miles per hour, and the other half at 60 miles per hour. If the whole trip was 20 miles, how many minutes did the train take to complete the trip?

_____ 20. Print your answer. $A\ B\ D$ is to $C\ B\ A$ as $Q\ R\ T$ is to:

_____ 21. If 2 is $A$ and 6 is $C$ and 8 is $D$ and 12 is $F$, how would you spell BEADED, using numbers instead of letters?

_____ 22. When Aunt Carrie makes soup, she puts in 1 bean for each 2 peas. If her soup contains a total of 300 peas and beans, how many peas are there?

_____ 23. No dog can sing, but some dogs can talk. If so, then:
(1) Some dogs can sing.
(2) All dogs can't sing.
(3) All dogs can't talk.

_____ 24. No man is good, but some men are not bad. Therefore:
   (1) All men are not bad.
   (2) No man is not bad.
   (3) All men aren't good.

_____ 25. The Potomac River and the Hudson River have a combined length of 850 miles, and the Hudson River is 250 miles shorter than the Potomac River. How many miles long is the Potomac River?

_____ 26. Smith and Jones went to the race track, where Smith lost 68 dollars on the first 2 races, losing 6 dollars more on the second race than he lost on the first one. But he lost 4 dollars less on the second race than Jones did. How much did Jones lose on the second race?

_____ 27. Stockings always have:
   (1) sexiness  (2) seams  (3) garters  (4) weight  (5) sheerness

_____ 28. In this series, what number comes next?
   9, 7, 8, 6, 7, 5 . . .

_____ 29. One bunch of bananas has one-third again as many bananas as a second bunch. If the second bunch has 3 less bananas than the first bunch, how many has the first bunch?

_____ 30. Birds can only fly and hop, but worms can crawl. Therefore:
   (1) Birds eat worms.
   (2) Birds don't crawl.
   (3) Birds sometimes crawl.

_____ 31. Boxes always have:
   (1) angles  (2) shapes  (3) wood  (4) string

_____ 32. What number is as much more than 10 as it is less than one-half of what 30 is 10 less than?

_____ 33. Smith gets twice as large a share of the profits as any of his three partners gets. The three partners share equally. What fraction of the profits is Smith's?

_____ 34. BIRD is to FISH as AIRPLANE is to:
   (1) boat  (2) whale  (3) dory  (4) ship  (5) submarine

_____ 35. These words can be arranged to form a sentence. If the sentence is true, write *T*. If the sentence is false, write *F*.
ONE IN IS NUMBER THAN MORE BOOKS BOOK

_____ 36. URBAN is to COUNTRY as RURAL is to:
(1) state   (2) capital   (3) city   (4) suburb   (5) population

_____ 37. IMPERIAL is to EMPIRE as COLONIAL is to:
(1) coup d'etat   (2) revolution   (3) capitalism   (4) colony
(5) territory

_____ 38. ELEPHANT is to KANGAROO as PACHYDERM is to:
(1) Australia   (2) mammal   (3) marsupial   (4) primate
(5) vertebrate

_____ 39. In this series, what number comes next?
20, 17, 18, 15, 16 . . .

_____ 40. In this series, what number comes next?
100, 52, 28, 16 . . .

_____ 41. In this group, which word does not belong?
(1) bridge   (2) river   (3) tunnel   (4) ferry   (5) boat

_____ 42. A LEXICON is a(n):
(1) lawbook   (2) ruler   (3) dictionary   (4) criminal
(5) atlas

_____ 43. These words can be arranged to form a sentence. If the sentence is true, write *T*. If the sentence is false, write *F*.
NEVER ONE TEN HAS MAN FINGERS

_____ 44. In this series, what number comes next?
6, 12, 9, 17, 13, 23 . . .

_____ 45. HOUND is to FOX as OUTLAW is to:
(1) bandit   (2) posse   (3) escape   (4) bank   (5) criminal

_____ 46. In this group, which word does not belong?
(1) then   (2) now   (3) soon   (4) because   (5) always

_____ 47. In this series, what number comes next?
11, 20, 29, 38 . . .

**68**

_____ 48. BEAT is to RATE as MAUL is to:
(1) melt   (2) hula   (3) haul   (4) pule   (5) dual

_____ 49. To PREVARICATE is to:
(1) lie   (2) plan   (3) thank   (4) compose   (5) forget

_____ 50. In this group, which word does not belong?
(1) telephone   (2) radio   (3) television   (4) communication
(5) telegraph

_____ 51. MINUTE is to GARGANTUAN as FRIGID is to:
(1) torpid   (2) turgid   (3) torrid   (4) turbid

_____ 52. In this series, what number comes next?
4, 6, 5, 8, 6 . . .

_____ 53. PORT is to SPURT as RIDE is to:
(1) hide   (2) crude   (3) rude   (4) pride

_____ 54. No snarks can sing, but some snarks can talk. Therefore (select one):
(1) All snarks can't talk.
(2) Some snarks can both sing and talk.
(3) Some snarks can neither sing nor talk.

_____ 55. My piece of pie is three times as large as your piece. Your piece is twice as large as Jack's piece. If my piece weighs 6 ounces, how much does Jack's piece weigh?

_____ 56. TENACIOUS means:
(1) murky   (2) fearful   (3) persistent   (4) irritating

_____ 57. How many miles can a car travel in 20 minutes if it travels half as fast as a train going 60 m.p.h.?

_____ 58. Cats always have:
(1) color   (2) eyes   (3) fur   (4) claws

_____ 59. _E_ is to _F_ as _B_ is to:
(1) D   (2) P   (3) A   (4) R

_____ 60. Joe lives between Peter and the library. The library is between Peter's house and the school. Therefore (select one):
(1) Joe lives between Peter's house and the school.
(2) The school is between Joe's house and Peter's house.
(3) The library is closer to Joe's house than it is to the school.

**69**

# COUNT THE CUBES

The Army General Intelligence Tests for many years included a test on counting cubes. This type of test is alleged to provide reliable data as to one's accuracy, powers of visual analysis, spatial reasoning, and ability to concentrate.

Below you'll find 15 figures. Each consists of two or more cubes. Count the number of cubes in each figure, and write your answer on the line under the figure.

TIME LIMIT: 2 MINUTES

*Answers on page 468*

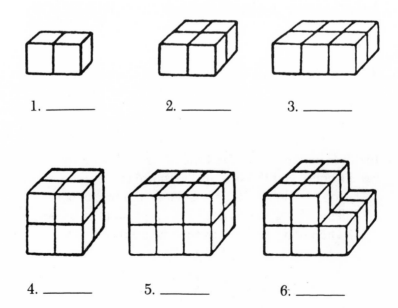

1. _____    2. _____    3. _____

4. _____    5. _____    6. _____

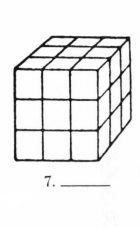

7. _____

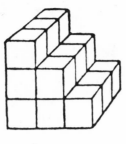

8. _____

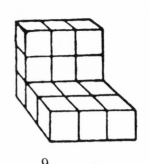

9. _____

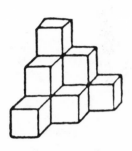

10. _____

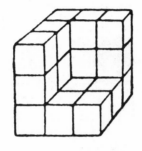

11. _____

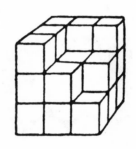

12. _____

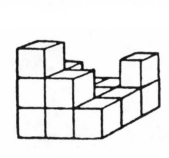

13. _____

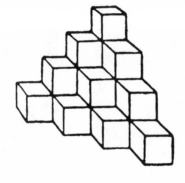

14. _____

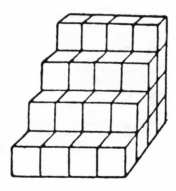

15. _____

# HOW SHARP IS YOUR MEMORY?

So you think you have a good memory? Try this test on for size. There are 21 designs on these two pages. Study them carefully for exactly *three minutes*. Then turn the page.

*Answers on page 469*

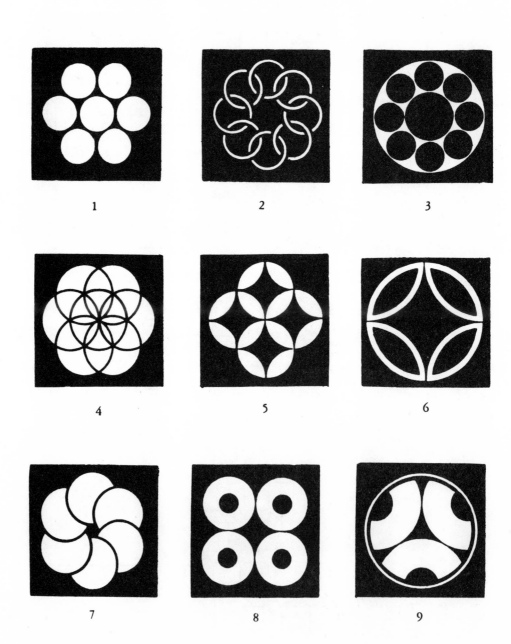

10

11

12

13

14

15

16

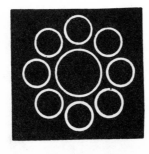

17

18

19

20

21

There are 21 designs on these two pages. The question is: Which of these designs exactly duplicates one of the designs on the preceding two pages.

If you recognize a design which duplicates a design on the preceding pages, circle the number below the design. If you're sure that the design does not duplicate a design on the preceding pages, place an X next to the number below the design. If you're not sure, do nothing.

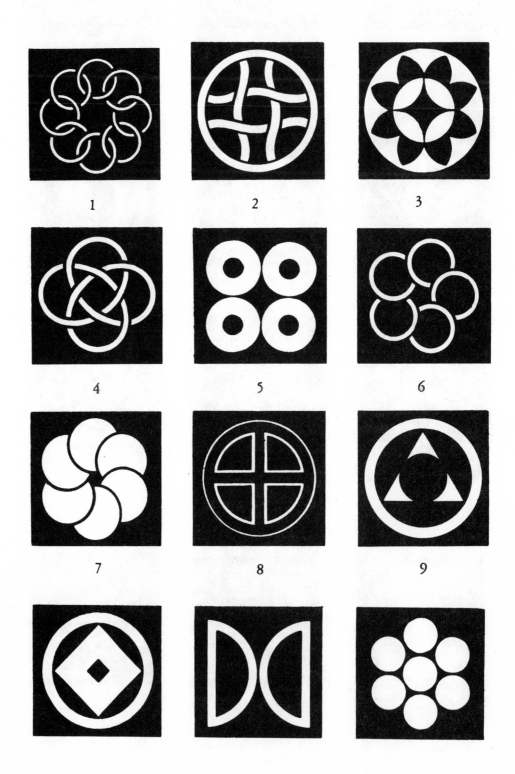

13

14

15

16

17

18

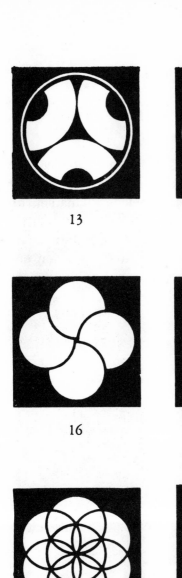

# DO YOU HAVE A HEAD FOR FIGURES?

Although this test does take for granted a certain elementary knowledge of arithmetic, this is in no sense an achievement test. It is designed to test your flair for mathematical reasoning rather than your knowledge of mathematical techniques and formulas.

Write your answer on the line provided before each question. Accuracy is more important than speed, but do not linger too long on any one question. You may do rough figuring in the margins or on a separate piece of paper.

TIME LIMIT: 40 MINUTES

*Answers on page 469*

_____ 1. If 4 apples out of a dozen are bad, how many are good?

_____ 2. In a box of 48 apples, 8 out of a dozen are good. How many in the box are bad?

_____ 3. What number is as much less than 60 as it is more than 50?

_____ 4. A girl spent half her money on lunch and half that amount on movies, which left her with 40 cents. How much did she spend on lunch?

_____ 5. How many hours will it take a car to go 400 miles at a speed of 50 miles per hour?

_____ 6. 36 is as much more than 29 as it is less than what number?

_____ 7. Your watch gains 4 minutes in a 24-hour day. If it reads 7:30½ at 7:30 A.M., how fast will it be at actual noon of the same day?

_____ 8. The sum of A plus B equals 116. A is less than C, but 4 more than B. What number does C equal?

_____ 9. If 7 men in 100 are criminals, how many men in 500 are not criminals?

_____ 10. Smith, a broker, bought 3 shares at 10 each which he sold at 6 each, and sold at 6 each what he bought at 5 each. If his total profit was 8, how many shares had he bought at 5?

_____ 11. How many hours will it take a jet plane to travel 400 miles at a speed of 600 miles per hour?

_____ 12. If 6½ yards of upholstery cloth cost 26 dollars, how much will 3½ yards cost?

_____ 13. If a grocer has enough eggs to last 300 customers 2 weeks, how long will the eggs last 400 customers?

_____ 14. Suppose A, B, and C are numbers. Suppose D is the sum of A, B and C. In that case, would D minus A equal B plus C?

_____ 15. Suppose A and B are numbers. Suppose D is the difference between A and B. In that case, would D plus A equal B, if B is greater than A?

_____ 16. It takes 10 ships 10 days to use 10 tanks of oil. How many days will it take 1 ship to use 1 tank of oil?

_____ 17. The winning horse in a race finished at 3:01 P.M., four lengths in front of the third horse, which finished two lengths behind the second horse. The second horse finished four-and-a-half lengths in front of the fourth horse, which ran the race in 61 and 310 seconds. In the last quarter of the race, each horse was traveling one length in one-fifth of a second. At what time did the race begin?

_____ 18. In this series, what is the next number?
1, 1, 2, 6 . . .

_____ 19. In a lot of 154 coats, there are 3 less white coats than red coats, but 5 more white coats than green coats. If all the coats are red, white or green, how many red coats are there?

_____ 20. Suppose the letters in this multiplication problem are numbers, and each dash represents a missing letter. Supply the missing letters.

$$
\begin{array}{r}
5 - 4 \\
\times\, C\ 5 \\
\hline
2 - A\ Y \\
- 1\ F\ 6 \\
\hline
- - 4\ 8\ - \\
\end{array}
$$

_____ 21. Supply the missing numbers in this multiplication problem.

$$
\begin{array}{r}
- - - \\
\times\ 6\ - \\
\hline
7 - 5\ 8\ - \\
- - - - - \\
\hline
- - - -\ 2\ 6 \\
\end{array}
$$

_____ 22. Suppose the letters in this multiplication problem are numbers. What number does each letter equal?

$$
\begin{array}{r}
F\ 1\ F \\
\times\ 2\ E \\
\hline
6\ 3\ C \\
D\ 2\ D \\
\hline
D\ 8\ B\ C \\
\end{array}
$$

# TEST YOUR LOGIC NO. 2

Each question below is self-explanatory. Write your answer on the line which precedes the question. Do not spend too much time on any one question; skip the difficult questions and return to them later if you have the time.

TIME LIMIT: 25 MINUTES

*Answers on page 469*

_____ 1. TRAIN is to TRACK as BUS is to:
(1) air (2) road (3) tire (4) bridge (5) depot

_____ 2. In this series, what number comes next?
2, 4, 7, 11 . . .

_____ 3. BIRD is to MIGRATE as BEAR is to:
(1) trap (2) forage (3) hibernate (4) mate (5) journey

_____ 4. In this group, which word does not belong?
(1) auto (2) truck (3) plane (4) bus (5) train

_____ 5. In the following series, how many numbers above 7 and below 19 are odd?

5  21  10  15  7  19  14  25  17  11  3  16  9  23  18

_____ 6. These words can be arranged to form a sentence. If the sentence is true, write *T*. If the sentence is false, write *F*.
ARE NOT ALL TALL MEN

_____ 7. WINDOW is to GLASS as BOOK is to:
(1) cardboard (2) alphabet (3) word (4) paper (5) print

_____ 8. In this series, what number comes next?
3, 7, 15, 31 . . .

_____ 9. 6 is to *F* as 11 is to what letter?

_____ 10. A SATURNINE aspect is:
(1) evil (2) morose (3) savage (4) astrological (5) jubilant

_____ 11. John is older than Peter. Jim is younger than Dennis. Dennis is older than Peter, but younger than John. Who is the oldest?

_____ 12. In this series, what number comes next?
1, 2, 2, 4, 8 . . .

_____ 13. In this group, which word does not belong?
(1) rubber (2) apples (3) maple (4) lumber (5) strawberries

_____ 14. POINT is to LINE as CIRCLE is to:
(1) pyramid (2) plane (3) ellipse (4) cone (5) cylinder

_____ 15. These words can be arranged to form a sentence. If the sentence is true, write _T_. If the sentence is false, write _F_.
NOT ONE TWO DOES HEADS HAVE woman

_____ 16. In this group, which word does not belong?
(1) earthquake (2) eclipse (3) flood (4) volcano (5) drought

_____ 17. In this series, what number comes next?
1, 9, 2, 18, 3 . . .

_____ 18. In this series, what number is wrong?
3, 9, 26, 81

_____ 19. SHOP is to HOPE as PLAN is to:
(1) plane (2) land (3) lain (4) lane (5) lope

_____ 20. An INGENUOUS person is:
(1) clever (2) inventive (3) patriotic (4) artless (5) false

_____ 21. HAIL is to SHALE as POUR is to:
(1) door (2) abhor (3) floor (4) spore (5) spout

_____ 22. SANGUINE means:
(1) blood-thirsty (2) thin (3) dark (4) hopeful (5) nasty

_____ 23. In this series, what letter comes next?
Y A W B . . .

_____ 24. In this series, what number is wrong?
10, 25, 40, 70, 100

_____ 25. If 117 is divisible by 3, write the number 3 on your answer sheet, unless 186 is divisible by 4, in which case write the number 5 on your answer sheet.

_____ 26. In this group, which word does not belong?
(1) cow (2) ermine (3) bear (4) sable (5) beaver

_____ 27. These words can be arranged to form a sentence. If the sentence is true, write *T*. If the sentence is false, write *F*.

IS FINGERS PLAYED WITH A THE PIANO NOT

_____ 28. If two trains traveling at 60 miles per hour toward each other are 30 miles apart, how long will it take them to meet?

_____ 29. If you had half as much money again in addition to what you have, you would have $1.20. How much have you?

_____ 30. DOCTOR is to SURGEON as SOLDIER is to:
(1) military (2) medicine (3) general (4) war (5) policeman

_____ 31. In this series, what number comes next?
144, 12, 81, 9, 121 . . .

_____ 32. What number is twice as much as what 20 is one-half of?

_____ 33. In this series, what number comes next?
E, 5, X, 24, H . . .

_____ 34. In this group, which word does not belong?
(1) botany (2) anatomy (3) geology (4) biology (5) zoology

_____ 35. CUPIDITY is:
(1) love (2) romanticism (3) avarice (4) cuteness (5) alcoholism

_____ 36. Animals always have:
(1) fur (2) mates (3) voices (4) hearts (5) claws

_____ 37. GRAPE is to WINE as WHEAT is to:
(1) bread (2) juice (3) rye (4) grain (5) food

_____ 38. In this group, which word does not belong?
(1) into (2) over (3) around (4) approximately (5) about

_____ 39. In this series, what number comes next?
24, 6, 12, 3 . . .

_____ 40. Letting 1 = a, 2 = b, 3 = c, etc., write the number which denotes the word "badge."

_____ 41. SPOILS is to VICTORY as PROFIT is to:
(1) defeat (2) triumph (3) cataclysm (4) adventure (5) sale

_____ 42. These words can be arranged to form a sentence. If the sentence is true, write *T*. If the sentence is false, write *F*.

SOME LAND WATER PLANES ON

_____ 43. In this group, which word does not belong?
(1) hatred (2) mockery (3) dislike (4) scorn (5) bitterness

_____ 44. A PANACEA is a:
(1) cure-all (2) disease (3) body organ (4) love sonnet
(5) declamation

_____ 45. 7 is to 49 as 10 is to:

_____ 46. In this series, what number comes next?
2, 8, 24, 48 . . .

_____ 47. In this series, which number is wrong?
7, 12, 18, 22, 25

_____ 48. In this series, what letter comes next?
1, B, 3, D, 5 . . .

_____ 49. CACOPHONY is to STENCH as SOUND is to:
(1) loudness (2) smell (3) taste (4) sight (5) fragrance

_____ 50. In this series, what letter comes next?
A A B D . . .

_____ 51. In this series, what number comes next?
1, 4, 2, 8, 4 . . .

_____ 52. First Avenue and Second Avenue have a combined length of 19 miles. First Avenue is 3 miles shorter than Second Avenue. How long is Second Avenue?

_____ 53. In this series, what letter comes next?
A G L P . . .

_____ 54. GLUTTONY is to INDIGESTION as FLOOD is to:
(1) rain (2) dam (3) destruction (4) earthquake (5) water

_____ 55. In this group, which object does not belong?
(1) rudder (2) oar (3) sail (4) paddlewheel

_____ 56. A PARADIGM is a(n):
   (1) rectangle (2) example (3) opposite (4) line (5) curse

_____ 57. Which number is wrong in this series?
   1, 6, 2, 12, 8, 24

_____ 58. These words can be arranged to form a sentence. If the sentence is true, write *T*. If the sentence is false, write *F*.
   WATER BIRDS OVER FLY NEVER

_____ 59. If 8 men out of 50 are blond, how many men in 1,000 are not blond?

_____ 60. ZOOLOGIST is to ANIMAL as CHEMIST is to:
   (1) formula (2) chemistry (3) chemical (4) scientist
   (5) alchemy

# DO YOU THINK STRAIGHT?

Despite painstaking investigations, uncertainty remains concerning just which ingredients make up the mixture of abilities we call intelligence. But you don't have to be a psychologist to know that reasoning power—like flour in a cake recipe—is the important element in the blend.

Speed and accuracy of inference, according to the best psychological studies, yield a rather reliable estimate of reasoning power. The questions which follow give you a chance to show how well you can reason by the inferential method.

Each set of statements is followed by one or more conclusions. You are to assume that the statements are correct. Judge each conclusion in relation to the statement that precedes it. Mark *T* on the line which precedes the conclusion if you think the statement makes the conclusion true; mark *F* if you think the conclusion is false, or if you cannot make a judgment on the basis of the preceding statement. Mark *all* conclusions either *T* or *F*.

TIME LIMIT: 20 MINUTES

*Answers on page 469*

1.  Elephants are animals. Animals have legs. Therefore:
    _____ Elephants have legs.

2.  My secretary isn't old enough to vote. My secretary has beautiful hair. Therefore:
    _____ My secretary is a girl under 21 years of age.

3.  Few stores on this street have neon lights, but they all have awnings. Therefore:
    _____ Some stores have either awnings or neon lights.
    _____ Some stores have both awnings and neon lights.

4.  All zublets have three eyes. This keptik has three eyes. Therefore:
    _____ This keptik is the same as a zublet.

5.  Potatoes are cheaper than tomatoes. I don't have enough money to buy two pounds of potatoes. Therefore:
    _____ I haven't enough money to buy a pound of tomatoes.
    _____ I may or may not have enough money to buy a pound of tomatoes.

6.  Willie Wilson is as good a hitter as Stan McStanley. Stan McStanley is a better hitter than most. Therefore:
    _____ Willie Wilson should lead the league.
    _____ Stan McStanley should lead the league, especially in home runs.
    _____ Willie Wilson is a better hitter than most.

7.  Good musicians play classical music. You have to practice to be a good musician. Therefore:
    _____ Classical music requires more practice than jazz.

8.  If your child is spoiled, spanking him will make him angry. If he is not spoiled, spanking him will make you sorry. But he is either spoiled or not spoiled. Therefore:
    _____ Spanking him will either make you sorry or make him angry.
    _____ It may not do any good to spank him.

9.  Squares are shapes with angles. This shape has no angles. Therefore:
    _____ This shape is a circle.
    _____ Any conclusion is uncertain.
    _____ This shape is not a square.

10. Greenville is northeast of Smithtown. New York is northeast of Smithtown. Therefore:
    _____ New York is closer to Greenville than to Smithtown.
    _____ Smithtown is southwest of New York.
    _____ New York is near Smithtown.

11. If green is heavy, red is light. If yellow is light, blue is medium. But green is heavy, or yellow is light. Therefore:
    _____ Blue is medium.
    _____ Yellow and red are light.
    _____ Red is light, or blue is medium.

12. You are in your car, and if you stop short you will be hit by a truck behind you. If you don't stop short, you will hit a woman crossing the road. Therefore:

_____ Pedestrians should keep off the roads.

_____ The truck is going too fast.

_____ You will be hit by the truck, or you will hit the woman.

13. I live between Joe's farm and the city. Joe's farm is between the city and the airport. Therefore:

_____ Joe's farm is nearer to where I live than to the airport.

_____ I live between Joe's farm and the airport.

_____ I live nearer to Joe's farm than to the airport.

14. A wise gambler never takes a chance unless the odds are in his favor. A good gambler never takes a chance unless he has much to gain. This gambler sometimes takes a chance against the odds. Therefore:

_____ He is either a good gambler or a wise one.

_____ He may or may not be a good gambler.

_____ He is neither a good gambler nor a wise one.

15. When B is Y, A is Z. E is either Y or Z, when A is not Z. Therefore:

_____ When B is Y, E is neither Y nor Z.

_____ When A is Z, Y or Z is E.

_____ When B is not Y, E is neither Y nor Z.

16. When B is larger than C, X is smaller than C. But C is never larger than B. Therefore:

_____ X is never larger than B.

_____ X is never smaller than B.

_____ X is never smaller than C.

17. As long as red is X, green must be Y. As long as green is not Y, blue must be Z. But blue is never Z when red is X. Therefore:

_____ As long as blue is Z, green can be Y.

_____ As long as red is not X, blue need not be Z.

_____ As long as green is not Y, red cannot be X.

18. Indians are sometimes Alaskans. Alaskans are sometimes lawyers. Therefore:

_____ Indians are not necessarily sometimes Alaskan lawyers.

_____ Indians can't be Alaskan lawyers.

19. Going ahead would not mean death without dishonor, but going backward would not mean dishonor without death. Therefore:
_____ Going backward would mean death without dishonor.
_____ Going ahead could mean dishonor without death.
_____ Going ahead could mean death without dishonor.

20. B platoon attacked the enemy and was wiped out, maybe. Smith, a member of B platoon, recovered in base hospital. Therefore:
_____ The rest of B platoon was wiped out.
_____ All of B platoon was wiped out.
_____ All of B platoon was not wiped out.

21. Awards were given only to honor students. John received an award. Therefore:
_____ John was not an honor student.

22. George does not play football well. None of the Central High School students plays football well. Therefore:
_____ George is a student at Central High School.

23. Only bright paints fade. None of the new paints are bright. Therefore:
_____ None of the new paints will fade.

24. Mary is taller than Grace. Helen is shorter than Grace. Therefore:
_____ Helen is taller than Mary.

25. All of the students wear caps. All of the caps are blue. Therefore:
_____ All of the students wear blue caps.

26. All of the trees near the house are green. Some of the trees near the house are oak. Therefore:
_____ None of the trees that are green are oak.

27. Some of the students who have books also have rulers. Some of those who have books also have pencils. Therefore:
_____ Some of those who have pencils also have rulers.

28. Hudson Street is parallel to River Drive. River Drive is perpendicular to Canal Street. Therefore:
_____ Canal Street is perpendicular to Hudson Street.

29. Not all of the buildings in town have shingle roofs. But all of them are built of brick. Therefore:
_____ There are some brick buildings in town without shingle roofs.

30. All of the tested students were accepted. Jim was not rejected. Therefore:
_____ Jim was tested.

31. Most of the old poles have been painted. Some of the old poles are broken. Therefore:
_____ Some of the painted poles are broken.

32. I like corn better than spinach. I like pudding better than corn. Therefore:
_____ I like pudding better than spinach.

33. Ridgefield is in the same longitude as Chittendon. Chittendon, which is as far east as Stratford, is west of Newport. Therefore:
_____ Ridgefield is west of Stratford.

34. John is taller than Jim, while Jim is taller than Bob. Dick and Bob are taller than Pearl. Therefore:
_____ John must be taller than Dick.

35. Jane was at the party only while Mary was there. Sam was Mary's escort and left with Mary before Tom came in. Therefore:
_____ Jane was not at the party when Tom was there.

# CIPHER TEST

Proficiency in working with numbers, letters, and other abstract symbols is a strong indicator of general reasoning ability. Such tasks as deciphering codes and unscrambling jumbled words require the ability to visualize and analyze, to think logically and clearly.

This test consists of three parts, each with a time limit. In the first part each letter or number represents another symbol; you're asked to decipher the codes. In the other two parts, you're asked merely to unscramble the letters.

*Answers on page 470*

## PART ONE

DIRECTIONS: Below are five messages given in code. Under each message there appears a translation. From the translation and code, you should be able to get some idea of the system which was employed in making the code. Using this system, it's up to you to make up the code words for the message "Bring Help."

TIME LIMIT: 10 MINUTES

1.   CODE:          RDMC RTOOKHDR
     TRANSLATION:   SEND SUPPLIES
"Bring Help" is: _____


2.   CODE:          BD DF ZB RU DF
                    EG HJ QS HJ MO FH
     TRANSLATION:   CEASE FIRING
"Bring Help" is: _____


3.   CODE:          HQHPB DSSURDFKIQJ
     TRANSLATION:   ENEMY APPROACHING
"Bring Help" is: _____


4.   CODE:          3 15 13 5   17 21 9 3 11
     TRANSLATION:   COME QUICK
"Bring Help" is: _____


5.   CODE:          WZMTVI HZYLGZTV
     TRANSLATION:   DANGER SABOTAGE
"Bring Help" is: _____

## PART TWO

DIRECTIONS: Below is a list of 15 birds, but the letters of each have been scrambled. Unscramble the letters and write the words they spell in the blank spaces. For example, EGOSO when unscrambled spells GOOSE.
TIME LIMIT: 2 MINUTES

1. _____ CKUD
2. _____ LULG
3. _____ NOBRI
4. _____ WROC
5. _____ NHE
6. _____ NOPEIG
7. _____ WKHA
8. _____ LOW
9. _____ RORTAP
10. _____ WARPSOR
11. _____ GEELA
12. _____ KHIECCN
13. _____ LEUBBRDI
14. _____ BBRCLIKDA
15. _____ KROTS

## PART THREE

DIRECTIONS: Below is a list of 25 animals, but the letters of each have been scrambled. Unscramble the letters and write the words they spell in the blank spaces. For example, OOMSE when unscrambled spells MOOSE.
TIME LIMIT: 2 MINUTES

1. _____ WOC
2. _____ TGERI
3. _____ SHERO
4. _____ YOMEKN
5. _____ BATRIB

6. _____ RELQUISR

7. _____ PHESE

8. _____ ACT

9. _____ UESMO

10. _____ FULFABO

11. _____ AMECL

12. _____ KKUNS

13. _____ KYDENO

14. _____ ILGOLAR

15. _____ HEPLETAN

16. _____ BERA

17. _____ OLIN

18. _____ HRPTENA

19. _____ MAALL

20. _____ LMEU

21. _____ PLATENOE

22. _____ BBOONA

23. _____ TOGA

24. _____ CRONOSHIRE

25. _____ REZAB

# DO YOU HAVE A MECHANICAL BENT?

Mechanical aptitude can mean a knack for handling tools, machinery, and physical objects generally. There is a level at which appreciation of mechanical principles is the important thing, rather than the trick of manipulating a monkey wrench.

This test attempts to measure not your manual and motor skills, but your ingenuity with spaces and forces, and your grasp of mechanical phenomena. Visualization and spatial reasoning contribute to your score.

On the line provided before each question, write the letter that corresponds to the answer you think best completes the statement.

NO TIME LIMIT

*Answers on page 470*

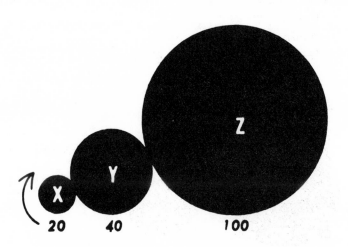

Assume that X, Y, and Z in the diagram above are gears. Gear X has 20 teeth, and drives Gear Y. Gear Y has 40 teeth, and drives Gear Z. Gear Z has 100 teeth.

_____ 1. If X turns in the direction shown by the arrow, Y will move:
   (a) In the same direction as the arrow.
   (b) In the opposite direction to the arrow.
   (c) Partly in the same direction as the arrow, and partly counter-clockwise.

_____ 2. If X turns in the direction shown by the arrow, Z will move:
   (a) In the same direction as the arrow.
   (b) In the opposite direction to the arrow.
   (c) Partly in the same direction as the arrow, and partly counter-clockwise.

_____ 3. If Z makes a complete turn, X will make:
   (a) 1/5 of a turn.
   (b) 5 turns.
   (c) 1¼ turns.


_____ 4. If X makes a complete turn, Z will make:
   (a) 1/5 of a turn.
   (b) 5 turns.
   (c) 1¼ turns.


_____ 5. If X makes a complete turn, Y will make:
   (a) 2 turns.
   (b) ½ turn.
   (c) 20 turns.


_____ 6. If a fourth gear is inserted between X and Y, Z will turn:
   (a) Faster.
   (b) Neither faster nor slower.
   (c) It depends on the size of the fourth gear.

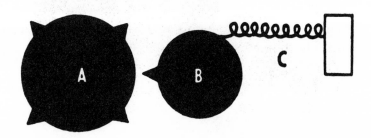

_____ 7. Examine the diagram above. Wheel A has four teeth and Wheel
       B has one tooth. When not being made to turn, B is snapped
       back to the original position by the pull of the steel spring C.
       Therefore:

   (a) Since A meshes with B, and since B cannot turn continuously
       because of the spring C, it follows that A cannot turn
       continuously.
   (b) If Wheel A turned clockwise more than once, then either B
       would stretch the spring too far and so force the apparatus to
       stop, or the spring would break under the tension.
   (c) Wheel A could keep turning, causing the tooth on B to move
       down and up four times to each revolution of A.

**93**

_____ 8. Take a look at the peculiar machine below. It is shown in starting position.

The ball pops out of the spout and falls on platform $p$, which causes the wheel B to partly turn. This causes platform $pp$ to tap the heavy pivoted beam C, one end of which is thus made to tap platform $ppp$, causing wheel D to partially turn. Could this machine work as described?

(a) No.

(b) No, because of friction.

(c) Yes, if the ball were heavy enough.

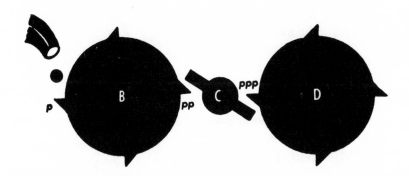

_____ 9. You want to get a stubborn screw out of your wall. It is already half out, but you have no screwdriver with which to finish the job. The best substitute tool is:

(a) A coin.

(b) A table knife.

(c) A penknife.

(d) Pliers.

_____ 10. You want to remove the nut from a rusty bolt sticking out of your stove. Since you have no pliers, you should use:

(a) A piece of wire looped around the nut.

(b) Scissors.

(c) A hammer.

(d) Your teeth.

_____ 11. You want to drive a nail into your closet wall, but have no hammer. You should use:

(a) A knife handle.

(b) A can opener.

(c) Heavy pliers.

(d) A riveting machine, if you happen to have one.

_____ 12. Your car has a flat rear tire on a country road, and you have no jack. You can change tires by:
   (a) Placing your spare tire on the road, then back your car until the flat tire is resting on the spare tire.
   (b) Scraping together a pile of stones or dirt, placing your spare tire on the mound, then backing your car until the flat tire is resting on the spare—and proceeding from there.
   (c) Scraping together a pile of stones or dirt, then backing your car so that the rear axle climbs the mound.

_____ 13. A box nailed together is stronger than the same box glued together.
   (a) Of course.
   (b) Of course not.
   (c) Not necessarily.

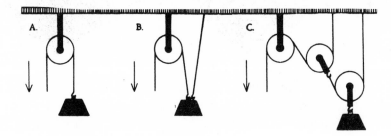

_____ 14. The diagram above shows three types of pulley arrangements. The pulleys weigh one pound each. The weights tip the scales at 500 pounds each. The arrangement which will require the least pull in the direction of the arrow in order to lift the weight is:
   (a) Pulley A.
   (b) Pulley B.
   (c) Pulley C.

# DO YOU HAVE PATTERN SKILL?

Tests of this kind were at one time great favorites with vocational counselors and personnel supervisors. If we are to believe the claims sometimes made for such tests, they can demonstrate a predilection for an enormous variety of tasks. These range from wrapping and packing to making the spatial adjustments required in handling tools. In any event, this test requires little mental effort and is amusing to take—but just what it measures is debatable.

Below you'll find seven pairs of circles. The second circle of each pair contains ruled lines. The first circle of each pair contains a pattern of x-marks. Each x-mark, if this circle were also ruled, would be situated at the point where two ruled lines meet. You must place the x-marks on the second circle at the corresponding points. Study the example:

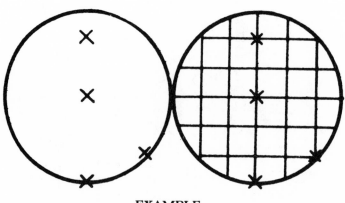

**EXAMPLE**

Here, the pattern of x-marks in the first circle has been duplicated in the second circle. Do the same for the seven pairs of circles below. Use no ruler or other mechanical aid. You must measure with your unaided eye.
TIME LIMIT: 5 MINUTES

*Answers on page 470*

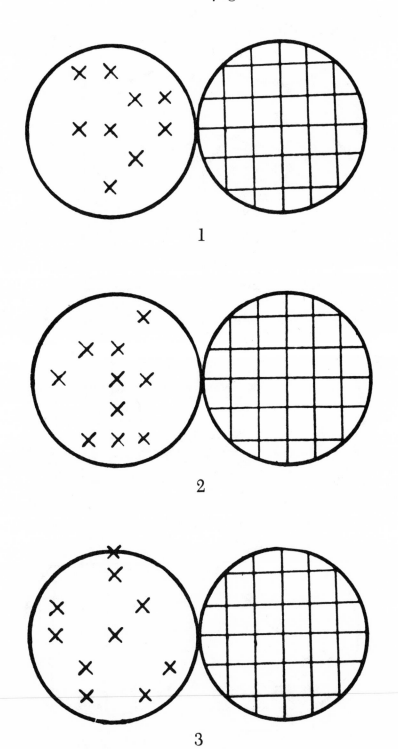

1

2

3

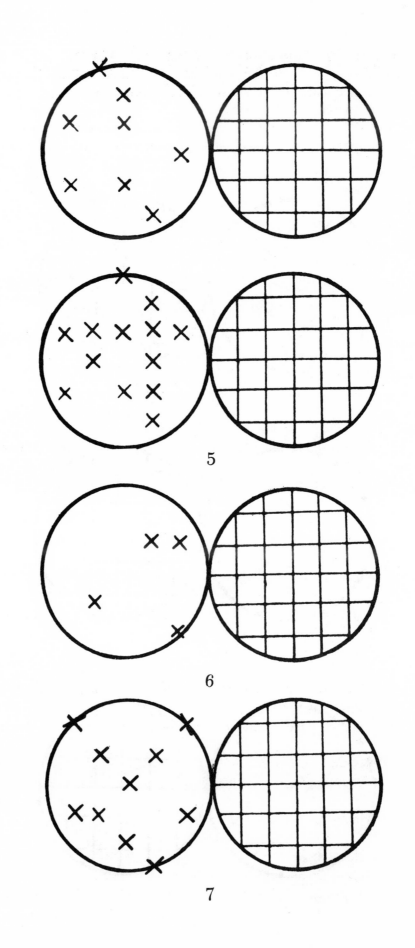

5

6

7

# TEST YOUR LOGIC NO. 3

Each question below is self-explanatory. Write your answer on the line which precedes the question. Do not spend too much time on any one question; skip the difficult questions and return to them later if you have the time.

TIME LIMIT: 25 MINUTES

*Answers on page 471*

_____ 1. RAKE is to LEAF as BROOM is to:
(1) marbles  (2) dust  (3) floor  (4) sweep  (5) bristle

_____ 2. In this group, which word does not belong?
(1) tuna  (2) whale  (3) shark  (4) herring  (5) swordfish

_____ 3. In this series, what number comes next?
8, 5, 3, 2 . . .

_____ 4. An ARDUOUS task is:
(1) lovable (2) spirited (3) difficult (4) dangerous (5) romantic

_____ 5. STRAP is to PAR as GREET is to:
(1) eat  (2) tee  (3) rap  (4) tea  (5) tree

_____ 6. These words can be arranged to form a sentence. If the sentence is true, write *T*. If the sentence is false, write *F*.
RUN DO GASOLINE NEED TO NOT CARS

_____ 7. If Alice had $12 more, she would have half again as much as Joyce. Together, the two girls now have $48. How much does Joyce have?

_____ 8. Which of the following words *cannot* be made from the letters of LEMONADE?
(1) almond  (2) emend  (3) nomad  (4) males  (5) demon

_____ 9. If 3 and 7 are prime integers, write A, unless 2408 is divisible by 6, in which case write Z.

_____ 10. BIRD is to FEATHERS as MAN is to:
(1) teeth  (2) skin  (3) hair  (4) nail  (5) feet

_____ 11. In this group, which word does not belong?
(1) producer (2) actor (3) composer (4) painter (5) sculptor

_____ 12. In this series, what number comes next?
6, 23, 91, 363 . . .

_____ 13. Which of these words most closely corresponds in meaning to
INEXORABLE?
(1) excruciating   (2) implacable   (3) remote   (4) perfect
(5) peerless

_____ 14. INCARCERATE is to PRISON as EDUCATE is to:
(1) jail   (2) teacher   (3) school   (4) pupil   (5) class

_____ 15. These words can be arranged to form a sentence. If the sentence
is true, write _T_. If the sentence is false, write _F_.
GREEN RED NOT ARE ONIONS

_____ 16. How many letters in this series follow vowels?
AQUITSPHUBRAISLE

_____ 17. If the 12th day of the month falls on Friday, on what day of the
week will the 29th fall?

_____ 18. A lake always has:
(1) fish   (2) algae   (3) a shore   (4) salt   (5) sand

_____ 19. PORCUPINE is to QUILLS as SKUNK is to:
(1) claws   (2) odor   (3) teeth   (4) stripe   (5) speed

_____ 20. In this group, which word does not belong?
(1) banjo   (2) mandolin   (3) harmonica   (4) lute   (5) guitar

_____ 21. In this series, what number comes next?
1000, 2000, 200, 400, 40 . . .

_____ 22. To EXASPERATE is to:
(1) terrify   (2) worsen   (3) annoy   (4) respire   (5) lie

_____ 23. TRAP is to STRIP as HACK is to:
(1) trip   (2) shack   (3) whack   (4) shock   (5) rack

_____ 24. These words can be arranged to form a sentence. If the sentence
is true, write _T_. If the sentence is false, write _F_.
FLY WINTER BIRDS IN NEVER SOUTH

_____ 25. If Milwaukee is north of Chicago and Chicago is east of Davenport, then Davenport is in what direction from Milwaukee?

**100**

_____ 26. No student over 18 cannot vote. Jane voted. Therefore:
  (1) Jane is over 18.
  (2) Jane is under 18.
  (3) Jane may or may not be over 18.

_____ 27. A pencil always has a(n):
  (1) eraser   (2) point   (3) lead   (4) trademark   (5) end

_____ 28. WORM is to APPLE as TERMITE is to:
  (1) nest   (2) tree   (3) insect   (4) larva   (5) destruction

_____ 29. In this group, which word does not belong?
  (1) unicorn   (2) roc   (3) phoenix   (4) dinosaur   (5) griffin

_____ 30. In this series, what number comes next?
  1/3, 7/12, 5/6, 13/12 . . .

_____ 31. John is two years older than Joe, three years older than Hank,
  and five years older than Willie. If Hank is twice Willie's age,
  how old is Joe?

_____ 32. In this group, which word does not belong?
  (1) zephyr   (2) sirocco   (3) nimbus   (4) gale   (5) squall

_____ 33. In this series, which number does not belong?
  10, 19, 28, 39, 46

_____ 34. In this series, what number comes next?
  1, —2, 0, —3, —1 . . .

_____ 35. In this series, what number comes next?
  10, 20, 32, 46 . . .

_____ 36. MAMMAL is to VERTEBRATE as INSECTIVORE is to:
  (1) mammal   (2) marsupial   (3) anteater   (4) primate
  (5) backbone

_____ 37. These words can be arranged to form a sentence. If the sentence
  is true, write _T_. If the sentence is false, write _F_.
  COLD SOME IS WATER VERY

_____ 38. No tove is blue; some toves are not green. Therefore:
  (1) All toves are either blue or green.
  (2) No tove is not blue.
  (3) Some toves are green.

_____ 39. Which of the following words *cannot* be made from the letters of ANCHORAGE?

(1) change  (2) charge  (3) coal  (4) chore  (5) crane

_____ 40. A fish always has:

(1) eyes  (2) fins  (3) smell  (4) teeth  (5) mass

_____ 41. In this group, which word does not belong?

(1) isthmus  (2) peninsula  (3) cape  (4) strait
(5) archipelago

_____ 42. In this series, which number does not belong?

1/10, 2, 21, 211, 2110

_____ 43. Which of these words most closely corresponds in meaning to ACUMEN?

(1) shrewdness  (2) charm
(3) decision  (4) yolk  (5) white

_____ 44. ACFJ is to BDE as MORV is to:

_____ 45. These words can be arranged to form a sentence. If the sentence is true, write *T*. If the sentence is false, write *F*.

WHITE BEAR FUR HAS NO

_____ 46. Some gnomes can speak and swim; no gnome cannot walk. Therefore:

(1) No gnomes can walk and swim.
(2) No gnome can speak and walk.
(3) All gnomes that speak can walk.

_____ 47. Jane had a bag of marbles. Her mother gave her 10 more marbles; Jane then gave half of her marbles to Mary. If she found that she now had three times as many marbles as when she'd started, how many did she have originally?

_____ 48. In this series, what number comes next?

1, —2, 6, —12, 36 . . .

_____ 49. In this group, which word does not belong?

(1) circle  (2) orb  (3) sphere
(4) ball  (5) globe

_____ 50. In this series, what number comes next?

180, 60, 63, 21, 24 . . .

_____ 51. Which of these words most closely corresponds in meaning to
COGENT?
(1) approximate   (2) valid
(3) congested   (4) integer
(5) critical

_____ 52. ITALIAN is to ROMAN as GREEK is to:
(1) empire   (2) Spartan
(3) Sicilian   (4) ancient
(5) nationality

_____ 53. These words can be arranged to form a sentence. If the sentence
is true, write _T_. If the sentence is false, write _F_.
IS DEAD ENGLISH A LANGUAGE

_____ 54. In this group, which word does not belong?
(1) ebony   (2) indigo   (3) raven
(4) sable

_____ 55. In this series, which number does not belong?
16, 12, 9, 4, 0

_____ 56. Which of the following words _cannot_ be made from the letters of
the word EXACTLY?
(1) latex   (2) lace   (3) lake   (4) cleat   (5) eclat

_____ 57. In this series, what letter comes next?
Z, B, X, D, V . . .

_____ 58. In this series, which letter does not belong?
A B E C I G O F U

_____ 59. To GARROTE is to:
(1) eliminate   (2) strangle
(3) squelch   (4) pilfer
(5) promote

_____ 60. Peter has 16 more apples than Joe, who has 10 more apples than
Sylvester. Together, the three boys have 66 apples. How many
does Sylvester have?

# SPOONERISMS

William Archibald Spooner was a British clergyman who lived from 1844 to 1930. He was a very nice man, but probably a little self-conscious. Very often, when he was speaking or lecturing, he would unwittingly switch his words around. His mistakes, which caused much laughter, have made him immortal.

On one occasion, Spooner, intending to announce to his congregation that they were about to sing the hymn "From Greenland's Icy Mountains," declared the title to be "From Iceland's Greasy Mountains."

It is reported that Spooner once referred to Queen Victoria as "our queer old dean."

This kind of mistake, switching around letters and thus changing the words, is called a spoonerism. Here are some others:

Shores of skells were fired in a bittle batter.

The picture is available in color and whack and blight.

Shellout falters.

He is a newted nose analyst.

President Hoobert Heever.

The Duck and Dooches of Windsor.

The sporks and foons.

You hissed my mystery lectures.

The rapes of grath.

A blushing crow.

The tons of soil.

His sin twister.

Outside, a roaring pain is falling.

I am grattered and flatified.

"Kinquering Kongs Their Titles Take"

"Is it kisstomary to cuss the bride?"

Hisses and kugs.

Sing a song of sixpence, a rocketful of pie.

Would you like metchup or custard on your hot dog?

As dizzy as the bay is long.

The new president was born in on the Swible.

Perhaps the most famous spoonerism is apocryphal. The story goes that the good reverend walked over to a lady in church and said, "Mardon me, padam, but this pie is occupewed. May I sew you to another sheet?"

Some vaudeville comic dreamed up this Spooneristic routine for a drunk:

"Now missen, lister, all I had was tee martoonis. Sough I theem under the affluence of inkahol, I'm not palf as hickled—half as packled—as thinkle peep—as theeple pink I am."

# UPROARIOUS JOKES

THE PRESIDENT of the congregation had to undergo surgery. The board met to decide how to show their concern. Finally, it was agreed that the secretary of the congregation would visit the president in the hospital.

Two days after the operation, the secretary visited the sickroom. "I bring you the good wishes of our board," he said. "We hope you get well and live to be 120 years old!"

The president smiled back weakly.

"And that's an official resolution," continued the secretary, "passed by a vote of twelve to nine."


A HENPECKED HUSBAND was suffering a torrent of abuse. His wife went on and on, becoming more and more furious until in a fit of frenzy she threatened to hit him on the head with a rolling pin.

Whereupon the cowed man slid under the bed and refused to reappear.

"Come out! You bum! Come out!" yelled the angry woman.

"I will *not*!" shouted the man from under the bed. "I'll show you who's boss in this house!"

THE NEW NEIGHBOR joined the mah johngg group for the first time, and all the ladies gaped at the huge diamond she wore.

"It's the third most famous diamond in the world," she told the women confidentially. "First is the Hope diamond, then the Kohinoor diamond, and then this one—the Rabinowitz diamond."

"It's beautiful!" admired one woman enviously. "You're so lucky!"

"Not so lucky," the newcomer maintained. "Unfortunately, with the famous Rabinowitz diamond, I have received the famous Rabinowitz curse."

"And what is that?" wondered the women.

The woman heaved an enormous sigh. "Mr. Rabinowitz," she said.

SAM BROMBERG HAD BEEN a cutter for some 20-odd years. All his life he had dreamed of owning a Cadillac.

But when Sam got to the point where he had actually saved up enough money to buy such a sumptuous car, he suddenly collapsed at his table and died.

His friends conferred about his burial. One of them spoke up and said, "You know, all his life Sam dreamed about owning a Cadillac. I think it would be fitting and proper if we took the money that he saved up and purchased the best Cadillac on the market and buried him in it." The other friends agreed.

On the day of the funeral, all Sam's friends gathered around the burial plot, which was about ten times as large as an ordinary grave. Six workmen had been employed to dig the grave. While the service was being intoned, the huge Cadillac was lowered from a crane into the grave.

One of the workmen lifted his head and marvelled at this brand new shining monster of a car coming down into the grave. In the front seat sat Sam all dressed up in white coat and tails. The workman nudged the man next to him and exclaimed, "Oh boy! That's the way to live!"

TWO OLD FRIENDS met, after not having seen each other for years. "Rosie! You look marvelous!" exclaimed Gussie.

"Yeh," said Rosie, "I'm feeling great. I'll tell you a secret. I'm having an affair."

Gussie smiled broadly. "Oh, that's marvelous! Who's catering?"

A RUSSIAN JEW had become successful. He was allowed to travel outside the country as a member of the Russian embassy. In England, he met up with some young Jewish Socialists, and found himself subject to many questions.

"Comrade," said one of the Britishers, "I understand you are a Jew; I understand you are a man of integrity. Now it would be of great interest to me to have your opinion of the Soviet attitude toward the Arab-Israeli conflict. Why do the Russians support the Egyptian fascists against the democratic Israelis?"

The Russian said nothing.

But the questioners continued. "I know your country has an official policy, and so does your party. But as a Jew you must have your own view of justice. Who do you think is right?"

The Russian maintained his silence.

But the young Englishmen persisted. "Surely you have some opinion?" they demanded.

Finally the Russian, up against the wall, replied, "Yes, I do have an opinion, but I do not agree with it."

MISS DANFORTH WAS a great racing fan. One afternoon, she decided to take her kindergarten class to the race track. She knew the experience would be exciting and she thought it would also be educational. As a matter of fact, the kids had a great time.

Before taking them back to school, she decided they had all better be taken to the bathroom. She asked one of the guards where the bathrooms were and if he would mind taking the little boys to the men's room while she escorted the girls to the ladies' room. He told the teacher that he couldn't leave his post, but since the children were so young and the boys were rougher than the girls he advised her to take them all into the men's room and it would be perfectly all right. He assured her that there was nobody in there at the time.

So Miss Danforth herded them all into the men's room, watching to be sure that every one of them was using the facilities. Suddenly her eyes swept downward from the even row of heads. Her eyes just about popped out of her head. She looked up in amazement, "Wh- who- are - you?"

The voice answered, "What the hell are you talking about, lady! I'm the guy who's riding Lazy Mare in the sixth."

A LOVELY BUT rather flat-chested young woman visited a physician for her periodic physical examination.

"Please remove your blouse," the doctor told her.

"Oh, no," the young lady protested, "I just couldn't!"

"Come, come," the doctor replied, "let's not make mountains out of molehills."

THE NEWLYWEDS had just moved into their first apartment, and had decided to begin married life with twin beds. During their first week in the apartment, the wife brought home and placed over her bed the motto: "I need thee every hour."

The husband promptly went out shopping and returned with a sign of his own, which read: "God give me strength."

MOORE SPOTTED MILLER at the clubhouse bar one afternoon and rushed over excitedly. "I've heard about the tragedy you experienced last weekend. It must've been terrible!"

Miller sipped his martini and nodded, lowering his head with the unpleasant memory. "I was playing a twosome with old Mr. Crawford," he murmured solemnly, "and the poor guy dropped dead on the seventh green."

"And I heard you carried him all the way back to the clubhouse," Moore said, admiration gleaming in his eyes. "That was quite a job. Old Crawford must've weighed at least 250 pounds."

"Oh," Miller replied, sipping again, "carrying him wasn't difficult. What tired me was putting him down at every stroke, and then picking him up again."

ON A SWANKY BEACH in Rhode Island, the local constable came up to a cute young thing and said, "Look, you're perfectly within the law wearing that abbreviated bikini, but just tell me, aren't you ashamed of yourself wearing so little clothing?"

The girl replied, "No sir, not at all! If I were," she said glancing down at her shapely thighs, "I'd wear more."

A TRAVELING SALESMAN walked into a hashery. He instructed the waitress, "Look, I want two eggs, and I want them fried very hard. I want two pieces of toast burnt to a crisp, and I want a cup of coffee weak, luke warm, and practically undrinkable."

"What!" exclaimed the waitress, "What kind of an order is that?"

"Never you mind," insisted the salesman, "just bring me what I asked for."

The waitress went back to the kitchen, told the chef there was a looney guy outside and gave him the order. The chef prepared everything just as it was ordered. The waitress brought the miserable breakfast back to the table, and said coolly, "Anything else, Sir?"

"Why, yes," said the salesman, "please sit down next to me and nag me. I'm homesick."

A POOR FARMER who had a huge family decided to take them out to the County Fair. Once there, everybody wanted to see the exhibit with the prize bull. But tickets were $1.00 each and the poor man was aghast at the thought of such an outlay. He approached the ticket hawker and said, "Mister, look, I've got a wife and 18 children. Couldn't you let us go in at half price?"

"Eighteen children?" gasped the amazed official. "Just wait here a minute and I'll bring the bull out to see you."

A WOMAN WAS TRYING to maneuver her car out of a parking space. She first crashed into the car ahead, then banged into the car behind, and finally struck a passing delivery truck as she pulled into the street. A policeman who had watched her bumbling efforts approached her. "All right, lady," he demanded, "let's see your license."

"Don't be silly, officer," she replied. "Who'd give *me* a license?"

"DOCTOR, I FEEL TERRIBLE," the staid businessman told his doctor. "Tell me what's wrong with me."

"First let me ask you a few questions," the doctor replied. "Do you drink much alcohol?"

"I have never touched the stuff in my life," the businessman replied indignantly.

"Do you smoke?" the doctor continued.

"I have never touched the filthy weed in my life."

"Do you stay up late at night?"

"Of course not!" the patient huffed. "I'm in bed every night by ten-thirty for a good night's rest."

"Well then," the doctor continued, "do you have sharp pains in the head?"

"Exactly!" the businessman replied. "I have pains in the head all the time."

"Just as I suspected," the doctor smirked. "Your halo is on too tight!"

A MAN CONSULTED a pychiatrist for help with various problems. The analyst said, "Stretch out here on the couch. Just relax and tell me about your early life. Just keep on talking. Say anything that comes to mind."

The man proceeded to spill out his life's story. Suddenly the analyst took out a big balloon and, sitting behind the patient, blew it up to full size. Then he stuck a pin in it. The balloon burst with a loud crash. The patient was startled. The doctor said sharply, "Now tell me, quick, what did you think about when you heard the loud explosion?"

"I thought of sex."

"Sex? At such a moment? You thought about sex?"

"Well," said the patient, "what's so surprising about that? It's all I ever think about."


FELIX SIMMONS was a nice guy, but a social flop. Although he was 35, he had never conquered his childhood habit of bedwetting. Finally, one of his dear friends told him, "Look, Felix, you might as well know the truth. We're all very fond of you, but nobody can stand to come into your house because it smells, and you're driving your wife up a wall. Why don't you see a psychiatrist about your problem. Enuresis is not too uncommon and it can be cured. Get it over with once and for all."

Felix was convinced. After six months of treatment he ran into the same friend. "Well, Felix, did you take my advice?"

"Yes," answered Felix, "I've been seeing a psychiatrist three times a week for four months now."

"Well, have you had any results?"

"Oh," beamed Felix, "great results!"

"You don't wet your bed anymore?"

"I still do, but now I'm proud of it."

AN INSURANCE AGENT was teaching his wife how to drive when the brakes of their car failed on a steep downhill grade.

"I can't stop!" shrieked the wife. "What'll I do now?"

"Brace yourself," her husband advised, "and try to hit something cheap."

THREE OLD MEN were sitting around drinking tea and philosophizing about life. One said, "You know, it is my opinion that the best thing there is in life is good health. Without good health, life isn't worth a darn."

The second took exception. "Well," he said, "I've known plenty of rich men who were sick, terribly sick. But they had lots and lots of money and they went to the best specialists. They went through all kinds of treatments and operations and they came out almost as good as new. The fact is that without money life isn't worth much. You can be as robust as a lion and still be miserable if you don't have a red cent. On the other hand, with money you can buy practically anything. In my opinion, the best thing in life is to have money."

The third one had listened patiently. And now he demurred, saying, "Yes, health is good, and money is good, but I've seen people with plenty of money who are utterly miserable, and I've seen people in good health who were miserable. The fact is that rich or poor, healthy or sick, life in itself is an enormous overwhelming misery. In my opinion, the best thing in life really is not to be born at all."

The other two responded to this remark by plunging themselves into deep contemplation. Finally, one broke the silence. "Yes, Danny, you're right. The best thing in life, as you say, is not to be born at all. But, tell me, who can be so lucky, one out of a million?"

MRS. MELTZER INVITED her new neighbor in for a cup of coffee, and to show her around the house.

"What a beautiful lamp!" admired the neighbor.

"Yes," said Mrs. Meltzer modestly, "I got it with Bleach-o detergent coupons."

"And I like that painting on the wall!" the neighbor went on.

"I got that with Bleach-o coupons, too."

"Oh, a piano! I've always wanted a piano."

"Well, as a matter of fact, I got that piano from Bleach-o coupons, too."

Then the neighbor tried one door handle that wouldn't budge. "What's in that room?" she asked full of curiosity.

"Bleach-o detergent! What else?"

Mo and Beck went to City Hall to apply for a wedding license. They were directed to the third floor where they had to fill out forms. When that was done, they were to take the forms to the sixth floor, pay a fee, and then they'd get their license.

They obediently filled out the forms, went up to the sixth floor and waited on a line. Eventually, they came to the front of the line, where the man looked over the forms.

"Beck?" he said. "Your legal name isn't Beck, is it? Go back to the third floor and fill out a new form with your real name, Rebecca."

So the couple went back downstairs, filled out another form, returned to the sixth floor, waited on line, and arrived before the man again.

This time the man got up to the part with Mo's name on it. He frowned, "Mo? That doesn't sound like an English name to me."

"Well, my real name is Michael," said Mo, "but I've always been called Mo—"

"Go back down to the third floor," interrupted the man, "and fill these forms out in full English!"

So the couple went down again, filled out another form, came back up to the sixth floor, waited again on line, and eventually arrived at the window. The names were okay this time, but this time the man found the address unacceptable. They had written 'Williamsburg, New York.' "Williamsburg is just a section of Brooklyn," said the man. "Go downstairs and rewrite the forms, and this time write 'Brooklyn, New York' instead of 'Williamsburg, New York.'"

Mo and Beck went through the whole procedure yet another time and returned to the sixth floor. Finally, after several hours at City Hall, everything seemed in order.

Mo sighed and turned to Beck. "It's worth it, sweetheart. Now our little boy will know that everything is legal."

The official glared at them. "Did I hear you say you have a little boy?" Mo admitted they did.

"You already have a baby and you're just getting a wedding license today? Do you know that makes your little boy a technical bastard?"

Mo was icy. "So?" he countered. "That's what the man on the third floor said *you* are, and *you* seem to be doing all right!"

THE HOT-TEMPERED GOLFER had spent 15 minutes in the rough unsuccessfully searching for a lost ball, and his patience was being worn to a frazzle. The caddy was no help.

Just as the linksman was about to give up the search in disgust, an elderly lady seated under a nearby tree called out to him: "Excuse me, sir, but will I be breaking the rules if I tell you where your ball is?"

IT WAS AFTER THE second world war had ended. Joe Dink was still in Japan waiting to be discharged. His wife, Irma Dink, was wild with anxiety and jealousy because she had read about the goings on between the American soldiers and the Japanese girls. Finally she could stand it no longer, and she wrote her husband. "Joe, hurry up and come back. What do those girls have anyway that the American girls don't?"

"Not a thing," wrote back Joe, "but what they have got, they've got here."

A MAN OBVIOUSLY three sheets to the wind staggered down the street and bumped into a woman of obvious respectability. "You horrible creature," she glowered. "You are the drunkest man I have ever seen."

The drunk turned slowly and said, "Lady, you're the ugliest woman I've ever seen! And that's worse, 'cause when I wake up tomorrow, I'm gonna be sober."

TWO BUSINESS PARTNERS had never had an argument in 20 years. One week one of the pair came down with a virus and missed a few days at the store.

On the fourth day of his absence the ailing partner received a call from his associate, who told him, "I just found $15,000 missing from the safe. What should I do?"

His partner replied quickly, "Put it back!"

THE HUSBAND CAME HOME drunk again. His wife couldn't stand it. She screamed at him, "If you don't stop this damnable drinking, I'm going to kill myself."

The hapless husband retorted, "Promises, that's all I get. Promises."

Two GOLFERS were marking time before they could tee off. "I suppose you heard," said one, "that Timothy Brown killed his wife."

"Yes, I heard something about it," responded the other, "but how? how did it happen?"

"Oh, with a golf club."

"Oh, is that so? How many strokes?"

A MAN WALKED into a hotel with a woman of dubious morals and stepped up to the desk to register. "Shall I call for the boy to take your baggage up for you?" asked the clerk.

"No thanks," replied the young man. "She can walk."

Two WOMEN of old acquaintance ran into each other on a downtown street. "Why, Mrs. Brown!" cried the first. "I haven't seen you in years! You look great, but whatever have you done to your hair? It looks exactly like a wig."

"To tell you the truth," said the second with some embarrassment, "it is a wig."

"Really? Well, you certainly can't tell!"

Two LABORERS STOPPED in front of a jewelry store window to admire a tray of sparkling diamonds. "How would you like to have your pick?" asked one.

"I'd rather have my shovel," replied the other. "I could get more that way."

# RAZZBERRY

RAZZBERRY is idiot's delight for misanthropes, misogynists, grouches, crabs, and sourpusses in general. It's your chance to get even with your worst enemy. But after all, it's all in the spirit of fun and everybody is given an equal portion of mud.

To get down to the dirty details:

The hostess first provides each player with a pencil and a sheet of paper. Then one of the players volunteers for martyrdom. Before he leaves the room, he announces that he represents a certain object. For example, he might say, "I am a chair," or "I am an overcoat," or "I am a pair of scissors." As he pronounces the phrase which is the death warrant to his self-esteem, he must immediately depart the scene.

Then his executioners go to work. The idea is to describe the personality of the vanished guest in terms of the object named. Each writes down as many descriptions on his or her piece of paper as time and ingenuity will permit. For example, suppose the victim proclaimed "I AM A BAG." When he is recalled after four minutes and the papers are read, he might hear the following accusations:

"You're a windBAG."

"You're a sham BAGatelle."

"You're just a one-BAGger."

"You're a BAG of bones."

"You're a cheap BAGgage."

"You're a BAGpipe that plays false notes."

"You're a BAG that's been punctured."

Or suppose a person said he was a piano. The following phrases might aptly describe him:

"You're a PIANO that's tight shut."

"You're a second-hand PIANO."

"You're an upright PIANO."

"You're a PIANO that's out of tune."

"You're a PIANO that needs moving."

"You're a PIANO with the soft pedal missing."

"You're a grand PIANO."

"You're a PIANO that won't play unless it's given money."

"You're a PIANO that needs dusting."

No matter how vile the defamation, it is assumed that "it" has waived all claim for libel. After the hostess reads the indictment, the accused is asked to choose which phrase he liked best. The author of the victim's choice in turn becomes a new sacrifice, and is given a scant minute to announce just what *he* represents.

It's a good game for getting even with a lot of people, and you'll be surprised at the cleverness with which most of us can dish it out. The trick, of course, is to be able to take it.

# "X-LY"

If you have any friends who think they have a flair for the dramatic, make them prove it by playing this game.

IT chooses an adverb—the juicier the better—but does not divulge his selection to the others. The adverb is dubbed "X-ly."

Each person tells IT to perform an act in the manner of the adverb he has chosen.

Suppose the word is "tenderly." IT may be ordered to walk X-ly, to talk X-ly, to drink X-ly, to ask for a date X-ly.

So he walks *tenderly*, then talks *tenderly*, then asks for a date *tenderly* . . . . . If you think that's easy, just try drinking *tenderly*!

The audience, of course, tries to guess the word in question from the actions of IT. The person who succeeds is the IT for the next game.

# UP, JENKINS!

This is a non-strenuous game, suitable for use after the heaviest refreshment—liquid or otherwise. All you need is a rectangular table, a coin, and enough guests to make two teams.

The members of each team sit together on one side of the table. Operations are started by giving the coin to one captain. The players on his team proceed to pass it from hand to hand, under the table, endeavoring to conceal its whereabouts by poker-faces and a minimum of motion.

After a suitable interval, the captain of the opposing team cries "Up, Jenkins!" At this command, the players on the coin-passing team must raise their clenched fists. At the signal "Down, Jenkins!" they slam down their *open* hands on the table. The person holding the coin attempts, of course, to conceal it under his palm, and tries to keep it from making a too obvious clink when it hits the table.

Then the opposing team goes into a one-minute huddle, trying to decide under which hand the coin lies. When they have reached a decision, the captain calls "Lift" to each one of the players on the other team, calling on them in any order his team desires. As each player's name is called, he lifts his hands.

The last hand to be called is the one that the captain *hopes* covers the coin.

If the Second Team guesses correctly, it scores 100. If not, it gets 10 points for each hand lifted before the coin was discovered. The first team to score 300 points, wins.

There's a load of fun in this game—in watching the opposing team try to read expressions—in the awkward fumblings—in the attempts to give false cues! Here's psychology at play in a big way!

# EYEFUL

The game of EYEFUL can be played by any number of people. It requires paraphernalia that can readily be found in the ordinary household. The object of the game is to test one's visual appreciation of quantity. Five objects are presented to the company. They are:

1)  A book
2)  A jar full of beans
3)  A box half full of cigarettes
4)  A pitcher half full of water and a small glass
5)  A bunch of spaghetti stalks tightly stuffed into a vase or bottle

The players, having been provided with pencil and paper, are asked to estimate how many pages there are in the book, how many beans there are in the jar; how many cigarettes there are in the box; how many tumblers of water the pitcher contains; and how many stalks of spaghetti are in the vase or jar. The hostess, of course, has accurately made all these computations in advance. The person who produces the closest estimate of the number of pages in the book gets the book as a prize and scores ten points. Runner-up position scores nine points; third place, eight points; and so on down the line. The bean expert gets the beans. The authority on liquid measure gets a long drink of water. The champion cigarette man gets a bunch of free smokes. The spaghetti connoisseur, who is doubtless a good cook, can try his art on the spaghetti. The vase stays put.

For all events, points are scored as outlined above. The guest with the highest score is awarded the baccalaureate degree B.E. (Best Estimator). As a grand prize, he or she can be given a recommendation to a Commissary Department, or a more munificent offering, if the hostess feels so inclined.

The number of items can be increased if desired. It is suggested that the hostess conceal the fact that prizes await individual winners.


# TEAKETTLE

IT leaves the room, and in his absence the company decides on two or more words which are pronounced alike but have different meanings, such as *sail* and *sale; two, too* and *to; root* and *route; ail* and *ale; new* and *knew.*

When IT returns, he hears this kind of double-talk, each person making a single contribution.

"I told him I'd *teakettle* him if he took me out in that *teakettle* again."
"Don't you like *teakettling?*"
"It *teakettles* me."

"Speaking of that, he's frightfully bloodthirsty; every time he goes on a picnic he *teakettles* hundreds of innocent little ants.

"My *teakettle* has runners."

Of course, the conversation has to be revealing enough to give ɪᴛ a chance to guess what *teakettle* is. Considerable ingenuity is required to keep it going after the first three or four sentences, and to play fair with ɪᴛ without making the game a give-away.

P. S. If you're going to stay up nights, we might as well tell you that the words used in the conversation above are *slay* and *sleigh*.


# GUATELAVIAN MURDER

This game is a natural for a large house or apartment with lots of rooms.

The guests are told that ɪᴛ has murdered someone!

Then, the lights are doused and the house plunged in blackest Stygian black. ɪᴛ makes a get-away. He gets three minutes to hide.

Then, with sound and fury—but no matches, candles or searchlights—the pack starts out in hot pursuit, spreading all over the house, groping for the culprit.

Somewhere, in some closet covered with the dust of ages, or perhaps in the bathtub, a hardy G-woman finds the murderer.

Is ɪᴛ apprehended and turned over to the police? No Siree! Not in Guatelavia! . . . . The posse, in strict Guatelavian fashion, is bribed, and hides right along with the murderer.

The second person who finds the hiding place acts in like manner—and so on, until the whole group is packed together.

The last one to discover the murderer et al. gets the booby prize and misses the fun.

The first one to find the hideout is the next murderer.

# APPROPRIATE ADVERBS

"I wish I'd made that bet," said the bookmaker, hoarsely.

♚

"Do you think you understand my painting?" asked Picasso, artfully.

♚

"Bing Crosby might get a sore throat," said Bob, hopefully.

"What an ample bosom!" he remarked, robustly.

♚

"But I don't want a spaniel, I want a corgi," said the pet-fancier, doggedly.

♚

"Your drip-dries are crumpled," said the laundress, ironically.

♚

"I only want 20,000 machine guns," said the dictator, disarmingly.

♚

"This is an imitation diamond," said the dealer, stonily.

♚

"I practiced three hours on my guitar," said the folk singer, pluckily.

"Dear Sirs, please send me your catalogue," he wrote, listlessly.

☖

"These pants are not short enough," said the young girl, hotly.

☖

"I wasn't there," she remarked, absently.

☖

"I must attend to my flock," said the vicar, sheepishly.

☖

"My Chinese necklace has been stolen," she said, jadedly.

☖

"How do you like my petticoat?" she asked, shiftlessly.

☖

"I am on the wrong street," said the Frenchman, ruefully.

☖

"I have flunked this lousy exam," said the student, testily.

☖

"My aim is true," said the swordsman, pointedly, as he lunged toward his
    opponent.

☖

"Have you anything by Hugo?" asked Les, miserably.

☖

"I've $400.00, any more?" asked the auctioneer, morbidly.

☖

"I don't *have* to do this for a living," she said, tartly.

"May I leave the room?" asked the schoolboy, highhandedly.

♕

"This ain't real turtle soup!" the woman said, mockingly.

♕

"He resembles a goat!" he chortled, satirically.

♕

"My pencil is dull," he remarked, pointlessly.

"I tore his valentine in two," she said, halfheartedly.

♕

"Press your own shirt!" she declared, flatly.

♕

"I'll drive the truck," he whispered, shiftily.

♕

"Yes, I've read *Gulliver's Travels*," he replied, swiftly.

♕

"I work as a ditch-digger", he announced, trenchantly.

♕

"We're out of pumpernickel," said the baker, wryly.

"Have you ever read Voltaire?" the teacher asked, candidly.

♛

"My dime rolled into the sewer," the boy cried, gratefully.

♛

"A mule is half donkey and half horse," he explained, crossly.

♛

"You still haven't learned how to bake," her husband sneered, crustily.

♛

"I hate shellfish!" she snapped, crabbedly.

♛

"My glands are swollen," she said, mumpishly.

♛

"I've got all the work I can handle," the doctor said, patiently.

♛

"I'll cut him to ribbons!" she scowled, mincingly.

♛

"I wish I could remember the name of that card game," she said, wistfully.

♛

"I slept in a draft last night," he remarked, stiffly.

♛

"I can't stand strawberries," she said, rashly.

♛

"May he rest in peace," the minister intoned, gravely.

# CROSSWORD PUZZLE NO. 1

*Answers on page 471*

**ACROSS**

1. National pastime
9. Period of the year
15. Zoological kingdom
16. Robe
17. Two-pronged instrument
18. Yardsticks
20. Wink
21. European blackbird
22. Devour
23. Swedish singer
24. Last
25. Masculine name
26. Wood of an E. Indian tree
27. Gasps
28. Fibrous Asiatic plant
29. In the thing
30. Centers
31. Defender of Troy
32. Attempts
33. Weight-raising device
34. Canarylike finches
36. Restrain
37. Thus
39. Inclining
40. Chemical element
41. Morass
42. Swelling
43. Factions
44. Full-grown pike
45. Employ
46. Pitchers
47. Drum major's stick
48. Spruce up
50. Heavenly
51. Equalizer
52. Gems
54. Peruse again
55. Lacking plant ovules

**DOWN**

1. Idle talker
2. Distillate of indigo
3. Auxiliary railroad track
4. Edit
5. Financial institution
6. High in the musical scale
7. Chinese weight
8. Bemoans
9. Little
10. Facility
11. Babylonian god of the sky
12. Ribbonlike flag
13. Genus of Australian shrubs
14. Cuddles up
19. Epochs
21. Burrows
24. Passengers
25. Cudgeler
27. Aim
28. Carousal
30. Brittle
31. Philippine Negritos
32. Verse of three measures
33. Europeans
34. Greeter
35. Not easily graspable
36. Edicts
37. Fleeting periods
38. Unity
40. Encounter
41. Vain
43. Turf
44. Former French statesman
46. Genus of tropical herbs
47. Feathered animal
49. Anglo-Saxon king
50. Letter
53. Pronoun

# CROSSWORD PUZZLE NO. 2

*Answers on page 471*

## ACROSS

1. Hew
5. Mexican fiber plant
10. A court, as of a college: slang
14. Italian coin
15. Angry
16. Impel
17. Affirm
18. Part of the skeleton
19. Plant of the bean family
20. Young animal
22. Something antiquated
23. Small table mat
24. Outer garment
25. Printer's measure
27. Beverage
28. Wedlock
32. Agitate
34. Scoff
36. Sane
37. Biblical country
39. Cossack
41. Hawaiian goose
42. Light boat
44. Surgical thread
46. Muscular twitching
47. Convey
49. Nevertheless
51. Pronoun
52. Crosspiece in a link
53. Ship's crane
55. One who glides over the ice
58. Erasure
61. Steamship
62. French novelist
63. Burden
64. Wide-mouthed pitcher
65. Levels with the ground
66. Cupid
67. Clever people
68. Put forth, as force
69. Pointed weapon

## DOWN

1. Common plastic earth
2. Bee structure
3. Mountain nymph
4. Talking bird
5. Hissing
6. Sarcasm
7. Chanted
8. Goddess of malicious mischief
9. French article
10. Interrogation
11. Vases
12. Hindu god of fire
13. Apportion
19. Floats aloft
21. Falsehoods
22. In behalf of
24. Twenty-fourth part
25. Dispossess
26. Pertaining to the cheek
28. Measure
29. Assist
30. Tutelar deities
31. Construct
33. Frog
35. Made comfortable
38. Fabulous animals
40. Supporter of a monarchy
43. Compound ether
45. Field of granular snow
48. Pelt
50. Named
53. Restrain from action
54. Coronet
55. Killed
56. Apteryx
57. Dillseed
58. Nap
59. Scent
60. Bird habitation
62. Negligent
65. Concerning

# CROSSWORD PUZZLE NO. 3

*Answers on page 471*

*Answers on page 471*

## ACROSS

1. Rodents
5. Tinges
10. Tolypeutine
14. Notice
15. Willowy
16. Slide
17. Control
19. Sheer
20. Service
21. Lavish
23. Custom
24. That which erodes
25. Allure
27. Pert girl
28. Cossack
32. Forth
33. Haughty
34. Bovine hybrid
35. Benefit
37. Kith
38. Stoop
39. Positive
40. Umbrella-shaped finial
41. Dye
42. Believe
43. Dray
44. Floating
46. Dutch measure
47. Value
50. Neckwear
53. Glasswort
54. Burlesque
56. Forest ox
57. Institute
58. A simple whole
59. Sutured
60. Pintails
61. Cloister

## DOWN

1. Travel
2. Whit
3. Allure
4. The greenbriers
5. American statesman
6. Inland islet
7. Requital
8. Chest
9. Sir: Sp.
10. The letter H
11. Stopple
12. Light breeze
13. Giddiness
18. Daughter of Chaos
22. Accessory
24. Politic
25. Phrase
26. Exaggerated
27. Nocturnal insect
29. Equal
30. Alnus
31. A red pigment
33. Locust
34. Pack
36. Moon investigator
37. Inferior parts
39. Arbitrate
42. Quell
43. Xerophyte
45. Grains
46. Masculine name
47. Assamese hill tribesmen
48. Division in a checker pattern
49. Farm utensil
50. Functions
51. The second part of a minuet
52. Bristle
55. Freeze

# CROSSWORD PUZZLE NO. 4

*Answers on page 471*

## ACROSS

1. Dinner
7. Beat severely: slang
15. Greek god
16. Antipathy
17. Whirlpool
18. Enemies of the Crusaders
19. Trouble
20. Legislative council
22. Chief Scandinavian god
23. A genus of perennial rosaceous herbs
25. Rough, steep rock
27. Beaches
30. Attempt
32. Intermittent fever
34. Roman emperor
35. Coarse flax
37. One who ornaments with raised work
39. Malt beverage
42. Tibetan antelope
44. Pacifier
45. Female sheep
46. Small migratory rodents of the Arctic region
49. Profit
51. Last name of character from "Arabian Nights"
52. Carry: colloq.
54. Running knot

58. Shrewd
60. Dress
62. Combat
63. Snare
65. Group of players
67. Three: prefix
68. Cause to explode
71. Bent
73. Opposed to feudal
74. Three in one
75. State of a benefice when occupied
76. Seasoned

## DOWN

1. Devastate
2. Lyric poems
3. Permeable
4. Higher part of musical scale
5. Sliding vehicle
6. Poisonous
7. Ship's ballast
8. Topaz humming bird
9. Spotted jewfish
10. Small nails
11. Inhabitants of the torrid zone
12. Pertaining to an Italian city: var.

13. A weight
14. Printer's measures
21. Memorable stage of history
24. Entangle
26. Pastes
28. Extracted
29. Sensitive
31. Hindu ascetic
33. Black
36. Accustomed
38. Unconcealed
39. Vestments
40. Feminine name
41. Array for war
43. Eager
47. Box for firecrackers: var.
48. Majestic
50. Fox
53. Before
55. Power obtained from an engine
56. Placid
57. Cut off the last syllable
59. Rare bear-like animal
61. People of a section in Europe
64. Two of a kind
66. Italian guessing game
68. Drop bait lightly on water
69. Cloth measure
70. Gunny cloth
72. Lubricant

# CROSSWORD PUZZLE NO. 5

*Answers on page 472*

## ACROSS

1. Stuff
5. Theatrical entertainment
10. Small open pie
14. Narrow path
15. Dye stuff
16. Genus of trees
17. Thought
18. Projects
19. Genus of the tea plant
20. Heedful
22. Bear witness
24. Obtain by injustice
25. Rod for chastisement
26. Stayed in expectation
28. At no time
31. Overturned
34. Hoarfrost
35. Exclamation of triumph
36. Meadow
37. Arabian garment
40. Snare
41. Minute fungoid growth
43. Object bearing resemblance to something else
45. Stake marking the turning point in an aeroplane race-course

47. Branch of a stag's horn
48. Microscopic organism
50. Mounts up
54. Composes
56. Word opposite to another in meaning
57. Mint
58. Pertaining to early Teutonic alphabet
60. Italian coin
61. Vanity box
62. Turkish imperial decree
63. Heroic
64. Ancient Greek township
65. Having a border
66. Search

## DOWN

1. A region
2. Root
3. Concerning
4. Leas
5. Appoint as a delegate
6. Revolve
7. Biblical character
8. Coined
9. Genus of geese
10. Tale bearer

11. Accomplishing
12. Chain of rock
13. A salver
21. Fragile
23. Source of light
25. Gave food to
27. Beverage
29. Large Australian bird
30. Network
31. Temporary abode
32. Term used in hailing a vessel
33. Safeguard of a liberty
37. Insect
38. Made equal
39. Vigilant
42. Schoolmaster
43. Collection of sayings
44. Golden thrushes
46. Negative word
47. Ridiculous
49. Weird
51. Long-billed fen fowl
52. Hawk's nest
53. Quick, smart blow
54. Congealed
55. Short epistle
56. Assisting officer
59. Small saddle horse

# CROSSWORD PUZZLE NO. 6

*Answers on page 472*

## ACROSS

1. Muscle
5. Pulley block end
9. Western state
13. Asterisk
17. Expect
18. Demolish
19. Roman emperor
20. Story
21. Wages
23. Brotherly
25. Birds' homes
26. Spices
28. Garden flowers
29. Combination form of *image*
31. Testaments
32. Slight flap
33. Stirred milk
37. Youth
38. Relinquishes
42. Corded fabric
43. Microbe
45. Did exist
47. Girl's name
48. Swiss mountains
50. Disposition
52. Pecks
54. Roof edge
55. Slumber
57. Bucket
59. Petitions
61. Colloquial for *to sift*
62. Large wasps
64. Distress signal
66. Ushers
68. Japanese porgy
69. Spurt
71. Owed
72. Garden plant
75. Cork
77. Hair
81. Nations
83. Claimant
85. Insoluble residue
86. Opposite of aweather
87. Assam silkworm
88. Contralto
89. Sea eagle
90. Wipes up
91. Talk noisily
92. Fewer

## DOWN

1. Next
2. Domicile
3. Epic poetry
4. Turmoil
5. Branch
6. Repents
7. Tendon
8. Involve
9. Open
10. Gull-like birds
11. Parrots
12. Torrid
13. Cone
14. Browns
15. Wings
16. Reluctance units in electricity
22. Employing
24. Cancel
27. Cabbage salad
30. Judge
32. Abbreviation for type of engineer
33. Sudden collapse
34. Familiar salutation
35. Higher
36. Falls
38. Riddle
39. Shine brightly
40. At no time
41. Cuts
44. Extinct bird
46. Cape
49. Determination
51. Arranges
53. Source
56. Variation synonym for *active*
58. Thread fold
60. Condiment
63. Polynesian tree
65. Evening meal
67. Threefold
69. Perpendicular
70. Latin for *earth*
72. Culmination
73. Fly
74. Twist
75. Ensile
76. Bridle strap
78. Unoccupied
79. Meshed fabrics
80. God of love
82. Male sheep
84. Make lace

**129**

# CROSSWORD PUZZLE NO. 7

*Answers on page 472*

## ACROSS

1. Sorrowful feeling
7. Strip of leather
12. Entire property
18. Notoriously bad
19. Dwelling place
20. Fostered
21. Pointed instrument
22. Out of order
23. Complain
24. Hotel
25. Naval petty officers
27. East Indian tree
29. Japanese coin
30. Barrel for herring
32. Baked desserts
33. Gull-like bird
34. Fondles
35. Ceases to please
37. Processions
39. Attains success
42. Female horses
43. Electronic device
47. Roads
48. Colloquial for *carried*
49. Courteous
50. Surgical thread
51. Melts
52. Meat pies
53. Sailor
55. Affray
56. Domesticated
59. Metallic rocks
60. Greater in amount
61. Coarse file
65. Malt beverage
66. Combustible matter
67. Invent
69. Northern constellation
70. Piebald horses
72. Choicest part
74. Educates
76. Tolerates
77. Cut
78. English chemist
79. Reposed
80. Heavenly bodies
81. Turkish coins

## DOWN

1. Sudden fright
2. Sphere of action
3. Direction
4. Possessed
5. Solitary
6. Spires
7. Disgraces
8. Large volumes
9. Lay waste
10. Long-eared equine
11. Annoyed
12. Commission
13. Look for
14. Strike gently
15. Get up
16. Doctrine
17. Paradises
26. Lubricates
28. Periods of time
31. Concise summary
33. Weeds
34. Book of Psalms
36. Genus of grasses
37. Father
38. Having toothed margin
39. Land measures
40. Small deer
41. Settled habit
42. Biblical character
44. Five hundred two
45. Consumed
46. Thing in law
48. Without melody
49. Archaic word for *gymnasium*
51. Conflagration
52. Combination form for *around*
54. Awakened
55. Furniture transporters
56. Small candle
57. Place in rows
58. Repairs
60. Apparatus for measuring
62. Girl's name
63. Spanish gentleman
64. Attitudes
66. Golf warning
67. Prima donna
68. God of love
71. Mild rebuke
73. Allow
75. Venomous serpent

# CROSSWORD PUZZLE NO. 8

*Answers on page 472*

## ACROSS

1. Small aperture
5. Desire
9. American Beauty
13. Military kit
17. Asiatic goat
18. Declare
19. Mohammedan ruler
20. To sheltered side
21. Ulster
22. Absolutely nothing
23. Tiny replica
25. Breed of dog
27. Installs
29. Sour fruit
30. Print measures
31. Daggers
32. Achieve
33. Muscle spasm
36. Not poetry
37. Choral composition
41. Lasso
42. Tilt
43. Stripped
44. Spanish word for *nurse*
45. Remains
46. Ceremonies
47. Young child
48. Roof walls
50. Biological factors
51. Army depot
52. Entrances
53. Cathedral parts
54. Progressed
55. Drain
56. Journal
57. Title of respect
58. Wiser
61. Narrow gradually
62. Freed on condition
66. Doorway registering device
68. Wicked
70. Rounded lump
71. Region
72. Roman road
73. Numeral
74. Uniform
75. Cry lustily
76. Orderly
77. Makes edging
78. Canvas shelter

## DOWN

1. Aryan aborigine
2. Wood-wind instrument
3. Foster
4. Radical
5. Mists
6. Beyond
7. Through
8. Rustings
9. Do over
10. Neglects
11. Transgressions
12. Silkworm
13. Registered rights
14. Astringent
15. West Indian fish
16. Alert
24. Arranges in rows
26. Little devil
28. Archaic word for *formerly*
31. Two-wheeled carts
32. Flutters
33. Black cloth
34. Latin
35. Aside
36. Interweaves
37. Quotes
38. Perfume
39. Vex
40. Increased
42. Precipitous
43. Lunch wagon
45. Lances
46. Very respectful
49. Munitions depot
50. Yawn
51. British title
53. Table linens
54. Conifer
56. Blanched
57. Bargains
58. Pierce
59. Subtle emanation
60. Matured
61. South American monkey
62. Fluid measure
63. Ardent affection
64. Paradise
65. Depression
67. Small bird
69. By way of

# CROSSWORD PUZZLE NO. 9

*Answers on page 472*

## ACROSS

1. Beetle
4. System
9. Rebuild
14. Wager
17. Fail
18. Earl-duck
19. Woolly lemur
20. Rooting call
21. Bang
23. Young sheep
24. Scratch together
25. Butterfly-fish
26. Lukewarmly
28. High in music
30. Imitating exactly
32. Frolic
33. Impassive
35. Execute
36. Perverse
38. Roughly outlined
40. Recounts
43. Temporary inactivity
45. Slumber
47. Profound
48. Extremely
49. Curves
51. Lamprey fisher
53. Abbreviation for southern state
54. Sums up
57. Instructor
59. Winter traveler
62. Lye-making vessel
64. Lengthy speeches
66. Twosome battles
67. Enfold
69. Covers with wax
70. Successor
71. At no specified time
74. Cotton fibre knots
75. Steal
78. Edible part of fruit
79. Guide
81. Therefore
83. Ocean movement
84. Lyric poem
85. Artifices
86. Thick slices
88. Letter of alphabet
89. Man's nickname
90. Widemouthed cooking vessels
91. Respites
92. Melancholy

## DOWN

1. Outwit
2. Rare for Heraldic bearing
3. Clinch
4. Word of surprise
5. Arouse to action
6. Hauling vehicle
7. Shade tree
8. Discount
9. Smidgen
10. Former capital of Burma
11. Snatch
12. Curb
13. Modern greeting
14. Printing for the blind
15. Acquire honestly
16. Ruffian
22. Nearly opaque
25. Propelled a boat
27. East Indian bird
29. Small tracts
31. Punch
33. Doubter
34. Milk products
36. Fundamental
37. Residence
38. Reconnoiter
39. Cheers
41. Flat
42. Boxes
44. Negative
46. Anchor bill
50. Tenderness
52. Horseman
55. Dillydallied
56. Discard
58. Infrequent
60. Culpability
61. Bombastic language
63. Head covering
65. Extremities
68. Jeopardy
70. Hoarse
71. Atop
72. Naked
73. Blunt
75. Cold wind of Peru
76. Thought
77. Hunger
80. Grassy field
82. Hovel
85. Trouble
87. Abbreviation for *steamship*

**132**

# CROSSWORD PUZZLE NO. 10

*Answers on page 472*

## ACROSS

1. Mast
5. Pack
9. Sudden onset
13. Coarse file
17. Rabbit
18. Solemn statement
19. City in Nevada
20. Again
21. Mass of sliding snow
23. Professional customers
25. Exclude
26. Condition of strain
28. Ahead of time
29. Soft metal
31. Prepared
32. Skill
33. Deer meat
37. Contend
38. Dispossesses
42. Animate
43. Copied
45. Transfer
46. Faucet
47. Stringed instrument
48. Cicatrix
49. Stout cord
50. Bakery product
51. Cyprinoid fish
52. Encircle
53. Central personage
54. Outward indication
55. Disorder
57. Sticky mixture
58. Violent stream
60. Pro, and ...............
61. French painter
63. Siesta
64. Tribunal
67. Colonist
69. Cringe
73. Fundamental
75. Count
77. Thread
78. Facility
79. Scent organ
80. Presently
81. Diving bird
82. Three at cards
83. Waste allowance
84. Period of fasting

## DOWN

1. Herringlike fish
2. Surface a street
3. Desert dweller
4. Kinsman
5. Native
6. Diplomacy
7. Different
8. At whatever time
9. Determine
10. Mixture of metals
11. Rind
12. Garden tool
13. Revolve
14. Declare
15. Find a buyer
16. Victim
22. Get up
24. Pluck
27. Uttered
30. Japanese drama
32. Military assistant
33. Well-grounded
34. Escape
35. Saltpeter
36. Mother-of-pearl
38. Railway station
39. Gambler's capital
40. Accepted
41. Exhausted
44. Cushion
45. Heart in anatomy
48. Endorse
49. Fragrant
50. Noncommissioned officer
52. Dwarf
53. Injure
54. Vestige
56. Shrewdness
57. Variegated
59. Forward
61. Discontinue
62. Trend
64. Cut down
65. Medley
66. City in Nevada
67. Rigel
68. Artifice
70. Decrease
71. Short jacket
72. Lease
74. Openwork fabric
76. Intersected

# CROSSWORD PUZZLE NO. 11

*Answers on page 473*

## ACROSS

1. Limbs
5. Dolt
8. Discolors
14. Posture
15. Especially liked
16. Small finch
17. Picket
18. Audience
19. Access
20. Inertness
22. Slang for *partners*
24. Lyric poem
25. Readjusts
27. Summon
28. Sack
31. Divisions
32. Fops
33. Exclamation of woe
35. The things
36. Deface
37. Plans
39. Globules of air
43. Decay
44. Mongrel dog
45. Reserve
46. Disliked
49. Water way
51. Emblem of dawn
52. Asiatic country
53. Bunched closely
55. Skill
56. Drive back
57. Web-footed fowl
61. Rag
63. Born
65. View amorously
66. Unburden
67. Weep
68. Portion of food
69. Soaks in liquid
70. Compass point
71. Collections

## DOWN

1. European vipers
2. Lifelike
3. Characteristic of man
4. Direct
5. Mimic
6. Harbors
7. Runs aground
8. Vehicles
9. Sealed cans
10. Social insect
11. Invasion
12. Slender, pointed rod
13. Makes hard
21. Church seat
23. Abbreviation for synonym of *dwelling*
26. Infect
27. Stone borders
28. Below standard
29. Malt drink
30. Fuel
32. Soft mass
34. Alert whistle
36. Wall painting
38. Pagan deity
39. Hustlers
40. Boy
41. Poetic for *evening*
42. Stitch
44. Rhythm
46. A chasm
47. Notoriously bad
48. Gossip
49. Sports prize
50. Limb
53. Crowds
54. Sentences
56. Cut with a sickle
58. S-shaped molding
59. Narrow strip
60. Snake-like fishes
62. Digit
64. Look

134

# CROSSWORD PUZZLE NO. 12

*Answers on page 473*

## ACROSS

1. Desire
5. Prayers
10. None better
14. Frosting maker
15. Scope
16. Dull pain
17. Waiter's item
18. Queerer
19. Colloquial for *gorilla*
20. Courageous
22. Shred
24. Silent greeting
25. Second-hand
27. Beverage vessels
29. Cattle thieves
33. Bang
34. Compass point
35. Novelist....................Wharton
37. Rigid
40. One of English architect brothers
42. Colloquial for *hoax*
44. Disfigurement
45. Forfeits
47. Bobbin
49. 100 Centiares
50. Colloquial for *dollar bills*

52. Sauntered
54. Wick-ed tallows
57. Rescue
58. King of Judah
59. Deficiency
61. Not rough
65. Twelve pairs per man
67. Elevate
69. Delineate
70. Groundless
71. Audible
72. The Old Sod
73. Garden vegetable
74. Aids
75. Wands

## DOWN

1. Association
2. 4840 sq. yards
3. Close by
4. Test
5. Continues
6. Youth
7. Terminates
8. Representative
9. Arrangement of parts
10. Pouch
11. Provident

12. Photograph
13. Baby-sits
21. ................ of Wight
23. Colloquial for *chums*
26. Falls in drops
28. Strokes lightly
29. Former Spanish coin
30. Unravel
31. Opportune
32. Closes
36. Derisive shouts
38. Passenger
39. Allen, the comedian
41. Repair
43. Raiders for food
46. Vend
48. Tender passion
51. Seek
53. Pawnbroker
54. Spanish-American savage
55. Away; off
56. Climb
60. German seaport
62. Threesome
63. Hog suet
64. She sheep
66. Clique
68. Plant juice

135

# CROSSWORD PUZZLE NO. 13

*Answers on page 473*

## ACROSS

1. Discharge
5. Indulge
10. Agitate
14. Floor
15. Fragrance
16. Lily-like plant
17. Ardor
18. More mature
19. Rip
20. Deferred
22. Renew
24. Seine
25. Accede
26. Agreements
29. Be prostrate
30. Imbibed
34. Greek god of war
35. Cushion
36. Hurry
37. Small enclosure
38. Knock lightly
39. Move swiftly on foot
40. Be indebted
41. Necessarily involve
43. A tippler
44. Dirk
45. Grates
46. Intimidate
47. Shifts

48. Flower part
50. Fish organ of locomotion
51. Elector
54. Maker
58. Pueblo Indian
59. Rough noise
61. Rise and fall of ocean
62. So be it
63. Implied
64. Augury
65. Shut up
66. Flat pieces of stone
67. Repose

## DOWN

1. Hastened
2. Robust
3. Egg shaped
4. Dwellers
5. Proofreading mark
6. Dry
7. Upper end
8. Come in sight
9. More scarce
10. Rags
11. Oil
12. Fly aloft
13. Withered
21. Yea

23. Auto type
25. Assist
26. Document
27. Field of combat
28. Pennies
29. Lick up
31. Reconcile
32. Fresher
33. Leg joints
35. Colloquial synonym
    for *chum*
36. Small cabin
38. Ascends
39. Line
42. Ordain
43. Sun
44. Member of legislative body
46. Fleshly
47. Contend
49. Tries
50. Irritates
51. Split
52. Dwelling place
53. Generous
54. Manger
55. Season
56. Lyric poems
57. Lease
60. South American plant
    resembling the potato

# CROSSWORD PUZZLE NO. 14

*Answers on page 473*

## ACROSS

1. Happy
5. Fall flower
10. Chilly
14. Capital of Peru
15. Raised platform
16. French girl friend
17. Metal
18. Farm building
19. Pleasant
20. National game
22. Furnace
24. Fuel
25. Placed down
26. An appendage in the throat
30. Corrupts
34. Bay window
35. Embankment
36. Abbreviation for an international labor organization
37. Arabian seaport
38. Satisfied
39. Principal
40. Dry
41. Pointer
42. ............... Cristo
43. Earthquake
45. Conductor
46. Beverages
47. Bind
48. Not fertile
51. Journeys ends
56. Norse navigator
57. Delineate
59. Actor's part
60. French spa
61. Russian leader
62. Soon
63. Asian weight
64. Irish poet
65. Recent reports

## DOWN

1. Fluent
2. Italian coins
3. Biblical prophet
4. European
5. Attack
6. Yet
7. High
8. Self
9. Molded again
10. Country in North America
11. Leave out
12. Vermin
13. Ruminant
21. Stew
23. Ireland
25. A pry
26. Drink to health
27. Command
28. Female relation
29. Sun Yat-............
30. Restrain
31. Foods; fare
32. Superior group
33. Sounder
35. Cripples
38. Quietly
39. Extinct bird
41. Capable
42. Obsolete word for *reward*
44. Wave hair
45. Flaxen goods
47. Silent
48. Curved
49. Operatic solo
50. Cereal
51. Miss Turner
52. Persia
53. Not any
54. Incandescence
55. Abbreviation for *senators*
58. Scottish for *wild*

# CROSSWORD PUZZLE NO. 15

*Answers on page 473*

**ACROSS**

1. Ox stall
5. John Jacob ..................
10. Half
14. Recent
15. On one of four suits
16. Steady
17. Tennis term
18. Smooths
19. Crack
20. Sociology
22. Excessively
24. Impulse
25. Befit
26. Connecticut city
29. Admitted
33. Anguish
34. Priggish person
35. Paddle
36. Male sheep
37. Frustrates
38. Beget
39. Uncle Tom's heroine
40. Places of squalor
41. Scolds
42. Render inedible
44. Rowdies

45. Grooves
46. Raccoon
47. Flexible
50. Moves to and fro
54. Chamber
55. Applause
57. Mr. Warren, C. J.
58. Colloquial for *one opposed*
59. Waken
60. Latvian capital
61. Affirmative votes
62. Horse
63. Rank admirer

**DOWN**

1. Clothed
2. Speed
3. Detail
4. Arab nomads
5. Appoint
6. Reservation
7. Browns
8. Queer
9. Reverberates
10. Erase
11. Always
12. Ground grain

13. Black
21. Three-spot
23. Depravity
25. Essences
26. Ventured
27. Century plant
28. Latin
29. Violation
30. Bringing about
31. Third from sun
32. Make ready
34. Gushes
37. Quivers
38. Strolls
40. Shock
41. Poke around
43. Athos, Porthos, ..................
44. Sent on course
46. Pursue
47. Entreat
48. Solitary
49. Jot
50. Swing about
51. Reclined
52. Therefore
53. Outside piece of log
56. Sheath

# CROSSWORD PUZZLE NO. 16

*Answers on page 473*

## ACROSS

1. Box
5. Jeer
10. Formerly
14. Ripped
15. Treadle
16. Spin
17. Vexes
18. Confuse
19. Final destiny
20. Renovate
22. Pastes
24. Blacken
25. Waster
26. Push
29. Prohibit
30. Distributed
34. Spouse
35. Name
36. Burrowing animal
37. Fairy
38. Dismissal
40. Girl's name
41. *Short dozen*
43. German councilor
44. Disorder
45. Novices
46. Sulky mood

47. Prescribed meals
48. Existed
50. Turf
51. Sharer
54. Traveler equipment
58. Region
59. Unyielding
61. Diminutive name
62. Unaccompanied male
63. Degraded districts
64. Observes
65. Style
66. Literary composition
67. Canvas shelter

## DOWN

1. Bustle
2. Gaze intently
3. Bowlike curvatures
4. Fidgety
5. Electrical discharge
6. Yield
7. Strange
8. Hawk
9. Vanishes
10. Commanded
11. Highest point
12. Congealed blood

13. Shade trees
21. Unit
23. Badge
25. Strived
26. Sugary
27. Steep
28. Bid
29. Vagrant
31. Assent
32. Smallest amount
33. Lock of hair
35. Private retreat
36. Wink
38. Varnish ingredient
39. Large tank
42. Electromotive force
44. Dwarfs
46. Dangers
47. Cur
49. Metrical writing
50. Foamy
51. Time elapsed
52. Colloquial for *artistic*
53. Harvest
54. Flat bean
55. In the shelter of
56. Valley
57. Toward the sunrise
60. Short for *Gustav*

**139**

# CROSSWORD PUZZLE NO. 17

*Answers on page 474*

Answers on page 474

## ACROSS

1. What person?
4. Good thing
8. Reside
13. Sultry
14. Prickly plant
15. Inspection
17. Eventually
18. Level
19. Compass point
20. College degree
21. Proposal
23. Baseball item
24. Domesticated mammal
25. In equal degree
27. ............. hot
28. Fe, fi, fo, .............
29. Tibia
30. Prank
32. Cabin
33. Blossom
34. Leave out
35. Source of heat
36. Organ of speech
39. Decompose
40. Colloquial for *tight place*
41. Hudson .............
42. Conclusion
43. Colloquial for *Arrested*
45. Mingle
46. Guardhouse
47. Suitable
48. Wisecrack
49. Refuse
50. Noisy
52. Remunerate
53. In support of
54. Edward
55. Perennial wise animal
56. Leverage
57. Spasms
59. In progress
60. Honey-maker
61. Oriental sailboat
62. No longer 59-Across
65. Male singers
67. Formerly
68. ............. Father
69. Pokes around
70. Lager
71. Attempt

## DOWN

1. For what reason?
2. Garden tool
3. Boy's name
4. Choose
5. Strongly liked
6. Partaker
7. Human beings
8. Imaginary vision
9. Occident
10. Mrs. Adam
11. Roman 51
12. Another *rotten apple*
16. Salary
22. Chafe
23. Except
24. Da Bums
25. Source of the oak
26. Pacific isles
28. Merriment
29. Bread roll
31. Pathetic
32. Sound of 60-Across
33. Lad
35. Mournful
36. Assessment
37. Unlace
38. Sharpened
40. Spout
41. Large
44. Box top
45. Flower month
46. Tough external covering
48. Lively
49. No idler
50. Bandit's haul
51. Proprietor
52. Iron
53. Enclosure
56. Bold
57. Bride's month
58. Chimney dust
60. Hoot; jeer
61. Long-sufferer
63. Pelt
64. Small .............
66. Nix

# CROSSWORD PUZZLE NO. 18

*Answers on page 474*

## ACROSS

1. Hashing
8. Juxtaposed
15. Sluggishness
16. Deterioration
17. Creaky
18. Obsequies
19. Stringed instrument
20. Shield
22. River in France
23. Mien
24. Certain securities
26. Kernel
27. Decree of the Sultan
29. Edible tuber
30. County in Ireland
32. Misled
34. Rescued
36. Stuffing again
38. Constituents of fats and oils
41. The stirrup bone
45. House plant
46. Abbreviation for medical group
48. Run off
49. Beverage
50. Tagged
53. Edge
54. Hottentot
56. Hindu queen
57. Bulging pot
58. Bower
60. Regularly progressive
62. Weights used in weaving
63. Medieval shoulder armor
64. Edible
65. Hatch again

## DOWN

1. Lost
2. Ask
3. Indifferent
4. Algonquian Indian
5. South American city
6. New Zealand palm
7. Mirth
8. Averred
9. Hesitation
10. Peg
11. Combining form for *oil*
12. Dutch Guiana
13. Obliteration
14. Erased
21. Sentries.
24. Pertaining to a compact between states
25. Fragrant
28. Pertaining to the dura mater
31. Lawful
33. Finial
35. Roman god
37. French striped cotton stuff
38. Slate gauge
39. Mythical winged shoes
40. Ingredient
42. Defile
43. Remove hair
44. Having divisions of a calyx
47. Sour ale
51. Arabian gazelle
52. Weird
55. Seaweed
57. River in Germany
59. A return in tennis
61. Vestment

# CROSSWORD PUZZLE NO. 19

*Answers on page 474*

**ACROSS**

1. Judgments
7. Wrong name
15. Soft felt hat
16. Sharp
17. Rubbed out
18. Small South American fishes
19. Congeals into hoarfrost
20. Fermented liquor
21. Torn
22. Cut to a steep slope
25. Malayan nipa palm
29. Sword handle
30. Large brilliant-colored fishes
35. In a gloomy manner
37. Hard money
38. Without limits of duration
39. Flattening by hammering
40. Fiends
41. Lively Spanish dance
42. Prophets
43. Bristle
44. Creates false impression
45. Observations
48. Inferior Mahometan magistrate
52. Large constellation

53. Bound with a band of cloth
58. Crystalline globulin
60. Mental condition
61. Revere
62. Extract forcibly
63. Respect
64. Proneness to anger

**DOWN**

1. Variation synonym of *to affirm*
2. Maori vegetable caterpillar
3. First man
4. Thorny flower
5. Frock
6. Melancholy
7. Very covetous
8. Commence
9. Alarm
10. Nothing
11. Sandy ridges
12. Wet spongy earth
13. Equable
14. Rhythmic silence in music
20. Lades
23. Game of skill
24. Slang for *predicted*

25. Gather together
26. Roman garments
27. Rugged mountain crest
28. Guiding
31. Punitive
32. Grapes
33. Door joint
34. Western North American perennial herbs
36. Perceive
37. Spanish word for *landmark*
39. West Indian basslike fish
41. Imaginary
43. Fairy
46. Variation synonym for *obeisance*
47. Heating apparatus
48. Grotto
49. The birds
50. Slight depression
51. Arrow poison
54. Genus of herbs
55. Flatter
56. Otherwise
57. Ruminant mammal
59. Metric measure
60. Encountered

# CROSSWORD PUZZLE NO. 20

*Answers on page 474*

## ACROSS

1. Sustain
5. Worthless
10. Boom
14. Entice
15. Pivot
16. Brink
17. Eskers; narrow ridges
18. Totaled
19. Latin for *public meetings*
20. Well being
22. Lifelike
24. Unwell
25. Book of maps
26. Promontories
30. Fumed
34. Associate
35. Theodore
36. Neckband
37. Rodent
38. Defender of his country
40. Before
41. Part of a flower
43. Blunder
44. Festive
45. Wading bird
46. Pen name
48. Dog genus
50. Phoebus
51. Neck feathers
54. Amanuenses
58. Competent
59. Loose Roman garment
61. Highest voice
62. Rend
63. Himalayan country
64. Food fish
65. Whirlpool
66. Slip
67. Agglomeration

## DOWN

1. Farm implement
2. Trick
3. Vocal
4. Faithlessness
5. Quack
6. Dissemble
7. Conclusion
8. Factors
9. Pertaining to a foot
10. Denial
11. Smell
12. Site of the Taj Mahal
13. Veritable
21. Whole of
23. Old Italian playing card
25. Speak to
26. Irritating
27. Elevate
28. Place for sacrifices
29. Mesh
31. Gather by degrees
32. Betimes
33. Reverie
36. To give out sparkles of light
38. Concerning punishment
42. Scornful imitation
44. Philistine giant
46. Part of a flower
47. Kind of beetle
49. Snug retreats
51. Abominate
52. In bed
53. Vested
54. Vehicle for sliding on snow
55. Color
56. Famous volcano
57. Cleansing agent
60. Japanese sash

# CROSSWORD PUZZLE NO. 21

*Answers on page 474*

## ACROSS

1. Battle
7. Rest
13. Halo
14. Famous
16. Army group
17. Marked with stripes
18. Likely
19. Interpose
21. Small enclosure
22. Riding whip
24. Classifies
25. Body of water
26. King of Tyre
28. Born
29. Menu
30. Root words
32. Demolish
34. Dessert
35. Arabian garment
36. Forsakes
40. Musical term
44. Harden
45. Greek letter
47. Nominator
48. Siamese coins

49. Impress
51. Resounded
52. Sesame
53. Son of Agamemnon
55. Philippine tree
56. South Pacific islands
58. Redecorate
60. Deserved
61. Imperial domains
62. Ecclesiastical councils
63. Attempts

## DOWN

1. An offender
2. Private chapel
3. Encountered
4. Spar
5. Bitter herbs
6. Bands terminating muscles
7. Narrates
8. Discharges
9. Tree
10. Unit
11. Harbor town
12. Understanding

13. Parisian criminal
15. Offer
20. Anger
23. Indulges
25. East Indian coasting vessel
27. Watered silk
29. Hut
31. Seine
33. Chinese dynasty
36. Microscopic marine or fresh water alga
37. Lures
38. Company that caters to soldiers
39. Coverlets
40. Race course near Liverpool
41. Erotic
42. Terms of land holdings
43. Musical instruments
46. Possessive pronoun
49. Scrutinized
50. Abounds
53. To and upon
54. Weakens
57. River in France
59. *Through* as a prefix

# CROSSWORD PUZZLE NO. 22

*Answers on page 474*

*Answers on page 474*

### ACROSS

1. Ruin
5. Eats
9. Solemnities
14. Of the mouth
15. French for *a main dish*
16. Maternal relative
17. Stamina
19. Gasified liquid
20. Repeat
21. Frivolous
22. Undisturbed
23. Black and blue
25. Gait
28. An adhesive
31. Decorates
35. Flower holder
37. Region
38. Be borne
39. Industry
40. Assignment of work
41. Sanction
42. Genus of swans
43. Legal witness
44. Textile screw pine
46. Underdone

48. A feline
50. Pass
55. Condiment
57. Unexpected
60. Nut
61. Curative
62. An African antelope
63. Very black
64. Weary
65. Alluvial fan
66. Grievous
67. Maple tree

### DOWN

1. South African Dutchmen
2. Female wild buffalo
3. Lowest point
4. To wash out
5. Gaunter
6. Forearm bone
7. Agreement
8. A metal
9. Enliven
10. Dead
11. Stirrup hoods

12. English school
13. Exhausted
18. Schisms
24. Refrigerant
26. Ellipsoid figure
27. Small drum
29. Snug retreat
30. Capture
31. Light carriage
32. Cleft
33. Same
34. Beggar
36. Wading bird
39. Solitary
43. Purposive
45. Things to be done
47. Grumble
49. Hoar frosts
51. Feminine name
52. Sudden fear
53. Intent look
54. Conger fisherman
55. Hastened
56. Polynesian volcano goddess
58. Biblical mount
59. Scent

**145**

# CROSSWORD PUZZLE NO. 23

*Answers on page 475*

## ACROSS

1. Small herrings
7. Saved
13. Shoulder ornament
14. Cafe entertainment
16. Japanese mile
17. Foundation
18. Obsolete synonym for *sandy*
19. Emmet
21. Colloquial for *young actress*
23. Ocean
24. Fly aloft
26. Arabian prince
27. Tunes
28. Chemical compound
30. Poetic form of *ever*
31. Higher up
32. Reply
34. South American timber trees
36. Regret
37. Indisposed
38. Takes out
42. More sedate
46. Originate
47. Sorrow

49. Gem
50. Belgian city
51. Diadem
53. Bark
54. American humorist
55. Curved tile
57. Inlet
58. Equipping
60. Greasy
62. Six
63. Agreement between nations
64. Unsatisfied
66. Burr plant
67. Sailors

## DOWN

1. Thorny
2. Colloquial for *parent*
3. Polish
4. Exclamation
5. Integument
6. Emitted vapor
7. Weigher
8. Peeler
9. Encourage
10. Raced
11. The eating away
12. Merit

13. Rubber
15. Annoys
20. Makes lace
22. Female ruff
25. Restrain
27. Power to act
29. Course
31. Book of maps
33. Born
35. Islet
38. Impair
39. Caustic
40. Marked with stripes
41. Variation synonym for *flail used in thrashing*
42. Thoughtful
43. One who accomplishes
44. Cheer
45. Refunded
48. Grain
51. French for *aunt*
52. Place in a row
55. Pegs
56. Feminine name
59. Turmeric
61. Tuber
65. Chemical symbol for *tellurium*

# CROSSWORD PUZZLE NO. 24

*Answers on page 475*

**ACROSS**

1. Daubed
8. Sailor
15. Graze
16. Quarantine
17. Little bone
18. Puts aside
19. Employ
20. Card games
22. Exist
23. Prong
25. Rows
26. Sea eagle
27. Occasion
29. Born
30. Elevctrical unit
31. Abandon
33. Poetic for *maidens*
35. Ditch around a castle
37. Civil wrong
38. Perfections
42. Unlimited quantities
46. Sign of the zodiac
47. Chart
49. Rye fungus
50. Poles

51. Divide
53. One of Columbus' ships
54. Join
55. Sovereignty
57. Rhythmic clapping
58. Makes public
60. Variation synonym of *feudal impost*
62. Part
63. Properties
64. Benne seeds
65. Most profound

**DOWN**

1. Jetted
2. Large
3. Jewish ascetics
4. Consumed
5. Law
6. Build
7. Hold
8. Abuse
9. Residue
10. Hinds
11. Ailing

12. Ancient French kingdom
13. Endless
14. Sows again
21. Marsh grass
24. Foes
26. Oriental
28. Runs
30. Violence
32. Japanese porgy
34. Low
36. Storms
38. Displays
39. Salamander
40. Perforates
41. Tunicate
43. Upset
44. Minorities
45. Most vapid
48. Opposed
51. Demonstration
52. Vex
55. Stalk
56. Ceremony
59. Candlenut tree
61. Circuit

147

# FUNERAL NOTICES

She was such a little seraph that her father, who is sheriff,
Really doesn't seem to care if he ne'er smiles in life again.
She has gone, we hope, to heaven, at the early age of seven
(Funeral starts off at eleven), where she'll nevermore have pain.

♚

Oh! bury Bartholomew out in the woods,
  In a beautiful hole in the ground,
Where the bumble-bees buzz and the woodpeckers sing,
  And the straddle-bugs tumble around;
So that, in winter, when the snow and the slush
  Have covered his last little bed,
His brother Artemas can go out with Jane
  And visit the place with his sled.

♚

Four doctors tackled Johnny Smith—
  They blistered and they bled him;
With squills and anti-bilious pills
  And ipecac, they fed him.

They stirred him up with calomel,
  And tried to move his liver;
But all in vain—his little soul
  Was wafted o'er The River.

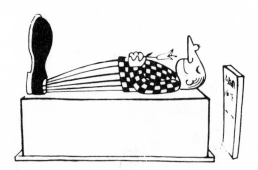

The death-angel smote Alexander McGlue,
  And gave him protracted repose;
He wore a checked shirt and a number twelve shoe,
  And he had a huge wart on his nose.
No doubt he is happier dwelling in space
  Over there on the evergreen shore.
His friends are informed that his funeral takes place
Precisely at quarter-past four.

# CLASSIC STANZAS

These verses are all well known, either for their brevity or their wit, which in some cases amount to the same thing.

### ODE ON THE ANTIQUITY OF FLEAS

Adam
Had' em!

👑

### ONTOLOGICAL REFLECTION ON THE MEANING OF EXISTENCE

I—
Why?

👑

### ODE ON THE CONDITION OF THE UNITED STATES
### AFTER SEVERAL YEARS OF PROHIBITION

Wet
Yet.

👑

Sir, I admit your general rule,
That every poet is a fool:
But you yourself may serve to show it,
That every fool is not a poet.

*Alexander Pope*

👑

### ODE TO THE BRAHMINS OF BOSTON

Here's to dear old Boston,
    The home of the bean and the cod;
Where the Lowells speak only to Cabots,
    And the Cabots speak only to God.

👑

### REFLECTIONS ON A PICNIC

Upon this theme I'll briefly touch:
Too far to go to eat too much.

👑

### OH, TO BE IN ENGLAND NOW THE WEATHER'S THERE!

Ah, lovely Devon . . .
Where it rains eight days out of seven!

### ODE ON GARRULITY

Whene'er a hen lays eggs, with each
She is impelled to make a speech.
The selfsame urge stirs human bones
Whenever men lay cornerstones.

Please wail one wail
For Adolph Barr;
He just would drive
A one-eyed car.

### ON LOVE

Love is like an onion
    You taste it with delight,
And when it's gone you wonder
    What ever made you bite.

### WORLD WAR III

I won't print and you won't see
The verses written on World War III

### REFLECTIONS ON HIGHWAY TRAVEL

Wherever the place,
    Whatever the time;
Every lane moves
    But the one where I'm.
                        *Ethel B. DeVito*

### LIFE'S SHORTEST STORY

The saddest words of tongue or pen
Perhaps may be "It might have been."
The sweetest words we know, by heck,
Are simply these: "Enclosed find check."

**150**

When two egotists meet
 It results in a tie:
A vocal dead heat,
 With an I for an I.

For a time newspapers across the country participated in an informal contest to see who could devise the cleverest verse offering advice to motorists. The following ditties were gleaned from among the best.

Oh shed a tear
 For Luther Stover;
He tried to toot
 Two State cops over.

He who stops to look each way
Will drive his car another day.
But he who speeds across the "stop"
Will land in some mortician's shop.

And he who starts his car in gear
May end his ride upon a bier.
And he who crashes through the red
May wake up once and find he's dead.

Bill Muffet said
 His car couldn't skid;
This monument shows
 It could and did.

O what a tangled web we weave
When first we practice to deceive!
But when we've practiced quite a while
How vastly we improve our style!

*J.R. Pope*

Great fleas have little fleas upon their back to bite 'em;
And little fleas have lesser fleas, and so *ad infinitum*.

Seven wealthy towns contend for Homer dead;
Through which the living Homer had to beg his bread.

### REFLECTIONS ON THE GRAPE

If all be true that I do think,
There are five reasons we should drink;
    Good wine—a friend—or being dry—
    Or lest we should be by and by—
    Or any other reason why.

*Henry Aldrich*

### ODE TO A PREACHER

I never see my rector's eyes,
He hides their light divine;
For when he prays, he shuts his own,
And when he preaches, mine.

## SWAN SONG

Swans sing before they die—
'Twere no bad thing
Should certain persons die
Before they sing.

## ODE TO YESTERYEAR

The good old days, the good old days,
We all so fondly speak of;
Which, if they ever should come back,
No one could stand a week of.

## REFLECTIONS ON BACHELORHOOD

A bachelor is a cagey guy
And has a load of fun:
He sizes all the cuties up
And never Mrs. one.

*John Wycherly*

## PHILOSOPHICAL REFLECTION ON AGING

King David and King Solomon
Lived merry, merry lives,
With many, many lady friends
And many, many wives;
But when old age crept onward,
With all its many qualms,
King Solomon wrote the Proverbs
And King David wrote the Psalms.

**153**

# MURDER IN THE LIBRARY

Mr. Parker was found dead in the library of his home on the evening of January 2, at 7:30 P.M. His death was reported to the police by a night watchman, who, because he was the only person other than the dead man in the immediate vicinity, was questioned by the inspector in charge as follows:

*Inspector:* What was your first knowledge of Mr. Parker's death?

*Watchman:* As I was walking past his house, I saw him seated in this chair. As I watched him, he raised a pistol to his head and shot himself.

*Inspector:* What did you do then?

*Watchman:* I rushed to the door and rang the bell, but I could get no response.

*Inspector:* How did you get into the house?

*Watchman:* I ran around the house trying the windows. I found an unlocked one in the rear and climbed through it.

*Inspector:* Did you close the window after you?

*Watchman:* No, I left it open.

*Inspector:* What did you do after that?

*Watchman:* I made my way with some difficulty to the library.

*Inspector:* Was it then that you telephoned headquarters?

*Watchman:* Yes.

*Inspector:* How did you know where the telephone was?

*Watchman:* As soon as I opened the library door and turned on the light, I saw it.

*Inspector:* How did you tear the pocket of your coat?

*Watchman:* I tore it climbing in the window.

*Inspector:* And you say you saw no one leave the house?

*Watchman:* No sir.

*Inspector:* What reason do you think Mr. Parker had for committing suicide?

*Watchman:* I am sure I don't know.

Because of an inconsistency in the watchman's answers, the inspector held him on suspicion.

### WHAT WAS THIS INCONSISTENCY?

*Answers on page 475*

# THE STYMIED SAVAGE

### WHAT DID THE MISSIONARY SAY?

*Answers on page 475*

# THE RIDDLE OF THE RED WINE

Two friars, Brother Boniface and the abbot, are seated at a table, upon which rests a pint jug of water and a pint bottle of red wine. The abbot pours a glass of wine and empties it into the jug of water. Then he fills a glass from the water jug and empties it into the bottle of wine.

"Tell me, Brother Boniface," the abbot demands, "have I taken more wine from the bottle than water from the jug? Or have I taken more water from the jug than wine from the bottle?"

CAN YOU ANSWER THE ABBOT'S QUESTIONS?

*Answers on page 475*

# RELATIVELY SIMPLE

WHAT RELATION IS ANN TO JOAN?

*Answers on page 475*

# SUBURBS

Five members of a club are named Surbiton, Ealing, Tottenham, Richmond, and Blackheath. Each of them, curiously, lives in a suburb which is a namesake of one of the others. Each of them, moreover, *works* in a second suburb which is also a namesake of one of the others. No two of them either live or work in the same suburb.

The gentleman who lives at Surbiton works at Richmond.

Mr. Richmond works at Blackheath.

The Blackheath resident works in the suburb which is the namesake of the Surbiton resident.

Mr. Ealing works in the suburb which is the namesake of the Blackheath resident.

### WHO WORKS AT EALING?

*Answers on page 475*

# KILLED IN ACTION

Five friends named Jones, Stacey, Young, Lewis, and Smith were involved in a battle, and one of the men was killed. The following facts are known:

(1) Jones was an ordained Catholic priest.

(2) The wife of the slain man was the sister of Mrs. Lewis.

(3) Mrs. Smith's beautiful daughter died of infantile paralysis.

(4) Stacey was sorry that Young did not return on the same boat with him.

(5) Mrs. Lewis always regretted that she had never had a niece or nephew.

### WHICH MAN WAS KILLED IN THE BATTLE?

*Answers on page 475*

# THE OHIO LIMITED

The Ohio Limited is controlled by an engineer, a fireman, and a guard, whose names are Brown, Jones, and Robinson, *not* respectively.

On the train are three passengers: Mr. Jones, Mr. Robinson, and Mr. Brown.

Mr. Robinson lives in Cleveland.

The guard lives halfway between Cleveland and New York.

Mr. Jones's income is $9,120.11 per year.

The guard earns in a year exactly one-third of the income of his nearest neighbor, who is a passenger.

The guard's namesake lives in New York.

Brown beat the fireman at billiards.

**WHAT IS THE NAME OF THE ENGINEER?**

*Answers on page 476*

# THE SIMPLE-MINDED MAID

A gentleman picked up the telephone just as his maid answered a call on another extension. The conversation he listened in on went as follows:

"Is Mr. Smith at home?"

"I will ask him, sir. What name shall I give him?"

"Quoit."

"What's that, sir?"

"Quoit."

"Would you mind spelling it?"

"*Q* for quick, *U* for umbrella, *O* for omnibus, *I* for idiot—"

"*I* for what, sir?"

"*I* for idiot, *T* for telephone. *Q,U,O,I,T*, Quoit."

"Thank you, sir."

The gentleman remarked to himself that his maid could not be too intelligent.

WHY?

*Answers on page 476*

# THE CHECKERBOARD

WHAT IS THE SOLUTION TO THE CHECKER PLAYER'S PROBLEM?

*Answers on page 476*

# THE STOLEN CAMEO

Sir Michael Farnsworth was elated. From some tumbledown shop in Leghorn he had brought back to England a cameo which he knew was a premier specimen. He presented his find for appraisal to Geoffrey Warren, senior member of Warren & Co., dealers in objets d'art for more than two hundred years. Mr. Warren, after careful scrutiny, acclaimed the carved piece a veritable masterpiece.

Sir Michael determined to deed the cameo to the British Museum.

Four days later, Sir Michael again appeared at Warren's. His gift had been accepted. The cameo wanted furbishing. Geoffrey Warren stated that he himself would attend to the matter, for he would not entrust so precious a piece to any but his own practiced hands. The same afternoon, a reporter from *The Times* obtained a statement from Mr. Warren. The old gentleman, departing from the conservatism of years, pronounced the Farnsworth cameo to be the finest specimen extant.

Two days later, Scotland Yard was notified that the solid house of Warren and Company had been despoiled of its greatest treasure. The Farnsworth cameo had been stolen. The police, after routine examination and routine questioning, rendered their routine report. Sir Michael was told that the house of Warren and Company would stand by its loss. The cameo was worth £5,000—£5,000 would be paid.

But Sir Michael was shocked far beyond the thought of money. He had been robbed of fame. Secretly he engaged one of the most brilliant private detectives in London. Within three hours he was informed that Geoffrey Warren himself had stolen the cameo.

At first Sir Michael wouldn't believe it. The thought was preposterous. The man had been entrusted with millions during his long, honorable career. Furthermore, the cameo, publicized throughout the world of art, was the only one of its kind and could never be resold. A collector, though he were in Tibet, would recognize it immediately. As to the idea that Geoffrey Warren had purloined the precious cameo simply for the joy of possession, that too was absurd. Had not Geoffrey Warren held within the palm of his hand for more than forty years the finest gems that existed? However, confronted with the accusation, Geoffrey Warren readily confessed.

The problem is to determine what motive impelled Mr. Warren to the theft of the cameo. The answer is not to be found in some extraneous circumstance, such as a personal grievance. A broad hint to the solution will be found in the fact that after the theft was discovered, Farnsworth and Warren remained good friends.

*Answers on page 476*

# THE SIX AUTHORS

Six authors are seated three on a side in a first-class railway compartment. Their names are Black, Brown, Gray, Green, Pink, and White. They are (but not respectively) an essayist, an historian, a humorist, a novelist, a playwright, and a poet.

Each has written a book which one or the other occupants of the compartment is reading.

Mr. Black is reading essays.

Mr. Gray is reading a book by the author sitting opposite to him.

Mr. Brown is sitting between the essayist and the humorist.

Mr. Pink is sitting next to the playwright.

The essayist is facing the historian.

Mr. Green is reading plays.

Mr. Brown is the novelist's brother-in-law.

Mr. Black, who is in a corner seat, has no interest in history.

Mr. Green is facing the novelist.

Mr. Pink is reading a book by the humorist.

Mr. White never reads poetry.

**IDENTIFY EACH OF THE SIX AUTHORS.**

*Answers on page 476*

# IN COLD BLOOD

Two sisters were married. The two couples jointly occupied a single apartment. The men, apart from being brothers-in-law, were otherwise unrelated. One night, while both men were asleep, one of the girls said to her sister: "Come with me." She led her into the chamber where the two men were sleeping, and having approached her own husband, she drew a dagger and plunged it into his vitals. He awoke, shouting in his death agony: "You are murdering me!" His brother-in-law, awakened by his cries, heard the woman announce coldly, "Yes, that's what I intend to do," and saw her again plunge the poniard up to its hilt into the victim's heart.

All the foregoing facts were established at the trial, not only by the evidence of the accused's sister and brother-in-law, but by the confession of the defendant herself. The jury duly brought in a verdict of "Guilty of murder in the first degree."

The judge stated that the verdict was unimpeachable, and while deploring the depravity of the defendant, he nevertheless stated to a crowded courtroom that under the law he found it impossible to pronounce sentence upon her. The accused then walked off scot-free.

Now take it for granted that the trial was held in due conformity with legal requirements. Take it for granted that the verdict could not be set aside for any legal technicality, and furthermore, take it for granted that the judge was fully competent and exercised unimpeachable judgment. In short, the difficulty did not arise from any deficiencies in either the processes of the law or the presiding tribunal. The dilemma arose solely out of the circumstances of the case.

**WHAT LOGICAL REASON COULD THE
JUDGE HAVE FOR REFUSING TO PRONOUNCE
SENTENCE UPON THE MURDERER?**

*Answers on page 476*

# DIRTY FACES

Two schoolboys were playing on the toolshed roof. Something gave way, and they were precipitated through the roof to the floor below.

When they picked themselves up, the face of one boy was covered with grime. The other boy's face was quite clean. Yet it was the boy with the clean face who at once went off and washed.

**HOW IS THIS TO BE EXPLAINED?**

*Answers on page 476*

# THE FIVE PEDAGOGUES

Dr. Mortarboard engages five instructors for his school: Mr. Botany, Mr. Geometry, Mr. French, Mr. History, and Mr. Syntax. Each is required to teach two of the subjects which correspond to their five names. No instructor, however, teaches the subject corresponding to his own name.

Mr. History plays cut-throat bridge with the two botany instructors.

Mr. Syntax is married to the sister of one geometry instructor, while his own sister is married to the other.

Mr. Botany knows no French, and Mr. French has no interest in syntax.

Mr. Geometry spends his holidays with the two history instructors.

Mr. History and Mr. Syntax share in the teaching of one subject.

French is not taught by the namesake of either subject taught by Mr. French.

All lessons in French and geometry take place at the same time.

**WHAT ARE THE TWO SUBJECTS WHICH THE
FIVE PEDAGOGUES RESPECTIVELY TEACH?**

*Answers on page 476*

# THE LEGIONNAIRES

WHERE DOES EACH LEGIONNAIRE COME FROM: RENO, MIAMI, BUFFALO, BANGOR. LOS ANGELES? EACH HAS A DIFFERENT HOME.

*Answers on page 476*

# AT CENTRAL STATION

All the trains from Central Station go to Fogwell. From Fogwell, some go on to Kemp; others, to Banstock and then to Midvale; others, to Greenfields and on to Deane. The fare is $3 to Kemp, Midvale, or Deane; elsewhere, $2.

Dan is in a hurry. He has bought a $2 ticket. The first train is going to Midvale, but Dan does not get on.

**WHAT IS DAN'S DESTINATION?**

*Answers on page 476*

# THE MAILBOX

Mr. Contango, a London businessman, went to Paris for a month's holiday. He gave Miss Smith, his secretary, the key to his office, asking her to carry on while he was away, and also to forward all letters. However, he omitted to give her the key to the mailbox.

At the end of some days, he rang up Miss Smith and inquired why he had received no letters. She explained that he had not left her the key. Mr. Contango promised to forward it at once.

The key was duly posted, but still no letters came for Mr. Contango. On returning home, therefore, he promptly sacked his secretary.

WAS HE JUSTIFIED IN DOING SO?

*Answers on page 477*

# THE DIFFICULT CROSSING

A farmer must transport a dog, a duck, and a bag of corn from one side of a river to the opposite bank. The craft he is using is very small—only large enough for him to take one of his possessions at any one time. If he leaves the dog alone with the duck, the dog is likely to make short work of the duck. If he leaves the duck alone with the corn, the duck will make short work of the corn.

WHAT IS THE LEAST NUMBER OF TRIPS THE FARMER CAN TAKE TO MANAGE SAFELY?

*Answers on page 477*

# THE FRATERNITY CONVENTION

It is the last day of the 1966 Convention of the She Delta Deck Fraternity held at St. Louis. The Convention has been in session for a full week. Friends and acquaintances mingle in the lounge, smoking and chatting. Six of the members of the Fraternity, peculiarly enough, bear the names of certain professions or trades. It is these six men with which this particular problem is concerned. Significant bits of their conversation are here recorded.

Mr. Grocer has been asked by Mr. Butcher to join him during the week in a round of golf. Mr. Grocer regrets he cannot accept.

Mr. Butcher replies, "How silly of me! You couldn't play golf now, anyhow. You told me you mashed your finger at your store under a tub of butter. Let me see it."

Mr. Doctor and Mr. Artist render the following colloquy:

Mr. Doctor: I go deep-sea fishing with the lawyer each weekend.

Mr. Artist: The doctor, the grocer, and I live in Milwaukee.

Mr. Baker has buttonholed Mr. Lawyer.

Mr. Baker: I got in a new and interesting case at the office. I'll drop in and tell you about it some time next week.

PROBLEM: Assume that none of these six men bears the name of his business or profession and assume that no two of these men are in the same business or profession, and further assume that one is a lawyer, one is a grocer, one is a doctor, one is an artist, one is a baker, and one is a butcher—

WHO IS THE LAWYER? WHO IS THE GROCER?
WHO IS THE ARTIST? WHO IS THE BAKER?
WHO IS THE BUTCHER? WHO IS THE DOCTOR?

*Answers on page 477*

# THE HORSE RACE

Three colts were running in a race. Their names were Tally-ho, Sonny Boy, and Regent. Their owners were Mr. Lewis, Mr. Bailey, and Mr. Smith, although not necessarily respectively.

Tally-ho unfortunately broke his ankle at the start of the race.

Mr. Smith owned a brown and white three-year-old.

Sonny Boy had previous winnings of $35,000.

Mr. Bailey lost heavily, although his horse almost won.

The horse that won was black.

This race was the first race run by Mr. Lewis's horse.

**WHAT WAS THE NAME OF THE HORSE THAT
WON, AND WHO WAS HIS OWNER?**

*Answers on page 478*

# THE STOLEN ANTIQUE

Three men—Mr. White, Mr. Black, Mr. Brown— and their wives were entertained at the home of a friend one evening. After the departure of the guests, the host and the hostess discovered that a valuable antique had been stolen. It later developed that one of the six guests was the thief.

It is known that:

The spouse of the thief lost money at cards that evening.

Because of partial paralysis of his hands and arms, Mr. Brown was unable to drive his car.

Mrs. Black and another female guest spent the entire evening doing a jig-saw puzzle.

Mr. Black accidentally spilled a drink on Mrs. White when he was introduced to her.

Mr. Brown gave his wife half of the money he had won to make up for her loss.

Mr. Black had beaten the thief in golf that day.

WHO WAS THE THIEF?

*Answers on page 478*

# FIVE MASTERS

"There's a prize," said Mrs. Prigg to her daughters, "for the girl who does best in a little test I've devised for you. These five postcards"—she arranged them on the piano—"are copies of paintings by Degas, Klee, Matisse, Picasso, and Renoir. Which is by whom? I've numbered the postcards from one to five. Here are pencil and paper. You will each make out a list, and the one who does best gets the prize."

Shortly afterwards Mrs. Prigg collected the lists. "You might have done worse," was her verdict, "but there must have been a lot of guesswork. No one gets the prize, however—all five of you have scored the same number of points."

The girls' lists were:

*Kitty*: (1) Renoir; (2) Matisse; (3) Picasso; (4) Degas; (5) Klee.
*Beryl*: (1) Matisse; (2) Picasso; (3) Renoir; (4) Degas; (5) Klee.
*Lorna*: (1) Degas; (2) Picasso, (3) Renoir; (4) Klee; (5) Matisse.
*Doris*: (1) Klee; (2) Matisse; (3) Degas; (4) Picasso; (5) Renoir.
*May*: (1) Degas; (2) Picasso; (3) Matisse; (4) Renoir; (5) Klee.

**ASSIGN THE APPROPRIATE NUMBER TO EACH ARTIST.**

*Answers on page 478*

# FIGHT TO THE FINISH

WHICH BOXER IS RELATED TO TIM?
WHAT IS THE RELATIONSHIP?

*Answers on page 478*

# IT REALLY HAPPENED ONE NIGHT

A charming hedonist, whom we'll call Winston, came home one night at about 2 A.M., rather tired after the revels of the night. He went to bed directly. About twenty minutes later, he got up, opened the local telephone book, and looked up the number of one Gerald Malcolm. He called, and a sweet soprano answered.

"Hello! Is this Mrs. Malcolm?" queried Winston.

"Yes."

"I would like to speak to Mr. Malcolm."

"He's asleep."

"But it's very important!" Winston insisted.

"Important! Well, hold the wire a moment and I'll awaken him."

Young Winston glued his ear to the receiver long enough to hear Mrs. Malcolm walking off spouseward. *Then he deliberately hung up!*

Now ruling out any hoax or wager, and hypothecating that Winston had never previously met or communicated with either Mr. or Mrs. Malcolm, and assuming that Winston acted premeditatedly and planned *everything* he did:

WHAT MOTIVE CAN YOU ASSIGN FOR HIS ACTION?

*Answers on page 478*

# THE MURDERED CARD PLAYER

Four men, whom we shall call Robert, Ronald, Ralph and Rudolph, were playing cards one evening. As a result of a quarrel during the course of the game, one of these men shot and killed another. From the facts given below, see if you can determine who the murderer and his victim were.

Robert will not expose his brother's guilt.

Rudolph had been released from jail on the day of the murder, after having served a three-day sentence.

Robert had wheeled Ralph, a cripple, to the card game at Ronald's house.

Rudolph had known Ronald for only five days before the murder.

Ralph had met Robert's father only once.

The host is about to give evidence against the murderer, whom he dislikes.

The murdered man had eaten dinner on the previous night with one of the men who did not customarily bowl with Ronald.

*Answers on page 478*

# THE FIRED WATCHMAN

Mr. Peabody was president of the Star Bottle Works. On Tuesday, at a directors' meeting, it was decided that Mr. Peabody should go to Chicago to close a large contract then pending. The office force soon learned of the projected trip, and the news soon leaked through to Jim Casey, night watchman of the bottle factory.

Jim, all in a tremor, hurried over to the main office and battled his way into the presidential office. Face to face with the president, he blurted out what was on his mind.

"Mr. Peabody," he said, "I heard you were going to Chicago. Don't do it, Mr. Peabody, please don't do it. I had a terrible dream last night that you were shot in Chicago by a gangster."

Just then Peabody's secretary entered to tell him that he would have to hurry to catch his train, whereupon the executive, paying no heed to the pleas of the watchman, grabbed his valise and rushed out.

Four days later, Peabody returned, hale and hearty. The contract had been signed. His first act was to dismiss Casey.

WHY?

*Answers on page 478*

# THE MUNICIPAL RAILWAYS

The illustration shows the plan of a city surrounded by pentagonal fortifications. Five railroad companies are clamoring for a concession to run a railway into the city. After deliberating, the mayor announces, "Let every one of them have a concession—but the line of one company must never cross the line of another!"

The letters in the diagram represent five railroad companies, and indicate just where each line must enter the city, and where the terminal belonging to that line must be located.

Trace out the route for the line A to A, B to B, C to C, and so on, so that one line does not cross another, or pass through another company's terminal.

*Answers on page 478*

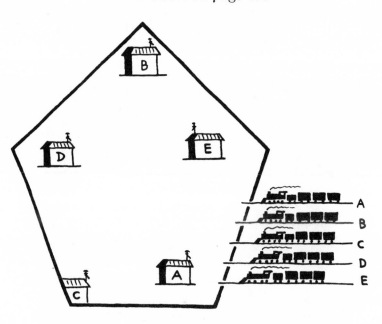

# THE DEAD TOURIST

Mr. and Mrs. Samuel Elkins, wealthy society folks, went on a trip to Switzerland to enjoy some mountain climbing.

A few weeks later, the attractive Mrs. Elkins, shrouded in heavy black, returned to her home in Boston, a widow. Mr. Elkins had missed his step while on a climbing expedition, and had been precipitated headlong down a glassy ravine to a horrible death at the base of the mountain. It was a terrible accident and a terrible ordeal for the stricken Mrs. Elkins, who was with him at the time and witnessed the tragedy.

About a month after her return, her friends, who had given her their deepest sympathy, were astounded to hear that she had been indicted for the murder of her husband. But they were more shocked when Mrs. Elkins broke down and confessed!

The police had received the tip-off from a certain Mr. Harper, head of a well-known travel agency. Mr. Harper had never left the United States.

HOW DID HE DEDUCE THAT MRS. ELKINS
HAD MURDERED HER HUSBAND?

*Answers on page 479*

# A NARROW ESCAPE

Mr. Drake was driving his car along a straight highway in Florida, which led due north to his destination, a town 20 miles north of his starting point. When he had gone approximately 19 miles, a fast-moving car passed his. As a result his car was forced a couple of yards off the highway, thereby scraping its side against some protruding bushes.

Drake stopped his car, and as he was looking out the window to ascertain whether any noticeable damage had been done by the bushes, he judged from the position of the sun that it was late in the afternoon and that he would have to hurry. A couple of minutes later he arrived at his destination, happy in the thought that he had escaped a possible serious accident.

**WHAT IS THE FALLACY IN THE ABOVE STORY?**

*Answers on page 479*

# THE LOST COIN

WHO IS ENTITLED TO THE COIN?

*Answers on page 479*

# THE ISLAND OF KO

On the island of Ko there are three types of inhabitants, physically indistinguishable from one another. They are known as the Reds, the Greens, and the Half-Breeds. A Red, when asked a question, invariably gives a truthful answer; a Green invariably gives an untruthful answer; a Half-Breed alternately lies and tells the truth, though one cannot tell whether his first answer will be a truthful one or not.

Three inhabitants—a Red, a Green, and a Half-Breed—were lounging on the beach. Their names (not necessarily respectively) were Tom, Dick, and Harry. A traveler accosted the first one and the following dialogue ensued:

"What is your name?"

"Tom, sir."

"Are you a Red, a Green, or a Half-Breed?"

"Green, sir."

"What is the name of your Red friend?"

"Dick, sir."

## WHAT ARE THE NAMES OF THE RED, THE GREEN, AND THE HALF-BREED?

*Answers on page 479*

# THE CARETAKER

Adam Smith was caretaker of an unoccupied old mansion from which all of the furniture had been removed, with the exception of the few pieces that graced the little back room in which Smith lived the life of a recluse. His only known contacts were with the little corner store and with the milk man, whom he paid each week. This person, upon finding that several bottles of milk were still standing on the stairs as he had left them and that there was no response to repeated knockings on the door, summoned the police. They entered the house and found the body of Smith hanging by the neck from the lofty chandelier in the center of the dusty and vacant ballroom.

It was a weird sight in the semi-darkness to see the limp figure of the man dangling in the empty center of what had once been a brilliant and beautiful salon. The police and the coroner, who had subsequently been called, cut down the body and made an examination. The man was suspended by his own belt and there was nothing further that they could observe except two cigarette stubs and an empty whisky flask on the floor, and the dust and cobwebs that covered the high ceiling and the barren walls.

Glad to be through with his unpleasant task, the coroner made the death certificate and assigned as cause of death "Suicide due to melancholia."

## WHAT WAS THE FALLACY IN THE CORONER'S EXPLANATION?

*Answers on page 479*

# THE MARINERS

There are three ships, the *Albatross*, the *Americus*, and the *Hispaniola*, on the sea sailing for the ports of Liverpool, New York, and Cherbourg, but not necessarily in that order. The ships are commanded by Captains Brine, Tarr, and Salt.

A few months ago Captain Tarr was the guest of Captain Brine on the *Albatross*.

The *Hispaniola* hit a derelict on her last crossing, and as a result was in dry dock for repairs for seven weeks previous to the present trip.

The *Albatross* has just passed the *Americus* in mid-ocean, and shipped a stowaway back by the *Americus*.

Mrs. Salt, who usually travels with her husband, was yesterday discharged from the hospital where she was treated for a week for a severe attack of ulcers. This unfortunate condition victimized her while she was three days from land and necessitated her immediate removal to the hospital when the ship docked.

The Captain of the *Americus* is preparing a report for his owners, Cartright and Smith, Ltd., of Liverpool, which he will deliver to their offices as soon as his ship docks.

**WHAT SHIP DOES CAPTAIN TARR COMMAND,
AND TO WHAT PORT IS IT BOUND?**

*Answers on page 479*

# THE VANISHED COIN

The eight members of an exclusive society in London known as the Collector's Club are each considered experts and connoisseurs of objets d'art, stamps, and coins.

The Club does not admit outsiders to its meetings, and even bars waiters from serving the bowls of fruit which invariably grace the long table at which the informal, fortnightly discussions are held.

One day one of the members met an acquaintance who also was a collector of coins. The friend, who had heard much about the famed discussions at the Club, was so insistent about being taken to a meeting that the member, succumbing to his friend's entreaties, obtained permission to have him attend.

During the meeting, Mr. Grant Lewis, a coin collector, just returned from a Continental tour, exhibited his prize find—an ancient, rare Phoenician coin. The coin passed from hand to hand and was closely scrutinized by all those present, amidst a continual barrage of questions directed at the proud Lewis. Lewis, urged to expatiate on the history of his rarity, surrendered to the importunities of his fellow members. He requested the silver piece in order to point out certain peculiarities; but no one had the coin.

Each averred he had passed it to another, so that from the maze of statements it was impossible to determine who actually had the coin last. Every inch of the carpet was examined, but the coin seemed to have vanished into thin air. Everyone volubly urged calm, thus indicating how upset the members actually were. Fear lest the scandal besmirch the honor of the venerable Collector's Club crowded out the suspicion that perhaps a hoax was being perpetrated, for the coin was worth a fabulous sum.

Finally, the demand was made that everyone submit to a personal examination. The suggestion was taken up and seconded with willingness by all—that is, all except the stranger. He demurred resolutely. Not only would he not submit to a search of his person, but he steadfastly refused to divulge any reason for his apparently stubborn refusal. The chairman threatened to inform the police. As the words fell from his lips, Grant Lewis reached forth nervously into the silver bowl for an apple. As he drew the fruit away, there to his amazement, at the bottom of the bowl, he saw his prize coin. Confusion succeeded bewilderment; and profuse apologies poured forth upon the stranger, who rose to explain.

The explanation for his refusing to be searched and refusing further to give a reason for his attitude was sound. All the facts necessary for a logical explanation of the stranger's actions are in the foregoing recital.

### WHAT SENSIBLE AND LOGICAL EXPLANATION
### DID THE STRANGER OFFER?

*Answers on page 479*

# THREE SONS

Smith, Sr., Brown, Sr., and Jones, Sr., each had a grown son. We may call the sons Smith, Jr., Brown, Jr., and Jones, Jr. One of the Juniors was a politician; another, a banker; and the third, a lawyer.

(1) The lawyer frequently played tennis with his father.

(2) Brown, Jr., called the politican a socialist.

(3) The politician's father played golf every Wednesday with another of the older men.

(4) Smith, Sr., had been a paralytic from youth.

**WHAT WAS THE NAME OF THE LAWYER?**

*Answers on page 480*

# THE MARKED FOREHEADS

A professor, wishing to determine who was the brightest among three of his cleverest students, named Alex, Joe, and Tom, arranged a little experiment. He had the three of them sit around a small circular table, each one facing the other two. Explaining that he was going to paste a little label on the forehead of each, he bade his three boys close their eyes. He told them that the labels would either be marked with a blue cross or a green cross. The challenge, he continued, consisted merely of this: that if any one of the students saw a green cross he should raise his hand, and that as soon as a student knew what color cross his forehead was marked with he should fold his arms on his chest.

While their eyes were shut, the professor proceeded to label each with a *green cross*. He then told the boys that all was set. They opened their eyes and each immediately raised his hand. After a lapse of a few minutes Alex folded his arms. The professor asked him how he was marked. Alex answered "Green."

CAN YOU EXPLAIN THE REASONING BY
WHICH HE MADE HIS DEDUCTION?

*Answers on page 480*

# THE BLIND BUTLER

WHAT IS THE LEAST NUMBER OF
SOCKS HE MUST BRING BACK?

*Answers on page 480*

# TRACKS IN THE SNOW

I WONDER WHAT MADE THOSE TRACKS IN THIS NEWLY FALLEN SNOW. THEY EXTEND CLEAR ACROSS TO THAT WOODSHED.

WHAT CAUSED THE TRACKS IN THE SNOW?

*Answers on page 480*

# AN EXERCISE IN LOGIC

Assume that the following statement is true: "John is over twenty-one if John can vote."

*Which of the following statements are then* necessarily *true also*?

(1) If John cannot vote, John is not over twenty-one.
(2) If John is over twenty-one, he can vote.
(3) If John is not over twenty-one, he cannot vote.
(4) Either John can vote or John is not over twenty-one.
(5) Either John cannot vote or he is over twenty-one.
(6) Either John can vote or he is over twenty-one.
(7) Either John cannot vote or he is not over twenty-one.

*Answers on page 480*

# THE SIX HOODLUMS

Serena Vashti Malloy, a rich dowager, was found murdered in her home in Chicago with a bullet through her heart. The local police ascertained that the murder was committed between 10 and 12 o'clock at night, and that the motive was robbery. They were also sure that the crime was committed by one of a notorious gang of local criminals.

They rounded up the gang, and at the preliminary arraignment each of the six suspects was questioned. Each of the men made two significant statements. In each case, one of the statements was true, and one of the statements was false. (The order of the statements as presented is not controlling.)

The judge, aware of this state of affairs, deliberated awhile and soon became rightfully convinced of the guilt of one of the men in particular. *Which one did he accuse?*

The statements follow:

*Mike:* Red didn't kill her. I never saw a gun in my life.

*Dan:* I was in Philly when it happened. Mat did it.

*Jim:* Mike pulled the trigger. All of us except Dan were in Chi when it happened.

*Spud:* Only one of us witnessed the murder. I was not even in town on the night of the killing.

*Mat:* Spud's the murderer. I was at the neighborhood movies, at the time, with some other one of the boys.

*Red:* Me and Mike were together from 10 to 12 away from the rest of the gang. Dan killed her.

**181**

*Answers on page 480*

# DR. LIMEJUICE

A statue of Dr. Limejuice, the temperance reformer, stands in Drinkwell marketplace. The other night two boys of Drinkwell School painted the doctor's nose red. One of them held a lantern, while the other did the actual painting.

The headmaster, having received a report from the police, sent for three boys, Sniggersby, Tittering, and Wallop. He proceeded to ask each of them three questions, putting the questions to the three boys in rotation. The questions, and the answers received, were as follows (but the order in which the boys were questioned is not necessarily that given above):

*Headmaster:* You are one of the two culprits?
*First Boy:* No, sir.
*Headmaster:* You are, then?
*Second Boy:* Yes, sir.
*Headmaster:* And you are?
*Third Boy:* No, sir.
*Headmaster:* Of those three statements, two at least are untrue?
*First Boy:* No, sir.
*Headmaster (reading):* "Sniggersby was holding the lantern." Is that true?
*Second Boy:* No, sir.
*Headmaster (reading):* "Tittering painted the statue." Is that true?
*Third Boy:* No, sir.
*Headmaster (reading):* "Wallop is not implicated." Is that true?
*First Boy:* No, sir.
*Headmaster (reading):* "You can rely on Sniggersby not to tell you a lie." Is that true?
*Second Boy:* Yes, sir.
*Headmaster (reading):* "And you can similarly rely on Wallop." Is that true?
*Third Boy:* Yes, sir.

Each of the suspects has now answered three questions. Wallop has lied twice, and the other two boys have each lied once.

## WHO HELD THE LANTERN, AND WHO PAINTED THE DOCTOR'S NOSE?

*Answers on page 481*

# THE STOLEN NECKLACE

WHICH MAN IS TELLING THE WHOLE TRUTH?

*Answers on page 481*

# THE NOBLES AND THE SLAVES

WHICH OF THE THREE AFRICANS ARE NOBLES?

*Answers on page 481*

# A SQUARE IN LINDLAND

Blotto Square is a tiny square in Lindland. There is only one house on each of its four sides. These sides may be called the north side, east side, south side, and west side.

The residents of the four houses are Mr. East, Mr. West, Mr. North, and Mr. South. They are (not necessarily respectively) a lawyer, a doctor, a sculptor, and an actor.

The resident on the north side of the square knows nothing about the law.

The doctor lives opposite Mr. South; the actor, opposite Mr. North.

The resident on the west side of the square has never passed an examination.

Mr. South, who has never been inside a theater, has enlisted the aid of the lawyer in an action now pending in the courts.

Mr. West is the actor's right-hand neighbor.

DRAW A PLAN OF BLOTTO SQUARE SHOWING
EACH RESIDENT'S HOUSE AND OCCUPATION.

*Answers on page 482*

# THE FOUR COEDS

WHAT IS THE ANSWER TO PROFESSOR
BROWN'S QUESTION?

*Answers on page 482*

# THE CLEVER BLIND MAN

Three men are seated around a circular table facing each other. They are told that a box in the room contains five hats—three white and two black. A hat is placed on each man's head. The remaining two hats are unseen. No man sees the hat that is placed on his own head.

One man is then asked what color hat he believes to be on his head. He looks at the other two hats before him on the heads of his companions, and then says he doesn't know.

The second man in reply to a similar question admits that he too, doesn't really know.

The question is then put once again, and the third man, *who is blind*, correctly announces the color of the hat on his head.

**CAN YOU TELL WHAT COLOR THAT HAT WAS
AND CAN YOU OUTLINE THE REASONING
WHICH THE BLIND MAN FOLLOWED?**

*Answers on page 482*

# THE FOOTBALL TOURNAMENT

An elimination tournament in football was held in which four colleges—Trinity, Tufts, Temple, and Tulane—participated. The winners of the first two games met in the third and final game to decide the championship. The colors of the various teams were brown, blue, red, and purple, and the competing captains were Albie, Barry, Bill, and Ben, though not necessarily respectively. The following facts are known:

(1) In the final game Albie's team made its only score by a touchdown on the first play, but missed the point after touchdown.
(2) The red team lost to Tufts in the first game.
(3) Ben's team defeated Tulane 12 to 0.
(4) The captain of the purple team saved his team from being scoreless in the third game by a 40-yard field goal.
(5) Ben's team did not play Trinity.
(6) Barry's team lost to the undefeated team.
(7) Albie did not see his former friend, the captain of the brown team.

WHO DEFEATED WHOM IN THE PLAY-OFF, AND
BY WHAT SCORE? WHO WAS THE CAPTAIN OF EACH
TEAM? WHAT WAS THE COLOR OF EACH TEAM?

*Answers on page 482*

# THE RAILROAD SIDING

E is an engine on the main line. A and B are boxcars on the two sidings. The segment C is long enough to contain only one boxcar or the engine.

You are required, by means of the engine, to move B to A and A to B and to leave E in its original position.

HOW WOULD YOU DO IT?

*Answers on page 483*

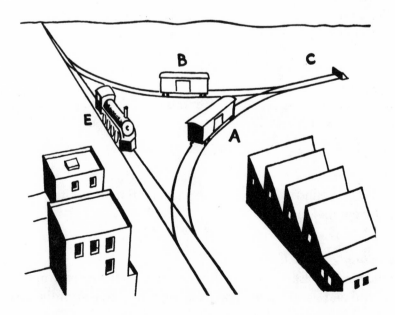

# NEWSPAPER BONERS

*From a Gettysburg paper:*

Blend sugar, flour and salt. Add egg and milk, cook until creamy in double boiler. Stir frequently. Add rest of ingredients. Mix well, serve chilled.

Funeral services will be held Thursday afternoon at 2 o'clock.

♚

*From the Waco News-Tribune:*

Every effort was made to restore the land to its frightful owners.

*From the Honolulu Star-Bulletin:*

A well-known beauty expert says that beauty is not a question of age. It is making the best of one's good paints.

♚

*From a Louisiana newspaper:*

The ladies of the Cherry Street Church have discarded clothing of all kinds. Call at 44 North Cherry Street for inspection.

♚

*From the Boston Globe:*

The blackground for the heated participation of whites in the anti-busing campaign is fear.

♚

*From a Wilmington, N.C. paper:*

Bathing in the Easter dew, these people believe, will make them beautiful and guard them against all ham for the rest of the year.

*From the Hollywood, Cal. Citizen-News:*
> You cannot encrust a teenager with the responsibility for making her own decisions.

☫

*From the Biloxi News:*
> The lawyer strode into the court carrying his grief case.

☫

*From the Tulsa, Okla. Daily World:*
> The author of *Forever Amber*, Kathleen Winsor, has written another book, *Star Money*, that is called a "20th-century Amber," and is supposed to out-smell the two million copies of the first book.

*From a Jefferson City, Mo. paper:*
> Columbia, Tenn., which calls itself the largest outdoor mule market in the world, held a mule parade yesterday headed by the Governor.

☫

*From the Malone, N.Y. Telegram:*
> William Andrews returned home yesterday from the hospital, where his left leg was placed in a cast following a fracture of the right ankle.

☫

*From the Philadelphia Inquirer:*
> After viewing the headless, armless and legless torso, the Coroner voiced the opinion that the real estate agent had been slain.

☫

*From a Norfolk newspaper:*
> James Farrell was born and educated in the public schools of Chicago.

*From a Portland newspaper:*
He was raised by his grandparents because his mother died in early infancy.

⬧

*From the Columbus Dispatch:*
Recovering from a head injury and shock caused by coming in contact with a live wife, Arthur E— left Mercy Hospital Wednesday.

⬧

*From a Kalamazoo paper:*
Nudism would be bared in Michigan under a bill introduced in the house Wednesday.

*From the Halstead, Kans. Independent:*
Mrs. E. Peterson was hostess to the Book-review Group Monday evening. Mrs. V. Chesky reviewed the book, *Three Little Pigs Stayed Home*. There were 19 present.

⬧

*From the Arkansas Post:*
The Secretary of State met today with the Crime Minister to discuss the situation in South Africa.

⬧

*From the Omaha Sunday World-Herald:*
Gene Autry is better after being kicked by a horse.

*From the Bonner Springs, Kans. Chieftain:*
The song fest was hell at the Methodist church Wednesday.

*From an El Paso paper:*
W.M. McG— lost a finger when a poisoned dog to which he was administering an anecdote bit him.

*From the Worcester, Mass. Sunday Telegram:*
State Senator Ernest A. Johnson, seeking re-election said, "I have made no wild promises, except one—honest government."

*From a New York paper:*
The bride was gowned in white lace. The bridesmaids' gowns were punk.

*From the Atlanta Free Press:*
To illustrate the points she was making, Ms. Crawford had a baby at the meeting.

*From the San Francisco Chronicle:*
If your gas range is not exactly level, the food cooked in the oven will not burn as evenly as it should.

*From the Los Angeles, Calif. News:*
   Fog and smog rolled over Los Angeles today, closing two airports and slowing snails to a traffic pace.

♔

*From the Kingsport, Tenn. Times:*
   The All-Girl Orchestra was rather weak in the bras section.

♔

*From the Pittsburgh Examiner:*
   We're still serving the same home-cooked chicken dinner we've been serving for the last 30 years.

♔

*From the classifieds in a New York paper:*
   Fine, gold jewelry, old and new. Why go elsewhere to be cheated when you can come here?

♔

*From a Reading, Pa. circular:*
   Elite laundry will not tear your clothes in machines. We do it carefully by hand.

♔

*From the Washington Post:*
   Adjacent to the library is a completely equipped lovatory.

*From the Greensboro, N.C. Record:*
   The slightly built general, with four rows of robbins on his chest, took the witness chair. ♔

*From the Rochester Times Union, an advertisement for a radio program:*
   Hear Mr. Blank. The complete dope on the weather.

# WHIMSICAL VERSE

The following stanzas, offered for your delectation, range in literary merit from slight to nil. Nevertheless, many have survived through generations which, in itself, attests to their appeal.

The savages closed around the tent;
  The lovers trembled in the gloom;
They knew their life was well-nigh spent,
  They knew they faced their doom.
He kissed the ringlets on her head,
  He crushed her in embrace of death;
And as he kissed her lips he said,
  *"There's garlic on your breath!"*

"I love the ground you walk on!" This was the tale he told.
For they lived up the Klondike, and the ground was full of gold!

They walked in the lane together,
  The sky was covered with stars;
They reached the gate in silence,
  He lifted down the bars.
She neither smiled nor thanked him
  Because she knew not how;
For he was just a farmer's boy,
  And she—a Jersey cow.

Divorced are Mr. and Mrs. Howell;
He wiped their car with her guest towel.

If all the land were apple-pie,
    And all the sea were ink;
And all the trees were bread and cheese,
    What should we do for drink?

I sneezed a sneeze into the air,
It fell to earth I know not where;
But hard and cold were the looks of those
In whose vicinity I snooze.

She took my hand with loving care;
She took my costly flowers so rare.
She took my candy and my books!
She took my eye with meaning looks.
She took all that I could buy,
And then she took the other guy.

A centipede was happy quite,
    Until a frog, in fun,
Said, "Pray, which leg comes after which?"
This raised her mind to such a pitch
She lay distracted in a ditch,
    Considering how to run.

Oh, what a blamed uncertain thing
    This pesky weather is:
It blew and snew and then it thew
    And now, by jing, it friz!

Yesterday upon the stair
I saw a man who wasn't there.
He wasn't there again today;
I wish to heck he'd go away.

I eat my peas with honey,
    I've done it all my life;
They do taste kind of funny,
    But it keeps them on the knife.

Here is a riddle most abstruse:
    Canst read the answer right?
Why is it that my tongue grows loose
    Only when I grow tight?

The bee is such a busy soul
It has no time for birth control;
And that is why in times like these
There are so many sons of bees.

This is the story of Johnny McGuire
Who ran through the town with trousers on fire.
He went to the doctor's and fainted with fright
When the doctor told him his end was in sight.

I often pause and wonder at fate's peculiar ways,
For nearly all our famous men were born on holidays.

# A DOLLAR BILL TURNS UPSIDE-DOWN

With this trick you can really astound your friends. All you need is a dollar bill.

First, place the dollar bill on a table or any other flat surface with the portrait facing you.

Fold it in half, by lifting the right-hand side of the bill and folding it over the left-hand side.

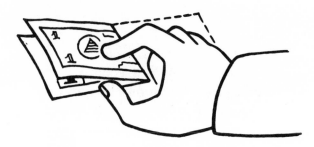

Now fold the bill once again, this time by lifting the top of the bill and folding it downward over the bottom.

Finally, turn the bill from left to right.

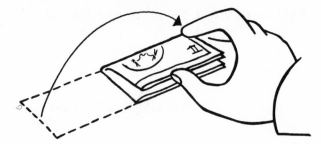

Then unfold it by lifting it up from the bottom.

When you unfold the bill, you will notice that the portrait is upside-down.

How, without lifting the bill off the table or turning it around, did you make the portrait point in the opposite direction? Well, in face you *have* turned it around. You did it on the second fold, when you folded the *top* of the bill on top of the *bottom*.

When you perform this trick, make the folds as quickly as you can, so that your audience cannot analyze how the trick is done.

# CARBON COPY

Here's a fascinating, mysterious trick that is bound to thrill your friends.

Ask someone at the table to write an initial on a lump of sugar, and then to place the sugar on the table face down so that the letter cannot be seen.... Then you take the lump of sugar and, without looking at it, drop it into a glass of water.... Now tell the party who has marked the sugar to close his fists.... Hold the glass of water containing the sugar above his clenched fists.... After the sugar has partly dissolved, tell your friend to open his fists. There on the palm of one hand, he'll find the imprint of the letter he wrote on the sugar, perfectly reproduced!

Here's the secret! . . . While your friend is writing down the initial, moisten the ball of your right thumb. Just a little bit of moisture is needed. When you pick up the lump of sugar, place your thumb against the initialed side as you drop the sugar into the glass. The imprint of the letter will remain on your thumb.

Then, grasp your friend's hands with both *your* hands and close *his* hands into fists, talking and explaining at the same time to distract his attention.

Meanwhile, you press your thumb against his palm *and he's a marked man!*

# PAPER TREE

Gather together about eight sheets of newspaper, some Scotch tape or paste, and a single-edged razor blade or a small, sharp knife. Your friends will marvel at how clever you are when you turn this material into a paper tree six feet high or more.

Paste four or more sheets of newspaper together with the Scotch tape or paste.

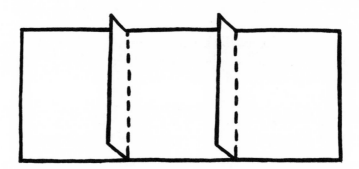

This results in a very long strip of newspaper, which you then roll up into a tube.

Seal the tube with paste or tape, so it won't unroll.

Now, use your razor blade or scissors to cut three small slits in the center of the paper tube. Make one vertical slit, about five inches in length. Make two horizontal slits, at the top and bottom of the vertical slit, about three inches long.

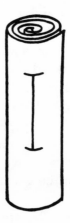

Make sure you cut all the way through to the center of the roll—but no further.

When you're finished cutting, spread back the leaves of paper which you have opened by your cuts.

Now bend the tube in half.

The portion of the newspaper roll which you have not cut should form two handles.

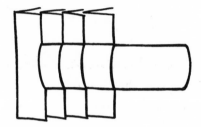

Hold both these handles in your left hand. With your right hand, very slowly and gently, pull out the section of the newspaper at the top, until it has gone high as it will go. To avoid tearing the paper, pull as gently as you can.

When you're finished, you will have a magic paper tree at least six feet high.

To make the paper tree collapse, simply push down gently from top to bottom, so that the paper telescopes once again into its original shape, in you left hand.

Then bend the two halves back into shape, so that you are left with a long roll, just like what you started with. In this shape, the tube can be easily stored. Keep a rubber band around it, so that the tube won't unravel.

# THE BUSINESS CARD TRICK

This amazing stunt is sure to arouse an enthusiastic response. Though it's easy to do, the effect is spectacular.

All you need is an ordinary 2″ by 3½″ business card and a pair of scissors. The object is to cut the business card in such a way so that you can put your head through it.

First fold the card in half the long way.

Then beginning from the folded edge, cut a series of slits along the entire width of the card, to within about ⅛ of an inch of the opposite side. Make your slits about ¼ of an inch apart.

Next, turn the card completely around so that the open edges are facing you. Cut more slits going in the opposite direction, the same way you made the others, stopping about ⅛ of an inch from the opposite edge of the card.

Finally, cut along the folded edge, beginning from the slit farthest on your right, and continuing to the slit farthest on your left. Be sure not to cut beyond those points, or you might accidentally cut the card into pieces.

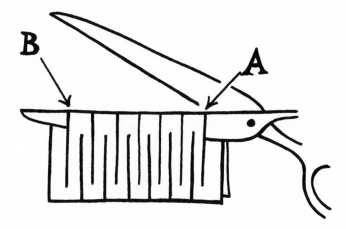

When you are finished, unfold the card carefully. It should look like this:

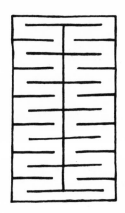

Now you are ready to put your head through the card. Gently slip your fingers into the long slit at the center of the card, and pull the card apart until it has opened as wide as it will go. You will find that you have created a hole so large that you can easily slide the card over your head and around your neck.

# STRANGE SQUARE

Get together a pencil, a piece of paper, a ruler, and scissors. Then draw and cut out a figure composed of five squares, as shown in this diagram.

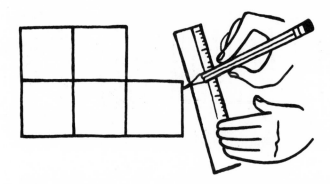

    The trick is to create a perfect square out of the figure, by making only two straight cuts with the scissors. In other words, you must cut the figure into three pieces, which when fitted together differently, form a perfect square.

    After you and your friends have all tried it and failed, make your cuts in the places indicated by the dotted lines.

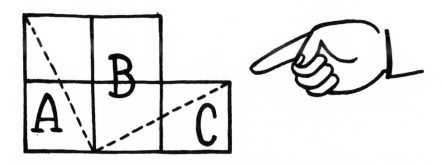

The pieces will fit together perfectly, to form a perfect square.

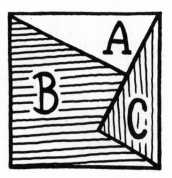

# THE GLASS PUZZLE

This trick is easy to do. The only materials necessary are three empty glasses, and three glasses filled with water.

Arrange the glasses in a row, in this order.

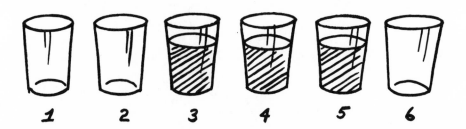

The trick is to arrange the six glasses so that they are standing alternately one with water, one empty; one with water, one empty; and so on. You are only allowed to move or touch one glass to accomplish this feat.

Let your friends try it first. Then, when they have given up in despair, you proceed to show them how.

Lift the glass that is standing fourth from the left (*Glass No. 4*). Pour the water in *Glass No. 4* into *Glass No. 1* (the first glass on the left). Then replace *Glass No. 4* in its original position. Your friends will find that the six glasses now stand in the correct alternating arrangement.

You have only moved one glass in the process.

# HOLE IN YOUR HAND

Prove to your friends that you can put a hole through someone's hand without his feeling it. All you need for this trick is a single sheet of paper.
Roll the piece of paper into the shape of a tube.

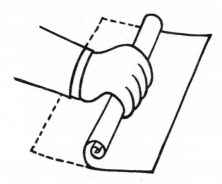

Now hold the tube up to one eye and look through it. Be sure to keep your other eye open.
Hold up your other hand with the palm facing you. Place this hand at eye level, right next to the middle of the tube. You are now looking through the tube with one eye, and looking at the palm of your other hand with the other eye.

Now you'll see an amazing thing: one of your hands has a hole in it!
Ask your friend to follow the same procedure. He'll see a hole in his hand, too.

# THE BOTTLED DOLLAR BILL

Start with two empty soda bottles of the same size, and a dollar bill that is as new and crisp as possible. Make sure the mouths of both bottles are dry, to prevent sticking. Then place the dollar bill across the mouth of one of the bottles. Balance the second soda bottle upside-down on top of the first, so that the two rims match together perfectly.

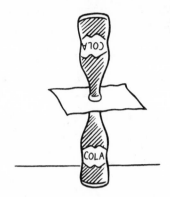

Your objective is to snatch the dollar bill from between the two bottles without upsetting either bottle. You are not allowed to touch the bottles.

"Impossible," you say. Well, try it and you'll see how simple it really is. Just hold the bill at one end with your left hand. Make sure to hold it very tightly. Then, with your right hand, strike the bill with a swift stroke, about half-way between the rims of the bottles and your left hand.

If you have held onto the bill tightly, and if you have struck it briskly enough, you will see the dollar bill slide smoothly out from between the two rims, causing barely a tremor in the precarious balance.

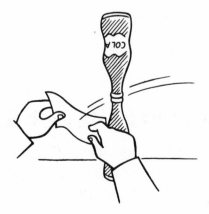

# WOULD YOU BELIEVE. . .

THERE'S NO LEAD IN A LEAD PENCIL.
*A pencil is filled with graphite.*

THERE'S NO SODA IN SODA WATER.
*It is water charged with carbon dioxide.*

THE FLYING FOX IS NOT A FOX, NOR DOES IT FLY.
*It is a large bat. It does not fly, it glides.*

PEANUTS ARE NOT NUTS.
*They are beans, and grow underground.*

THE LADYBIRD IS NOT A BIRD.
*It is a beetle.*

A GUINEA PIG IS NOT A PIG.
*It is a rodent.*

DRESDEN CHINA DOES NOT COME FROM DRESDEN.
*It is made in the town of Meissen, Germany.*

THERE IS NO TEA IN BEEF TEA.
*It is made from beef, and is served as broth.*

KID GLOVES ARE NOT MADE OF KID.
*They are made of lambskin.*

A TITMOUSE IS NOT A MOUSE.
*It is a small bird.*

ROSE FEVER HAS NOTHING TO DO WITH ROSES.
*It is caused by spring grasses.*

GINGERBREAD IS NOT BREAD.
*It is a kind of cake.*

A PRAIRIE DOG IS NOT A DOG.
*It is a rodent.*

SEALING WAX CONTAINS NO WAX.
*It is made of shellac, Venice turpentine and cinnabar.*

JOHNNYCAKE IS NOT CAKE.
*It is a kind of bread.*

CATGUT DOES NOT COME FROM A CAT.
*It is obtained from sheep.*

THE SILVERFISH IS NOT A FISH.
*It is an insect.*

ARABIC FIGURES WERE NOT DEVISED BY THE ARABS.
*They were created by the early scholars of India.*

CAMPHOR BALLS DO NOT CONTAIN CAMPHOR.
*They are made of naphthalene.*

THE RED SEA IS NOT RED.
*It is bluish green, like most bodies of water.*

HUDSON SEAL IS NOT SEAL.
*It is dyed muskrat.*

PANAMA HATS ARE NOT MADE IN PANAMA.
*They are manufactured in Ecuador.*

GROUNDHOGS ARE NOT HOGS.
*They are rodents.*

A WALKING LEAF IS NOT A LEAF.
*It is an insect.*

HUSH PUPPIES ARE NOT PUPPIES.
*They are a kind of food made from deep-fried batter.*

A SEA LION IS NOT A LION.
*It is a seal.*

# PENCIL BOXING

This game is played by two opponents. The object of the game is to form boxes, by drawing at each turn one line connecting two dots. The lines may be horizontal or vertical, but not diagonal.

The first player draws his line anywhere on the diagram that he chooses. Then his opponent draws one line, also placing it anywhere on the diagram that he wants to. The players take turns drawing connecting lines.

Each time that a player completes one box, he gets one point. Each player should try to avoid forming the third side of a box, since that will give his opponent the opportunity to complete the box by drawing in its fourth side.

In order to keep score, every time a player scores a point, he must draw his initial inside the box he has formed.

When all the dots in the diagram have been completed, the players count the number of times their initials appear on the diagram. The player with the most number of points, or, in other words, the most number of boxes bearing his initial, wins the game.

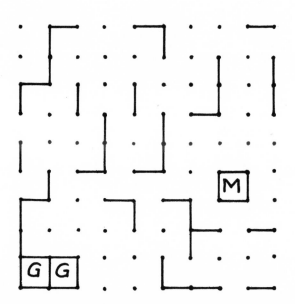

Three diagrams have been provided. You can easily draw more of these diagrams if you are interested in playing more of these delightful games.

The first two diagrams provided in this book are each composed of 100 dots, 10 on a line. This forms a game of 100 boxes. The third game is somewhat larger, consisting of 260 boxes. You might try playing with the larger diagram by having each player make two strokes on each turn, instead of one, for the first twenty strokes. This will speed up the game and make it more interesting.

Remember, if you are playing with two strokes to a turn and you use your two strokes to make two sides to the same box, your opponent will be able to close your box on his very next turn. So be careful to use your two strokes on two different boxes.

## GAME ONE

## GAME TWO

## GAME THREE

# BATTLESHIP

Battleship is one of the most exciting pencil games ever invented. All you need is a pencil and a piece of paper.

Each player begins by taking a piece of paper and drawing boxes just like those in the diagram.

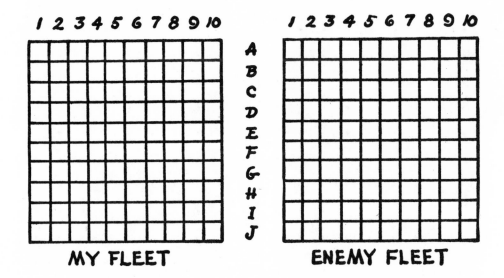

MY FLEET                    ENEMY FLEET

The diagram consists of two squares, each composed of one hundred boxes. The boxes should be numbered at the top of the large square, from *1* to *10*. Alongside each box, from the top of the large square to the bottom, run the letters *A* through *J*. Now you can easily identify any box, by calling it, for example, *D-7*, which would signify the fourth box down and the seventh box in.

Each player should mark the square on his left *My Fleet*, and the square on his right *Enemy Fleet*.

The idea of the game is as follows: Each player begins with a fleet composed of one Battleship, one Cruiser, and two Destroyers. A Battleship is four boxes in length; a Cruiser, three; and a Destroyer, two. Before the game begins, each player marks in the disposition of his naval fleet in the square designated as *My Fleet*.

A player can place his ships in any position that he desires. The diagram will show you one way in which a fleet can be positioned: The fleet is indicated by gray boxes. This is done by shading in the boxes with your pencil. The ships may be laid in diagonally, horizontally, or vertically, as shown in the illustration. The only restriction is that the ships may not touch one another; each ship must be separated by at least one blank box.

The players sit so that they cannot see each other's charts. The game starts as soon as the two players have finished positioning their fleets.

The object of the game is to sink the enemy fleet. This is done by calling out the letter and number of a specific box. This is the equivalent of a naval salvo. If you happen to call out the letter and number of a box on which an enemy ship is placed, you make a *Hit*. However, one *Hit* is not enough to sink a whole ship. In order to sink a ship, you must have hit each and every box on which the ship is positioned. A Destroyer can be sunk in two *Hits*; but it takes four *Hits* to sink a Battleship.

The game proceeds like this: The first player calls out four different boxes, in turn. As he calls each one, he marks the box that he has called with an *X* on his *Enemy Fleet* chart. In this way, he can keep track of which boxes he has already called.

For example, a player might call out the boxes *I-3*, *D-4*, *E-5*, and *B-8*. He would then mark those boxes with an *X* on his *Enemy Fleet* chart, as in the illustration.

When the first player has completed his first call, his opponent must report whether any *Hits* have been made. He could reply, for example, "*No Hits*," "*One Hit on a Battleship*," or "*Two Hits on a Cruiser*."

Then it is the second player's turn to call out four boxes. He also records *his* calls on his *Enemy Fleet* chart, and his opponent must tell him whether any *Hits* have been made.

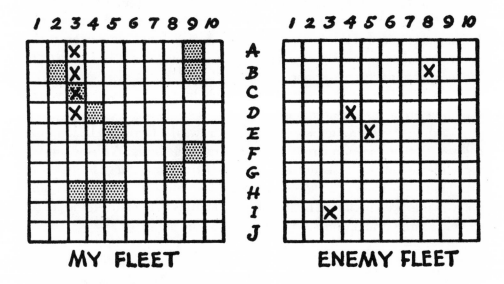

MY FLEET          ENEMY FLEET

In the sample illustration, the second player has called out the boxes *A-3*, *B-3*, *C-3*, and *D-3*, and he has scored a *Hit* on the first player's Battleship.

The game proceeds in this way, with each player keeping track of the boxes he himself calls out, and the boxes his opponent has called out. As the game goes on, each player begins to figure out where his opponent's ships are positioned.

When a player has lost a ship, he is only entitled to three salvos. Each time he loses another ship, the number of calls he is allowed to make is reduced by one. When one of the players has succeeded in sinking all four of his opponent's ships, he has won the game.

# JAILHOUSE

This is an exciting word game for two players. One player is the *Jailer*; his opponent is the *Guesser*.

The *Jailer* picks out a word and gives the *Guesser* three hints as to what the word is. The hints are as follows: First, the *Jailer* shows the *Guesser* how many letters there are in the word by drawing one dash for each letter in the word on a piece of paper.

Second, the *Jailer* shows the *Guesser* what the first letter of the word is, by printing that letter on the paper above the first dash.

Thirdly, the *Jailer* prints the last letter of the word above the last dash.

In addition, if either the first letter or the last letter, or both, appear somewhere in the word a second time, these letters must be printed by the *Jailer* above the dash corresponding to their position in the word.

For example, if the word were ORANGE, the *Jailer's* clues to the *Guesser* would look like this: O _ _ _ _ E .

If the word were RECEIVE, the clues would look like this: R E _ E _ _ E.

Before the guessing starts, the *Jailer* draws a framework of a jail on the paper—just a simple box. Then the *Guesser* calls out a letter which he thinks might be in the word. If he calls out a letter which belongs somewhere in the word, the *Jailer* must write down that letter, as many times as it appears in the word, above its corresponding dash.

But if the *Guesser* calls out a letter which does not appear in the word, the *Jailer* proceeds to put him in jail!

With the first wrong guess, the *Jailer* draws the *Guesser's* head inside the box. With the second wrong guess, he draws the body. With the third, a leg; with the fourth, the second leg. With the fifth wrong guess, he draws an arm, and with the sixth, the other arm. After seven wrong guesses, the *Guesser* is locked in the jail by the *Jailer*, who puts in the bars of the jail by drawing three straight lines down in front of the jail.

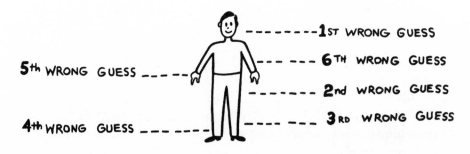

If the *Guesser* guesses the correct word before he is locked in jail by the *Jailer*, he wins the game and becomes the *Jailer* for the next game. If he does not guess the word and gets locked in jail, the *Jailer* remains the *Jailer* for the next game, until the *Guesser* succeeds in guessing the correct word.

# PENCIL POLO

This is a fascinating pencil game for two players. Five diagrams have been provided for you, and when you have used these up, it is easy to draw some more yourself.

The first player starts at the bottom box. He may move one, two, or three boxes up the ladder towards the GOAL. He makes his move by writing an X in one, two, or three consecutive boxes on the ladder, beginning with the bottom box.

The players take turns. The second player, on his turn, places an O in one, two, or three consecutive boxes on the ladder.

The object of the game is to land in the box marked GOAL.

For example, suppose the first player has put two X's in the two bottom boxes. His opponent, on his turn, must place an O in the third box from the bottom. Of course, he may also put an O in the fourth box from the bottom, if he desires, and also in the fifth box from the bottom. In other words, he may move upward one square, two squares, or three squares on each of his turns.

Each player must try to determine what his best move will be so that eventually he can land in the GOAL SQUARE at the top.

# PUNS

Puns have been decried by some purer-than-thous as the lowest form of humor, but we agree with Edgar Allan Poe who wrote: "Of puns it has been said that those who most dislike them are those who are least able to utter them."

In any case, puns have been the darling of the literati for as far back as goeth the memory of man. Even Queen Elizabeth allegedly succumbed to the temptation when she told Lord of Burleigh:

> *"Ye be burley, my Lord of Burleign, but ye shall make*
> *less stir in our realm than my Lord of Leicester."*

Other well-known personalities who have contributed to the lore of pundom, are:

GROUCHO MARX: When shooting elephants in Africa, I found the tusks very difficult to remove; but in Alabama, the Tuscaloosa.

F. P. ADAMS: Take care of your peonies and the dahlias will take care of themselves.

S. J. PERELMAN: Doctor, I've got Bright's disease and he's got mine.

SYDNEY SMITH: (upon observing two housewives yelling at each other across a courtyard) These women will never agree, for they are arguing from different premises.

PETER DE VRIES: The things my wife buys at auction are keeping me baroque.

F. P. ADAMS: Those Spanish senoritas are a snare Andalusian.

F. P. ADAMS: A group of Basques, fleeing before the enemy, were penned into a narrow mountain pass and wiped out. Which is what comes of putting all your Basques into one exit.

JIMMY DURANTE: (after blundering into the dressing room of the operatic contralto Helen Traubel) Nobody knows the Traubel I've seen.

BENNETT CERF: A relative and namesake of Syngman Rhee, former president of South Korea, was visiting our country to learn the magazine business, and got a job on what was at that time America's most popular picture periodical. On his first assignment, however, he lost himself in the mazes of New York City, until at last a Missing Persons Bureau investigator found him in a bar and cried: "Ah, sweet Mr. Rhee of *Life*, at last I've found you!"

MAX BEERBOHM: (declining a hike to the summit of a Swiss Alp) Put me down as an anticlimb Max.

WALTER WINCHELL: (explaining why he always praised the first show of a new theatrical season) Who am I to stone the first cast?

GEORGE KAUFMAN: (concerning a young Vassar coed who had eloped) She put the heart before the course!

*And here are some delights from lesser-known punsters:*

JIM HAWKINS: There's a vas deferens between children and no children.

JACK THOMAS: (Title for guidebook) Paris by Night and Bidet.

PHILIP GUEDALLA: (Replying to a slanderous attack on the Church) Any stigma will do to beat a dogma.

SAM HOFFENSTEIN: A teen-age girl attributed the loss of a current boyfriend to "only a passing fanny."

Four dons were strolling along an Oxford street one evening, discussing collective nouns: a covey of quail, an exaltation of larks, etc. As they conversed, they passed four ladies of the evening. One of the dons asked, "How would you describe a group like that?"

One suggested: "A jam of tarts?"

A second offered: "A flourish of strumpets?"

A third chimed in with: "An essay of Trollope's?"

The first then countered with: "A frost of hoars?"

Then the dean, the eldest and most scholarly of the four, apparently closed the discussion with: "I wish that you gentlemen would consider 'An anthology of pros.'"

Whereupon a voice behind them broke in with: "Surely you have overlooked the obvious: 'A pride of loins.'"

At a dinner party, the hostess-mother was listening with clearly evident delight to the compliments of a Mr. Campbell, which, by the way, the English pronounce by suppressing the "p" and "b". Her daughter on the other hand was enthusiastically flirting with a gentleman named Nathaniel. Disturbed by her daughter's marked sprightliness, the mother frowned in severe reproach. Whereupon the daughter scribbled a note on a piece of paper and handed it to her mother:

*Dear Ma, don't attempt my young feelings to trammel,*
*Nor strain at a Nat while you swallow a Campbell.*

Three brothers went to Texas to begin raising cattle, but they couldn't think of an appropriate name for their ranch. They wrote to their father back in Boston, and he wrote back: "I'd call it Focus, for that's where the sun's rays meet."

At a sidewalk cafe in Paris, a man ordered a cocktail for his female companion and a glass of water for himself. Ordering a second round, he told the waiter: "The lady will have another cocktail, and I'll have more of the Seine."

"One man's Mede is another man's Persian."

"Are you Shah?"

"Sultanly."

The owner of an Indianapolis antique shop dubbed his store: "Den of Antiquity." And the inmates of the Iowa State Penitentiary refer to their domicile as "The Walled-Off Astoria."

Well, as Clifton Fadiman states, of such puns we may say that their special virtue is to be tried and found wanton. Mr. Fadiman, however, has been guilty of penning the following:

In a Skid Row saloon, the patrons often enter optimistically and leave mistyoptically.

A combined charity drive represents an effort where everyone puts all their begs into one ask-it.

A gentleman crossing the English River Mersey and noting its muddy condition remarked, "Evidently the quality of Mersey is not strained."

♚

Bennett Cerf tells of the man who poured pickle juice down a hill just to see if dill waters run steep.

And there was the wit who complained that he was always hearing his own stories told back to him: "A plain case of the tale dogging the wag."

Speaking of dogs, there was the gentleman who came into his house dripping wet and disheveled. His sympathetic wife exclaimed, "Oh dear, it's raining cats and dogs outside!"
"You're telling me," the man replied, "I just stepped in a poodle."

♚

The tale of the king and his fool illustrates some of the dangers of pundom. The monarch, tired of his clown, told the inveterate punster: "Unless you make a pun at once— and a good one—you shall be hanged."
"Very well," said the fool. "Name a subject."
"Myself," said the monarch. "The king."
"The king," punned the clown, "is not a subject."
"Well then," said the king, struggling to conceal his irritation, "why do you make fun of my figure?"
"Sire", said the punster, "everyone likes to make fun at someone else's expanse."
"As to royalty," pursued the king, "why do you say that Queen Elizabeth was greater than Joan of Arc?"
"Joan of Arc was a wonder," replied the clown. "But Queen Elizabeth was a Tudor."
"Enough!" cried the king, "Hang him!"
But as the noose was drawn around the punster's neck, the king said, "I'll grant you your life on one condition: that you promise never to make another pun."
"I promise, your Majesty," said the jester. "No noose is good news."
So they hanged him.

# HOW TO SOLVE THREEZIES

You are given a sequence of three letters. You are to list all the words you can think of which contain these letters *in exact sequence*.

The sequence may seem quite unlikely. For example, a sequence of letters RRH at first blush might seem completely hopeless, yet with a little thought you may come up with the word *Catarrh* and possibly with the word *Myrrh*. If the given three letters were MBS, you might find that out of this strange sequence you can form the word *Numbskull*.

The rules of the game are very simple. You may use only one form of the word. For example, if the threezies were NDL, a proper answer would be *Fondly*. But then you couldn't count the word *Fondle*, since both these words have the same root. However, where words have completely different meaning, then they may both be used even though the roots are similar. So, if the threezies were RTH, you could score with the word *Forth* and also with the word *Forthright*.

Proper names are off limits. Hyphenated words are allowed.

♔

# L U M

There are at least 32 words which contain the letter sequence L U M. How many can you find? List them below.

If you get 15, that's fine; 22 is excellent; and 25 is superb.

*Answers on page 483*

| 1. _____ | 12. _____ | 22. _____ |
| 2. _____ | 13. _____ | 23. _____ |
| 3. _____ | 14. _____ | 24. _____ |
| 4. _____ | 15. _____ | 25. _____ |
| 5. _____ | 16. _____ | 26. _____ |
| 6. _____ | 17. _____ | 27. _____ |
| 7. _____ | 18. _____ | 28. _____ |
| 8. _____ | 19. _____ | 29 _____ |
| 9. _____ | 20. _____ | 30. _____ |
| 10. _____ | 21. _____ | 31. _____ |
| 11. _____ | | 32. _____ |

# L T I

There are at least 10 words which contain the letter sequence L T I. How many can you find? List them below.

A score of 6 is good; 8 is excellent.

*Answers on page 483*

1. _____    4. _____    8. _____
2. _____    5. _____    9. _____
3. _____    6. _____    10. _____
                 7. _____

# E C H

There are at least 14 words which contain the letter sequence E C H. How many can you find? List them below.

If you can fill in the spaces below with 9 of them, that's swell; 10 is terrific; and 12 is super.

*Answers on page 483*

1. _____    6. _____    10. _____
2. _____    7. _____    11. _____
3. _____    8. _____    12. _____
4. _____    9. _____    13. _____
5. _____                     14. _____

# H O U

There are at least 12 words which contain the letter sequence H O U. How many can you find? List them below.

A score of 5 is fair; 8 is excellent; and 10 is really top-notch.

*Answers on page 483*

1. _____    5. _____    9. _____
2. _____    6. _____    10. _____
3. _____    7. _____    11. _____
4. _____    8. _____    12. _____

# C L E

There are at least 14 words which contain the letter sequence C L E. How many can you find? List them below.

A score of 8 is fine; 10 is great; and 12 is sensational.

*Answers on page 483*

1. _____
2. _____
3. _____
4. _____
5. _____

6. _____
7. _____
8. _____
9. _____

10. _____
11. _____
12. _____
13. _____
14. _____

# O R S

There are at least 20 words which contain the letter sequence O R S. How many can you find? List them below.

If you get 8, that's pretty good; 12 is excellent; and 18 rates you with the pros.

*Answers on page 483*

1. _____
2. _____
3. _____
4. _____
5. _____
6. _____
7. _____

8. _____
9. _____
10. _____
11. _____
12. _____
13. _____

14. _____
15. _____
16. _____
17. _____
18. _____
19. _____
20. _____

# O C H

There are at least 12 words which contain the letter sequence O C H. How many can you find? List them below.

A score of 6 is good; 8 is very good; and 10 is excellent.

*Answers on page 483*

1. _____
2. _____
3. _____
4. _____

5. _____
6. _____
7. _____
8. _____

9. _____
10. _____
11. _____
12. _____

(DIRECTIONS FOR SOLVING THREEZIES ARE ON PAGE 218)

# N D A

There are at least 23 words which contain the letter sequence N D A. How many can you find? List them below.

If you can fill in the spaces below with 15 of them, that's good; 18 is dandy; and 20 or more is fantastic.

*Answers on page 483*

1. _____
2. _____
3. _____
4. _____
5. _____
6. _____
7. _____
8. _____

9. _____
10. _____
11. _____
12. _____
13. _____
14. _____
15. _____

16. _____
17. _____
18. _____
19. _____
20. _____
21. _____
22. _____
23. _____

# A R D

There are at least 39 words which contain the letter sequence A R D. How many can you find? List them below.

If you can fill in the spaces below with 20 of them, that's fine; 25 is terrific; and 30 is splendid.

*Answers on page 483*

1. _____
2. _____
3. _____
4. _____
5. _____
6. _____
7. _____
8. _____
9. _____
10. _____
11. _____
12. _____
13. _____

14. _____
15. _____
16. _____
17. _____
18. _____
19. _____
20. _____
21. _____
22. _____
23. _____
24. _____
25. _____
26. _____

27. _____
28. _____
29. _____
30. _____
31. _____
32. _____
33. _____
34. _____
35. _____
36. _____
37 _____
38. _____
39. _____

(DIRECTIONS FOR SOLVING THREEZIES ARE ON PAGE 218)

# L I A

There are at least 14 words which contain the letter sequence L I A. How many can you find? List them below.

If you get 7, that's fair; 9 is splendid; and 12 is absolutely magnificent.

*Answers on page 484*

| | | |
|---|---|---|
| 1. _____ | 6. _____ | 10. _____ |
| 2. _____ | 7. _____ | 11. _____ |
| 3. _____ | 8. _____ | 12. _____ |
| 4. _____ | 9. _____ | 13. _____ |
| 5. _____ | | 14. _____ |

# T O O

There are at least 14 words which contain the letter sequence T O O. How many can you find? List them below.

A score of 8 is good; 11 is great; and 12 is fantastic.

*Answers on page 484*

| | | |
|---|---|---|
| 1. _____ | 6. _____ | 10. _____ |
| 2. _____ | 7. _____ | 11. _____ |
| 3 _____ | 8. _____ | 12. _____ |
| 4. _____ | 9. _____ | 13. _____ |
| 5. _____ | | 14. _____ |

# M P U

There are at least 10 words which contain the letter sequence M P U. How many can you find? List them below.

A score of 5 is very good; and 7 is excellent; and 9 is fabulous.

*Answers on page 484*

| | | |
|---|---|---|
| 1. _____ | 4. _____ | 8. _____ |
| 2. _____ | 5. _____ | 9. _____ |
| 3. _____ | 6. _____ | 10. _____ |
| | 7. _____ | |

(DIRECTIONS FOR SOLVING THREEZIES ARE ON PAGE 218)

# N T R

There are at least 32 words which contain the letter sequence N T R. How many can you find? List them below.

A score of 18 is fine; 22 is grand; and 26 or more is superb.

*Answers on page 484*

1. _____
2. _____
3. _____
4. _____
5. _____
6. _____
7. _____
8. _____
9. _____
10. _____
11. _____

12. _____
13. _____
14. _____
15. _____
16. _____
17. _____
18. _____
19. _____
20. _____
21. _____

22. _____
23. _____
24. _____
25. _____
26. _____
27. _____
28. _____
29. _____
30. _____
31. _____
32. _____

# R T I

There are at least 37 words which contain the letter sequence R T I. How many can you find? List them below.

A score of 20 is good; 25 is very good; 28 is super; and 34 or more is stupendous.

*Answers on page 484*

1. _____
2. _____
3. _____
4. _____
5. _____
6. _____
7. _____
8. _____
9. _____
10. _____
11. _____
12. _____

13. _____
14. _____
15. _____
16. _____
17. _____
18. _____
19. _____
20. _____
21. _____
22. _____
23. _____
24. _____
25. _____

26. _____
27. _____
28. _____
29. _____
30. _____
31. _____
32. _____
33. _____
34. _____
35. _____
36. _____
37. _____

(DIRECTIONS FOR SOLVING THREEZIES ARE ON PAGE 218)

# R S I

There are at least 31 words which contain the letter sequence R S I. How many can you find? List them below.

A score of 18 is fairly good; 23 is exceptional; and 26 or more is worthy of a medal!

*Answers on page 484*

1. _____
2. _____
3. _____
4. _____
5. _____
6. _____
7. _____
8. _____
9. _____
10. _____

11. _____
12. _____
13. _____
14. _____
15. _____
16. _____
17. _____
18. _____
19. _____
20. _____
21. _____

22. _____
23. _____
24. _____
25. _____
26. _____
27. _____
28. _____
29. _____
30. _____
31. _____

# M P L

There are at least 34 words which contain the letter sequence M P L. How many can you find? List them below.

A score of 20 is very good; 24 is above average; and 28 or over is an outstanding score.

*Answers on page 484*

1. _____
2. _____
3. _____
4. _____
5. _____
6. _____
7. _____
8. _____
9. _____
10. _____
11. _____

12. _____
13. _____
14. _____
15. _____
16. _____
17. _____
18. _____
19. _____
20. _____
21. _____
22. _____
23. _____

24. _____
25. _____
26. _____
27. _____
28. _____
29. _____
30. _____
31. _____
32. _____
33. _____
34. _____

(DIRECTIONS FOR SOLVING THREEZIES ARE ON PAGE 218)

# E M O

There are at least 28 words which contain the letter sequence E M O. How many can you find? List them below.

A score of 14 is good; 20 is wonderful; and 23 is magnificent.

*Answers on page 484*

1. _____
2. _____
3. _____
4. _____
5. _____
6. _____
7. _____
8. _____
9. _____

10. _____
11. _____
12. _____
13. _____
14. _____
15. _____
16. _____
17. _____
18. _____
19. _____

20. _____
21. _____
22. _____
23. _____
24. _____
25. _____
26. _____
27. _____
28. _____

# E P T

There are at least 28 words which contain the letter sequence E P T. How many can you find? List them below.

A score of 16 is pretty good; 19 is superior; and 22 or more is outstanding.

*Answers on page 485*

1. _____
2. _____
3. _____
4. _____
5. _____
6. _____
7. _____
8. _____
9. _____

10. _____
11. _____
12. _____
13. _____
14. _____
15. _____
16. _____
17. _____
18. _____
19. _____

20. _____
21. _____
22. _____
23 _____
24. _____
25. _____
26. _____
27. _____
28. _____

(DIRECTIONS FOR SOLVING THREEZIES ARE ON PAGE 218)

# LVE

There are at least 15 words which contain the letter sequence L V E. How many can you find? List them below.

A score of 8 is fine; 10 is grand; and 12 is super-duper.

*Answers on page 485*

| | | |
|---|---|---|
| 1. _____ | 6. _____ | 11. _____ |
| 2. _____ | 7. _____ | 12. _____ |
| 3. _____ | 8. _____ | 13. _____ |
| 4. _____ | 9. _____ | 14. _____ |
| 5. _____ | 10. _____ | 15. _____ |

# OMI

There are at least 25 words which contain the letter sequence O M I. How many can you find? List them below.

A score of 15 is good; 18 is very good; and 22 is stupendous.

*Answers on page 485*

| | | |
|---|---|---|
| 1. _____ | 9. _____ | 18. _____ |
| 2. _____ | 10. _____ | 19. _____ |
| 3. _____ | 11. _____ | 20. _____ |
| 4. _____ | 12. _____ | 21. _____ |
| 5. _____ | 13. _____ | 22. _____ |
| 6. _____ | 14. _____ | 23. _____ |
| 7. _____ | 15. _____ | 24. _____ |
| 8. _____ | 16. _____ | 25. _____ |
| | 17. _____ | |

# API

There are at least 19 words which contain the letter sequence A P I. How many can you find? List them below.

A score of 10 is average; 13 is above average; and 16 is tops.

*Answers on page 485*

| | | |
|---|---|---|
| 1. _____ | 7. _____ | 14. _____ |
| 2. _____ | 8. _____ | 15. _____ |
| 3. _____ | 9. _____ | 16. _____ |
| 4. _____ | 10. _____ | 17. _____ |
| 5. _____ | 11. _____ | 18. _____ |
| 6. _____ | 12. _____ | 19. _____ |
| | 13. _____ | |

(DIRECTIONS FOR SOLVING THREEZIES ARE ON PAGE 218)

# EVE

There are at least 25 words which contain the letter sequence E V E. How many can you find? List them below.

A score of 15 is fine; 18 is grand; and 22 is superb.

*Answers on page 485*

1. _____
2. _____
3. _____
4. _____
5. _____
6. _____
7. _____
8. _____

9. _____
10. _____
11. _____
12. _____
13. _____
14. _____
15. _____
16. _____
17. _____

18. _____
19. _____
20. _____
21. _____
22. _____
23. _____
24. _____
25. _____

# LEM

There are at least 13 words which contain the letter sequence L E M. How many can you find? List them below.

A score of 7 is good; 9 is first-rate; and 11 is top-notch.

*Answers on page 485*

1. _____
2. _____
3. _____
4. _____

5. _____
6. _____
7. _____
8. _____
9. _____

10. _____
11. _____
12. _____
13. _____

# AWB

There are at least 10 words which contain the letter sequence A W B. How many can you find? List them below.

A score of 6 is good; 8 is excellent.

*Answers on page 485*

1. _____
2. _____
3. _____

4. _____
5. _____
6. _____
7. _____

8. _____
9. _____
10. _____

(DIRECTIONS FOR SOLVING THREEZIES ARE ON PAGE 218)

# O L E

There are at least 25 words which contain the letter sequence O L E. How many can you find? List them below.

   If you can come up with 14, that's pretty good; 17 is excellent; and 20 is really marvelous.

*Answers on page 485*

| | | |
|---|---|---|
| 1. _____ | 9. _____ | 18. _____ |
| 2. _____ | 10. _____ | 19. _____ |
| 3. _____ | 11. _____ | 20. _____ |
| 4. _____ | 12. _____ | 21. _____ |
| 5. _____ | 13. _____ | 22. _____ |
| 6. _____ | 14. _____ | 23. _____ |
| 7. _____ | 15. _____ | 24. _____ |
| 8. _____ | 16. _____ | 25. _____ |
| | 17. _____ | |

# M P O

There are at least 19 words which contain the letter sequence M P O. How many can you find? List them below.

   A score of 9 is good; 11 is first-rate; and 13 or more is top-notch.

*Answers on page 485*

| | | |
|---|---|---|
| 1. _____ | 7. _____ | 14. _____ |
| 2. _____ | 8. _____ | 15. _____ |
| 3. _____ | 9. _____ | 16. _____ |
| 4. _____ | 10. _____ | 17. _____ |
| 5. _____ | 11. _____ | 18. _____ |
| 6. _____ | 12. _____ | 19. _____ |
| | 13. _____ | |

(DIRECTIONS FOR SOLVING THREEZIES ARE ON PAGE 218)

# ANAGRAMS & PALINDROMES

An anagram is, plain and simple, a rearrangement of the letters of a word or words to make another word or words. The word SMILE, for example, yields the anagram *slime*, as well as *miles* and *limes*.

One of the earliest and best-known anagrams was created from the question that Pilate asked Jesus:

*Quid est veritas?* [What is truth?]

THE ANSWER:
*Est vir qui adest.* [It is the man who is here.]

Consider the following quatrain in which the letters P T S and O have been used to form five different words:

> *Oh, landlord, fill our thirsting* POTS,
> *Until the* TOPS *flow over;*
> *Tonight, we* STOP *upon this* SPOT,
> *Tomorrow,* POST *for Dover.*

Many have been frustrated by the tricky task of making one word out of *new door*. If the solution eludes you, see the bottom of the next page.

Anagrams have inspired linguistic jugglers to various creative efforts, for better or verse. To wit:

A VILE *young lady* on EVIL *bent,*
*Lowered her* VEIL *with sly intent.*
"LEVI," *she said,* "*It's time to play.*
*What shall we do to* LIVE *today?*"
"*My dear,*" *said he,* "*do as you please.*
"*I'm going to eat some* IVEL *cheese!*"

(Ivel cheese is a fictitious *fromage* made in the valley of the non-existent Ivel river.)

**229**

Here are some other unusually apt anagrams:

| | |
|---|---|
| THE EYES | *They see.* |
| A SHOPLIFTER | *Has to pilfer.* |
| THE COUNTRYSIDE | *No city dust here!* |
| THE MONA LISA | *No hat, a smile.* |
| THE NUDIST COLONY | *No untidy clothes!* |
| THE UNITED STATES OF AMERICA | *Attaineth its cause:* *freedom!* |

An anagram that reads the same backwards and forwards—the word *toot*, for instance—is called a palindrome.

The story goes that the first palindrome ever fashioned was uttered by the first man. Adam allegedly introduced himself to Eve thus:

"MADAM, I'M ADAM."

Here are a few small ones:

STEP ON NO PETS.

LIVE NOT ON EVIL.

DRAW, O COWARD!

'TIS IVAN ON A VISIT.

WAS IT A RAT I SAW?

**230**

One word.

YREKA BAKERY
*(an actual bakery at
322 W. Miner St., Yreka, California)*

A palindrome of great historical interest is the classic supposedly uttered by Napoleon:

"ABLE WAS I ERE I SAW ELBA."

A palindrome that might be instrumental in celebrating a Black Mass is this exhortation to Satan:

LIVE O DEVIL! REVEL EVER! LIVE! DO EVIL!

And here's one that offers a revolutionary method for keeping trim:

DOC, NOTE I DISSENT: A FAST NEVER PREVENTS
A FATNESS. I DIET ON COD.

But undoubtedly the cleverest palindrome ever penned in English was the work of some anonymous genius who apotheosized the Panama Canal in seven words which, however you look at them, yield the same pithy statement:

A MAN, A PLAN, A CANAL—PANAMA!

# RAILROAD FLATS

Many old tenements were divided into "railroad flats," apartments in which all rooms led from one central hallway. In this maze of "rooms," enter through the windows at the top and find the way to the door at the bottom. A solution in 12 minutes is fair; 8 minutes, good; and 6 minutes or less is an express run.

*Answers on page 486*

# INCA STINKER

Like an archeologist, you start at the top and dig your way down to paydirt.
Six minutes is an average time for this one, and 3 minutes or less is superb.

*Answers on page 486*

# SECRET GARDEN

Here's a bouquet of unusual flowers. Hidden within are many paths, but only one leads from top to bottom. A solution in 15 minutes is fair; 10 minutes is very good; and 8 minutes or less is magnificent.

*Answers on page 486*

# THE EYES HAVE IT!

Here's a maze that looks back at you. There's one sure thing—you won't sail through this one. Twenty minutes is a reasonable time; 15 minutes is just peachy; and 12 minutes or less is an eye-catching accomplishment.

*Answers on page 486*

# MAP PROBLEM

Three highways enter this maze at the top, but only one exits at the bottom. There are overpasses and underpasses, and some streets are one-way. A trip completed in 12 minutes is slow but sure; 10 minutes, a bit better; and 8 minutes or less—slow down, you're speeding!

*Answers on page 487*

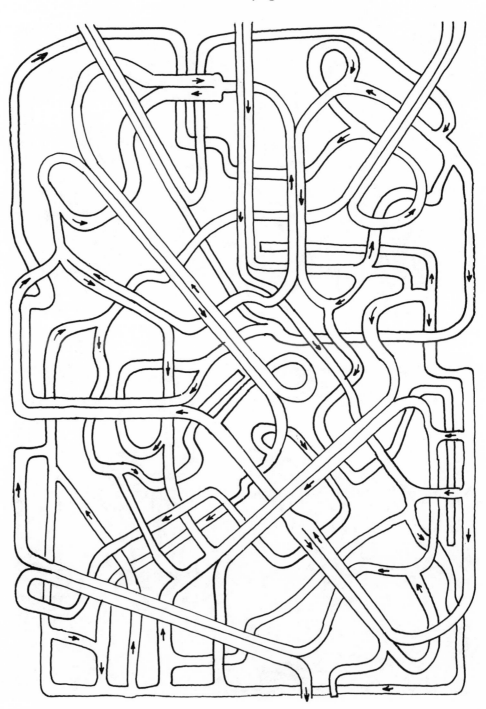

# THIRD DIMENSION

The third dimension is depth, and you'll find yourself in deep trouble before you can steer a course through this jumble of objects. If you're home free in 12 minutes, that's mediocre; 10 minutes is good; and 8 minutes or less is sensational.

*Answers on page 487*

# SIX TRICKS

Start at the top, move from one to six in order, and exit at the bottom. This over-and-under puzzle requires that *no path be followed more than once*. Twenty-two minutes is maximum for this one; 18 minutes is quite good; and a solution in 15 minutes or less adds up to quite a trick.

*Answers on page 487*

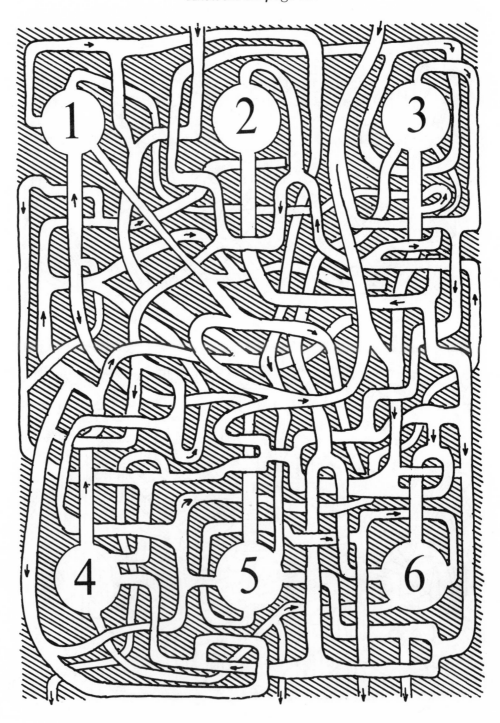

# PERSIAN SCRIPT

These thick and thin curves may remind you of Arabic writing, but they'll certainly spell trouble before you find your way through to the bottom. A solution in 12 minutes is so-so; 10 minutes is much better; and 8 minutes or less is remarkable.

*Answers on page 487*

# COLLYWOBBLES

Some say you get the collywobbles, some say the collywobbles get you. Anyway, get through this one in 12 minutes for a passing grade; 10 minutes for an excellent score; and 6 minutes or less for a mark of distinction.

*Answers on page 488*

# TEN TIMES SQUARE

Here's a city map with ten plazas. Traffic must follow the arrows in the plazas, as well as in the side streets. If your journey home takes 15 minutes, you're late for dinner; 10 minutes, you're right on time; and 7 minutes or less, you've got time to spare.

*Answers on page 488*

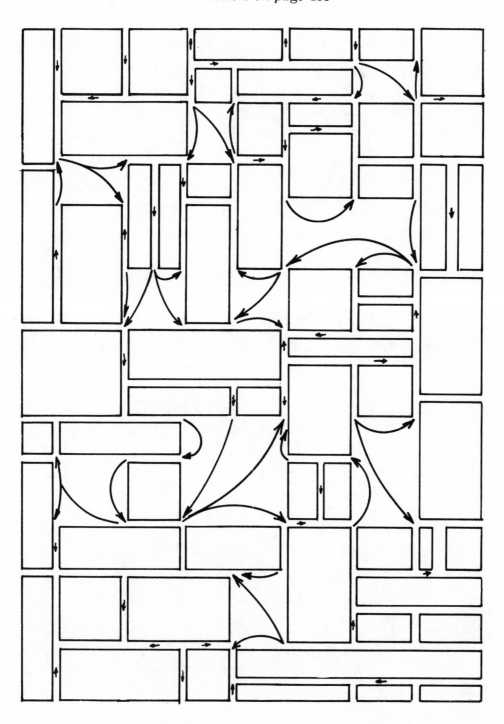

# TIPTOE

There are no tulips to tiptoe through in this garden, but there are leaves and flowers galore. A 15-minute trip is only a garden-variety feat; 11 minutes smells sweeter; and 9 minutes or less shows a fertile mind.

*Answers on page 488*

# MEDAL OF HONOR

Here's a fancy medal on a ribbon, but what's that mess below it? You'll have to muddle through to find out. Sixteen minutes is a respectable time for this one; 12 minutes is a lot better; and if you can zig-zag through in 10 minutes or less, you deserve a medal.

*Answers on page 488*

# CITY BLOCKS

This perplexing puzzler should be enough to send even the most clear-eyed city dweller back to the country. If escape from this cityscape takes you more than 15 minutes, you're in the woods; 12 minutes, you're on the right road; and 10 minutes or less—you must be a city slicker.

*Answers on page 489*

# SCROLLWORK

This ornamental scrollwork would form an easy labyrinth if it weren't for those pesky one-way arrows. A journey of 15 minutes is an acceptable performance; 12 minutes, a jolly-good show; and 10 minutes or less, a cause for applause.

*Answers on page 489*

# ALPHABLITZ

Don't look for words here, just for a way out the bottom. If you find it in 10 minutes, that's only fair; 8 minutes is much better; and for 6 minutes, words are inadequate to describe your wit.

*Answers on page 489*

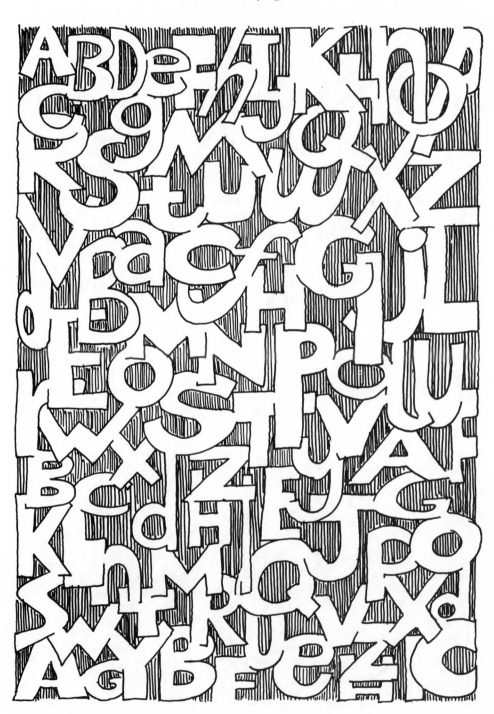

# BOUQUET

Like a drop of rain, enter through the flower and get down through the roots. This is a three-dimensional maze, so you may go over or under. If you can find the route in 15 minutes, you've got nothing to be ashamed of; 12 minutes is good; 10 minutes or less and you come up roses.

*Answers on page 489*

# BINGO

Start at the top, find a path to "B," then to "I," and so on, to spell BINGO. Important: *you can't take the same path twice.* After you've made BINGO, exit at the bottom. A solution in 20 minutes or less is something to brag about.

*Answers on page 490*

# PARALLEL PATHS

Parallel lines never meet, so there's only one clear path from top to bottom. If you find it in 12 minutes, you're doing swell; 10 minutes, you're ahead of the game; and success in 7 minutes or less is an unparalleled accomplishment.

*Answers on page 490*

# RHYTHMS

This maze may be easier than it looks. Give it a try, you'll catch the rhythm. A 10-minute journey is just average; 8 minutes, an excellent time; and success in 6 minutes or less is noteworthy.

*Answers on page 490*

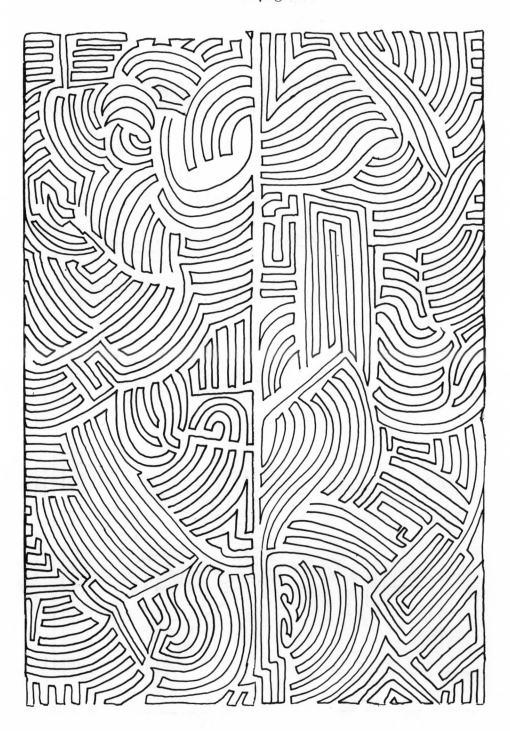

# PANIC BUTTONS

If you can't find your way from top to bottom, there are 35 panic buttons to push. But you should be able to wend your merry way through this maze in 15 minutes. If you succeed in 10 minutes, you're cool and collected; and in 7 or less, you're an iceman.

*Answers on page 490*

# ZIGZAG

Up, down, and around go the paths of this maze. Be careful not to zig when you should zag, and you'll find the route to the bottom soon enough. A 12-minute journey is fair; 10 minutes is an excellent time; and a solution in 8 minutes or less is—well, amazing!

*Answers on page 491*

# ORBITS

A circle has no beginning and no end. Your troubles start at the top and end at the bottom of this maze. In between, you're in orbit. Spin through in 20 minutes for a passing grade; 15 minutes for hearty congratulations; and 10 minutes or less for resounding cheers.

*Answers on page 491*

# NIGHTMARE

Ever see one of these in your dreams? You will if you don't solve it in less than 12 minutes. Ten minutes and you earn sweet dreams; 7 minutes or less, and the maze fairy will give you a quarter.

*Answers on page 491*

# CLASSIC CIRCLES

Some of the earliest mazes were in the form of a circle. Try these circuits on for size. From top to bottom in 9 minutes is not a dizzying feat; 7 minutes is more impressive; and if you can swirl through in 5 minutes or less, you are, like the circle, just perfect.

*Answers on page 491*

# REVENGE

If you look at this pattern for long enough, you'll begin to see the swastikas repeated. Start at the top and make your way down to the southern front. Victory in 22 minutes isn't bad; 17 minutes is superior; and 14 minutes or less is exceptional.

*Answers on page 492*

# ANCIENT FRAGMENT

Here's an artifact that looks like it might contain the outline of some strange idol. If you search through this one for more than 20 minutes, you're wandering in the desert; 15 minutes is good; and if you find the promised land in 12 minutes or less, that's ideal!

*Answers on page 492*

# BERTILLON SYSTEM

A Frenchman named Bertillon devised a system for criminal identification that was the forerunner of our fingerprint system. Follow the giant's fingerprints from top to bottom for a positive identification. If you can do it in 12 minutes or less, you're a sleuth first-class.

*Answers on page 492*

# ON THE MARCH

This crowd is up to no good. To slip through you'll have to step on a few toes. If you can shoulder your way to the bottom in 10 minutes, that's not bad; 8 minutes, that's good; and if you can push through in 5 minutes or less, you're liable to start a riot.

*Answers on page 492*

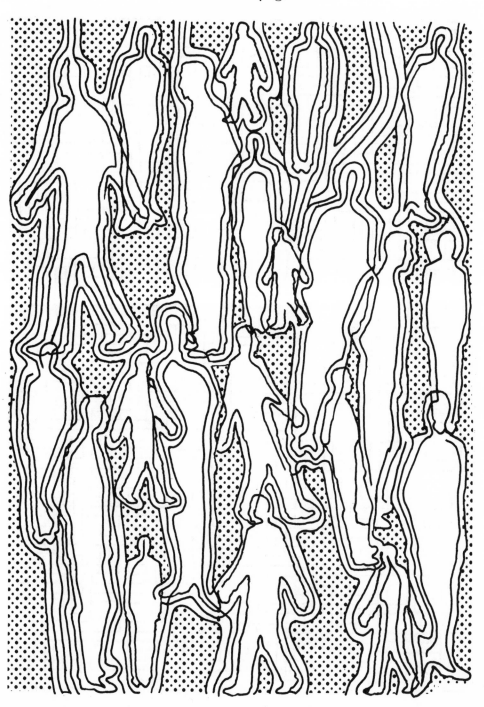

# ON THE SQUARE

A square is two-dimensional, and so is this maze: you can't go under another passageway. A solution in 10 minutes is fair and square; in 7 minutes, excellent; in 5 minutes or less, simply magnificent!

*Answers on page 493*

# REPEAT PATTERN

Template patterns are repeated over and over to form this maze. Enter anywhere you like at the top, but naturally there's only one way to the bottom. Find it in 12 minutes and you're doing well; 8 minutes, even better; and 5 minutes or less, you're an old hand at this game.

*Answers on page 493*

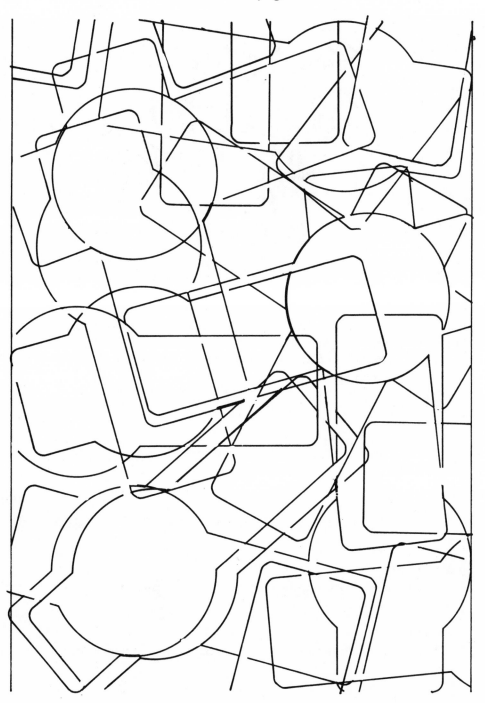

# CRACKS FROM THE CRITICS

**DOROTHY PARKER**
*The House Beautiful* is the play lousy.

**ROBERT GARLAND**
This show has to be seen to be depreciated.

**J. NORMAN LYND**
The quartet sang a derangement of an old favorite.

**ROBERT BENCHLEY**
*Perfectly Scandalous* was one of those plays in which all of the actors unfortunately enunciated very clearly.

**DOROTHY PARKER**
Katherine Hepburn (in *The Lake*) runs the gamut of emotions from A to B.

**MONTY WOOLLEY**
For the first time in my life I envied my feet. They were asleep.

**JOHN ANDERSON**
The audience was so quiet, you could hear a pun drop.

**ANONYMOUS**
If I've said anything to insult you, believe me, I've tried my best.

**262**

**ANONYMOUS**
As a playwright, he's an archaeologist—his career lies in ruins.

**ANONYMOUS**

I just saw Isherwood's play *I Am a Camera*.
No Leica.

**ANONYMOUS**

It's a TV drama with comic relief, but the only relief came during an unexpected and, unfortunately, shortlived blackout.

**EUGENE FIELD**

The actor who took the role of *King Lear* played the king as though he expected someone to play the ace.

**BROOKS ATKINSON**

When Mr. Wilbur calls his play *Halfway to Hell*, he underestimates the distance.

**PERCY HAMMOND**

I have knocked everything but the chorus girls' legs, and here God anticipated me.

**FRANK NUGENT**

A run of DeMille picture—March comes in like a lion and goes out like a ham.

**ANONYMOUS**

Last night the High School band played Beethoven. Beethoven lost.

**ALEXANDER WOOLLCOTT**

The scenery was beautiful—but the actors got in front of it.

**ANONYMOUS**

The trapeze artist was light on his feat.

# BLANKIES IN VERSE

*Blankies in Verse* is a word game based on anagrams, such as TEA, ATE, EAT. Each Blankie is a short poem in itself. In each poem, a number of words have been omitted. Each omitted word is indicated by a number of dashes, each dash representing a single letter. For example, a series of three dashes would indicate a three-letter word; a series of four dashes, a four-letter word, etc. Look for a definite clue within the poem to help you get started.

*Answers on page 493*

1. The hockey player says, as he _ _ _ _ _ a long rest,

   "I will _ _ _ _ _ my life that I am the best.

   But I'll _ _ _ _ _ no more, nor swing my stick

   Till you feed me a _ _ _ _ _ that's four inches thick!"

   ♚

2. The robin comes first when spring is here;

   For the _ _ _ _ _ worm he cocks his ear.

   He'll catch him 'neath a _ _ _ _ _ of earth,

   Then _ _ _ _ _ the news, for what it is worth.

   ♚

3. The convict, wearing _ _ _ _ _ and ball,

   Dug a hole so deep and so very tall,

   Clear down to _ _ _ _ _; and then he said,

   "Oh, my _ _ _ _ _' back, it sure feels dead!"

   ♚

4. _ _ _ _ _ are wise and stalk their prey

   Only at night, and never by day.

   The old cow _ _ _ _ _ her calf to sleep;

   Life is _ _ _ _ _ in the forest deep.

5. The beauty Queen had won the crown;

   Upon the _ _ _ _ _ _ she settled down.

   'Twas _ _ _ _ _ _ choice to scream with fear *(2 wds.)*

   But an angry _ _ _ _ _ _ had jabbed her rear.

♔

6. A teller of _ _ _ _ _ _ who lived alone

   Scratched his words on a _ _ _ _ _ _ made of stone.

   A _ _ _ _ _ _ crust he would _ _ _ _ _ _ each day,

   But at _ _ _ _ _ _ he survived in this very strange way.

♔

7. The Mexican boy had a _ _ _ _ _ _ full of glory;

   He fought in a battle so bloody and gory.

   He was _ _ _ _ _ _ with a knife, all set to attack

   Till his _ _ _ _ _ _ awakened him out of the sack!

♔

8. At festive _ _ _ _ _ _ there presides a host;

   While the _ _ _ _ _ _ carves and serves the roast.

   And out in the _ _ _ _ _ _ is next week's dinner,

   Who sadly _ _ _ _ _ _ and wants to be thinner!

♔

9. The typer and _ _ _ _ _ _ was good at his work

   Till a _ _ _ _ _ _ with bullets was aimed at this clerk.

   The killer, a _ _ _ _ _ _ who just went berserk

   Is a _ _ _ _ _ _ in jail now, the poor little jerk.

10. The _ _ _ _ _ _ _ flicks his tongue with such malice

While all those _ _ _ _ _ _ _ drink from the chalice.

Not one _ _ _ _ _ _ _ this terrible sin,

Nor sees the creature slithering in.

♚

11. The red-head from the _ _ _ _ _ _ _ -full state

_ _ _ _ _ _ _ into the party some two hours late,

Well _ _ _ _ _ _ _ in her jeans and drunk from beer.

"Oh, you're in the _ _ _ , _ _ _ ,"
    was hissed in her ear. ( 2 wds. )

♚

12. The King was so _ _ _ _ _ _ and so wicked and old,

He drank all his _ _ _ _ _ _ from mugs of pure gold.

His haughty bold _ _ _ _ _ _ was as sharp as an eagle;

His courtiers feared this fat ruler so _ _ _ _ _ _ .

♚

13. _ _ _ _ _ _ Dame was the name of a lovely goose

Who _ _ _ _ _ _ _ in her _ _ _ _ _ _ _ free and loose.

Through fences of wire a _ _ _ _ _ _ _ she spied—

In spite of the _ _ _ _ _ _ _ she flew to his side.

♚

14. The old Latin scholar, _ _ _ _ _ _ _ and enthralled,

Looked up where a _ _ _ _ _ _ _ of Caesar's installed

The crowd roared with laughter at this poor old bloke,

_ _ " _ _ _ _ _ , Brute" were the words that he spoke.

15. The mountain _ _ _ _ _ _ _ have oaken wood floors

With _ _ _ _ _ _ _ of brass on all of the doors.

The racers stay here whenever it snows;

They bring in skis and a _ _ _ _ _ _ _ of clothes.

♚

16. In robe of black with _ _ _ _ _ _ of red,

The _ _ _ _ _ _ sat down and blessed the bread.

When served dessert, he gave a grin—

The _ _ _ _ _ _ fruit was served to him.

♚

17. _ _ _ _ , the new head of the school _ _ _ _ ,

Had a meeting with mothers on one wintry day.

With a _ _ _ _ of the gavel, she said with a smirk

"We're _ _ _ to go broke if we don't get to work!"

♚

18. The _ _ _ _ were crude and made of thatch—

No doors to _ _ _ _ nor windows to latch.

In wind and rain they could not sleep

And _ _ _ _ _ they lived in the jungle so deep.

♚

19. The _ _ _ _ _ of horses strutted and pranced;

The circus seal was _ _ _ _ _ and danced.

The lion's _ _ _ _ _ was snarling and mad—

The diet of _ _ _ _ _ had made her mad.

**267**

# MALAPROPISMS

When what someone says is pertinent and to the point it may be said to be apropos. When it is the opposite of these things, it is malapropos.

In 1775, the year Richard Sheridan's comedy *The Rivals* was first presented, the world was given its model of linguistic maladroitness forevermore—the tongue-tied and muddle-headed Mrs. Malaprop. Her chronic misuse and abuse of the English language gave birth to the term *malapropism*, some choice examples of which are offered below.

Strategy is when you are out of ammunition but keep right on firing so that the enemy won't know.

If your father were alive, he'd be turning over in his grave.

Your whole fallacy is wrong!

Gender in English tells us if a man is male, female, or neuter.

Don't pay any attention to him—don't even ignore him!

The driver swerved to avoid missing the jaywalker.

*Leo Rosten*

He gets up at six o'clock in the morning no matter what time it is.

*Leo Rosten*

An oral contract isn't worth the paper it's written on.

*Samuel Goldwyn*

Don't blame God; He's only human.

*Leo Rosten*

Every man loves his native land whether he was born there or not.

*Thomas Fitch*

Let us be happy and live within our means, even if we have to borrow money to do it with.

*Artemus Ward*

You can observe a lot by watching.

*Yogi Berra*

Rome is full of fallen arches.

God Bless the Holy Trinity.
 *A placard which actually led a parade of devout Catholics some years ago in Dublin.*

The climate of the Sahara is such that its inhabitants have to live elsewhere.

I don't want any yesmen around me. I want everyone to tell me the truth— even though it costs him his job.

*Samuel Goldwyn*

*No one* goes to that restaurant anymore; it's too crowded.

*Yogi Berra*

♚

We're overpaying him, but he's worth it.

*Samuel Goldwyn*

♚

A lot of people my age are dead at the present time.

*Casey Stengel*

♚

Washington's farewell address was Mount Vernon.

*Leo Rosten*

♚

There's a dirge of good music on the radio.

♚

Let's not downgrade this up.

♚

Get on your bicycle and run like crazy.

♚

Gentlemen, you may include me out.

*Samuel Goldwyn*

♚

You've no idea what a poor opinion I have of myself, and how little I deserve it.

*W.S. Gilbert*

♚

It's a pretty big town for a town of its size.

♚

**270**

A practical nurse is one who marries a rich patient.

# DEFYING GRAVITY

To set up this trick, you need two glasses and two wooden kitchen matches. Place the two glasses upside down on a table. Place one match between the two glasses, and press the glasses closely together so that the match is held up by the sides of the glasses.

Your object is to remove one of the glasses without having the match fall to the table. You may not touch the suspended match with anything but one other match.

Let some of your friends try it first. When they have given up, you can proceed to amaze them.

First, light the second match. Using the lit match, light the head of the suspended match.

Wait a moment until the entire match head has turned black. Then blow out the flame. Wait again for one more second for the match to cool and stick. Then remove the glass which is not touching the match head.

You will see that the burnt match head has adhered to the glass. Now you can safely remove the other glass without causing the match to fall.

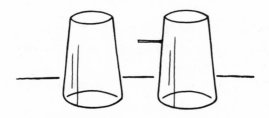

# FAIR AND SQUARE

Arrange four matches, as in the diagram below.

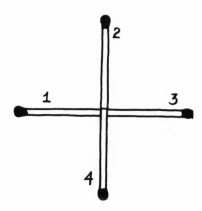

You challenge anyone to move *one* match *and only one match* to form a perfect square!

This is done by moving *Match No. 4* downward, leaving a square in between the ends of the four matches, as illustrated below.

In performing this trick—and it's a humdinger!—you must take care to arrange the matches in the first place so that *Match No. 4* alone lies between *Matches No. 1* and *No. 3*, making it unnecessary to move *Match No. 2* in order to complete the square.

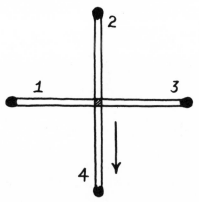

# USE ONE MATCH TO LIFT TEN

Challenge your friends to arrange ten matches on a table in such a way that they can be lifted up all at once by using one more matchstick. For this trick all you need are eleven matchsticks.

When your friends have exhausted their ingenuity, you show them how.

First, put one match down on the table. Arrange the other nine matches across the first match.

When you have arranged them properly, stand back for a moment to let your friends get a good look. Then place the 11th match on top of your arrangement. Make sure that it is lying parallel to the first match lying at the bottom of the pile. Place the head of the last match opposite the plain end of the first match, so that the parallel matchsticks are lying as flat as possible.

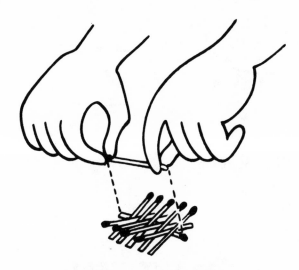

Using the thumb and forefinger of each hand, press the ends of the two parallel matchsticks together as tightly as you can. The nine matchsticks in the middle are now being held in a vise by the two matches at the top and bottom. You will be able to lift them all, none spilling apart.

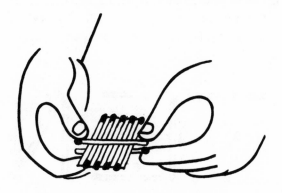

# SWEET FIRE

All you need for this stunt is a few lumps of sugar, a cigarette, and some matches.

The challenge is to make a lump of sugar burn. Sugar contains alcohol, which burns easily once combustion is started. But if you try simply putting a lighted match to the sugar, it will merely char.

Let your audience attempt to light the sugar first. While they are fumbling around with their matches, quietly slip a sugar cube out of the sugar bowl, and dip the corner of the cube into some cigarette ash, which you should have in an ashtray you left on the table.

When your friends have given up, calmly light the corner of the sugar cube which you have dipped in the ash with a lighted match, and watch as it comes into flame.

# MAKE TEN

This trick is always good for a laugh. All you need is nine matchsticks.

Challenge your friends to take nine matches and make ten. Your friends will, of course, laugh at you, and tell you it is impossible. But the joke will be on them when you show them how it is done.

Simply set up the matches as shown below.

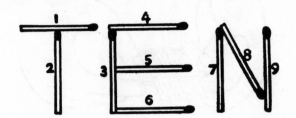

# PAGE THE SURVEYOR!

Arrange eight matches so as to form the figure illustrated immediately below.

Tell your friends this represents a field bequeathed by a farmer to his sons. As can readily be seen, this field is easily divisible into three equal parts.

The hitch is this: the farmer went and died and left *four* sons.

Now the trick is to divide the plot of ground into FOUR EQUAL PARTS, each the same shape.

. . . To do the job, you are given four matches. You can dispose these matches in any way you choose; but unfortunately you can't move land, so the eight original matches must stay put.

The figure below demonstrates how the deed is done. Note that two matches are broken in half.

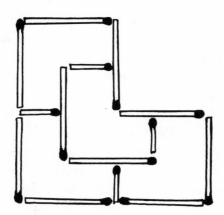

# HOW TO SOLVE ACROSS-TICS

In the world of puzzle ratios, where the crossword puzzle would be held equivalent to a game of checkers, the ACROSS-TIC would be equivalent to a game of chess. It is the development *par excellence* of the word game.

If you've never done ACROSS-TICS before, a new glamorous world in puzzledom is now discovered for you.

The first thing to understand is that the diagram does not in any way resemble a crossword puzzle diagram. The words read only from left to right, and do not interlink.

The ACROSS-TIC contains a quotation from a book or a poem. The black squares in the diagram indicate the end of a word. If there's a white square at the end of the line and the next line following begins with a white square—then two possibilities exist. The white square at the end of the first line may actually be the end of a word, and the white square on the following line may represent the first letter of a new word. Or it may be that all the white squares—those which end the first line and those which begin the following line—constitute a single word. This uncertainty constitutes one of the bafflements of the ACROSS-TIC puzzle.

With each ACROSS-TIC, you will find a list of definitions. The dashes alongside the definition indicate the number of letters in that particular word. The first thing you do is to read the definition and try to guess the word. It is a wise procedure to first run through all the definitions, in more or less rapid order, and then to write down those definitions which you are reasonably sure of.

Under each dash, you'll find a number. This number indicates a particular square in the diagram. You now fill in the letters of the words you have solved in the proper squares of the diagram. This will yield many hints towards a solution of other definitions. For example, if there's a three-letter word and you found that the first two letters are T H, the overwhelming likelihood is that the third box contains the letter E. Finding this E you now transcribe this particular letter by placing it on one of the dashes in the definition list. You do this by consulting the letter in the particular box in which you have written the E. If, for example, the box contains the keyed letter Q, you then know that the letter you wrote down is keyed to *Definition Q* and is to be placed in *Definition Q*.

By working this way, back and forth, you will be able to fill in letters from the diagram on the definition lines; and from the definition lines into the diagram. In other words, one solution helps the other.

Now and then, you will be forced to make a guess. Where, for example, in a five-letter word, the first two letters are G H, and the fourth one an S, it's a pretty safe bet that the word will be G H O S T. But where a four-letter words starts with the letters B A N, the fourth letter might be E, D, G, K or S; and you may be obliged to guess. This guessing is a temporary measure—a trial-and-error piece of business—which you employ until you find out for

276

sure what the letter is. ACROSS-TIC puzzlers must be constantly armed with a nice, big eraser.

There's still another help you get in solving an ACROSS-TIC. The ACROSS-TIC gets it name and its particular flavor because of the fact that the initial letters of the given definitions, if read down, yield the name of the author of the quotation, followed by the name of the book or the name of the piece from which the quotation was taken. This may vary somewhat. The ACROSS-TIC may be the full name of the author, or just the last name of the author, or an initial or initials of the author followed by the last name. This may be followed by a designation of the kind of literary composition from which the quotation is taken, like *Shakespeare Play Macbeth*, or *Kilmer Poem Trees*. Where the author is anonymous, the name of the author would, of course, be omitted. What must be kept in mind is that the ACROSS-TIC device is used in a free manner, and there is no hard and fast rule which will indicate what the initial letters are going to spell out. However, you can be assured that the source of the quotation will always appear in the ACROSS-TIC.

Although some of the definitions will at first sight appear impossible of solution and beyond your ken of knowledge, you will find that that merely makes the puzzle intriguing. A good ACROSS-TIC solver never employs encyclopedias or other reference books. It's considered cricket to check your definition in a dictionary for the purpose of authenticating your solution at any point in the game. But the ACROSS-TIC is not an exercise in research—it's rather a game, a pleasant pastime with a great amount of challenge. You will find that, although you may be obliged at the start to resort to reference helps, the real fun comes when you can dope out the solution of an "impossible definition" through conjecture and by force of your fuller experience in dealing with word structure.

Definitions are based on those found in *Webster's International Dictionary, Second Edition*. Where the word *compound* appears after a definition, it indicates that the word is hyphenated. Where a bracket contains a phrase like *four words*, it means that the definition consists of four words, like the expression *Out of this world*. No obsolete or archaic words or spellings are used at any time in the ACROSS-TIC puzzle.

*Pleasant sailing!*

# ACROSS-TIC NO. 1

DEFINITIONS                                    WORDS

**A**  Early form of Sanskrit          ___ ___ ___ ___ ___
                                        102  64  42  26  169

**B**  Site of crucial battle (333     ___ ___ ___ ___ ___
       B. C.) won by Alexander          97  192  66  146  53
       the Great

**C**  Only actress to win two         ___ ___ ___ ___ ___ ___ ___ ___ ___ ___ ___ ___ ___ ___
       "Best Supporting" Oscars         147 190 125  54 177   4  32  75 108  44 152 184  90  18
       (2 wds.)

**D**  U. S. national monument         ___ ___ ___ ___ ___ ___ ___ ___ ___ ___ ___
       in New Mexico (2 wds.)           120 160  76 126  10 145 165 109 178  40  24

**E**  Serpent                         ___ ___ ___ ___ ___ ___ ___ ___
                                        103  16 187  52 132  28 195 122

**F**  1953 Fred Astaire movie         ___ ___ ___ ___ ___ ___ ___ ___ ___ ___ ___ ___
       (2 wds.)                          36 153 106 133   1 113  69 186  58 193  23  85

**G**  U. S. national forest in        ___ ___ ___ ___ ___ ___ ___
       Idaho & Wyoming                  116 198 156 130  51   5  83

**H**  Low-grade iron ore              ___ ___ ___ ___ ___ ___ ___ ___
                                         74 188  13 144  98  30 123  61

**I**  Weary, drawn, and tired         ___ ___ ___ ___ ___ ___ ___
       in appearance; author of         171 163  99 114 158  35 142
       *She* and *King Solomon's
       Mines*

**J**  Collections of property;        ___ ___ ___ ___ ___ ___ ___
       large landholdings               180   9 170 121 139  94  77

**K**  River embankment                ___ ___ ___ ___ ___
                                         29 140 105  62  89

**L**  Suited to a purpose             ___ ___ ___ ___ ___ ___ ___ ___
                                        155  22   6  67 115 100  80 200

**M**  Female silent movie star        ___ ___ ___ ___ ___ ___ ___
       Mabel . . .                      183  34  65 175 128 101  86

**N**  Famous conservationist;         ___ ___ ___ ___ ___ ___ ___ ___ ___ ___ ___ ___ ___ ___
       twice governor of Pa. (2         39 182 143  59 194   3  48 176 136 151 162 111  70  96
       wds.)

**O**  Released; detached              ___ ___ ___ ___ ___ ___ ___ ___ ___
                                        134 164  37 174 189  14 117 161 179

**P**  Circumference                   ___ ___ ___ ___ ___
                                         12  82  46 112  95

**Q**  Petty swindler; con man         ___ ___ ___ ___ ___ ___ ___
       (colloq.)                         91   8  55 181 135  38 199

**R**  Mythological poetry of          ___ ___ ___ ___
       Scandinavia                       20 107  45  84

**S**  Large diving bird of the        ___ ___ ___ ___ ___ ___
       hawk family                      150 138  63  19  79  92

**T**  Famous fat, jolly               ___ ___ ___ ___ ___ ___ ___ ___
       Shakespearean character         167  43 196 149 119 141   2  56

**U**  Metallic musical                ___ ___ ___ ___
       instrument, often used           33  49 166 131
       with drums

**V**  Gaseous hydrocarbons            ___ ___ ___ ___ ___ ___ ___
                                         57  31 127 118 137   7 197

**W**  Gaelic                          ___ ___ ___ ___
                                        154  60  25 148

**X**  Active volcano in               ___ ___ ___ ___ ___ ___
       California                       104  47 185 159  71  11

| Y | Engrossed; purpose; meaning | $\underline{81}$ $\underline{50}$ $\underline{17}$ $\underline{172}$ $\underline{73}$ $\underline{110}$ |
| Z | Measuring point in the Roman calendar | $\underline{68}$ $\underline{41}$ $\underline{88}$ $\underline{157}$ $\underline{21}$ |
| $Z^1$ | Gallows | $\underline{93}$ $\underline{191}$ $\underline{27}$ $\underline{124}$ $\underline{168}$ $\underline{78}$ |
| $Z^2$ | Feeling; perception; meaning | $\underline{173}$ $\underline{15}$ $\underline{129}$ $\underline{72}$ $\underline{87}$ |

*Answers on page 493*

|   |   |   |   |   |   | 1 F |   |   | 2 T | 3 N | 4 C | 5 G |   |
|---|---|---|---|---|---|---|---|---|---|---|---|---|---|
| 6 L | 7 V | 8 Q | 9 J | 10 D | 11 X |   |   | 12 P | 13 H | 14 O | 15 $Z^2$ | 16 E | 17 Y | 18 C |
|   |   | 19 S | 20 R | 21 Z | 22 L | 23 F | 24 D | 25 W | 26 A | 27 $Z^1$ | 28 E | 29 K | 30 H | 31 V |
| 32 C |   |   | 33 U | 34 M | 35 I |   | 36 F | 37 O | 38 Q |   |   | 39 N | 40 D |
| 41 Z | 42 A |   |   | 43 T | 44 C | 45 R |   | 46 P | 47 X | 48 N |   |   | 49 U |
| 50 Y |   |   | 51 G | 52 E | 53 B |   | 54 C | 55 Q | 56 T | 57 V |   |   | 58 F |
|   | 59 N | 60 W | 61 H | 62 K |   | 63 S | 64 A | 65 M | 66 B | 67 L | 68 Z |
|   | 69 F | 70 N | 71 X | 72 $Z^2$ | 73 Y | 74 H |   | 75 C | 76 D | 77 J | 78 $Z^1$ | 79 S |
|   | 80 L | 81 Y | 82 P | 83 G |   |   | 84 R | 85 F | 86 M |   | 87 $Z^2$ | 88 Z | 89 K |
| 90 C | 91 Q | 92 S |   | 93 $Z^1$ | 94 J | 95 P | 96 N | 97 B | 98 H | 99 I |   | 100 L |
| 101 M | 102 A | 103 E | 104 X | 105 K | 106 F | 107 R |   | 108 C | 109 D |   | 110 Y | 111 N |
| 112 P | 113 F | 114 I | 115 L |   | 116 G | 117 O | 118 V | 119 T |   | 120 D | 121 J | 122 E |
| 123 H |   | 124 $Z^2$ | 125 C |   | 126 D | 127 V | 128 M | 129 $Z^2$ | 130 G | 131 U | 132 E |
|   | 133 F | 134 O | 135 Q |   | 136 N | 137 V | 138 S | 139 J | 140 K | 141 T | 142 I |
| 143 N | 144 H | 145 D | 146 B | 147 C | 148 W | 149 T |   | 150 S | 151 M |   | 152 C | 153 F |
| 154 W |   | 155 L | 156 G | 157 Z | 158 I | 159 X |   | 160 D | 161 O |   | 162 N |
| 163 I | 164 O |   | 165 D | 166 U | 167 T | 168 $Z^1$ | 169 A | 170 J |   | 171 I | 172 Y |
|   | 173 $Z^2$ | 174 O | 175 M | 176 N | 177 C | 178 D |   | 179 O | 180 J | 181 Q | 182 N | 183 M | 184 C |
| 185 X |   | 186 F | 187 E | 188 H | 189 O |   | 190 C | 191 $Z^1$ | 192 B |   | 193 F |
| 194 N | 195 E | 196 T | 197 V |   | 198 G | 199 Q | 200 L |

(DIRECTIONS FOR SOLVING ACROSS-TICS ARE ON PAGE 276)

# ACROSS-TIC NO. 2

DEFINITIONS                                    WORDS

A   1935 Katherine Hepburn
    movie (2 wds.)           ——  ——  ——  ——  ——  —  —  ——  ——  ——
                             86  30  124 148 118 98  7  183 74  60

B   Disreputable; vulgar     ——  ——  ——  ——  ——  ——  ——
                             160 201 51  67  174 22  95

C   Stiff fabric of silk, nylon,
    etc.                     ——  ——  ——  ——  ——  ——  ——
                             94  165 52  66  193 134 206

D   Having a horny covering
    on the feet              ——  ——  ——  ——  ——  ——
                             115 73  12  199 39  152

E   Major Pacific fleet
    anchorage, W W II        ——  ——  ——  ——  ——  ——
                             13  196 78  110 143 32

F   Oared                    ——  ——  ——  ——  ——
                             137 48  16  111 87

G   Official misconduct or
    neglect                  ——  ——  ——  ——  ——  ——  ——  ——  ——  ——
                             182 29  72  187 204 53  166 130 89  10

H   Unyielding; rock-hard    ——  ——  ——  ——  ——  ——  ——
                             59  178 68  157 140 19  101

I   Bantered; needled; having
    bands                    ——  ——  ——  ——  ——  ——
                             26  100 194 153 55  162

J   Heavy gaseous element    ——  ——  ——  ——  ——
                             49  185 125 20  34

K   17th century French dance ——  ——  ——  ——  ——  ——  ——
                             80  17  40  104 147 120 71

L   Witchcraft; talisman;
    black magic              ——  ——  ——  ——  ——
                             105 69  177 159 15

M   Dictionary               —  ——  ——  ——  ——  ——  ——
                             6  127 186 205 14  175 79

N   Wagner opera (2 wds.)    ——  ——  ——  ——  ——  —  ——  ——  ——  ——  ——  ——
                             90  171 119 180 82  3  168 64  131 45  31  114

O   Felon                    ——  ——  ——  ——  ——  ——  ——
                             58  173 93  81  207 149 135

P   Leading contemporary
    (1933 - ) Soviet poet    —  ——  ——  ——  ——  ——  ——  ——  ——  ——  ——
                             9  154 192 88  97  109 77  203 133 138 37

Q   Gained; caught in a seine ——  ——  ——  ——  ——  ——
                             113 161 11  76  188 106

R   Placing stress upon      ——  ——  ——  ——  ——  ——  ——  ——  ——
                             83  35  155 24  141 169 191 42  103

S   Examination by touch     ——  ——  ——  ——  ——  —  ——  ——  ——  ——  ——  ——
                             27  108 151 128 50  1  84  65  139 25  189 57

T   Coroner's investigation  ——  ——  ——  ——  ——  ——  ——
                             56  176 96  150 36  190 126

U   By-product               ——  ——  ——  ——  ——  ——  ——
                             91  179 170 18  85  44  116 197

V   U. S. inventor (1818-1903)
    of machine gun           ——  ——  ——  ——  ——  ——  —
                             43  33  163 129 144 117 4

W   Large wine bottle        ——  ——  ——  ——  ——  ——  ——  ——
                             38  132 23  136 47  181 112 200

X   Bring into harmony       ——  ——  ——  ——  ——  ——
                             61  107 21  167 184 75

Y   Type of temporary bridge
    built on cylinders       ——  —  ——  ——  ——  ——  ——
                             145 5  122 202 164 198 62

Z   " . . . did from their color
    fly," *Julius Caesar* (3 wds.) —  ——  ——  ——  ——  ——  ——  ——  ——  ——  ——  ——  ——
                             2  63  142 54  195 92  121 28  46  99  146 158 172

$Z^1$    Uttered mournful, long
         cries

        102  156   8   70   41  123

## Answers on page 494

| | | | | | 1 S | 2 Z | 3 N | | 4 V | 5 Y | 6 M | 7 A |
|---|---|---|---|---|---|---|---|---|---|---|---|---|
| 8 $Z^1$ | 9 P | 10 G | | 11 Q | 12 D | 13 E | 14 M | 15 L | | 16 F | 17 K | 18 U |
| | 19 H | 20 J | 21 X | | 22 B | 23 W | 24 R | 25 S | 26 I | | 27 S | 28 Z |
| 29 G | 30 A | 31 N | 32 E | 33 V | 34 J | 35 R | 36 T | | 37 P | 38 W | | 39 D |
| 40 K | 41 $Z^1$ | 42 R | | 43 V | 44 U | 45 N | 46 Z | | 47 W | 48 F | 49 J | |
| 50 S | 51 B | 52 C | 53 G | 54 Z | 55 I | | 56 T | 57 S | | 58 O | 59 H | 60 A |
| | 61 X | 62 Y | | 63 Z | 64 N | 65 S | 66 C | 67 B | 68 H | 69 L | 70 $Z^1$ | 71 K |
| | 72 G | 73 D | 74 A | 75 X | 76 Q | 77 P | 78 E | 79 M | 80 K | | 81 O | 82 N |
| 83 R | 84 S | | 85 U | 86 A | 87 F | | 88 P | 89 G | | 90 N | 91 U | |
| 92 Z | 93 O | 94 C | 95 B | | 96 T | 97 P | 98 A | 99 Z | 100 I | 101 H | 102 $Z^1$ | |
| 103 R | 104 K | 105 L | 106 Q | | 107 X | 108 S | 109 P | 110 E | 111 F | | 112 W | 113 Q |
| 114 N | | 115 D | 116 U | 117 V | 118 A | 119 N | 120 K | | 121 Z | 122 Y | 123 $Z^1$ | |
| 124 A | 125 J | 126 T | 127 M | 128 S | 129 V | 130 G | 131 N | 132 W | 133 P | 134 C | | 135 O |
| 136 W | 137 F | 138 P | 139 S | 140 H | 141 R | 142 Z | 143 E | 144 V | 145 Y | | 146 Z | 147 K |
| | 148 A | 149 O | 150 T | 151 S | 152 D | | 153 I | 154 P | | 155 R | 156 $Z^1$ | 157 H |
| 158 Z | 159 L | 160 B | 161 Q | 162 I | | 163 V | 164 Y | | 165 C | | 166 G | 167 X |
| 168 N | 169 R | | 170 U | 171 N | 172 Z | 173 O | 174 B | 175 M | 176 T | 177 L | 178 H | |
| 179 U | 180 N | 181 W | 182 G | | 183 A | 184 X | | 185 J | 186 M | 187 G | 188 Q | 189 S |
| 190 T | 191 R | 192 P | 193 C | | 194 I | 195 Z | 196 E | 197 U | | 198 Y | 199 D | |
| 200 W | 201 B | 202 Y | 203 P | 204 G | 205 M | 206 C | 207 O | | | | | |

(DIRECTIONS FOR SOLVING ACROSS-TICS ARE ON PAGE 276)

# ACROSS-TIC NO. 3

DEFINITIONS        WORDS

**A**   Show business superstar, made broadway debut in *Word I* (full name, 2 wds.)
187   27   64   219   178   10   93   171   205   214

**B**   Cutting into; sharp, penetrating
53   189   67   1   158   31   141   118

**C**   Having a ribbed surface
32   213   131   57   201   112

**D**   1932 Marx Brothers movie (2 wds.)
137   84   154   99   26   167   8   38   203   211   157   119   59

**E**   Command; urgent, necessary, compelling
58   179   159   80   176   33   125   5   200   140

**F**   "The fairest meadow . . .," Oliver Wendell Holmes, *Chanson* (3 wds.)
150   60   107   73   3   217   132   82   48   25   161   191   139

**G**   Anesthetic
111   18   126   76   183

**H**   Bulging; protuberant (said of the moon)
120   177   101   164   63   98   17

**I**   1938 Broadway musical hit by Cole Porter (4 wds.)
81   151   22   117   66   170   36   110   138   97   6

**J**   Former official native name for Tokyo
186   116   202   45

**K**   Slipknot loop used by hangman
54   174   68   11   102

**L**   Jewish university located in New York City
190   122   162   37   13   75   92

**M**   Temple on the Acropolis
136   121   29   108   44   210   91   149   193   15

**N**   Distribute; assign
105   69   144   41   130   218   185   24

**O**   Based on hearsay
96   175   42   168   30   103   14

**P**   Plant of the milkweed family
194   207   52   77   148   61   46   115   95   156   181

**Q**   Protested; demurred; spoke against
160   195   19   87   135   47   127   9

**R**   Political party of Hamilton and Adams (1789-1816)
83   71   12   212   89   109   197   163   206   147

**S**   Pervade; pass through; enter stealthily
74   23   133   172   215   51   104   88   146   199

**T**   Aircraft engine housing
34   208   72   166   90   4   155

**U**   ". . . hard lodging and thin weeds," *Love's Labour's Lost* (3 wds.)
79   143   16   50   124   35   188   173   106   56   180   128   100   40

**V**   Uneasy; fearful; worried
129   86   21   169   43   204   196   62   209   184   7   153

**W**   Scene of major Civil War battle, 1864 (2 wds.)
28   114   2   198   70   142   94   123   216

**X**   "This diamond he greets . . .," *Macbeth*, (3 wds.)
78   55   182   85   65   145   192   49   152   134   39   113   20   165

*Answers on page 494*

| | | | | 1 B | | 2 W | 3 F | 4 T | 5 E | 6 I | 7 V |
|---|---|---|---|---|---|---|---|---|---|---|---|
| 8 D | 9 Q | | 10 A | 11 K | | 12 R | 13 L | 14 O | | 15 M | 16 U | 17 H |
| 18 G | | 19 Q | 20 X | 21 V | 22 I | 23 S | 24 N | 25 F | 26 D | | 27 A | 28 W |
| 29 M | 30 O | 31 B | 32 C | 33 E | 34 T | 35 U | | 36 I | 37 L | 38 D | 39 X | |
| 40 U | 41 N | 42 O | 43 V | 44 M | 45 J | 46 P | | 47 Q | 48 F | 49 X | | 50 U |
| 51 S | 52 P | 53 B | 54 K | | 55 X | 56 U | | 57 C | 58 E | 59 D | 60 F | 61 P |
| 62 V | 63 H | 64 A | | 65 X | 66 I | | 67 B | 68 K | 69 N | 70 W | 71 R | 72 T |
| 73 F | 74 S | 75 L | 76 G | 77 P | 78 X | | 79 U | 80 E | 81 I | 82 F | | 83 R |
| 84 D | 85 X | | 86 V | 87 Q | 88 S | 89 R | 90 T | | 91 M | 92 L | 93 A | 94 W |
| 95 P | 96 O | | 97 I | 98 H | 99 D | 100 U | | 101 H | 102 K | | 103 O | 104 S |
| 105 N | 106 U | 107 F | 108 M | 109 R | 110 I | 111 G | 112 C | | 113 X | 114 W | 115 P | 116 J |
| 117 I | 118 B | 119 D | | 120 H | 121 M | 122 L | 123 W | 124 U | | 125 E | 126 G | 127 Q |
| | 128 U | 129 V | 130 N | 131 C | 132 F | 133 S | 134 X | 135 Q | 136 M | | 137 D | 138 I |
| 139 F | 140 E | 141 B | 142 W | 143 U | | 144 N | 145 X | 146 S | 147 R | 148 P | 149 M |
| 150 F | 151 I | | 152 X | 153 V | 154 D | 155 T | | 156 P | 157 D | 158 B | 159 E | 160 Q |
| 161 F | 162 L | 163 R | 164 H | 165 X | 166 T | | 167 D | 168 O | 169 V | | 170 I | 171 A |
| | 172 S | 173 U | | 174 K | 175 O | 176 E | | 177 H | 178 A | 179 E | 180 U | 181 P |
| 182 X | 183 G | 184 V | 185 N | 186 J | | 187 A | 188 U | 189 B | 190 L | | 191 F | 192 X |
| | 193 M | 194 P | | 195 Q | 196 V | 197 R | 198 W | 199 S | 200 E | 201 C | 202 J |
| 203 D | 204 V | 205 A | 206 R | | 207 P | 208 T | 209 V | | 210 M | 211 D | 212 R |
| 213 C | 214 A | 215 S | 216 W | | 217 F | 218 N | 219 A | | | | |

(DIRECTIONS FOR SOLVING ACROSS-TICS ARE ON PAGE 276)

# ACROSS-TIC NO. 4

| | DEFINITIONS | WORDS |
|---|---|---|

**A** Tie down, as over a ship's hatch
___ ___ ___ ___ ___ ___
62 83 193 107 11 39

**B** Playful webfooted, furry mammal related to the mink and weasel
___ ___ ___ ___ ___
141 189 44 115 12

**C** 1941 Barbara Stanwyck-Gary Cooper movie (3 wds)
___ ___ ___ ___ ___ ___ ___ ___ ___ ___
20 9 176 143 89 102 182 98 35 70

**D** Evil spirit
___ ___ ___ ___ ___ ___ ___ ___ ___
82 36 14 170 71 153 114 208 138

**E** "Best men are moulded . . .," *Measure for Measure* (3 wds.)
___ ___ ___ ___ ___ ___ ___ ___ ___ ___ ___
45 63 207 129 73 93 5 186 27 111 197

**F** Brood or nest of pheasants
___ ___ ___ ___
130 38 152 164

**G** Baseball or football arenas
___ ___ ___ ___ ___ ___
150 171 106 124 26 49

**H** "Their images I loved . . .," Shakespeare, *Sonnets* (4 wds.)
___ ___ ___ ___ ___ ___ ___ ___ ___ ___ ___
85 60 205 34 140 103 4 50 25 196 123

**I** Not concentrated; spread out; scattered
___ ___ ___ ___ ___ ___ ___
132 13 177 101 68 58 185

**J** Reveal; make known
___ ___ ___ ___ ___ ___
81 10 33 133 154 108

**K** Pitcher who hurled four no-hit games (2 wds.)
___ ___ ___ ___ ___ ___ ___ ___ ___
149 19 46 178 86 69 134 157 165

**L** Designating the sweat glands
___ ___ ___ ___ ___ ___ ___
175 24 1 88 59 187 120

**M** Obstructed; delayed; blocked
___ ___ ___ ___ ___ ___ ___
151 23 119 53 203 173 28

**N** 1949 Broadway musical (3 wds.)
___ ___ ___ ___ ___ ___ ___ ___ ___ ___ ___ ___
125 184 29 109 139 55 94 76 169 3 163 79

**O** Famous singing group in the opera *Lucia*
___ ___ ___ ___ ___ ___
8 190 54 195 180 128

**P** Subordinate associate; helper
___ ___ ___ ___ ___ ___ ___
74 144 160 211 84 147 91

**Q** Outstanding U. S. female tennis star (1923 - ) (2 wds.)
___ ___ ___ ___ ___ ___ ___ ___ ___ ___ ___
21 87 142 113 118 212 145 179 181 95 40 2

**R** Famous U. S. aircraft carrier sunk in W W II; a New York main thoroughfare
___ ___ ___ ___ ___ ___ ___ ___ ___
97 201 30 188 57 210 112 161 75

**S** Fitted one within another
___ ___ ___ ___ ___ ___
209 105 16 183 199 67

**T** Capital of ancient Media
___ ___ ___ ___ ___ ___ ___ ___
155 135 96 7 43 110 66 77

**U** Place from which a pilot or captain conns a ship
___ ___ ___ ___ ___ ___ ___ ___ ___
174 136 65 47 202 172 92 117 192 56

**V** Sugar compound
___ ___ ___ ___ ___ ___ ___ ___ ___ ___
206 159 121 99 200 166 18 137 156 51

**W** Wobble; sway; waver
___ ___ ___ ___ ___ ___
122 61 131 37 168 48

| | | |
|---|---|---|
| **X** | Large constellation south of Hercules | $\overline{148}\ \overline{17}\ \overline{198}\ \overline{72}\ \overline{42}\ \overline{167}\ \overline{204}\ \overline{90}\ \overline{32}$ |
| **Y** | Grim; ghastly; horrible | $\overline{78}\ \overline{127}\ \overline{104}\ \overline{15}\ \overline{41}\ \overline{162}\ \overline{146}$ |
| **Z** | British poet (1878-1917): "Adlestrop," "The Owl," "Lights Out" (2 wds.) | $\overline{22}\ \overline{191}\ \overline{6}\ \overline{31}\ \overline{80}\ \overline{52}\ \overline{64}\ \overline{126}\ \overline{100}\ \overline{158}\ \overline{194}\ \overline{116}$ |

*Answers on page 494*

| 1 L | 2 Q | 3 N | 4 H | 5 E | ■ | 6 Z | 7 T | 8 O | ■ | 9 C |
|---|---|---|---|---|---|---|---|---|---|---|
| 10 J | 11 A | 12 B | 13 I | 14 D | 15 Y | 16 S | ■ | 17 X | 18 V | 19 K | 20 C | 21 Q |
| 22 Z | 23 M | ■ | 24 L | 25 H | 26 G | 27 E | 28 M | ■ | 29 N | 30 R | 31 Z | 32 X |
| 33 J | 34 H | 35 C | 36 D | 37 W | 38 F | 39 A | 40 Q | ■ | 41 Y | 42 X | 43 T | ■ |
| 44 B | 45 E | 46 K | 47 U | 48 W | 49 G | 50 H | 51 V | 52 Z | ■ | 53 M | 54 O | 55 N |
| 56 U | 57 R | 58 I | 59 L | 60 H | 61 W | ■ | 62 A | 63 E | 64 Z | ■ | 65 U | 66 T |
| 67 S | 68 I | 69 K | 70 C | 71 D | ■ | 72 X | 73 E | ■ | 74 P | 75 R | 76 N |
| 77 T | 78 Y | 79 N | 80 Z | 81 J | 82 D | 83 A | 84 P | ■ | 85 H | 86 K | ■ | 87 Q |
| 88 L | ■ | 89 C | 90 X | 91 P | ■ | 92 U | 93 E | ■ | 94 N | 95 Q | 96 T | 97 R |
| 98 C | 99 V | ■ | 100 Z | 101 I | 102 C | 103 H | 104 Y | 105 S | ■ | 106 G | 107 A |
| 108 J | 109 N | 110 T | 111 E | ■ | 112 R | 113 Q | 114 D | 115 B | ■ | 116 Z | 117 U | 118 Q |
| 119 M | 120 L | 121 V | 122 W | 123 H | 124 G | ■ | 125 N | 126 Z | 127 Y | 128 O | ■ | 129 E |
| 130 F | 131 W | ■ | 132 I | 133 J | 134 K | ■ | 135 T | 136 U | 137 V | 138 D | 139 N |
| 140 H | 141 B | 142 Q | 143 C | 144 P | ■ | 145 Q | 146 Y | ■ | 147 P | 148 X | 149 K | 150 G |
| 151 M | 152 F | 153 D | 154 J | 155 T | 156 V | ■ | 157 K | ■ | 158 Z | 159 V | 160 P | 161 R |
| 162 Y | ■ | 163 N | 164 F | 165 K | 166 V | 167 X | 168 W | ■ | 169 N | 170 D | ■ | 171 G |
| 172 U | 173 M | ■ | 174 U | 175 L | 176 C | 177 I | 178 K | 179 Q | 180 O | ■ | 181 Q | 182 C |
| ■ | 183 S | 184 N | 185 I | ■ | 186 E | 187 L | 188 R | 189 B | 190 O | 191 Z | ■ | 192 U |
| 193 A | 194 Z | 195 O | 196 H | 197 E | ■ | 198 X | 199 S | ■ | 200 V | 201 R | 202 U | 203 M |
| ■ | 204 X | 205 H | 206 V | ■ | 207 E | 208 D | 209 S | 210 R | 211 P | 212 Q | ■ |

# ACROSS-TIC NO. 5

| | DEFINITIONS | WORDS |
|---|---|---|

**A** Medicinal
‾96‾ ‾192‾ ‾109‾ ‾49‾ ‾5‾ ‾170‾

**B** Wandering; homeless
‾31‾ ‾100‾ ‾176‾ ‾140‾ ‾62‾ ‾73‾ ‾124‾

**C** 1934 Broadway musical hit by Cole Porter (2 wds.)
‾30‾ ‾148‾ ‾59‾ ‾38‾ ‾61‾ ‾119‾ ‾179‾ ‾40‾ ‾9‾ ‾88‾ ‾198‾ ‾166‾

**D** Legendary drug which brings forgetfulness
‾76‾ ‾32‾ ‾139‾ ‾173‾ ‾6‾ ‾105‾ ‾110‾ ‾58‾

**E** Common prefix meaning prelude or within
‾164‾ ‾136‾ ‾14‾ ‾183‾ ‾120‾

**F** Group of Norwegian islands
‾116‾ ‾147‾ ‾89‾ ‾28‾ ‾135‾ ‾52‾ ‾101‾ ‾162‾

**G** Sentinel
‾69‾ ‾163‾ ‾34‾ ‾155‾ ‾84‾ ‾115‾ ‾50‾

**H** Legal order which prevents or restrains
‾67‾ ‾122‾ ‾3‾ ‾152‾ ‾57‾ ‾95‾ ‾181‾ ‾189‾ ‾39‾ ‾63‾

**I** Harmonious; in agreement with
‾71‾ ‾184‾ ‾82‾ ‾26‾ ‾125‾ ‾121‾ ‾149‾ ‾94‾ ‾42‾

**J** Mythical monster with features of an eagle, horse and lion
‾15‾ ‾81‾ ‾112‾ ‾102‾ ‾123‾ ‾64‾ ‾45‾ ‾132‾ ‾47‾ ‾185‾

**K** Family of Jewish patriots, who revolted in 175 B. C.
‾168‾ ‾93‾ ‾154‾ ‾99‾ ‾177‾ ‾157‾ ‾16‾ ‾86‾ ‾144‾

**L** Anxious; impatient; showing keen desire
‾106‾ ‾194‾ ‾77‾ ‾143‾ ‾17‾

**M** Outstanding male red-headed U. S. pre-W W II tennis player (2 wds.)
‾27‾ ‾141‾ ‾68‾ ‾195‾ ‾158‾ ‾85‾ ‾130‾ ‾169‾

**N** Congenital scaly skin disease
‾70‾ ‾107‾ ‾51‾ ‾159‾ ‾29‾ ‾2‾ ‾190‾ ‾197‾ ‾91‾ ‾134‾

**O** Large U. S. national forest in Arizona
‾60‾ ‾113‾ ‾18‾ ‾4‾ ‾97‾ ‾146‾ ‾126‾ ‾48‾

**P** "The world . . . to make thee rich," *Romeo and Juliet* (3 wds.)
‾117‾ ‾90‾ ‾142‾ ‾44‾ ‾25‾ ‾80‾ ‾87‾ ‾8‾ ‾104‾ ‾193‾ ‾171‾ ‾35‾

**Q** Popular type of pasta
‾127‾ ‾53‾ ‾138‾ ‾98‾ ‾22‾ ‾75‾ ‾191‾ ‾13‾

**R** "They kept the . . . of their way," Gray, *Elegy* (2 wds.)
‾79‾ ‾137‾ ‾7‾ ‾21‾ ‾186‾ ‾161‾ ‾36‾ ‾156‾ ‾74‾ ‾118‾ ‾41‾ ‾133‾ ‾167‾ ‾103‾

**S** Ornamental stand or compartmented dish
‾24‾ ‾114‾ ‾46‾ ‾37‾ ‾12‾ ‾165‾ ‾72‾

**T** Light, sweet white Italian wine
‾43‾ ‾129‾ ‾54‾ ‾172‾ ‾153‾ ‾150‾ ‾78‾

**U** Ambassador's residence; person or group sent on an official mission
‾111‾ ‾55‾ ‾1‾ ‾160‾ ‾66‾ ‾188‾ ‾128‾

**V** Covered with scales
‾174‾ ‾151‾ ‾196‾ ‾131‾ ‾23‾ ‾175‾ ‾10‾ ‾65‾

**W** Duty; tax
‾178‾ ‾83‾ ‾33‾ ‾19‾ ‾187‾ ‾108‾

**X** Projecting platform for a ship's gun
‾145‾ ‾182‾ ‾56‾ ‾20‾ ‾180‾ ‾11‾ ‾92‾

| 1 U | 2 N | | 3 H | 4 O | 5 A | 6 D | 7 R | 8 P |
|---|---|---|---|---|---|---|---|---|
| 9 C | 10 V | 11 X | 12 S | 13 Q | 14 E | 15 J | 16 K | 17 L | 18 O |
| 19 W | 20 X | 21 R | 22 Q | 23 V | 24 S | 25 P | 26 I | 27 M | 28 F |
| 29 N | 30 C | 31 B | 32 D | 33 W | 34 G | 35 P | 36 R | 37 S | 38 C |
| 39 H | 40 C | 41 R | 42 I | 43 T | 44 P | 45 J | 46 S | 47 J |
| 48 O | 49 A | 50 G | 51 N | 52 F | 53 Q | 54 T | 55 U | 56 X | 57 H |
| 58 D | 59 C | 60 O | 61 C | 62 B | 63 H | 64 J | 65 V | 66 U | 67 H |
| 68 M | 69 G | 70 N | 71 I | 72 S | 73 B | 74 R | 75 Q | 76 D | 77 L |
| 78 T | 79 R | 80 P | 81 J | 82 I | 83 W | 84 G | 85 M | 86 K | 87 P |
| 88 C | 89 F | 90 P | 91 N | 92 X | 93 K | 94 I | 95 H | 96 A | 97 O | 98 Q |
| 99 K | 100 B | 101 F | 102 J | 103 R | 104 P | 105 D | 106 L | 107 N | 108 W |
| 109 A | 110 D | 111 U | 112 J | 113 O | 114 S | 115 G | 116 F | 117 P | 118 R |
| 119 C | 120 E | 121 I | 122 H | 123 J | 124 B | 125 I | 126 O | 127 Q | 128 U |
| 129 T | 130 M | 131 V | 132 J | 133 R | 134 N | 135 F | 136 E | 137 R | 138 Q |
| 139 D | 140 B | 141 M | 142 P | 143 L | 144 K | 145 X | 146 O | 147 F | 148 C | 149 I | 150 T |
| 151 V | 152 H | 153 T | 154 K | 155 G | 156 R | 157 K | 158 M | 159 N |
| 160 U | 161 R | 162 F | 163 G | 164 E | 165 S | 166 C | 167 R | 168 K | 169 M |
| 170 A | 171 P | 172 T | 173 D | 174 V | 175 V | 176 B | 177 K | 178 W | 179 G |
| 180 X | 181 H | 182 X | 183 E | 184 I | 185 J | 186 R | 187 W | 188 U | 189 H | 190 N |
| 191 Q | 192 A | 193 P | 194 L | 195 M | 196 V | 197 N | 198 C |

(DIRECTIONS FOR SOLVING ACROSS-TICS ARE ON PAGE 276)

# ACROSS-TIC NO. 6

DEFINITIONS WORDS

A Small European falcon
——— ——— ——— ——— ——— ——— ———
19 58 106 85 94 29 47

B Smart; a-one; excellent (colloq.)
——— ——— ——— ——— ———
169 177 73 128 82

C To mate individuals of the same or closely related stocks
——— ——— ——— ——— ——— ——— ———
183 64 81 15 136 175 28

D Italian librettist and composer ("Rinaldo," etc.) (2 wds.)
——— ——— ——— ——— ——— ——— ——— ——— ——— ——— ——— ———
89 25 113 184 192 56 108 39 147 7 101 133

E Troublemaker; rascal; imp
——— ——— ——— ——— ——— ——— ———
153 14 110 59 131 165 122

F Close-fitting Scottish trousers
——— ——— ——— ——— ———
145 33 93 8 163

G Native of Riga
——— ——— ——— ———
187 138 92 53

H Famous U. S. novelist and playwright ("Stage Door," "So Big," etc.) (2 wds.)
——— ——— ——— ——— ——— ——— ——— ——— ——— ———
180 52 24 65 74 130 6 116 194 157

I Belgian town, site of crucial W W I battle
——— ——— ——— ——— ———
188 98 10 115 123

J Mussed; disordered
——— ——— ——— ——— ——— ——— ———
68 159 77 148 97 20 176

K Stout rope; ship's cable
——— ——— ——— ——— ——— ———
107 91 16 139 117 174

L Turn; female tennis star
——— ——— ——— ——— ———
126 60 9 182 40

M "To bandy word for word and . . .," *Taming of the Shrew* (3 wds.)
——— ——— ——— ——— ——— ——— ——— ——— ——— ——— ——— ——— ———
151 125 189 37 88 49 67 18 70 160 45 172 3

N Sharp; vivid; to a high degree
——— ——— ——— ——— ——— ——— ———
75 143 152 55 119 171 36

O 1959 Broadway musical hit
——— ——— ——— ——— ——— ——— ———
132 173 21 41 168 185 111

P Group of ancient Hebrews which rejected oral laws (plural)
——— ——— ——— ——— ——— ——— ——— ——— ——— ———
57 156 71 48 109 1 120 32 162 141

Q 1941 Barbara Stanwyck - Cary Grant movie (3 wds.)
——— ——— ——— ——— ——— ——— ——— ——— ——— ———
105 129 84 186 27 195 80 42 114 154

R Hollow and curved
——— ——— ——— ——— ——— ——— ———
76 69 134 44 178 13 149

S Class of crustaceans having two sets of feet
——— ——— ——— ——— ——— ——— ——— ———
99 179 31 146 63 191 12 167

T Medieval musical instrument (2 wds.)
——— ——— ——— ——— ——— ——— ——— ——— ——— ——— ———
30 124 190 137 104 166 5 100 54 142 155 22

U Only racehorse ever to defeat Man O'War (1919); overturn
——— ——— ——— ——— ———
46 164 193 23 181

V Dressed; clad
——— ——— ——— ——— ——— ——— ———
34 102 79 87 161 61 127

W Formation within the body of stony deposits
——— ——— ——— ——— ——— ——— ——— ——— ———
83 50 170 103 72 38 4 95 62

**X** Long, slender animal growth used for grasping, feeling, moving, etc.

———  ———  ——  ——  ——  ———  ——  ——
140 118 26 35 96 158 78 11

**Y** " . . . forever in thine east," Tennyson, *Tithonus* (4 wds.)

——  —  ——  ———  ——  ——  ———  ——  ———  ——  ———  ———
43 2 86 112 17 66 144 90 121 51 150 135

## Answers on page 495

| | | 1 P | 2 Y | 3 M | 4 W | 5 T | 6 H | 7 D | | | 8 F |
|---|---|---|---|---|---|---|---|---|---|---|---|
| 9 L | 10 I | 11 X | | | 12 S | 13 R | 14 E | 15 C | 16 K | 17 Y | 18 M | 19 A |
| 20 J | 21 O | | | 22 T | 23 U | 24 H | | 25 D | 26 X | | | |
| 27 Q | | | 28 C | 29 A | 30 T | 31 S | 32 P | 33 F | 34 V | 35 X | 36 N | |
| | 37 M | 38 W | 39 D | | | 40 L | 41 O | 42 Q | 43 Y | | | 44 R |
| 45 M | 46 U | 47 A | 48 P | | | 49 M | 50 W | 51 Y | 52 H | | | 53 G |
| 54 T | 55 N | 56 D | 57 P | 58 A | 59 E | 60 L | 61 Y | 62 W | | | 63 S | 64 C |
| | | 65 H | | | 66 Y | 67 M | 68 J | | | 69 R | 70 M | |
| | 71 P | 72 W | 73 B | 74 H | 75 N | 76 R | 77 J | 78 X | 79 V | 80 Q | | |
| 81 C | 82 B | | | 83 W | 84 Q | 85 A | 86 Y | 87 V | 88 M | 89 D | | |
| 90 Y | 91 K | 92 G | 93 F | 94 A | 95 W | 96 X | 97 J | | | 98 I | 99 S | 100 T |
| 101 D | | | 102 V | 103 W | 104 T | 105 Q | | | 106 A | 107 K | 108 D | 109 P |
| 110 E | 111 O | | | 112 Y | 113 D | 114 Q | 115 I | | | 116 H | 117 K | 118 X |
| 119 N | | | 120 P | 121 Y | 122 E | 123 I | 124 T | 125 M | 126 L | 127 V | | |
| 128 B | 129 Q | 130 H | 131 E | 132 O | | | 133 D | 134 R | 135 Y | 136 C | 137 T | 138 G |
| 139 K | 140 X | 141 P | | | 142 T | 143 N | 144 Y | | | 145 F | 146 S | 147 D |
| 148 J | 149 R | | | 150 Y | 151 M | | | 152 N | 153 E | 154 Q | | |
| 155 T | 156 P | 157 H | | | 158 X | 159 J | 160 M | 161 V | 162 P | 163 F | 164 U | 165 E |
| 166 T | 167 S | 168 O | 169 B | 170 W | 171 N | | | 172 M | 173 O | 174 K | 175 C | |
| | 176 J | 177 B | 178 R | 179 S | 180 H | 181 U | 182 L | 183 C | 184 D | 185 O | 186 Q | 187 G |
| 188 I | | | 189 M | 190 T | 191 S | 192 D | 193 U | 194 H | 195 Q | | | |

**289**

(DIRECTIONS FOR SOLVING ACROSS-TICS ARE ON PAGE 276)

# ACROSS-TIC NO. 7

DEFINITIONS WORDS

**A** Famous U. S. battleship, sunk at Pearl Harbor; famous musical
151 185 72 44 132 162 192 18

**B** Sight; outlook; scene
35 154 91 131 8

**C** Dead; lifeless; lacking spirit or vitality
45 166 102 4 59 116 23 82 186

**D** Potentate; rich, important personage
201 158 12 144 108

**E** Harsh, rasping sound
113 177 26 48 136 196 146 182

**F** Made harmonious in color, appearance, or sound
15 111 170 87 159

**G** Tyrant; harsh ruler; one who uses power unjustly
98 199 193 9 115 19 129 40 86

**H** Avenger; person or thing that habitually defeats one
25 197 39 120 160 97 140

**I** Soft cotton cloth, often used for sleepwear, baby clothes, etc.
152 110 128 99 195 85 32 168 43 58 122

**J** Ardent lover in Shakespearean tragedy
49 169 183 14 164

**K** 1948 Astaire-Garland movie (2 wds.)
61 133 198 67 126 148 75 184 29 79 123 3

**L** Hypothesis; assumption
47 66 157 150 200 94 81 20 194 188 77

**M** Ancient language and tribe of Asia Minor and Syria
2 88 139 70 105 161 36

**N** William . . .: English dramatist (1640? - 1716)
104 27 167 101 10 114 181 56 156

**O** Make thin or slender; draw out
21 134 63 109 57 7 38 143 73

**P** Drunkard
103 34 138 130 175 16 96

**Q** 10th century British king
117 22 1 187

**R** Turnip having a large, yellow root
37 191 83 11 135 51 178 95

**S** Choral number from "Guys and Dolls" (3 wds.)
31 71 176 107 6 179 80 125 92 145 141 13 55

**T** Harmful
180 42 190 142 137 76 65 165 89

**U** Outside a city
202 173 119 189 64 127 53 93

**V** Agreement; combination into a pleasing, tuneful whole
84 62 174 118 149 54 33

**W** Embedded; fixed firmly
68 52 163 153 74 46 100 203 28

**X** Act having no legal force; zero
69 41 155 106 24 124 171

Y   Government by women   $\overline{78}$ $\overline{5}$ $\overline{112}$ $\overline{50}$ $\overline{17}$ $\overline{172}$ $\overline{60}$ $\overline{121}$ $\overline{90}$ $\overline{147}$ $\overline{30}$

*Answers on page 495*

| | | 1 Q | 2 M | 3 K | 4 C | | 5 Y | 6 S | 7 O | | 8 B | 9 G |
| 10 N | 11 R | 12 D | 13 S | 14 J | | 15 F | 16 P | | 17 Y | 18 A | 19 G |
| 20 L | | 21 O | | 22 Q | 23 C | 24 X | 25 H | 26 E | 27 N | | 28 W | 29 K |
| 30 Y | | 31 S | 32 I | 33 V | | 34 P | 35 B | 36 M | 37 R | | 38 O | |
| 39 H | 40 G | 41 X | 42 T | 43 I | 44 A | 45 C | 46 W | | 47 L | 48 E | 49 J | 50 Y |
| 51 R | 52 W | | 53 U | 54 V | 55 S | | 56 N | 57 O | 58 I | 59 C | 60 Y | 61 K |
| | 62 V | | 63 O | 64 U | 65 T | 66 L | 67 K | | 68 W | 69 X | 70 M | 71 S |
| | 72 A | 73 O | 74 W | 75 K | 76 T | 77 L | 78 Y | | 79 K | 80 S | | 81 L |
| 82 C | | 83 R | 84 V | 85 I | 86 G | 87 F | | 88 M | 89 T | | 90 Y |
| 91 B | 92 S | 93 U | 94 L | 95 R | 96 P | 97 H | 98 G | 99 I | | 100 W | 101 N | 102 C |
| 103 P | | 104 N | 105 M | 106 X | 107 S | | 108 D | 109 O | | 110 I | 111 F | 112 Y |
| 113 E | | 114 N | 115 G | 116 C | 117 Q | 118 V | 119 U | 120 H | 121 Y | 122 I | 123 K |
| 124 X | 125 S | 126 K | | 127 U | 128 I | 129 G | 130 P | | 131 B | 132 A | 133 K | 134 O |
| | 135 R | 136 E | 137 T | 138 P | 139 M | 140 H | | 141 S | 142 T | 143 O | | 144 D |
| 145 S | | 146 E | | 147 Y | 148 K | 149 V | 150 L | | 151 A | 152 I | | 153 W |
| 154 B | 155 X | 156 N | | 157 L | 158 D | 159 F | 160 H | | 161 M | 162 A | | 163 W |
| 164 J | 165 T | 166 C | 167 N | 168 I | | 169 J | 170 F | | 171 X | 172 Y | 173 U | 174 V |
| | 175 P | 176 S | 177 E | 178 R | | 179 S | 180 T | 181 N | 182 E | | 183 J | 184 K |
| 185 A | 186 C | | 187 Q | 188 L | 189 U | | 190 T | 191 R | 192 A | 193 G | | 194 L |
| 195 I | | 196 E | 197 H | 198 K | 199 G | 200 L | 201 D | 202 U | 203 W | |

**291**

(DIRECTIONS FOR SOLVING ACROSS-TICS ARE ON PAGE 276)

# ACROSS-TIC NO. 8

DEFINITIONS          WORDS

**A**   Highly emotional; showing deep feeling

208   94   56   12   214   143   219

**B**   Daughter of Hera and Zeus; goddess of youth (Greek myth)

40   123   59   180

**C**   Geometric figure consisting of a closed curve

116   181   176   19   49   127   70

**D**   Famous Finnish athlete, held world record for mile run 1923-1931 (2 wds.)

83   50   6   194   88   224   128   158   45   175

**E**   Make free; admit to citizenship; allow to vote

167   204   2   51   210   32   124   174   79   75   107

**F**   Withdraw; quit; go to bed

187   39   99   21   168   52

**G**   Faulty development; muscle or tissue degeneration

114   183   212   217   109   13   119   78   28

**H**   Popular contemporary comic strip artist, creator of "Doonesbury" (2 wds.)

102   86   139   215   34   77   120   185   148   61   201   14

**I**   "Sit patiently and . . . the morning's danger," *Henry V* (2 wds.)

193   53   72   48   131   82   42   223   206   186   20   165

**J**   U. S. national forest in North Carolina

89   64   26   153   43   130   161   145   218

**K**   Storehouse for weapons; military meeting-hall

133   115   200   63   93   166

**L**   Counselor; wise old man

202   154   90   22   135   38

**M**   First (1925) joint theatrical venture of Hammerstein and Rodgers (2 wds.)

155   190   138   7   188   33   125   169   57   179   18   76

**N**   British King, 9th century, father of Alfred the Great

192   105   164   10   60   209   141   27   178

**O**   Pouchlike; resembling a part filled with fluid

15   46   110   191   221   162   97

**P**   Overprotect; treat tenderly

98   35   189   65   113   151

**Q**   "The sad review . . . like the morning dew," *Campbell, The Pleasures of Hope* (4 wds.)

213   91   122   4   211   118   54   106   31   150   156   71   17   216   203

**R**   1931 Marx Brothers movie (2 wds.); shenanigans

66   184   44   81   8   147   95   74   137   23   117   172   55   126

**S**   Rash; imprudent; unwise

67   136   96   5   177   220   152   108   157   36   182

**T**   British governesses

101   16   80   47   199   132   142

**U**   Feminine; characteristic of a woman or women

225   3   196   149   173   92   112   207

**V**   Moslem title of honor; pilgrim to Mecca

171   144   9   69   100

**W**   Of, or caused by, an upright position

121   84   62   160   25   134   170   11   163   195   129

*Answers on page 495*

| | | | | | | | | | | | | | |
|---|---|---|---|---|---|---|---|---|---|---|---|---|---|
| 1 X | 2 E | | 3 U | 4 Q | 5 S | | 6 D | 7 M | 8 R | | 9 V | 10 N | |
| 11 W | 12 A | 13 G | 14 H | 15 O | | 16 T | 17 Q | 18 M | 19 C | 20 I | | 21 F | |
| 22 L | | 23 R | 24 X | | 25 W | 26 J | 27 N | 28 G | | 29 X | 30 Y | 31 Q | |
| 32 E | 33 M | | 34 H | 35 P | 36 S | | 37 X | 38 L | 39 F | | 40 B | 41 X | |
| 42 I | 43 J | 44 R | | 45 D | 46 O | 47 T | 48 I | | 49 C | 50 D | 51 E | 52 F | |
| 53 I | 54 Q | 55 R | | 56 A | 57 M | 58 Y | 59 B | 60 N | 61 H | | 62 W | 63 K | |
| | 64 J | 65 P | 66 R | 67 S | 68 Y | | 69 V | 70 C | 71 Q | 72 I | 73 X | 74 R | |
| 75 E | 76 M | | 77 H | 78 G | 79 E | 80 T | 81 R | | 82 I | 83 D | | 84 W | |
| 85 Y | 86 H | 87 X | 88 D | 89 J | 90 L | | 91 Q | 92 U | 93 K | | 94 A | 95 R | |
| 96 S | 97 O | 98 P | 99 F | 100 V | 101 T | 102 H | | 103 X | 104 Y | | 105 N | 106 Q | |
| 107 E | 108 S | 109 G | | 110 O | 111 X | 112 U | 113 P | 114 G | 115 K | 116 C | 117 R | 118 Q | |
| | 119 G | 120 H | 121 W | 122 Q | 123 B | 124 E | 125 M | 126 R | | 127 C | 128 D | 129 W | |
| 130 J | | 131 I | 132 T | 133 K | 134 W | 135 L | 136 S | 137 R | | 138 M | 139 H | 140 X | |
| | 141 N | 142 T | 143 A | 144 V | 145 J | 146 Y | 147 R | | 148 H | 149 U | 150 Q | 151 P | |
| 152 S | 153 J | 154 L | 155 M | | 156 Q | 157 S | 158 D | | 159 X | 160 W | 161 J | 162 O | |
| | 163 W | 164 N | 165 I | 166 K | | 167 E | 168 F | 169 M | | 170 W | 171 V | 172 R | |
| | 173 U | 174 E | 175 D | 176 C | 177 S | | 178 N | 179 M | 180 B | 181 C | 182 S | | |
| 183 G | 184 R | 185 H | | 186 I | 187 F | 188 M | | 189 P | 190 M | 191 O | 192 N | 193 I | |
| 194 D | 195 W | 196 U | 197 X | | 198 X | 199 T | 200 K | | 201 H | 202 L | 203 Q | | |
| 204 E | 205 Y | 206 I | 207 U | 208 A | | 209 N | 210 E | 211 Q | 212 G | | 213 Q | 214 A | |
| | 215 H | 216 Q | 217 G | 218 J | 219 A | 220 S | 221 O | 222 Y | 223 I | 224 D | 225 U | | |

(DIRECTIONS FOR SOLVING ACROSS-TICS ARE ON PAGE 276)

# ACROSS-TIC NO. 9

DEFINITIONS                                    WORDS

**A**  10th century French king,
       founder of dynasty
       (2 wds.)
       — — — — — — — — —
       184 90 193 172 71 32 163 50 4

**B**  Odorless, colorless
       hydrocarbon used as a
       refrigerant and fuel
       — — — — — —
       141 18 37 87 171 122

**C**  Popular comic strip artist
       who created "Steve
       Canyon" and "Terry and
       the Pirates" (2 wds.)
       — — — — — — — — — — —
       130 104 187 27 144 61 77 3 42 198 182 97

**D**  Exist innately as a born-in
       quality; stick to
       — — — — — —
       60 189 169 115 136 26

**E**  1930 Marion Davies movie
       (3 wds.)
       — — — — — — — — —
       155 73 168 52 109 126 15 89 33

**F**  Variety of cucumber,
       often pickled
       — — — — — — —
       190 92 11 127 62 201 116

**G**  Star Brooklyn Dodger
       Pitcher of 1940's (2 wds.)
       — — — — — — — — — — — —
       53 31 153 186 195 146 106 84 121 44 1 105

**H**  Curving inward, as a beak
       — — — — —
       107 132 29 83 156

**I**  Former official native
       name for Tokyo
       — — — — —
       6 124 142 75 96

**J**  "Like a . . . in the light of
       thought," Shelley, *To A
       Skylark* (2 wds.)
       — — — — — — — — — —
       111 34 173 80 10 68 158 120 164 192

**K**  Character in the opera
       *Parsifal*
       — — — — — — — —
       170 5 143 99 152 72 63 88

**L**  "On the . . . of Pallas,"
       Poe, *The Raven* (2 wds.)
       — — — — — — — — — —
       150 129 45 98 191 114 64 35 162 9

**M**  Crossbar connecting the
       wheels of a carriage or
       wagon
       — — — — — — — —
       85 149 137 101 43 12 167 66

**N**  Opera by Gluck
       — — — — — — —
       70 16 91 128 39 183 157

**O**  Superior ability, skill, or
       valor
       — — — — — — —
       79 28 119 176 203 51 103

**P**  Illumination of the dark
       side of the moon by
       reflected light from our
       planet
       — — — — — — — — —
       95 8 147 36 174 108 197 46 139 76

**Q**  Norse conqueror of
       Normandy; first Duke of
       Normandy (911-927)
       — — — — —
       145 14 65 47 117

**R**  U. S. national monument
       in Nebraska (2 wds.)
       — — — — — — — — — — —
       161 166 188 30 179 86 118 196 56 7 134

**S**  Present for sale or
       approval; tender; bid;
       present
       — — — — —
       181 74 110 23 125

**T**  Impossible!
       — — — — —
       94 138 59 178 13

**U**  Group of plants found in
       water, including seaweed,
       etc.
       — — — — —
       194 20 140 54 154

**V**  1948 Broadway musical by
       Lerner and Weill (2 wds.)
       — — — — — — — —
       48 93 100 180 21 81 202 160

| | | |
|---|---|---|
| **W** | Austrian composer and conductor Gustav . . . (1860-1911) | 40 185 25 159 78 177 |
| **X** | Cheered up; made proud or joyful | 41 200 165 58 131 17 |
| **Y** | Elk; wapiti | 22 135 82 55 151 |
| **Z** | Made of a common edible grain | 133 102 24 175 49 |
| **Z¹** | James M. . . .: partner of Nathaniel Currier | 113 123 19 69 |
| **Z²** | Light, dry white wine; of a German river region | 112 2 148 57 38 199 67 |

*Answers on page 496*

| 1 G | 2 Z² | 3 C | 4 A | | 5 K | 6 I | | 7 R | 8 P | 9 L | 10 J | 11 F | 12 M |
|---|---|---|---|---|---|---|---|---|---|---|---|---|---|
| | 13 T | 14 Q | 15 E | 16 N | 17 X | | 18 B | 19 Z¹ | 20 U | 21 V | | 22 Y | 23 S |
| | 24 Z | 25 W | 26 D | | 27 C | 28 O | 29 H | 30 R | 31 G | | 32 A | 33 E | 34 J |
| 35 L | 36 P | | 37 B | 38 Z² | 39 N | | 40 W | 41 X | 42 C | 43 M | 44 G | 45 L | |
| 46 P | 47 Q | 48 V | 49 Z | 50 A | 51 O | 52 E | | 53 G | 54 U | 55 Y | | 56 R | 57 Z² |
| 58 X | 59 T | 60 D | 61 C | 62 F | 63 K | 64 L | 65 Q | 66 M | | 67 Z² | 68 J | 69 Z¹ | |
| 70 N | 71 A | 72 K | | 73 E | 74 S | | 75 I | 76 P | 77 C | 78 W | 79 O | 80 J | 81 V |
| 82 Y | 83 H | | 84 G | 85 M | 86 R | | 87 B | 88 K | | 89 E | 90 A | 91 N | 92 F |
| | 93 V | 94 T | 95 P | | 96 I | 97 C | | 98 L | 99 K | 100 V | 101 M | | 102 Z |
| 103 O | | 104 C | 105 G | | 106 G | 107 H | 108 P | | 109 E | 110 S | | 111 J | 112 Z² |
| 113 Z¹ | 114 L | 115 D | | 116 F | 117 Q | 118 R | 119 O | 120 J | 121 G | | 122 B | 123 Z¹ | 124 I |
| 125 S | | 126 E | 127 F | 128 N | 129 L | 130 C | 131 X | 132 H | | 133 Z | 134 R | | 135 Y |
| 136 D | | 137 M | 138 T | 139 P | 140 U | 141 B | 142 I | | 143 K | 144 C | 145 Q | | 146 G |
| 147 P | | 148 Z² | 149 M | 150 L | 151 Y | 152 K | 153 G | 154 U | 155 E | 156 H | 157 N | 158 J | |
| 159 W | 160 V | 161 R | 162 L | | 163 A | 164 J | 165 X | 166 R | 167 M | | 168 E | 169 D | 170 K |
| 171 B | | 172 A | 173 J | | 174 P | 175 Z | | 176 O | 177 W | 178 T | 179 R | 180 V | |
| 181 S | 182 C | | 183 N | 184 A | 185 W | 186 G | | 187 C | 188 R | 189 D | 190 F | 191 L | 192 J |
| 193 A | | 194 U | 195 G | 196 R | | 197 P | 198 C | 199 Z² | | 200 X | 201 F | 202 V | 203 O |

**295**

(DIRECTIONS FOR SOLVING ACROSS-TICS ARE ON PAGE 276)

# ACROSS-TIC NO. 10

| | DEFINITIONS | WORDS |
|---|---|---|
| A | Moslem leader or ruler | ___ ___ ___ ___<br>104 183 28 65 |
| B | Coarse perennial plants of the nettle family | ___ ___ ___ ___ ___ ___<br>64 51 106 216 16 209 |
| C | 1939 Broadway musical hit by Jerome Kern (4 wds.) | ___ ___ ___ ___ ___ ___ ___ ___ ___ ___ ___ ___ ___<br>123 61 41 214 53 144 196 184 11 33 204 105 71 97 |
| D | Shameful behavior; dishonor; wickedness | ___ ___ ___ ___ ___ ___<br>182 160 113 77 191 21 |
| E | Family name of three well-known U. S. writers (Kathleen, Frank, Charles G.) | ___ ___ ___ ___ ___ ___<br>135 54 20 75 185 170 |
| F | Pertaining to the structure and shape of rock bodies | ___ ___ ___ ___ ___ ___ ___ ___ ___ ___ ___<br>167 74 132 6 217 49 112 86 207 151 36 |
| G | German existentialist (1889 - ) philosopher Martin . . . | ___ ___ ___ ___ ___ ___ ___ ___ ___<br>13 122 159 148 84 179 44 205 67 |
| H | Vertical arrangement of leaves or flowers on stems | ___ ___ ___ ___ ___ ___ ___ ___ ___ ___ ___<br>163 92 39 180 63 119 193 134 72 171 2 |
| I | Large marine snail with a spiral shell | ___ ___ ___ ___ ___<br>149 199 26 78 56 |
| J | Results; brings about; causes | ___ ___ ___ ___ ___ ___ ___<br>91 212 164 40 15 140 59 |
| K | Notwithstanding; despite that; in addition, besides | ___ ___ ___ ___ ___ ___<br>157 42 18 102 188 125 |
| L | Concealed dungeon | ___ ___ ___ ___ ___ ___ ___ ___ ___<br>89 126 1 31 50 208 103 152 66 |
| M | Cane or switch made from a common climbing palm | ___ ___ ___ ___ ___ ___<br>25 124 176 80 99 111 |
| N | Seaport in West Italy; common breed of small chicken | ___ ___ ___ ___ ___ ___ ___<br>52 24 108 194 82 187 131 |
| O | "That one talent which is . . .," Milton, *On His Blindness* (3 wds.) | ___ ___ ___ ___ ___ ___ ___ ___ ___ ___ ___<br>145 96 34 198 81 120 10 213 107 85 156 |
| P | Industrial city in Wisconsin | ___ ___ ___ ___ ___ ___ ___<br>138 201 23 130 88 162 95 |
| Q | 1955 Broadway play by S. N. Behrman | ___ ___ ___ ___ ___<br>129 114 17 43 175 |
| R | Major Canadian city, river, and Indian tribe | ___ ___ ___ ___ ___ ___<br>192 38 22 146 139 202 |
| S | Salve or ointment | ___ ___ ___ ___ ___ ___ ___<br>100 147 215 7 57 166 94 |
| T | Paraphrases; states differently; edits | ___ ___ ___ ___ ___ ___ ___<br>118 161 133 48 8 206 76 |
| U | "Lean-looked prophets whisper . . .," *Richard II* (2 wds.) | ___ ___ ___ ___ ___ ___ ___ ___ ___ ___ ___ ___ ___<br>62 117 154 142 46 178 79 203 121 30 218 186 5 |
| V | Group; mass; total | ___ ___ ___ ___ ___ ___ ___ ___ ___ ___<br>177 87 136 58 200 101 37 115 169 128 9 |
| W | Supporting frameworks; railroad bridges | ___ ___ ___ ___ ___ ___ ___ ___<br>98 109 195 32 12 158 143 68 |
| X | Large Indian city (population over 500,000) opposite Calcutta | ___ ___ ___ ___ ___ ___<br>4 211 27 150 110 73 |

Answers on page 496

**Y** Persons highly sensitive to fine arts, beauty, culture, etc.

—219 —47 —190 —137 —14 —69 —174 —93

**Z** Cruel; lacking compassion

—60 —19 —172 —116 —168 —153 —83 —197

**Z¹** Nation-wide Laurel and Hardy fan club named after their 1934 movie (4 wds.)

—29 —141 —189 —210 —45 —155 —3 —173 —70 —90 —127 —35 —165 —55 —181

Grid:

Row 1: 1 L | 2 H | 3 Z¹ | 4 X | 5 U | 6 F | 7 S | 8 T | 9 V | 10 O
Row 2: 11 C | 12 W | 13 G | 14 Y | 15 J | 16 B | 17 Q | 18 K | 19 Z | 20 E | 21 D
Row 3: 22 R | 23 P | 24 N | 25 M | 26 I | 27 X | 28 A | 29 Z¹ | 30 U | 31 L | 32 W | 33 C
Row 4: 34 O | 35 Z¹ | 36 F | 37 V | 38 R | 39 H | 40 J | 41 C | 42 K | 43 Q | 44 G
Row 5: 45 Z¹ | 46 U | 47 Y | 48 T | 49 F | 50 L | 51 B | 52 N | 53 C | 54 E | 55 Z¹ | 56 I
Row 6: 57 S | 58 V | 59 J | 60 Z | 61 C | 62 U | 63 H | 64 B | 65 A | 66 L | 67 G | 68 W
Row 7: 69 Y | 70 Z¹ | 71 C | 72 H | 73 X | 74 F | 75 E | 76 T | 77 D | 78 I | 79 U | 80 M
Row 8: 81 O | 82 N | 83 Z | 84 G | 85 O | 86 F | 87 V | 88 P | 89 L | 90 Z¹ | 91 J | 92 H | 93 Y
Row 9: 94 S | 95 P | 96 O | 97 C | 98 W | 99 M | 100 S | 101 V | 102 K | 103 L | 104 A
Row 10: 105 C | 106 B | 107 O | 108 N | 109 W | 110 X | 111 M | 112 F | 113 D | 114 Q | 115 V | 116 Z | 117 U
Row 11: 118 T | 119 H | 120 O | 121 U | 122 G | 123 C | 124 M | 125 K | 126 L | 127 Z¹ | 128 V
Row 12: 129 Q | 130 P | 131 N | 132 F | 133 T | 134 H | 135 E | 136 V | 137 Y | 138 P | 139 R
Row 13: 140 J | 141 Z¹ | 142 U | 143 W | 144 C | 145 O | 146 R | 147 S | 148 G | 149 I | 150 X
Row 14: 151 F | 152 L | 153 Z | 154 U | 155 Z¹ | 156 O | 157 K | 158 W | 159 G | 160 D | 161 T
Row 15: 162 P | 163 H | 164 J | 165 Z¹ | 166 S | 167 F | 168 Z | 169 V | 170 E | 171 H | 172 Z
Row 16: 173 Z¹ | 174 Y | 175 Q | 176 M | 177 V | 178 U | 179 G | 180 H | 181 Z¹ | 182 D | 183 A | 184 C
Row 17: 185 E | 186 U | 187 N | 188 K | 189 Z¹ | 190 Y | 191 D | 192 R | 193 H | 194 N | 195 W | 196 C | 197 Z
Row 18: 198 O | 199 I | 200 V | 201 P | 202 R | 203 U | 204 C | 205 G | 206 T | 207 F | 208 L | 209 B
Row 19: 210 Z¹ | 211 X | 212 J | 213 O | 214 C | 215 S | 216 B | 217 F | 218 U | 219 Y

(DIRECTIONS FOR SOLVING ACROSS-TICS ARE ON PAGE 276)

# ACROSS-TIC NO. 11

DEFINITIONS          WORDS

**A**   Smooth, hard-twisted wool yarn, often used in clothing

—167 —104 —118 —63 —14 —86 —188

**B**   Serving to prove

—102 —24 —151 —54 —142 —112 —133 —183

**C**   Plethora; sudden outpouring; flash flood

—165 —123 —53 —20 —146

**D**   Foolishness; nonsense (colloq.)

—103 —125 —198 —5 —181 —35 —184 —159

**E**   " . . . the wood ere thou canst limn with it?," Thompson, *The Hound of Heaven* (3 wds.)

—64 —12 —80 —193 —101 —157 —3 —177 —75 —196 —71 —31

**F**   Inflexible; hardhearted; stubborn

—89 —140 —55 —114 —186 —178 —28 —189

**G**   Any of the cud-chewing animals; meditative, thoughtful

—124 —100 —139 —38 —7 —158 —90 —176

**H**   Person of high ideals; moral teacher

—197 —136 —29 —41 —56 —107 —13 —156

**I**   Famous golfer who has won over $1 million in prizes (2 wds.)

—108 —79 —135 —34 —18 —152 —173 —131 —50 —91

**J**   Digestive chamber of an animal's stomach

—65 —99 —168 —121 —1 —145 —185 —11

**K**   Contemporary British composer, singer, recording star, and Broadway playwright

—19 —141 —26 —179 —52 —122

**L**   Lacking self-confidence; shy; timid

—155 —62 —46 —116 —98 —8 —83 —40 —195

**M**   Outstanding U. S. female tennis star, 1938-40 national titlist (2 wds.)

—76 —15 —147 —61 —194 —4 —36 —97 —126 —150 —174

**N**   Orange-yellow color; plant of the iris family; food flavor used in bouillabaise

—160 —6 —30 —115 —82 —68 —137

**O**   Start; initial stage

—39 —69 —190 —119 —96

**P**   Ancient stringed musical instruments

—67 —32 —92 —164 —130

**Q**   Establish limits; state the meaning of

—120 —49 —105 —23 —77 —149

**R**   Tristram's beloved

—134 —113 —21 —170 —88 —74

**S**   In Greek myth, the god of the east wind

—154 —81 —48 —109 —72

**T**   Solitary; hermit

—57 —9 —93 —180 —169 —166 —47

**U**   Black and lustrous; famous poem by Edgar Allan Poe

—45 —106 —153 —128 —95

**V**   Correct a text

—111 —129 —44 —175 —171

| | Clue | Letters |
|---|---|---|
| **W** | U. S. gunboat, sunk by the Japanese in 1937 | 191 138 42 17 87 |
| **X** | Esoteric; concealed; mysterious | 94 51 2 161 127 37 |
| **Y** | Framework of a ship's sails | 110 27 148 78 60 132 70 |
| **Z** | "That I am meek and gentle with . . . ," says Antony (2 wds.) | 43 73 16 66 25 182 144 59 162 85 172 10 33 |
| **Z¹** | Salt or ester derived from the hard, glassy mineral found in quartz, flint, and sand | 187 58 22 192 163 143 84 117 |

*Answers on page 496*

| 1 J | | 2 X | 3 E | 4 M | 5 D | 6 N | 7 G | 8 L | 9 T | 10 Z | | 11 J | 12 E |
|---|---|---|---|---|---|---|---|---|---|---|---|---|---|
| 13 H | 14 A | | 15 M | 16 Z | 17 W | 18 I | 19 K | | 20 C | 21 R | | 22 Z¹ | 23 Q |
| 24 B | 25 Z | | 26 K | 27 Y | 28 F | 29 H | | 30 N | 31 E | 32 P | 33 Z | 34 I | 35 D |
| 36 M | 37 X | 38 G | 39 O | 40 L | | 41 H | 42 W | 43 Z | 44 V | 45 U | 46 L | 47 T | 48 S |
| 49 Q | 50 I | 51 X | 52 K | | 53 C | 54 B | 55 F | | 56 H | 57 T | 58 Z¹ | 59 Z | 60 Y |
| 61 M | 62 L | 63 A | 64 E | | 65 J | 66 Z | | 67 P | 68 N | 69 O | 70 Y | | 71 E |
| 72 S | | 73 Z | 74 R | | 75 E | 76 M | 77 Q | | 78 Y | 79 I | | 80 E | 81 S |
| 82 N | 83 L | | 84 Z¹ | 85 Z | 86 A | 87 W | | 88 R | 89 F | | 90 G | 91 I | 92 P |
| | 93 T | 94 X | 95 U | 96 O | 97 M | 98 L | 99 J | 100 G | 101 E | 102 B | | 103 D | 104 A |
| | 105 Q | 106 U | 107 H | 108 I | 109 S | 110 Y | 111 V | | 112 B | | 113 R | 114 F | 115 N |
| 116 L | 117 Z¹ | 118 A | 119 O | 120 Q | | 121 J | 122 K | | 123 C | 124 G | 125 D | 126 M | 127 X |
| 128 U | 129 V | 130 P | | 131 I | 132 Y | | 133 B | 134 R | 135 I | 136 H | 137 N | 138 W | 139 G |
| | 140 F | 141 K | 142 B | 143 Z¹ | 144 Z | 145 J | 146 C | | 147 M | | 148 Y | 149 Q | 150 M |
| 151 B | 152 I | 153 U | 154 S | 155 L | | 156 H | 157 E | 158 G | 159 D | | 160 N | 161 X | 162 Z |
| 163 Z¹ | 164 P | 165 C | 166 T | | 167 A | 168 J | 169 T | 170 R | 171 V | | 172 Z | 173 I | 174 M |
| 175 V | 176 G | 177 E | 178 F | 179 K | 180 T | 181 D | | 182 Z | 183 B | | 184 D | 185 J | 186 F |
| 187 Z¹ | | 188 A | 189 F | 190 O | 191 W | 192 Z¹ | 193 E | 194 M | | 195 L | 196 E | 197 H | 198 D |

(DIRECTIONS FOR SOLVING ACROSS-TICS ARE ON PAGE 276)

# ACROSS-TIC NO. 12

DEFINITIONS                    WORDS

**A** Famous character in Dostoevsky's *Crime and Punishment*
83  135  7  28  119  59  170  143  15  95  78

**B** Nashville's "Grand Old . . ."
19  156  49  162

**C** Exultant; taking malicious pleasure in one's own success
189  133  42  84  152  110  18  129

**D** Spent the summer
116  70  142  169  154  62  8  105  126

**E** Gilbert and Sullivan operetta
164  107  56  67  127  81  96  14  46

**F** Inept; gauche; clumsy
190  145  11  31  50  185  165

**G** ". . . of our discontent made glorious summer," *Richard III* (4 wds.)
128  101  40  68  109  136  71  29  61  92  3  144  112  168

**H** Fishermen's barbed spears
82  13  175  99  64

**I** Spacious, often tree-lined area for public traffic; wide roadway
174  17  22  125  148  43  89  111  192

**J** Kurt Weill-Maxwell Anderson Broadway musical success (4 wds.)
113  160  87  179  32  55  47  74  197  147  93  2  137  98

**K** Brought a vessel into or nearer the wind
94  21  149  131  48  86

**L** Island known for its huge lake of asphalt
33  77  158  85  124  4  138  166

**M** System using and combining known data to form new information
104  184  167  45  9  151  108  176  75

**N** Literary blunders or goofs; mistakes
155  38  24  132  103  54

**O** Swiss canton, population 75,000
20  44  173  181  63  139

**P** Capital of Outer Mongolia (2 wds.)
123  5  117  80  140  39  69  182  100

**Q** Civil War name given to a deserter or shirker
25  130  159  53  122  146  10  115

**R** Process of cell division
51  16  88  106  193  35  183

**S** Picked out in a crowd or group; spotted
150  188  12  79  195  91

**T** Camping or hiking necessity
157  76  1  60  178  163  41  97

**U** Indian name for a river landing-place or crossing
171  194  58  30

**V** Quivering
26  121  57  114  172  134  34

**W** "This is the forest primeval, the . . . ," Longfellow, *Evangeline* 2 wds.)
102  141  27  191  120  196  153  66  73  52  186  90  6  37

Answers on page 497

**X** Divert; amuse; please; delight

$\overline{187}$ $\overline{118}$ $\overline{180}$ $\overline{23}$ $\overline{177}$ $\overline{36}$ $\overline{65}$ $\overline{72}$ $\overline{161}$

| 1 T | 2 J | 3 G | 4 L | 5 P | 6 W | 7 A | 8 D | 9 M | 10 Q | 11 F |
|---|---|---|---|---|---|---|---|---|---|---|
| 12 S | 13 H | 14 E | 15 A | | 16 R | 17 I | | 18 C | 19 B | |
| 20 O | 21 K | 22 I | 23 X | 24 N | 25 Q | 26 V | 27 W | 28 A | 29 G | 30 U |
| 31 F | 32 J | 33 L | 34 V | | 35 R | 36 X | 37 W | | 38 N | 39 P | 40 G |
| | 41 T | 42 C | 43 I | 44 O | 45 M | 46 E | 47 J | 48 K | | 49 B | 50 F |
| 51 R | 52 W | 53 Q | | 54 N | 55 J | 56 E | | 57 V | 58 U | 59 A | 60 T |
| 61 G | 62 D | 63 O | 64 H | | 65 X | 66 W | 67 E | | 68 G | 69 P | 70 D |
| | 71 G | 72 X | 73 W | 74 J | | 75 M | 76 T | 77 L | 78 A | 79 S | 80 P |
| 81 E | | 82 H | 83 A | 84 C | 85 L | 86 K | 87 J | 88 R | 89 I | 90 W | 91 S |
| | 92 G | 93 J | | 94 K | 95 A | 96 E | 97 T | 98 J | | 99 H | 100 P |
| 101 G | 102 W | | 103 N | 104 M | 105 D | | 106 R | 107 E | 108 M | 109 G | 110 C |
| 111 I | 112 G | | 113 J | 114 V | 115 Q | 116 D | | 117 P | 118 X | |
| 119 A | 120 W | 121 V | 122 Q | 123 P | 124 L | 125 I | 126 D | 127 E | 128 G | 129 C | 130 Q |
| 131 K | | 132 N | 133 C | 134 V | 135 A | 136 G | 137 J | 138 L | 139 O | | 140 P |
| 141 W | 142 D | | 143 A | 144 G | | 145 F | 146 Q | 147 J | | 148 I |
| | 149 K | 150 S | 151 M | 152 C | 153 W | 154 D | 155 N | | 156 B | 157 T | 158 L |
| 159 Q | 160 J | 161 X | | 162 B | 163 T | 164 E | 165 F | | 166 L | 167 M | 168 G |
| 169 D | 170 A | 171 U | | 172 V | 173 O | 174 I | | 175 H | 176 M | 177 X | 178 T |
| 179 J | | 180 X | 181 O | 182 P | | 183 R | 184 M | 185 F | 186 W | 187 X | 188 S |
| | 189 C | 190 F | 191 W | 192 I | 193 R | | 194 U | 195 S | 196 W | 197 J |

# ACROSS-TIC NO. 13

DEFINITIONS        WORDS

**A**   Parasitic plant which grows on another plant

—96 —122 —110 —42 —172 —207 —216 —12

**B**   U. S. national monument in California (2 wds.)

—89 —218 —30 —10 —206 —66 —125 —81 —151 —178 —113 —143 —159 —51

**C**   Famous race horse, 1941 Triple Crown winner

—170 —50 —210 —71 —5 —106 —86 —197 —147

**D**   Get in the way of; block, restrain

—164 —111 —136 —20 —33 —196

**E**   Study of the problems of aged people

—17 —182 —79 —137 —53 —37 —220 —161 —108

**F**   Rodgers and Hart hit song from "Pal Joey"; enchanted

—158 —72 —208 —185 —179 —134 —22 —123 —41

**G**   Book, movie, and Broadway play by Clarence Day (3 wds.)

—4 —160 —104 —40 —188 —24 —130 —84 —57 —177 —225 —93 —29 —114

**H**   Coarse, abusive, insulting language

—202 —144 —15 —59 —219 —92 —213 —35 —115

**I**   Bubble; churn and foam; boil up

—117 —169 —56 —19 —217 —80

**J**   Natural unsaturated hydrocarbon found in shark livers

—116 —25 —140 —204 —156 —64 —76 —175

**K**   U. S. national forest in Washington state, named after a famous conservationist (2 wds.)

—145 —128 —184 —2 —87 —32 —121 —47 —189 —97 —171 —7 —152 —77

**L**   Gathered or derived from many sources

—228 —21 —146 —209 —101 —83 —223 —60

**M**   "This seat of Mars, . . . ," *Richard II* (3 wds.)

—95 —180 —199 —54 —131 —6 —191 —85 —174 —120 —141 —31 —107

**N**   Having a collar-like or ringlike band around the neck

—61 —165 —195 —73 —26 —14 —190 —149

**O**   Narrow strip of land which connects two larger ones, e.g., Panama

—62 —48 —194 —212 —227 —74 —28

**P**   To wink

—224 —154 —133 —109 —3 —163 —94

**Q**   Hearty, loud burst of laughter

—211 —118 —82 —70 —46 —150

**R**   Hard, chewy British candies (plural)

—222 —192 —58 —183 —34 —75 —13

**S**   South-west African native or language

—45 —173 —67 —9 —187 —214 —201 —103 —49

**T**   Chemical compound, related to but physically different from another

—16 —129 —91 —105 —181 —119

**U**   Painfully; persistently; annoyingly

—90 —162 —142 —18 —65 —168 —138 —198 —102

**V**   Common sugar

—215 —126 —78 —203 —157 —221 —36

**W**   Lines of junction, as in cloth

—176 —43 —155 —52 —167

**X**    Extract by boiling down

<u>98</u> <u>112</u> <u>153</u> <u>1</u> <u>186</u> <u>55</u>

**Y**    Lydian queen served by Hercules (Greek mythology)

<u>124</u> <u>11</u> <u>39</u> <u>68</u> <u>132</u> <u>205</u> <u>99</u>

**Z**    Structural unit of the body's nervous system

<u>166</u> <u>135</u> <u>193</u> <u>88</u> <u>38</u> <u>23</u>

**Z¹**    Hall of Fame fullback from Stanford U., once scored 40 points in a professional game (2 wds.)

<u>27</u> <u>139</u> <u>100</u> <u>226</u> <u>8</u> <u>148</u> <u>69</u> <u>63</u> <u>127</u> <u>44</u> <u>200</u>

*Answers on page 497*

---

Grid (cell number and letter):

Row 1: 1 X · 2 K · 3 P · 4 G · 5 C · 6 M · 7 K · 8 Z¹

Row 2: 9 S · 10 B · 11 Y · 12 A · 13 R · 14 N · 15 H · 16 T · 17 E · 18 U · 19 I · 20 D

Row 3: 21 L · 22 F · 23 Z · 24 G · 25 J · 26 N · 27 Z¹ · 28 O · 29 G · 30 B · 31 M · 32 K

Row 4: 33 D · 34 R · 35 H · 36 V · 37 E · 38 Z · 39 Y · 40 G · 41 F · 42 A · 43 W · 44 Z¹ · 45 S

Row 5: 46 Q · 47 K · 48 O · 49 S · 50 C · 51 B · 52 W · 53 E · 54 M · 55 X · 56 I

Row 6: 57 G · 58 R · 59 H · 60 L · 61 N · 62 O · 63 Z¹ · 64 J · 65 U · 66 B · 67 S · 68 Y

Row 7: 69 Z¹ · 70 Q · 71 C · 72 F · 73 N · 74 O · 75 R · 76 J · 77 K · 78 V · 79 E · 80 I

Row 8: 81 B · 82 Q · 83 L · 84 G · 85 M · 86 C · 87 K · 88 Z · 89 B · 90 U

Row 9: 91 T · 92 H · 93 G · 94 P · 95 M · 96 A · 97 K · 98 X · 99 Y · 100 Z¹ · 101 L · 102 U

Row 10: 103 S · 104 G · 105 T · 106 C · 107 M · 108 E · 109 P · 110 A · 111 I · 112 X · 113 B

Row 11: 114 G · 115 H · 116 J · 117 I · 118 Q · 119 T · 120 M · 121 K · 122 A · 123 F · 124 Y · 125 B · 126 V

Row 12: 127 Z¹ · 128 K · 129 T · 130 G · 131 M · 132 Y · 133 P · 134 F · 135 Z · 136 D · 137 E

Row 13: 138 U · 139 Z¹ · 140 J · 141 M · 142 U · 143 B · 144 H · 145 K · 146 L · 147 C · 148 Z¹ · 149 N

Row 14: 150 Q · 151 B · 152 K · 153 X · 154 P · 155 W · 156 J · 157 V · 158 F · 159 B · 160 G · 161 E

Row 15: 162 U · 163 P · 164 D · 165 N · 166 Z · 167 W · 168 U · 169 I · 170 C · 171 K · 172 A · 173 S

Row 16: 174 M · 175 J · 176 W · 177 G · 178 B · 179 F · 180 M · 181 T · 182 E · 183 R · 184 K

Row 17: 185 F · 186 X · 187 S · 188 G · 189 K · 190 N · 191 M · 192 R · 193 Z · 194 O · 195 N · 196 D

Row 18: 197 C · 198 U · 199 M · 200 Z¹ · 201 S · 202 H · 203 V · 204 J · 205 Y · 206 B · 207 A · 208 F · 209 L

Row 19: 210 C · 211 Q · 212 O · 213 H · 214 S · 215 V · 216 A · 217 I · 218 B · 219 H · 220 E · 221 V

Row 20: 222 R · 223 L · 224 P · 225 G · 226 Z¹ · 227 O · 228 L

(DIRECTIONS FOR SOLVING ACROSS-TICS ARE ON PAGE 276)

# ACROSS-TIC NO. 14

DEFINITIONS          WORDS

**A**   Sprinkle; moisten; dampen

— — — — —
136 77 172 16 117

**B**   Pioneer U. S. comic strip artist, creator of "The Yellow Kid" (2 wds.)

123 90 129 35 185 164 72 18 200 145 5 79 189 154 47

**C**   Toward the rear (nautical term)

105 159 48 141 82

**D**   1953 Clark Gable movie (4 wds.)

19 66 127 3 201 190 124 52 40 88 107 32

**E**   Eliminates; gets rid of (3 wds.)

167 39 148 46 112 13 125 62 1 139 93 151

**F**   Famous confederate general (1817-1872) in Civil War

160 111 71 87 8

**G**   Perform a lawn chore; install new grass

10 61 99 176 25 155

**H**   Talkative; wordy

177 23 106 192 157 67 41

**I**   Colorless, oily hydrocarbon used in resins

49 195 26 178 96 175

**J**   U. S. national forest in Alabama

103 152 181 184 17 33 92

**K**   Character in the opera *Cavalleria Rusticana*

114 168 50 101 9 126 153

**L**   Prayer

188 15 118 76 43 179

**M**   Having a good memory; holding on to

204 120 74 11 156 84 128 162 100

**N**   Gershwin show-stopper with which Ethel Merman began her Broadway career (3 wds.)

21 34 161 130 80 6 149 110 60 183

**O**   Swedish runner who held world record for mile, 1943-44 (2 wds.)

81 24 199 137 56 166 191 64 98 150 113 37 12

**P**   Indian watercourse; gully

102 97 138 28 144 197

**Q**   "The . . . ," 1968 Howard Sackler prize-winning play on Broadway (3 wds.); Caucasian fistic contender

182 65 163 75 59 89 2 194 173 116 143 53 78 95

**R**   The edible underground stem of the taro; source of poi

108 22 42 131

**S**   The area above or at the head of a glacier

31 171 70 55

**T**   "No . . . his wrath allay," Scott, *Rokeby* (2 wds.)

36 63 180 186 7 170 174 142 29 198 44 121

**U**   Reduces; drops; brings down; lessens

169 27 187 140 69 202

**V**   Fuel and anesthetic of the olefin series

68 158 94 205 57 193 135 83

**W**   Foul-smelling; injurious

54 14 122 147 109 91 133 38

**X** "To sail beyond the sunset, . . . of all the western stars," Tennyson, *Ulysses* (3 wds.)

73  4  119  146  104  30  86  134  196  115  51

**Y** Minor female character in *The Merchant of Venice*

45  203  132  165  20  58  85

*Answers on page 497*

| | | | | | | | | | | | | |
|---|---|---|---|---|---|---|---|---|---|---|---|---|
| 1 E | 2 Q | 3 D | 4 X | ■ | 5 B | 6 N | 7 T | 8 F | 9 K | 10 G | 11 M | 12 O |
| ■ | 13 E | 14 W | 15 L | 16 A | ■ | 17 J | 18 B | 19 D | 20 Y | 21 N | 22 R | 23 H |
| 24 O | 25 G | 26 I | ■ | 27 U | 28 P | 29 T | ■ | 30 X | 31 S | 32 D | 33 J | 34 N |
| 35 B | ■ | 36 T | 37 O | ■ | 38 W | 39 E | 40 D | 41 H | ■ | 42 R | 43 L | 44 T |
| 45 Y | 46 E | 47 B | 48 C | 49 I | 50 K | 51 X | ■ | 52 D | 53 Q | ■ | 54 W | 55 S |
| 56 O | 57 V | 58 Y | ■ | 59 Q | 60 N | 61 G | 62 E | ■ | 63 T | 64 O | 65 Q | 66 D |
| ■ | 67 H | 68 V | 69 U | 70 S | 71 F | 72 B | ■ | 73 X | 74 M | ■ | 75 Q | ■ |
| 76 L | 77 A | 78 Q | 79 B | 80 N | 81 O | 82 C | 83 V | ■ | 84 M | 85 Y | 86 X | 87 F |
| 88 D | ■ | 89 Q | 90 B | 91 W | 92 J | ■ | 93 E | 94 V | 95 Q | ■ | 96 I | 97 P |
| 98 O | 99 G | 100 M | ■ | 101 K | 102 P | ■ | 103 J | 104 X | 105 C | 106 H | 107 D | 108 R |
| ■ | 109 W | 110 N | ■ | 111 F | 112 E | 113 O | ■ | 114 K | 115 X | 116 Q | ■ | 117 A |
| 118 L | 119 X | 120 M | 121 T | 122 W | 123 B | 124 D | 125 E | 126 K | ■ | 127 D | 128 M | 129 B |
| 130 N | 131 R | 132 Y | 133 W | 134 X | 135 V | ■ | 136 A | 137 O | 138 P | 139 E | 140 U | 141 C |
| ■ | 142 T | 143 Q | 144 P | 145 B | ■ | 146 X | 147 W | 148 E | 149 N | ■ | 150 O | 151 E |
| 152 J | 153 K | 154 B | 155 G | ■ | 156 M | 157 H | 158 V | ■ | 159 C | 160 F | ■ | 161 N |
| 162 M | 163 Q | 164 B | 165 Y | 166 O | 167 E | 168 K | 169 U | 170 T | 171 S | 172 A | ■ | 173 Q |
| 174 T | 175 I | ■ | 176 G | 177 H | 178 I | 179 L | 180 T | 181 J | 182 Q | ■ | 183 N | 184 J |
| 185 B | 186 T | ■ | 187 U | 188 L | 189 B | 190 D | 191 O | ■ | 192 H | 193 V | ■ | 194 Q |
| 195 I | ■ | 196 X | 197 P | 198 T | ■ | 199 O | 200 B | 201 D | 202 U | 203 Y | 204 M | 205 V |

(DIRECTIONS FOR SOLVING ACROSS-TICS ARE ON PAGE 276)

# ACROSS-TIC NO. 15

DEFINITIONS                                    WORDS

A   Well-known U. S. Indian       ___ ___ ___ ___ ___ ___ ___ ___
    tribe; most famous Charlie    103 158  32  97  79   7  131 118
    Barnet recording

B   Sin; crime; act which         ___ ___ ___ ___ ___ ___ ___
    causes resentment or           89  53 100  30 144  10 110
    anger

C   Major river of western        ___ ___ ___ ___ ___
    Europe beloved by the          50 116 156  17 104
    Germans

D   Knob; knot; swelling;         ___ ___ ___ ___
    point of concentration         70 168 136  16

E   Send out; give forth;         ___ ___ ___ ___
    discharge                      49  15 160  90

F   "The . . . winds slowly o'er  ___ ___ ___ ___ ___ ___ ___ ___ ___ ___
    the lea," Thomas Gray,        130 153  35 178 189 162  25 183  94  59
    *Elegy* (2 wds.)

G   Spaced in from a margin;      ___ ___ ___ ___ ___ ___ ___ ___
    made a hollow in              140 170  39  44 193  73   3  83

H   Juniors and seniors,          ___ ___ ___ ___ ___ ___ ___ ___ ___ ___ ___ ___ ___
    collectively                  139  76 108  62  31 146 122   9 195 167 184  99  43

I   Gertrude Lawrence and         ___ ___ ___ ___ ___ ___ ___ ___ ___ ___ ___ ___
    Yul Brynner duet from          45   2  69 151 129 113  28 171  86 182 121  47
    "The King and I" (3 wds.)

J   Poem by Robert Louis          ___ ___ ___ ___ ___ ___ ___
    Stevenson; funeral mass       126 181 138  14  42 176  88

K   Outstanding Japanese          ___ ___ ___ ___ ___ ___ ___ ___
    admiral of W W II;            185   5 107 125  87  96  77  54
    commanded enemy forces
    at Midway

L   "Flow gently, sweet . . .":   ___ ___ ___ ___ ___
    river in Robert Burns' song    21  33 159 106  98

M   Salamander                    ___ ___ ___ ___
                                  179 194 169  24

N   Declare to be genuine or      ___ ___ ___ ___ ___ ___
    true; witness; certify         84  60  18 143 124  72

O   Colloquial term for a wife    ___ ___ ___ ___ ___ ___ ___ ___ ___ ___
    (2 wds.)                       51 123   4 166  34 187  61 149 191 155

P   Title role played by          ___ ___ ___ ___ ___ ___ ___ ___
    Chuck Connors in a long-       63 165 154  20  52 142 134  82
    running television series

Q   To be about to happen; to     ___ ___ ___ ___ ___ ___
    be imminent                    38  75 174  26 161 180

R   To do something               ___ ___ ___ ___ ___ ___ ___ ___
    superficially, not seriously   23 147 175  95 109  56 120  68
    (2 wds.)

S   Yield; concede; allow an      ___ ___ ___ ___ ___ ___
    opponent to win (2 wds.)       36 192 117  67 128  22

T   Understanding or              ___ ___ ___ ___ ___ ___ ___
    agreement between              66 135 190 173  46 127 112
    nations

U   Common term for a gray        ___ ___ ___ ___ ___
    or brown cat with dark        115  19 150  65 133
    stripes

V   Crush; make helpless; rout    ___ ___ ___ ___ ___ ___ ___ ___ ___
                                   12  48 172 132  29 177 152  41  85

**W** George . . . : Pulitzer Prize-winning U. S. poet

‾‾ ‾‾ ‾‾ ‾‾ ‾‾
101 148 141 64 13

**X** The press and journalists, collectively (2 wds.)

‾‾ ‾‾ ‾‾ ‾‾ ‾‾ ‾‾ ‾‾ ‾‾ ‾‾ ‾‾ ‾‾ ‾‾
186 163 37 27 111 57 81 6 145 92 1 74

**Y** Frank Sinatra and Gene Kelly starred in this musical; naval song (2 wds.)

‾‾ ‾‾ ‾‾ ‾‾ ‾‾ ‾‾ ‾‾ ‾‾ ‾‾ ‾‾ ‾‾ ‾‾ ‾‾
58 164 105 91 188 102 80 71 8 40 93 157 119

**Z** Send money in payment; forgive, pardon

‾‾ ‾‾ ‾‾ ‾‾ ‾‾
55 137 11 114 78

## Answers on page 497

| 1 X | 2 I | 3 G | ■ | 4 O | 5 K | 6 X | 7 A | ■ | 8 Y | 9 H | 10 B | ■ |
| 11 Z | 12 V | 13 W | 14 J | 15 E | 16 D | 17 C | 18 N | 19 U | 20 P | ■ | 21 L | 22 S |
| 23 R | ■ | 24 M | 25 F | 26 Q | 27 X | 28 I | ■ | 29 V | 30 B | 31 H | 32 A | ■ |
| 33 L | 34 O | 35 F | ■ | 36 S | 37 X | 38 Q | 39 G | 40 Y | 41 V | 42 J | 43 H | 44 G |
| 45 I | ■ | 46 T | 47 I | 48 V | 49 E | 50 C | ■ | 51 O | 52 P | 53 B | 54 K | 55 Z |
| 56 R | ■ | 57 X | 58 Y | 59 F | ■ | 60 N | 61 O | 62 H | 63 P | 64 W | ■ | 65 U |
| 66 T | 67 S | 68 R | ■ | 69 I | 70 D | ■ | 71 Y | 72 N | 73 G | 74 X | 75 Q | 76 H |
| 77 K | ■ | 78 Z | 79 A | ■ | 80 Y | 81 X | 82 P | 83 G | ■ | 84 N | ■ | 85 V |
| 86 I | 87 K | 88 J | 89 B | 90 E | 91 Y | ■ | 92 X | 93 Y | 94 F | 95 R | 96 K | 97 A |
| 98 L | 99 H | ■ | 100 B | 101 W | 102 Y | 103 A | 104 C | ■ | 105 Y | 106 L | 107 K | 108 H |
| 109 R | 110 B | 111 X | 112 T | ■ | 113 I | 114 Z | 115 U | 116 C | ■ | 117 S | 118 A | 119 Y |
| 120 R | 121 I | 122 H | 123 O | 124 N | ■ | 125 K | 126 J | 127 T | 128 S | 129 I | 130 D | 131 A |
| 132 V | 133 U | ■ | 134 P | 135 T | 136 D | ■ | 137 Z | 138 J | 139 H | 140 G | 141 W | 142 P |
| 143 N | 144 B | 145 X | ■ | 146 H | 147 R | 148 W | 149 O | 150 U | 151 I | 152 V | ■ | 153 F |
| 154 P | ■ | 155 O | 156 C | 157 Y | 158 A | 159 L | 160 E | 161 Q | 162 F | ■ | 163 X | 164 Y |
| ■ | 165 P | 166 O | 167 H | ■ | 168 D | 169 M | 170 G | ■ | 171 I | 172 V | 173 T | 174 Q |
| ■ | 175 R | 176 J | 177 V | 178 F | 179 M | 180 Q | ■ | 181 J | 182 I | 183 F | 184 H | 185 K |
| ■ | 186 X | 187 O | 188 Y | 189 F | 190 T | ■ | 191 O | 192 S | 193 G | 194 M | 195 H | ■ |

**307**

(DIRECTIONS FOR SOLVING ACROSS-TICS ARE ON PAGE 276)

# ACROSS-TIC NO. 16

DEFINITIONS WORDS

**A** Show business awards
(colloq.)

—— —— —— —— —— ——
121 77 133 21 103 66

**B** Besought

—— —— —— —— —— —— —— ——
79 155 59 201 99 13 168 112

**C** Encase

—— —— —— —— —— —— ——
146 10 84 52 122 70 173

**D** Species of wheat

—— —— —— —— ——
191 58 1 25 172

**E** Cancel out

—— —— —— —— —— —— ——
192 50 118 24 110 41 145

**F** Conformity of a report to
actual past events and
facts

—— —— —— —— —— —— —— —— —— —— ——
109 62 177 29 182 199 7 164 92 71 151

**G** "Nymph, in thy . . . be all
my sins remembered,"
says Hamlet

—— —— —— —— —— —— ——
30 61 176 189 195 90 8

**H** Necessary assets or means

—— —— —— —— —— —— —— —— —— —— ——
67 125 194 31 180 44 141 159 83 200 94

**I** Deviating from a norm

—— —— —— —— —— —— —— —— ——
165 36 97 6 153 82 107 143 56

**J** Historical novel by
Kenneth Roberts (3 wds.)

—— —— —— —— —— —— —— —— —— —— —— ——
46 93 140 53 150 76 32 131 156 3 197 114

**K** "City for . . . ," 1940 James
Cagney-Ann Sheridan
movie

—— —— —— —— —— —— —— ——
193 198 48 128 35 106 88 19

**L** Toothed wheel

—— —— —— —— —— —— ——
85 27 91 124 184 160 69

**M** Sway; wave

—— —— —— —— —— —— —— ——
132 75 154 42 142 96 9 171

**N** In short bursts; made up
of abrupt, brief sounds

—— —— —— —— —— —— —— ——
87 179 104 28 115 4 144 57

**O** Pass; avoid

—— —— —— —— —— —— ——
60 134 20 98 45 113 163

**P** Make more intense;
*extend*

—— —— —— —— —— ——
49 38 17 149 86 161

**Q** U. S. Revolutionary War
hero (1738-1789) (2 wds.)

—— —— —— —— —— —— —— —— —— ——
55 181 72 152 33 166 102 5 123 158

**R** Tontine specialty

—— —— —— —— —— —— —— —— ——
119 80 108 175 167 162 22 37 89

**S** Small cup or mug

—— —— —— —— —— ——
65 139 23 12 178 126

**T** Brash, bold behavior

—— —— —— —— —— —— —— —— —— ——
130 26 95 51 64 120 183 11 170 78

**U** Leading all the rest;
having top priority

—— —— —— —— —— —— —— —— ——
147 111 169 73 100 138 2 40 190

**V** Necessity

—— —— —— —— —— —— —— —— ——
136 47 174 129 68 34 188 16 202

**W** Hardens

—— —— —— —— —— —— —— ——
81 39 18 127 196 116 186 101

**X** Easily visible portion of
the constellation Taurus

—— —— —— —— —— —— —— ——
148 43 135 157 15 105 185 63

**Y** Drives out

—— —— —— —— —— ——
74 187 117 14 54 137

| 1 D | 2 U | 3 J | 4 N | 5 Q | 6 I | | 7 F | 8 G |
|---|---|---|---|---|---|---|---|---|
| 9 M | 10 C | 11 T | | | 12 S | 13 B | 14 Y | 15 X | 16 V | 17 P |
| 18 W | 19 K | | 20 O | 21 A | 22 R | 23 S | 24 E | 25 D | | 26 T |
| 27 L | 28 N | 29 F | 30 G | 31 H | | 32 J | 33 Q | | 34 V | 35 K |
| 36 I | 37 R | 38 P | 39 W | 40 U | 41 E | 42 M | 43 X | | 44 H | 45 O | 46 J |
| 47 V | 48 K | 49 P | 50 E | 51 T | 52 C | 53 J | 54 Y | 55 Q |
| 56 I | 57 N | 58 D | 59 B | 60 O | 61 G | 62 F | 63 X | 64 T | 65 S | 66 A |
| 67 H | 68 V | 69 L | 70 C | | 91 F | 72 Q | 73 U | | 74 Y | 75 M |
| 76 J | 77 A | 78 T | | 79 B | 80 R | | 81 W | 82 I | 83 H | 84 C |
| 85 L | | 86 P | 87 N | 88 K | 89 R | 90 G | 91 L | 92 F | 93 J | 94 H |
| 95 T | 96 M | 97 I | 98 O | 99 B | 100 U | 101 W | | 102 Q | 103 A | 104 N |
| 105 X | 106 K | 107 I | 108 R | 109 F | 110 E | 111 U | | 112 B | 113 O | 114 J | 115 N |
| 116 W | 117 Y | 118 E | 119 R | 120 T | 121 A | | 122 C | 123 Q | 124 L | 125 H | 126 S |
| 127 W | 128 K | 129 V | 130 T | | 131 J | 132 M | 133 A | 134 O | 135 X | 136 V | 137 Y |
| 138 U | 139 S | 140 J | 141 H | 142 M | 143 I | 144 N | 145 E | | 146 C |
| 147 U | 148 X | 149 P | 150 J | 151 F | | 152 Q | 153 I | 154 M | | 155 B |
| 156 J | 157 X | 158 Q | 159 H | 160 L | 161 P | 162 R | 163 O | 164 F | 165 I | | 166 Q |
| 167 R | 168 B | | 169 U | 170 T | 171 M | 172 D | 173 C | 174 V | 175 R | 176 G | 177 F |
| 178 S | 179 N | 180 H | | 181 Q | 182 F | | 183 T | 184 L | 185 X |
| 186 W | 187 Y | 188 V | 189 G | 190 U | 191 D | 192 E | 193 K | 194 H | | 195 G |
| 196 W | | 197 J | 198 K | 199 F | 200 H | 201 B | 202 V |

(DIRECTIONS FOR SOLVING ACROSS-TICS ARE ON PAGE 276)

# JOVIAL JOKES

Two men sat down in a restaurant and ordered their main dishes. Then they closed their menus. The waiter said, "Thank you, gentlemen. And would any of you wish a beverage with your meal?"

One man said, "Well, I usually have coffee, but today I think I'll have a glass of milk."

The other man said, "That sounds good. I'll have milk, too. But make sure the glass is clean!"

"Very good," said the waiter, and he left.

Soon he came back with a tray and two glasses of milk, and said, "Here you are, gentlemen. Now which one asked for the clean glass?"

Max had been living with his shrewish wife for thirty years. But he couldn't stand the nagging any longer. He consulted his friend John about what to do.

"Why not do her in?" suggested John.

"If I do that I'll be thrown in jail. I don't want to spend the rest of my life in prison."

John considered, then he said, "Well, why don't you buy her a car? She can't drive. Maybe she'll have an accident, and her death won't be on your head."

So Max bought his wife a little sportscar. But when he met John a week later, he still looked sad. "She drives it perfectly," said Max. "I threw my money away."

John knew what was wrong. "That car you bought her was too small. Why don't you get her a large car that will be hard to handle? She's bound to get into an accident with a big sedan."

So Max bought his wife a huge Cadillac. But that didn't work either. "She drives that one perfectly, too," he told John a week later. "What do I do now?"

"Well, there's one other thing you can try. Splurge and get her a Jaguar."

So Max bought his wife a Jaguar. A week later, he was all smiles.

"So what happened?" John asked him.

"Wonderful!" exclaimed Max. "One bite, and she was finished!"

Goldberg walked into his partner's office at Goldberg and Cohen Dressmakers. "I have in my office an order from Marshall Field and Company in Chicago!" he exclaimed.

"I don't believe it," said Cohen.

"You don't believe it? Well, here, take a look at the cancellation."

AFTER MANY YEARS of not having seen each other, Deborah ran into Rhea at—of all places—a bar mitzvah reception her boyfriend had invited her to.

The women shed tears, and immediately fell into deep conversation. Suddenly, the bar mitzvah boy walked in, to the applause of the assembled guests.

"Look at that poor boy!" Deborah whispered. "His face is so full of pimples, you could almost throw up looking at him!"

Rhea was scandalized. "It so happens," she announced haughtily, "that that's my boy, David!"

Deborah's face turned bright red, then she asserted effusively, "You know, darling, on him they're becoming."

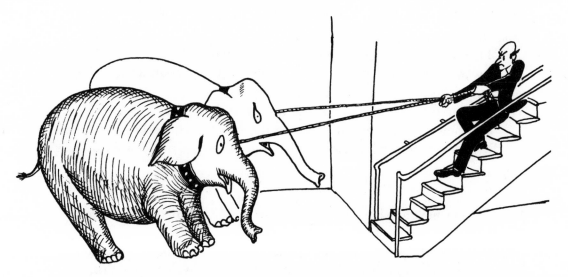

DANNY WAS an inveterate bargain hunter. He hadn't a penny to his name, but whenever he saw a bargain he couldn't resist it.

One day a friend of his came to see him. Jim said, "Danny, I've got a terrific bargain for you. A boatload has arrived for the Barnum and Bailey Circus and they have an overstock. They've got an elephant on board, a baby elephant, that's worth at least $2,000 and I can land it for you for only $300."

Danny looked at Jim as if he were half crazy. "What! An elephant! An elephant in my one-room apartment? You must be out of your mind! In the first place, there's no room for it. And in the second place, how could I feed it? In the third place, what could I do with it? Don't be nuts!"

"But," persisted Jim, "I'm telling you this elephant is worth 2,000 bucks and I can get it for you for a mere 300, maybe even for 250."

Danny was adamant. "Get the hell out of here, will you? You're off your rocker. I don't need an elephant. I don't want an elephant. Leave me alone with elephants."

But Jim knew his friend and he continued hammering away. "Listen, Danny," he said, "the fact is they have an overstock. You know, I think if I put it to 'em I could get you two elephants for the same 200 bucks."

"Now you're talkin'," said Danny.

SADIE WASN'T FEELING WELL, and she knew she should see a doctor. So she asked her friend Becky the name of the doctor she used.

"His name's Feinstein," said Becky, "but you should know he's expensive."

"How expensive?" asked Sadie.

"Well, it's fifty dollars for the first visit, and twenty-five for every visit after that."

So Sadie went off to see Dr. Feinstein. When her turn came to be examined, she smiled brightly and said to the nurse, "Hi, honey. Here I am again!"


SADIE WEINTRAUB asked for two bagels.

"That'll be twenty cents, please," said the baker.

"Twenty cents!" exclaimed Sadie. "Why, that's ten cents a bagel! The man across the street only charges *six* cents!"

"So, buy them across the street," shrugged the baker.

"But they're all out of bagels across the street," said Sadie.

"Lady, when I'm all out of bagels, I only charge a nickel apiece."


TWO MEN SAT next to each other on the train to Miami. Since it was a long trip, both were willing to chat.

One man, obviously wealthy, opened the conversation, "I'm looking forward to being at my vacation home again. I can't wait to go golfing. I love golf. Do you play?"

The other man did not want to appear uncivilized, so he said, "Of course. I love to golf also. Why, every afternoon since my retirement I've played."

"Oh, then you must be pretty good!" said the rich man. "I play in the low seventies myself," he added modestly.

"Oh, so do I," said the second man. "Of course, if it gets any colder, I go right back to the hotel!"


AN OLD WOMAN living in New York died at the age of seventy-seven, leaving a grieving husband of sixty-eight years to survive her.

However, when a reporter came to interview the husband about their fifty years of marriage, he surprised him in the living room with the maid on his lap, his arms entwined around her.

"I can't believe my eyes," squawked the reporter. "After fifty years of marriage, and your wife hardly buried!"

The widower dropped his arms abruptly and did some fast thinking. "In my grief," he said finally, "do I know what I'm doing?"

Sammy finally managed to get the new receptionist to agree to a date. The next morning, he looked pleased as punch. He told his friend Bernie all about it.

"You know that beautiful new receptionist? Well, I went out with her last night, and let me tell you, she's a living doll," Sammy bragged.

"What did you do?" asked Bernie.

"Well, I took her to dinner and a show, and then we went up to her apartment, and we got intimate. And I must say, she's a million times better than my wife, Molly."

"Gee, she sounds wonderful!" said Bernie. "Do you mind if I ask her out?"

"No, of course not," said Sammy. "Have yourself a ball!"

So two nights later Bernie took her out. The next morning, Sammy went to Bernie's office to get a report.

"Ah, Sammy," Bernie began. "She was a lot of fun, but how can you compare her to your wife, Molly?"

Mrs. Rosenbush was negotiating for a mink stole at Mendel's. She asked a lot of questions.

"If I buy the coat and I get caught in the rain," she asked the salesmen, "will it get ruined?"

"Look, lady," answered Mr. Mendel, "did you ever see a mink carrying an umbrella?"

Two neighborhood cronies were gossiping one morning when a third lady eagerly joined the group.

"Have I got a story!" interrupted the newcomer. "Poor old Linsky just tripped at the top of the stairs, fell down to the bottom, hit his head, and died."

"Died?" exclaimed the other ladies.

"Yes," asserted the talebearer. "And he broke his glasses, too."

313

ABE SAID to his friend Willie, "Willie, lend me twenty dollars."

Willie took out his wallet and handed Abe a ten dollar bill.

"Willie," said Abe, "I asked you for twenty."

"Yes, I know," said Willie. "This way you lose ten and I lose ten."

IN THE DAYS OF PIONEERING the wild old West, Jake and Izzy were traveling through Colorado by stagecoach. Suddenly the coach stopped, and Jake realized that robbers were about to stage a hold-up.

Quickly, Jake took some money from his wallet and handed it to his companion. "Izzy," he explained, "here is the fifty dollars I owe you."

MR. AND MRS. MANDELBAUM decided the only solution to their marital problems was in divorce. So they went to see the rabbi.

The rabbi was concerned about the three children and was reluctant to see the family broken up. He thought that if he could stall the couple maybe they would work it out together.

"Well," said the rabbi, "there's no way of dividing three children. What you'll have to do is live together one more year. You'll have a fourth child, and then, it will be easy to arrange a proper divorce. You'll take two children, and he'll take two."

"Nothing doing," said Mrs. Mandelbaum. "Rabbi, if I depended on him, I wouldn't even have had these three!"

AT A DINNER PARTY, the hostess served the appetizers herself, carrying the tray around to each guest. One man, however, declined.

"But you must!" insisted the lady.

"Really, they're delicious," replied the guest, "but I've had six already."

"Actually, you had seven," advised the hostess, "but who's counting?"

ABE WAS ON HIS WAY to the Coast when his train was derailed and fell into a ravine. All around him, passengers lay dead; he couldn't see a sign of life anywhere, but miraculously he himself was unhurt. However, he couldn't find a single door or window through which he could extricate himself. He was stuck in the car in danger of suffocation. After several hours, a rescue crew arrived and started breaking through a window to reach him.

"We're from the Red Cross," they announced.

Abe waved them off, "I gave already at the office."

TWO BANKERS, Morris and Harry, decided to take a vacation together and get away from it all. They rented a cabin on a lake so they could go fishing.

The first morning of their vacation, the pair got into the boat and made their way out into the middle of the lake. Suddenly a large motorboat sped by, and the force of its wake caused the smaller craft to capsize.

"Help me, Morris! I can't swim very well," shouted Harry.

Morris could swim, but the problem was that Harry was twice his size. He'd never be able to rescue him. So he hollered, "I'll go get help. Do you think you can float alone?"

Harry was indignant. "Morris, how can you talk about business at a time like this?"

ESSIE AND GERT went to visit their neighbor Rosie, who had just come home from the hospital with her triplets.

"Oh, Rosie, it's wonderful!" sighed Essie. "Imagine having triplets! I hear it's pretty rare."

Rosie replied smiling, "Rare? The doctor told me it's practically a miracle! He told me triplets happen only once in one million, six hundred and eighty times!"

"My God!" cried Gert. "Rosie, when did you ever have time to do your housework?"

**315**

SHEILA JOINED THE GIRLS for mah johngg one day sporting a huge diamond ring. All the ladies were envious. Finally, one of them asked where she'd gotten it.

"Well," said Sheila, "my mother-in-law gave me a thousand dollars in trust before she passed away. She said that when she dies, I should buy her a beautiful stone for her memory. So I did!"

A MOTHER TORE INTO her son's bedroom and shook her son who was lying in bed. "Mike," she said, "you've got to go to school. Enough of this nonsense, get up and go to school."

Mike growled, "I don't wanna go to school."

She shook him once again and said, "Mike, I'm telling you, you've gotta get up and go to school."

Mike said, "Why?"

"Well," she yelled, "I'll give you three good reasons. In the first place, I pay taxes; in the second place, you're 50 years old; and in the third place, you're the principal."

MINNIE AND MAX had been married for 18 years. As Minnie grew older and less attractive, Max became disinterested and his libido started to wane dramatically. In desperation, Minnie hauled him before a marriage counselor. The marriage counselor listened patiently to Minnie's complaints and to Max's protestations. Max said he was being nagged unmercifully; Minnie said that Max was causing her anguish.

Finally the marriage counselor issued a verdict. "Max," he said, "from now on, no matter how you feel, you must give Minnie her conjugal rights at least semi-annually."

Minnie was delighted and they left the counselor's chambers. On the way downstairs she nudged Max, "Tell me Max, how many times a week is semi-annually?"

SAMMY STEPPED UP to his friend who sold hot dogs from a pushcart and said casually, "So, Morris, how's business?"

Morris was open with his friend. "Oh, business is pretty good. I even was able to put a thousand dollars into my savings account!"

Sammy was quick to try to take advantage of this opportunity, "So, Morris, could you lend me a hundred?"

Morris didn't hesitate. "I'm sorry, but I'm not allowed to."

"You're not *allowed* to? What do you mean by that?"

"Well, I made an agreement with the bank. They agreed they won't go into the hot dog business, and I agreed not to lend money."

A MAN CAME INTO a grocery store and asked for five cents worth of salt. The proprietor asked, "What kind of salt do you want?"

"What kind of salt do I want? I want salt, plain and simple. How many kinds of salt are there!"

"Ha ha," chuckled the store owner, "what you don't know about salt! You come with me." And he took him downstairs and showed him a cellar that contained no less than 40 or 50 barrels of salt. The customer was amazed. "All these are different salts?" he asked.

"Yes, they're all different. We have salt for all kinds of prices and uses."

"My goodness, you're a specialist. I suppose, if you have all these barrels of different kinds of salt, you must sell one hell of a lot of salt. You must really know how to sell salt!"

"Oh," said the other, "me—I'm not so good at selling salt, but the guy who sold it all to me, boy! Can *he* sell salt!"

TWO PARTNERS IN THE GARMENT industry were having business problems; it looked as if they might have to declare bankruptcy. But at the brink, a particular line of dresses seemed to lure a buyer. A West Coast outlet wanted to buy the whole line, at a price which would put the partners well into the black. The partners were overjoyed.

"The only thing is," warned the buyer, "I have to have the deal approved by the home office. I'm sure they'll agree, but I do have to check with them. I'm going back tomorrow. If you don't hear from me by Friday closing time, you can be sure everything's okay."

The week went by slowly; and Friday crawled. The two men sat without moving at their desks, unable to concentrate on any kind of work. Without this deal, they would definitely go under. They sweated the hours out, minute by minute.

Two o'clock went by, three o'clock, then four o'clock, and now they were close to pay dirt. Four-thirty came, and they were holding their breath. Suddenly, a messenger burst into the office. "Telegram!" he said. The men froze in terror.

Finally, one of the partners stood up. Slowly he opened the telegram, and read it quickly.

Then came a shriek of joy. "Harry! Good news! Your brother died!"

**317**

Two chums were having a private little conversation. "Do you know," said one, "I'm amazed at how popular I am, and I cannot for the life of me understand why the men cluster around me. Tell me the truth, Jane, is it my complexion?"

"No," said Jane.

"Well, do you think it's my figure?"

"No," came the reply.

"Well, is it my personality?"

"No, not really."

"Well, I give up."

"Uh, huh!" exclaimed the other, "Now you got it!"

An American girl married a Greek millionaire and moved to Athens. One day soon after the wedding her mother called her from Boston and told the maid she'd like to speak to Mrs. Adrianopolis.

"I'm sorry," the maid replied, "but she's in bed with peritonitis."

"Well," the mother snapped indignantly," if it isn't one Greek, it's another!"

Two city men pulled up in front of a ramshackle country house and found a stubble-faced farmer on the front porch. "Hey, mister," the driver shouted, "can you change a twelve-dollar bill?"

The farmer rose and nodded. "Sure thing, but I have to go inside to get the money."

The driver's companion said, "What a jackass! But what are you planning to do now?

"I'm giving him a ten," the driver snickered. "I'll mark up the zero to look like a two. He'll never know the difference."

The farmer came out of the house with a battered wallet, took the bill the driver offered without examining it, and put it into his pocket. Then he looked at the driver and said, "How do you want the change? Two sixes or three fours?"

ALL THE GIRLS from the office poured into a crowded cafeteria for the coffee break. One of the girls lit a cigarette and blew ring after ring of smoke. An elderly lady, sitting next to her, was supremely annoyed. "Miss," she said, "that smoking is a horrible habit. I would rather commit adultery than smoke."

"So would I," answered the girl, "but, you know, there just isn't time during a coffee break."

DEEP IN THE Tennessee hills, a farmer's mule kicked his mother-in-law to death. An enormous crowd of men turned out for the funeral. The minister, examining the crowd outside the church, commented to a farmer friend, "This old lady must have been mighty popular. Just look at how many people left their work to come to her funeral."

"They're not here for the funeral," snickered the friend. "They're here to buy the mule."

THE ADMIRAL WAS ABOARD his flagship in a Mediterranean port. The captain of one of the cruisers made a very sloppy job of it when it was up to him to bring his ship into berth.

The captain knew he had made a foul-up, and dreaded the wrath of his commanding officer. Finally, the message came from the flagship. It was but one word, "Good."

Fifteen minutes later, the confused captain was startled by the delivery of another message from the admiral. It ran: "To previous message, please add the word 'God!'"

"SOME YOUNG MAN is trying to get into my room through my window," screamed a spinster into the telephone.

"Sorry, lady," came back the answer, "you've got the fire department. What you want is the police department."

"Oh, no," she pleaded, "I want the fire department. What he needs is a longer ladder."

**319**

# GOING TO THE DOGS

On this and the following pages, you will find pictures of 18 varieties of man's best friend. Under each is a brief description, and under that, a line of blanks. The number of blanks corresponds to the number of letters in the name of the breed. How many can you identify?

A score of 9 is fair; 12 is good; and 15 is doggone swell.

*Answers on page 498*

This bird dog has been trained to indicate to its master when it has spotted game. It is nearly two feet tall, and weighs 35-55 pounds.

1.   THIS DOG IS AN

_ _ _ _ _ _
_ _ _ _ _ _.

Except for a tuft of hair on its head and some fuzz along the lower half of its tail, this Latin American dog is "bald."

2.   THIS DOG IS A

_ _ _ _ _ _
_ _ _ _ _ _ _.

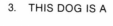

This hunting dog, known also as the Highland Greyhound or the Staghound, has a rough, wiry coat about three or four inches in length. He is usually from 30 to 32 inches in height, and weighs between 85 and 110 pounds.

3.   THIS DOG IS A

_ _ _ _ _ _ _
_ _ _ _ _ _ _ _

This dog, probably of British origin, was once known as "the retired gentleman's shooting dog," because of his value for pheasant and cock shooting. He is slow-moving, large-bodied, and short-legged. His head resembles that of a St. Bernard.

5.   THIS DOG IS A

_ _ _ _ _ _ _
_ _ _ _ _ _ _

This Scottish breed became fashionable for the nobility in the 19th century. He is twice as long as he is high, and his whole face is commonly obscured by a thick fringe of hair.

4.   THIS DOG IS A

_ _ _ _
_ _ _ _ _ _ _

This former hunting dog's beauty and quality as a pet have made it one of the most popular American breeds. It is about 15 inches tall, with long, floppy ears and large, round eyes.

6.   THIS DOG IS A

_ _ _ _ _ _
_ _ _ _ _ _ _

This large Scottish-bred dog is known for its gorgeous long coat, its amazing ability to perform tricks, and its gracefulness. It has a very affectionate nature, making it an excellent dog for children.

Bred in the Swiss Alps, this large, powerful dog was once used to aid travelers. It is over two feet tall, and sometimes weighs close to 200 pounds.

7.   THIS DOG IS A

_ _ _ _ _ _.

9.   THIS DOG IS A

_ _ _ _ _
_ _ _ _ _ _ _.

Bred in England, Holland, and Japan of Chinese ancestors, this toy breed is essentially a house dog. Weighing only 14-18 pounds, it has large, soft eyes and a square, short muzzle.

This tall, thin dog has been famous for its racing and hunting skill for centuries. His keen eyesight and great speed allow him to easily bring down his quarry.

8.   THIS DOG IS A

_ _ _.

10.   THIS DOG IS A

_ _ _ _ _ _ _ _ _.

This compact, curly-coated dog is extremely intelligent and has exceptional ability in small game hunting. It stands 15-18 inches high, and weighs 25-40 pounds. His good nose and fondness for water make him one of the most easily trained of the retrievers.

11.  THIS DOG IS A

_ _ _ _ _
_ _ _ _ _ _

This large, short-haired dog is known for its incredible sense of smell and its characteristic of standing stiffly, with its nose in the air and its tail straight out, when it scents its prey.

13.  THIS DOG IS A

_ _ _ _ _ _ _

This large English water dog is popular in England and America because of his beauty and sweet disposition. He averages about 27 inches in height, and weighs about 120 to 140 pounds. His coat is flat, dense, and oily in nature.

12.  THIS DOG IS A

_ _ _ _ _ _ _ _ _ _

Long-bodied and low-hung, this popular dog has been nicknamed "the sausage dog," or described as "half-a-dog high and a dog-and-a-half long" because of its strange appearance. He is considered the national dog of Germany.

14.  THIS DOG IS A

_ _ _ _ _ _ _ _ _.

This statuesque-looking dog, despite its large size, makes an excellent apartment dog as well as a country pet. He is nearly 3 feet tall, and has a square-looking build.

15. THIS DOG IS A

_ _ _ _ _
_ _ _ _

This bright red-colored breed is valued today mostly for its beauty, but it once was a popular hunting dog. One of the pointing breeds, he is sturdy, swift, and very affectionate.

17. THIS DOG IS AN

_ _ _ _ _
_ _ _ _ _ _.

This smooth-coated hunting dog is known for its keen sight and nose, and for its ability to drive a fox from its hole. Plucky and courageous, it is a great favorite in England.

16. THIS DOG IS A

_ _ _
_ _ _ _ _ _ _.

America's most popular breed, this thick-coated dog is considered the most intelligent of the species. Active and elegant-looking, its coat is often clipped in various fanciful designs.

18. THIS DOG IS A

_ _ _ _ _ _.

# FAMOUS WOMEN

On this and the following pages, you will find pictures of 18 famous women of a number of nationalities and periods in history. It's an unusual batch, including monarchs, writers, painters, teachers, and even a saint. How many can you identify?

Beneath each picture is a brief clue to the woman's identity. Fill in your answer in the blank line provided.

A score of 10 is fine; 12 is superior; and 14 is really excellent.

*Answers on page 498*

This 19th-century English woman was the founder of modern nursing. She was nick-named "The Lady With the Lamp" because she believed that a nurse's duty was to care for the sick night and day.

1. HER NAME WAS:

_____

This English queen reigned from 1558 to 1603. The daughter of Henry VIII and Anne Boleyn, she ruled England during one of its greatest cultural periods, an age to which historians have given her name.

2. HER NAME WAS:

_____

Her first work, *Uncle Tom's Cabin*, was published serially in an abolitionist paper in 1851-1852. The enormous success of the book edition and stage dramatization fanned the feelings which led to the Civil War.

3.   HER NAME WAS:

_____

This American woman, nearly blind herself, was responsible for teaching Helen Keller to speak and read, and remained Helen's constant companion through-out her life.

5.   HER NAME WAS:

_____

Rosine Bernard was the real name of this French actress of Jewish descent. The most famous actress of the late 19th and early 20th centuries, she is perhaps best known for her portrayal of Phèdre and of Dõna Sol in Hugo's *Hernani*.

4.   HER NAME WAS:

_____

This French novelist's real name was Amandine Aurore Lucie Dupin. She wrote over 80 novels, many of which expressed her serious concern with social reform. *The Haunted Pool* (1890) is considered by many to be her masterpiece.

6.   HER NAME WAS:

_____

This Spanish queen ruled Castile jointly with her husband, Ferdinand. The patron of Columbus, the Catholic Queen, as she was known, encouraged great cultural achievement and exploration during her reign.

7.   HER NAME WAS:

_____

This French saint and national heroine, born around 1412, is known as the "Maid of Orleans." When she was 16, she heard voices exhorting her to aid the Dauphin, later Charles VII, in regaining his throne from the British.

9.   HER NAME WAS:

_____

This 19th century English novelist is today considered one of the masters of the English novel. Her comedies of manners depict the self-contained world of provincial ladies and gentleman, as in *Pride and Prejudice,* her best-known work.

8.   HER NAME WAS:

_____

Born Marie Josephe Rose Tascher de La Pagerie, this creole woman of Martinique was married to Napoleon Bonaparte in 1796, and ruled as empress of France until the marriage was annulled in 1809 because of her alleged sterility.

10.   HER NAME WAS:

_____

This 19th-century English woman, a poet herself, had a famous love affair with another poet, Robert, in defiance of her father, which resulted in their elopement to Italy. Her greatest poetry, *Sonnets from the Portuguese,* was inspired by her own love story.

11.  HER NAME WAS:

_____

This 19th century American writer is best remembered for her authorship of one of most popular girls' books ever written, *Little Women,* in which the character of Jo March is largely autobiographical.

13.  HER NAME WAS:

_____

The daughter of James V of Scotland and Mary of Guise, this woman, born in 1542, became Queen of Scotland while still in her infancy. In 1558 she was married to the Dauphin of France, thus making her also Queen of France. A series of unsuccessful attempts to raise herself to the English crown led to her beheading on the orders of Queen Elizabeth in 1587.

The famous solution to the 18th-century bread famine in France, "Let them eat cake," is unjustly attributed to this French queen, the wife of Louis XVI, but it is certain that her insensitive attitude toward her subjects was one factor leading up to the French Revolution, as well as to her own execution.

**328**

12.  HER NAME WAS:

_____

14.  HER NAME WAS:

_____

The daughter of an American Indian chief, whose name means "playful one," this woman used to visit the English colony at Jamestown in Virginia. The story of how she saved the life of Captain John Smith, though still disputed among historians, is probably true.

15.   HER NAME WAS:

_____

The major literary contribution of this 19th-century English writer is the frightening novel *Frankenstein*. She also wrote several other works of fiction, as well as editing the works of her famous husband, Percy.

17.   HER NAME WAS:

_____

This 17th century English actress began her incredible career by selling oranges at the Theatre Royal. After her debut in 1665, she quickly became one of the most popular actresses of the time. In 1669, she became the mistress of Charles II, and bore him two sons, one of whom was created the duke of St. Albans.

16.   HER NAME WAS:

_____

*The Horse Fair,* in the Metropolitan Museum, is probably this 19th-century French artist's best-known work. Her conscientious pictures of animal life gained her wide popularity, particularly in the United States and England.

18.   HER NAME WAS:

_____

# CORPORATE IDENTITY

Below you will find 24 symbols, each one of which is used as a special insignia to designate a noted company, generally of international reputation. You have probably seen most of these symbols at one time or another. How many can you identify?

A score of 7 is average, 10 is good, 14 is better than most, and 19 puts you in a very special category.

*Answers on page 498*

1. _____

2. _____

3. _____

4. _____

5. _____

6. _____

7. _____

8. _____

9. _____

10. _____

11. _____

18. _____

12. _____

19. _____

13. _____

20. _____

14. _____

21. _____

15. _____

22. _____

16. _____

23. _____

17. _____

24. _____

# PENMAN'S PUZZLE

The 18 authors pictured below all had a significant impact on the development of literature—in fiction, non-fiction, and poetry. They represent the literature of a number of nationalities and periods in history. Read the clues below the pictures and see if you can recognize who they are.

A score of 10 rates a National Book Award; 12 earns a Pulitzer Prize; and a score of 16 merits a Nobel Prize in literary scholarship.

*Answers on page 499*

He used the pseudonym Diedrich Knicker-bocker when he wrote his satirical "History of New York," which has been called the first great work of comic literature by an American. He is best known today for his stories "Rip Van Winkle" and "The Legend of Sleepy Hollow."

1. HIS NAME WAS:

_____

He began his career as a military man and later became a journalist, but he was, above all, a master poet and short-story writer. His major poems include "To Helen," "Annabel Lee," and "The Raven"; among his macabre tales are "The Murders in the Rue Morgue" and "The Pit and the Pendulum."

2. HIS NAME WAS:

_____

He was the first American whose bust was placed in the Poets' Corner of Westminster Abbey. "Evangeline," "The Song of Hiawatha," and "Paul Revere's Ride" are among his best-known poems.

3.　HIS NAME WAS:

A principal figure of ancient Greek literature, he has been called the first European poet. Modern scholars are generally agreed that he lived before 700 B.C., was possibly blind, and wrote two of the masterpieces of Greek epic poetry, the *Iliad* and the *Odyssey*.

5.　HIS NAME WAS:

In *Don Quixote*, his masterpiece, the whole fabric of 16th-century Spanish society is laid out in satirical form. This book, and other of his works, had an indelible effect on the development of the European novel.

4.　HIS NAME WAS:

England's first Nobel Prize winner for literature, his stories and poems are mainly concerned with colonial India. His romantic imperialism, expressed in such poems as "The White Man's Burden," made him extremely popular with the English. He is also known for his children's stories, including "The Jungle Book."

6.　HIS NAME WAS:

**333**

This 19th-century Norwegian poet and dramatist was far ahead of his time in social criticism and the development of drama. His plays, which had a profound effect on the course of European drama, often focused on the plight of the 19th-century female, as in *A Doll's House* and *Hedda Gabler*.

7.   HIS NAME WAS:

_____

This 19th-century Russian novelist and philosopher is commonly agreed to be one of the world's best writers. His two greatest works, *Anna Karenina* and *War and Peace*, represent in detail his philosophy of morality and of history.

9.   HIS NAME WAS:

_____

This English journalist and publisher did not turn to novel-writing until he was nearly 60 years old. His greatest works, *Robinson Crusoe* and *Moll Flanders*, were not published under his name, but as authentic memoirs, intending to gull the reader into believing his fictions true.

8.   HIS NAME WAS:

_____

This German's genius embraced almost every field of human endeavor, including painting, music, science, and literature. His dramatic poem, *Faust*, recast the traditional legend as a philosophic and poetic masterpiece. His *The Apprenticeship of Wilhelm Meister* became the prototype of the German novel of character development.

10.   HIS NAME WAS:

_____

He first appeared in London periodicals under the pseudonym Boz, with his small sketches of London life. His novels, including *Pickwick Papers, Great Expectations,* and *A Christmas Carol,* made him the most popular novelist of his day, both in England and the United States.

11.   HIS NAME WAS:

_____

This English poet is known as an early leader of the school of Romanticism. His poems, such as "She Dwelt Among the Untrodden Ways," "The Solitary Reaper," and "The World Is Too Much With Us," displayed a seriousness tempered with tenderness and a love of simplicity.

13.   HIS NAME WAS:

_____

This 17th-century Frenchman started out as an actor, but quickly developed his skills as a director, stage manager, and playwright. Under royal patronage, his troupe produced such classics as *Le Misanthrope, L'Avare (The Miser),* and *Le Bourgeois Gentilhomme (The Would-Be Gentleman).*

12.   HIS NAME WAS:

_____

This Russian poet and prose writer was born of a noble family, but was imprisoned in his youth for his revolutionary writings. His two masterpieces, *Eugene Onegin,* a novel, and *The Queen of Spades,* a short story, were both adapted as operas by Tchaikovsky.

14.   HIS NAME WAS:

_____

**335**

In his masterpiece, *Prometheus Unbound,* he illustrates his philosophy, embodying faith in the perfectability and ultimate progress of man. His shorter poems include "To a Sky-lark," "When the Lamp is Shattered," and "The Indian Serenade."

15.　HIS NAME WAS:

_____

Francois Marie Arouet was the real name of this French philosopher and author. Imprisoned several times in his youth, he spent the rest of his life fighting what he felt were judicial injustices. His best-known work is *Candide,* a satirical novel.

17.　HIS NAME WAS:

_____

This American poet, essayist, and lecturer was one of the first proponents of transcendentalist thought. Among his famous lectures, collected in his series, *Essays,* are "The Over-Soul," "Self-Reliance," and "Compensation." One of his best-known poems is "The Concord Hymn."

16.　HIS NAME WAS:

_____

This Italian poet of the Middle Ages wrote his greatest work, *The Divine Comedy,* as a memorial to his dead idol, Beatrice. The work is divided into three parts, relating the poet's symbolic journey through Hell, Purgatory, and Heaven, through which he is led by Beatrice.

18.　HIS NAME WAS:

_____

# ANIMAL QUIZ

Here are pictures of 18 animals. Read the clue under each one and see if you can fill in the missing blanks. The number of blanks corresponds to the number of letters in the animal's name.

If you can identify 10, you're a clever fox; get 12 and you're as wise as an owl; get 14, and you're king of the beasts.

*Answers on page 499*

The smallest of the anthropoid apes, this animal is found in southeast Asia and the East Indies. It has a slender, tail-less body and extremely long arms, which enables it to swing through the trees with speed and agility.

1.   THIS ANIMAL IS A

      _ _ _ _ _ _.

This animal, found in North America and the Galapagos Islands, is a terrestrial form of turtle, inhabiting dry or desert regions. It is encased in a hard shell, and can withdraw its head into its shell when frightened.

2.   THIS ANIMAL IS A

      _ _ _ _ _ _ _ _.

Found in Africa, Southwest Asia, and West India, this animal has a yellow or brown short-haired coat and a black or tawny long mane. It is know as the "king of the jungle."

3.   THIS ANIMAL IS A

_ _ _ _.

This massive herbivore has very thick, often folded skin and horns. It is a native of Africa, India, and Southeast Asia, and is fond of wallowing in mud and water.

5.   THIS ANIMAL IS A

_ _ _ _ _ _ _ _ _.

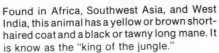

This mammal from North America, Europe, Asia, and Africa, was once considered a rodent, but is now placed in the separate category Lagomorpha. It closely resembles a rabbit but has longer ears, and can travel at up to 30 miles per hour.

4.   THIS ANIMAL IS A

_ _ _ _.

This animal has an appetite for insects, particularly termites and ants. Its long snout and tongue enable it to burrow under the earth for its dinner.

6.   THIS ANIMAL IS AN

_ _ _ _ _ _ _ _.

**338**

This gregarious mammal is a relative of the whale and the porpoise. It averages 5 to 14 feet in length, has a pointed snout, and is especially abundant in the Mediterranean region.

7.   THIS ANIMAL IS A

— — — — — — —.

This large, clumsy-looking beast adores honey and hibernates in the winter. This breed is extinct in much of Europe, but can be found in Russia and North Asia.

9.   THIS ANIMAL IS A

— — — — —
— — — —.

Of African or Asian origin, this member of the cat family is distinguished by its thick, often yellow fur patterned with black rosettes. It can reach as much as 7½ feet in length, and preys on monkeys, birds, and reptiles.

8.   THIS ANIMAL IS A

— — — — — — —.

This marsupial, also known as the brush kangaroo, can leap 25 feet at a bound. A native of Australia and Tasmania, it feeds on grass and other vegetation and is usually found in the plains.

10.   THIS ANIMAL IS A

— — — — — — —.

This wild animal from the forests of Europe is thought to be the forefather of the common domesticated pig. It is valued for its flesh and its fat, and is also hunted for sport in Europe.

This small, burrowing rodent hails from the Andes of Bolivia, Chile, and Peru. It is also raised on farms in the United States for its soft, gray pelt, one of the costliest of all furs.

11.   THIS ANIMAL IS A

— — — —
— — — —.

13.   THIS ANIMAL IS A

— — — — — — — — —.

Native to South America and the United States, this nocturnal marsupial has coarse fur of mixed white-tipped and black-tipped hair. It is hunted for sport, food, and its fur for making clothes.

This animal, also known as the Australian bear, sleeps in the day and feeds at night, using its sharp claws to climb trees in search of food. The female has a pouch in which it carries its young.

12.   THIS ANIMAL IS AN

— — — — — — —.

14.   THIS ANIMAL IS A

— — — — —   — — — —.

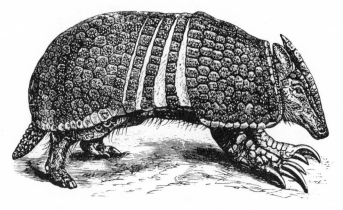

This nocturnal member of the dog family is found in southeast Europe, Asia, and Africa. It resembles a small wolf, and preys on carrion and small and large animals, often traveling in packs.

15.   THIS ANIMAL IS A

— — — — —.

This strange mammal's head and body are almost entirely covered by an armor of bone and horny material, and can roll itself into a tight ball for protection. It is found mostly in the area from Patagonia northward to parts of the south and southwest United States.

17.   THIS ANIMAL IS AN

— — — — — — — —.

A native of South America, especially in the Andes Mountains, this hoofed mammal somewhat resembles a sheep. Used as a pack animal since the days of the Incas, it is also valued for its flesh, wool, and milk.

16.   THIS ANIMAL IS A

— — — — —.

This short-tailed member of the cat family has soft, thick, black-marked beige to gray fur and tufted ears. It can be found in the Alps, Scandinavia, and north Russia, and is related to the American bobcat.

18.   THIS ANIMAL IS A

— — — —.

# CRAZY EIGHTS

This is an exciting card game for two or three players.

You deal out seven cards to each player face down. You place the rest of the deck face down in the middle of the table. This pile is then called the "Dig Pile."

The idea of the game is to get rid of all your cards.

Choose for dealer: Deal out one card to each player. The one who gets the highest card becomes the dealer.

The player to the left of the dealer starts the game. He places any one of his cards face upward next to the Dig Pile. The next player must then play a legal card, if he can. What is a legal card? Let's say that the first player has thrown down a 4 of Diamonds. A legal card would be any 4—either the 4 of Spades, the 4 of Hearts, the 4 of Clubs, or any Diamond. If the second player holds none of these cards, he must then go to the Dig Pile and pull cards until he finds a card which is valid. However, if he holds an 8—one of the four Crazy Eights—he may play the 8 at any time. And furthermore, when he plays the 8 he may call out any suit—Diamonds, Hearts, Clubs, or Spades—and the next player must follow the suit that has been called, or else must go to the Dig Pile.

In other words, an 8 acts as a Joker and can be transmuted into any suit at the whim of he who plays it.

After any single player has disposed of all his cards, the round stops. The winning player then scores the total amount of cards in his opponent's hands. Let's say Player 1 holds six cards and Player 2 holds two cards, then the winning player scores 8 points. As soon as any player scores 21 points, he wins the game.

There is one further catch in the rules. Should one player go out and any other player be caught with an 8 in his hand, he loses double the amount of cards he holds. For example, if a player holds three cards and one of them is an 8, he loses 6 points to the winner.

One other rule: A player who holds an 8 need not play it. He may keep on pulling cards at will from the Dig Pile. At rare times this is good strategy; most of the time it isn't.

Crazy Eights should be played quickly. Then it is fun—lots of fun.

# I DOUBT IT

This terrific card game may be played by anywhere from four to ten players.

First deal out all the cards to the players, face down, one at a time.

The object of the game is to get rid of all the cards in your hand.

The game starts with the player to the left of the dealer calling out *Ace*. If this player has an *Ace*, he now places it, face down, in the center of the table. If he has several *Aces*, he can place all of them at the center of the table, calling out "*Two Aces*," or "*Three Aces*."

If this player has no *Aces*, he has two alternatives: he can call out "*Pass*," signifying that he has no *Aces* and that the next player should take his turn; or he can place a different card, face down, in the middle of the table and *pretend* that his card (or cards) is an *Ace*. This, of course, is where the game gets really tricky. The player can place one, two, three, or four cards in the middle of the table, calling out "*One Ace*," "*Two Aces*," "*Three Aces*," or "*Four Aces*," as the case may be. But only some of these cards, or perhaps none of them, may actually be *Aces*.

If no one questions the authenticity of the player's claim, the next player gets the chance to play a *Two*. The game progresses with each player taking his turn, right up to the *King*, and then back to the *Ace*, and around again.

But if anybody thinks that one of the other players is bluffing when he puts his cards in the middle of the table, he calls out "*I doubt it!*" At this point, the game is halted and the dealer turns up the cards that were put in the middle of the table by the accused player.

If the card or cards actually are what the player said they were, then the challenger must take *all* the cards from the pile in the middle of the table, and put them in his hand.

If the card or cards are *not* what the accused player claimed they were when he put them down, then the *bluffer* must take all the cards in the pile and put them in his hand, even if some of his cards were called correctly. If he has called even one out of four cards incorrectly, he is to be treated just as if he called all the cards incorrectly.

The game continues in this way, from *Ace* through *King*, and then back to *Ace* again, until someone has gotten rid of every card in his hand. That player wins the game.

# TWO-ACE CHARLIE

If your living room is choked with propriety and your guests are all sitting about like second cousins at a funeral, there is no game that will pep them up like TWO-ACE CHARLIE. It goes to work on a crowd in easy doses and gets the sedate excited without their knowing it. Indeed, it is a peach of a game for any group that craves a little gambling.

Before playing TWO-ACE CHARLIE, the hostess should have on hand a few rolls of pennies with which to make change, and two decks of bridge cards. If the company is more adventurous, nickels can be used instead of pennies, and if we happen to be writing for millionaires, no one's going to stop them from playing around with silver dollars. Anyhow, checks and specie are traded in for common coin—let us say, pennies.

The two decks are run through—the Aces, Kings, Queens, and Jacks being separated from the other cards. The two Kings of Clubs are removed, so that one pack consists of 30 "picture" cards and Aces and the other pack of 72 "number" cards.

Both packs are generously shuffled and placed in the center of the table. The game is begun by dealing a single card from the Number Pile to each player, who is then required to ante into the pot the number of pennies equal to the number of pips on the card he has been dealt. For example, if Gladys is dealt a trey, she contributes three cents to the pot. If George has the tough luck to pull a ten he is soaked for a dime. After this preliminary deal, the players throw their cards face up into the Discard Heap. Then the game starts in earnest.

Each player in turn gets a chance. The first player picks a single card from the Picture Pile, turns it up in full view, and throws it into the Discard Pile. If it happens to be a Jack, he is privileged to contribute further to the pot. The exact amount of his charity is determined by his picking a second card, this one from the Number Pile. He puts into the pot pennies equal to the number on the card which he has picked.

Now suppose, on the other hand, he picks a Queen. This is a lucky break and entitles him to a dividend. The number of pennies he draws out of the pot is determined by the number on the second card which he picks. This second card, of course, is taken from the Number Pile.

The draw of a King is still luckier—that is, provided the King has red hair. If a player picks a King of Hearts or a King of Diamonds, he is entitled to take out of the pot double the pennies on his number card. On the other hand, the black King, which appears only twice in the deck, is not only a sign of evil, but is an out-and-out misfortune. The victim perforce must pick three number cards in a row and must pay for each one of them.

If a player picks an Ace, he is on the road to bonanza. On that round, he does no more. *He doesn't draw a number card.* He doesn't put anything into the pot, nor does he draw therefrom. He simply sits still, waits, hopes, prays—prays for a second Ace on his next turn, which will entitle him to appropriate the whole pot—every last cent of it. When an Ace is picked, the drawer of it retains it and places it face up in front of him.

If eight Aces appear on the table, each one in front of a different player, then, of course, no one can possibly become Two-Ace Charlie, and at that point a new deal is in order. All the "number cards" and all the "picture cards," *including the eight Aces,* are separated and placed in two stacks, as heretofore set forth. The pot remains. The next player takes his turn as usual.

If the pot is emptied, a new pot is started. This means that the players are again dealt a single card which determines how much each initially contributes to the new pot.

If at any point during the game there are no more cards in the Picture Pile, the deal does not end. The pot remains as is, and the cards in the Discard Heap are assorted and shuffled, after which the next play continues as usual. In this case, each player retains his aces.

TWO-ACE CHARLIE can be played with any number of people up to fifteen. Playing with pennies, financial catastrophes should be rare. There *should* be a good deal of excitement.

# IRISH BULLS

An Irish bull is a grotesque blunder in language, differing from a malapropism in that the blunder lies not in the misuse of words, but in a complete confusion of ideas—which usually results in a joining of two mutually exclusive concepts. Webster defines an Irish bull as "an expression containing apparent congruity but actual incongruity of ideas," and gives us this almost perfect example: "He remarked in all seriousness that it was hereditary in his family to have no children."

The Irish bulls that follow could easily challenge Webster's best.

"Mercy me!" Mrs. Murphy said to her husband, "but wasn't that a terrible thunder and lightning storm we had last night."

"You don't say!" replied Murphy. "Why didn't you wake me? You know I can't sleep when it thunders like that!"

"Begorra, Willie," Mike exclaimed as he finished a final pint and rose unsteadily to his feet, "but I haven't the faintest notion where I left my cap. Have you seen it?"

"I have," replied Willie. "It's on your head."

"Indeed it is! And it's a good thing you found it, or I'd have gone off without it."

"Your money or your life!" cried the stick-up man, brandishing a revolver. "Take my life," replied Casey. "I'm saving my money for my old age."

"Dear Molly," wrote O'Neill, "this is the fourth letter I've written to you asking for your hand in marriage. If you still refuse, please return this letter unopened."

♚

"Why do Irishmen always enjoy a brawl?" asked the American tourist.

"That's simple," replied O'Leary. "An Irishman is never at peace except when he's fighting."

"Callahan!" cried Hogan, after his friend had tripped and fallen into the gutter. "Are you all right?"

"I can't answer you," replied Callahan, "I've been knocked speechless."

♚

"Abstinence is a fine thing," observed Paddy. "But it must always be practiced in moderation."

♚

"You're such a pest," the father scolded his misbehaving child. "The next time I take you out I'll leave you home."

♚

"An Irishman," noted Flynn, "will die before he'd let himself be buried in any but an Irish cemetery."

**347**

# JUGGLING JUGS

Two merchants in partnership have purchased an eight-quart jug of olive oil. They want to divide the oil into two equal parts. However, all they have on hand for purposes of measuring are two jugs—one of which holds five quarts, and the other three quarts.

At first it seems impossible to effect an even division of four quarts each by using the three containers on hand; but they finally manage to do it.

CAN YOU?

*Answers on page 499*

# THE SMALL GAME HUNTERS

HOW MANY QUAIL DID GERALD SHOOT?

348

*Answers on page 499*

# LATE FOR TEE

CAN YOU ANSWER JOE'S QUESTION?

*Answers on page 499*

# THE STEEL BEAM

A steel beam balances on a scale with three-quarters of a beam and a ¾-pound weight.

HOW MUCH DOES THE BEAM WEIGH?

*Answers on page 500*

# COUNT THE TRAINS

CAN YOU ANSWER TOM'S QUESTION?

*Answers on page 500*

# SCALING THE ORCHARD WALL

A boy wishing to get to the top of an orchard wall found that the ladder he had brought, when placed upright against the wall, just reached to the top. So he pulled the foot of the ladder out exactly 10 feet, and supported it on a box two feet high. The top of the ladder then reached exactly to the top of the wall.

WHAT WAS THE HEIGHT OF THE WALL?

*Answers on page 500*

# THE CYCLISTS AND THE FLY

Two cyclists, 20 miles apart, start at the same instant and ride towards each other along a straight road at a speed of 10 miles per hour. At the same instant a fly on the forehead of one of the riders starts to fly at 15 miles per hour toward the other rider, alights on his forehead, and then immediately flies back to the first rider. The fly travels back and forth over the continuously decreasing distance between the two riders until the two riders meet.

HOW FAR HAS THE FLY FLOWN WHEN ALL
ITS JOURNEYS ARE ADDED TOGETHER?

*Answers on page 500*

# APPOINTMENT IN ABILENE

Percy Poppon had an appointment in Abilene at two o'clock in the afternoon. If he left home and traveled at 15 miles per hour, he would arrive at one o'clock; if he traveled at 10 miles per hour he would not arrive until three o'clock.

**WHAT WAS THE DISTANCE FROM HIS HOME TO ABILENE?**

*Answers on page 500*

# THE STRANDED TEDDY BEAR

Father takes little Oswald to the zoo. Ozzie is especially attracted by the fierce alligators who lie exposed in the shallow water of a circular moat.

We now interrupt this story with some simple figures: The moat is six feet deep. In the center of it, there is a concrete island, which is exactly 11 feet away from the outer edge of the moat.

Little Ozzie gets sort of bumptious and flings his teddy bear onto the island. He cries his head off, so his Pa decides to do something about the situation.

Scurrying around, Father finds a nine-foot plank and a 10-foot plank, but nothing to nail or bind them together. However, with the aid of these two pieces of wood, he somehow contrives to retrieve the teddy bear 11 feet away.

HOW DOES HE DO IT?

*Answers on page 500*

# THE FORTY-TWO BEERS

In Guatelavia, the standard dollar is worth 100¢. In the bordering country of Tinto, the standard dollar is also worth 100¢. In fact, both dollars contain the same gold equivalent and are of exact value.

However, because of conditions of foreign exchange, the Guatelavian dollar is worth only 90¢ in Tinto, while the Tintoese dollar is worth but 90¢ in Guatelavia.

One day a smart Yankee with an enormous thirst drops into a Guatelavian cafe and orders a 10¢ beer. He hands over the single Guatelavian dollar that he has in his pocket, and asks for 90¢ in change in Tintoese money. Since the Tintoese dollar is only worth 90¢ in Guatelavia, the barkeep gives him a full Tintoese dollar.

Whereupon our friend hops across the border and makes for the nearest saloon. He orders a beer and hands the bartender in Tinto a Tintoese dollar—the one he got in Guatelavia—demanding 90¢ change in Guatelavian money. Since, as aforesaid, the Guatelavian dollar is worth only 90¢ in Tinto, he receives a full Guatelavian dollar for his change.

Things look pretty bright for the Yankee, and he keeps up the transaction the whole day long, imbibing exactly 42 beers. When he is done, he finds that he has the same Guatelavian dollar that he started out with.

Now apparently the Guatelavian cafe sold 21 beers at the ordinary price and made a profit; and apparently the Tintoese saloon sold 21 beers with a profit, and evidently the American financial wizard got 42 beers without expending a single penny . . . So the question remains:

WHO PAID FOR THEM THERE BEERS?

*Answers on page 500*

**353**

# THE DARING YOUNG MAN

HOW DOES THE YOUNG MAN CROSS THE BRIDGE SAFELY?

*Answers on page 501*

# THE ARTIST'S CANVAS

An artist has an oddly shaped piece of canvas that contains exactly 81 square inches.

The small square piece projecting at the top is one inch on a side. It is attached to a square of 16 square inches, which is in turn attached to a larger square of 64 square inches. The artist wants to make a nine-by-nine square canvas for his painting.

**HOW CAN HE DIVIDE THE CANVAS INTO THE SMALLEST NUMBER OF PIECES THAT WILL FIT TOGETHER TO MAKE A PERFECT SQUARE?**

*Answers on page 501*

*Answers on page 501*

# THE EGG MAN

An egg man sold to Mr. Jones half his stock of eggs and half an egg. He then sold to Smith half of his remaining stock and half an egg. Then Robinson bought half of the eggs which he had left and half an egg. Finally Brown bought the rest of his stock, namely 33 eggs.

**HOW MANY EGGS DID THE EGG MAN HAVE TO START WITH?**
**HE DID NOT SELL ANY BROKEN EGGS!**

*Answers on page 501*

*Answers on page 501*

**355**

# THE COMMUTER

CAN YOU TELL HOW MUCH TIME BROWN
SPENT WALKING UNTIL HE MET HIS CAR?

*Answers on page 501*

# THE PENSIONER

A pensioner remembered that he was sent to school when he was four-and-a-half years of age, and that he stayed at that same school for one-sixth of his life. Then he remained in the army for one-fifth of his life, and when he left the army he spent one-quarter of his life as a clerk. At present he had already spent one-third of his life in retirement.

**WHAT WAS THE PENSIONER'S AGE?**

*Answers on page 501*

# THE FRUIT PEDDLERS

Three fruit peddlers stood beside their pushcarts hawking their wares. They were each selling apples and each pushcart carried an identical price sign. The signs were the kind which are generally used by fruit peddlers. Similar signs may be seen every weekday in every marketplace in the land.

The first peddler had fifteen apples to sell; he sold them all.

The second peddler had fourteen apples to sell; he sold them all.

The third peddler had thirteen apples to sell; he sold them all.

At the end of the day, they found that each had realized exactly the same amount of money for his apples.

The apples were not sold by weight or by measure. None of the apples was rotten; none of the apples was given away; none of the peddlers ate any of his apples; nor was any peddler given counterfeit money.

**HOW DO YOU ACCOUNT FOR THE STRANGE RESULTS?**

*Answers on page 501*

# THE TEACHER'S DILEMMA

A teacher is trying to figure out how many students he can put in the classroom without having more than two students in any one row, including all the diagonal rows.

**CAN YOU HELP HIM OUT? TWO STUDENTS HAVE ALREADY BEEN SEATED, SO NO MORE STUDENTS ARE PERMITTED IN THAT CORNER-TO-CORNER DIAGONAL.**

*Answers on page 501*

357

# THE SCHOLARSHIP EXAMINATION

Five boys sat for a scholarship examination. In each of five subjects—Latin, English, science, mathematics, and history—60 marks were divided among the five boys. Each boy was awarded at least one mark in each subject. Each boy, curiously enough, was first in one subject, second in another, third in another, fourth in another, and fifth in yet another. Their aggregate marks, however, differed. The scholarship award was based on aggregate marks.

The following facts were reported:

Alfred took third place in Latin. In English, however, he scored 27 marks against David's 26.

Bertram scored 12 marks in science and was bottom but one in mathematics, scoring only 2.

Cyril was bottom in history, with 10 marks.

David, with 18 marks, took third place in mathematics.

Egbert took top place in history, but was bottom in science, with only 9 marks.

The top mark in Latin was 14.

**WHO WON THE SCHOLARSHIP, AND WHAT WERE THE AGGREGATE MARKS OF THE WINNER AND HIS RIVALS?**

*Answers on page 502*

# THE DRY GOODS DEALER

A dry goods dealer has a five-yard piece of 36-inch wide material. A lady wishes to purchase one and one-half yards. Neither a yardstick nor a tape measure, nor any other measuring device is available.

**HOW IS THE DIFFICULTY SOLVED?**

*Answers on page 502*

# THE SWISS MILKMAIDS

**WHICH GIRL HAS THE HEAVIEST MILK CAN?**

**WHICH THE LIGHTEST?**

*Answers on page 502*

# MRS. ADDEM'S CHILDREN

Mrs. Addem's age is three times the sum of the ages (in years) of her children.

This ratio will, of course, decrease from year to year. In 11 years' time Mrs. Addem's age will equal the sum of her children's ages.

The age (in years) of the eldest child is equal to the product of the ages of the other two.

No two children were born in the same year.

**WHAT ARE THE CHILDREN'S AGES?**

*Answers on page 502*

**359**

# THE ROPE LADDER

HOW MANY LADDER RUNGS WILL BE
SUBMERGED TWO HOURS LATER?

*Answers on page 502*

# BOOTS

Mr. Cobblewell, a bootmaker, sold a pair of boots to a well-dressed stranger, who tendered a $50 bill in payment. As he had no change, Mr. Cobblewell went next door and had his friend Plaster, the druggist, change the bill. The price of the boots was $46. The stranger took his change and left.

Shortly afterwards Plaster appeared in Cobblewell's shop in a state of much agitation to explain that the $50 bill he had been given was counterfeit. Naturally, Cobblewell had no option but to replace it with a good $50 bill.

### HOW MUCH HAS COBBLEWELL LOST?

*Answers on page 502*

# THE LILY POND

A certain pond in Central America is a perfect circle twenty feet in diameter. Every year a magnificent water-lily appears in the exact center of the pond. The lily grows with a remarkable rapidity, doubling its area every day; at the end of exactly twenty-one days, the lily fills the entire area of the pond. Then it dies away and for twelve months no more is seen of it.

### AT THE END OF HOW MANY DAYS FROM ITS FIRST APPEARANCE DOES THE LILY OCCUPY HALF THE AREA OF THE POND?

*Answers on page 502*

# THE CAT IN THE WELL

Through some misadventure, a cat fell down a well. The well was 18 feet deep. The cat managed to climb out, but only after experiencing great difficulty, since the sides of the well were damp and slippery.

For every minute of effort, the cat gained three feet. It was then too tired to struggle further and rested. During that next minute of rest, the cat slid back two feet.

**HOW LONG DID IT TAKE THE CAT TO GET OUT OF THE WELL?**

*Answers on page 502*

# THE PROBLEM OF THE CHAINS

A mechanic has six pieces of chain, each containing five links. He wants to make a continuous piece of 30 links.

It costs 20 cents to cut a link open, and it costs 50 cents to weld the opening back again. A new continuous chain, all in one piece, can be bought for $4.

**HOW MUCH CAN BE SAVED IF THE CHAIN IS PUT TOGETHER IN THE MOST ECONOMICAL MANNER?**

*Answers on page 502*

# THE TWO CANOES

At precisely the same moment, two boys start paddling their canoes from opposite sides of a river. One boy paddles faster than the other. They meet at a point 410 feet from one of the shores.

After each arrives at his destination, he remains there for 10 minutes. Then he starts on his return trip.

The canoes again meet, this time at a point 230 feet from one of the shores.

**WHAT IS THE EXACT WIDTH OF THE RIVER?**

*Answers on page 502*

*Answers on page 502*

# THE FOUR GOATS

A farmer has four goats tethered one at each corner of a square field 100 feet by 100 feet. The tethers are of such a length that each goat can graze over a sector of 50 feet radius. The goats therefore are compelled to leave uneaten a portion in the center of the field.

Three of the goats are sold, and the farmer lengthens the tether of the remaining goat. He finds that he has made the rope just long enough to allow the goat to graze over an area equal to the combined area the four goats had previously grazed over.

**WHAT WAS THE LENGTH OF THE TETHER?**

*Answers on page 503*

*Answers on page 503*

# THE BLIND ABBOT

An old medieval tale tells of a blind abbot who had 20 prodigal monks under his care. He and his charges lived in the top story of a square tower which was arranged in nine cells. He himself occupied the center cell.

Each night it was his habit to patrol the abbey and to count his charges in order to make sure that the monks were all at home. His own peculiar method of tallying was to count nine heads for each wall. If he got a full count, he took it for granted that all were present.

Now a certain sly fellow arranged the beds so that two of the boys could leave of a night and make whoopee without the old codger suspecting any A.W.O.L.

On another night, this shrewd young fellow even contrived to bring in four comrades from a neighboring monastery for a party. He arranged the group so cleverly that when the abbot made his evening round, he still counted only nine heads along each wall.

A few months later, the boys decided to give a grand blow-out. They increased the attendance to 32, but still the abbot did not sense that anything was amiss.

And as a grand finale, they held one big gala super-affair, which 36 monks attended, but still the blind abbot counted but nine heads along each wall.

Now the problem is to discover how that wily brother arranged the monks in each cell so that 18, 20, 24, 32, and 36 friars were present, although the blind abbot in each case counted nine heads along each wall of the tower.

*Answers on page 503*

# THE COUNTERFEIT COIN

A king of ancient days once wished to reward one of his wise men, so he had his servants lay before the sage nine coins and a balance scale.

Addressing the object of his largesse, the king said, "There are nine coins here. Eight of them are made of pure gold. One of them has been debased by a lesser metal, which of course, does not weigh as much as gold.

"Now," continued the king, "you will determine your own reward. If you weigh each coin separately, you will, of course, find out which coin weighs the least, and that one will obviously be the counterfeit coin. But if you proceed in that manner you will be obliged to use the balance scale nine times. You would then achieve the worst result, for every time you use the scale, you lose one coin. You can take 15 minutes to think over how to proceed. Since you are a very wise man, you will manage to use the balance scale the fewest possible number of times."

The sage retired for a few minutes, and then came back and addressed himself to the king. "Sire," he said, "I am now ready to pick the counterfeit coin." And he proceeded to do this, using the scale the least number of times necessary to determine which of the nine coins was the counterfeit.

### HOW DID HE CONTRIVE TO FIND OUT?
### HOW MANY TIMES DID HE USE THE SCALE?

*Answers on page 503*

# THE WHIFFLEBIRD

ON WHAT DAY HAD THE WHIFFLEBIRD EATEN
EXACTLY HALF THE LEAVES ON THE TREE?

*Answers on page 503*

# THE FISHERMEN

Two fishermen caught a large fish and wished to know its weight, but did not have a scale on hand. So they set a plank up as a see-saw, and with one fisherman standing on each end, they moved the plank until it was exactly balanced. Keeping the plank in the same position, they then changed places, and the lighter man put the fish on his side of the plank. This brought the balance exactly right again. The weights of the fishermen were 120 and 150 lbs.

**WHAT WAS THE WEIGHT OF THE FISH?**

*Answers on page 504*

# THE VICTORY COLUMN

In a public square stands a column commemorating a great victory. The shaft of the column is 200 feet high and 30 feet in circumference.

The shaft is wreathed in a spiral garland which passes around the shaft exactly five times.

**WHAT IS THE LENGTH OF THE GARLAND?**

*Answers on page 504*

# THE ESCAPING PRISONER

A convict escapes from prison and has a half hour's start on two guards and a bloodhound who race after him. The guards' speed is four miles per hour; the dog's speed is 12 miles per hour; but the prisoner can do only three miles per hour. The dog runs up to the prisoner and then back to the guards, and so on back and forth until the guards catch the prisoner.

HOW FAR DOES THE DOG TRAVEL ALTOGETHER?

*Answers on page 504*

# THE SAHARA EXPEDITION

Charles Wayne Looksee, noted African explorer, is preparing to fulfill his life's ambition—to chart the trackless sands of the Sahara. A trip straight across the desert would be hazardous enough, but Looksee's journey will be doubly dangerous, since he must travel a roundabout route so as to make observations.

One of Looksee's biggest problems is equipment. For the automobile, he buys special heat-resistant tires, each of which is guaranteed to last 12,000 miles. It is extremely important that he does not load his car with any more weight than is necessary, so he determines to rely completely on the guarantee. Now the problem is:

WHAT IS THE LEAST NUMBER OF TIRES THE
EXPLORER MUST BUY TO CARRY HIM THROUGH
THE 27,000-MILE JOURNEY? AND WHY?

*Answers on page 504*

# A CASE OF ORANGES

Four women—Mary, Jane, Kate, and Eliza—chipped in and bought a case containing 233 oranges. They divided them up in proportion to the amount of money each woman chipped in.

Mary received 20 more oranges than Jane, 53 more than Kate, and 71 more than Eliza.

**HOW MANY ORANGES DID EACH WOMAN RECEIVE?**

*Answers on page 505*

# SMOKE GETS IN YOUR EYES

**HOW MANY CIGARETTES CAN THEY MAKE FROM THE BUTTS?**

*Answers on page 505*

# NAME THE CARDS

CAN YOU NAME THE THREE CARDS?

*Answers on page 505*

# THE HORSE TRADER

A horse trader brings a string of horses to a horse fair. As admission charge, he gives up one of his horses. At the fair, he sells one half of those remaining; and on the way out, he is charged one horse as a trading fee.

He proceeds to a second fair where like conditions prevail. There he pays one horse to get in, sells half of the horses he still has on hand, and pays a single horse as trading fee.

And, not content, he proceeds to a third fair. Here again he pays one horse to get in, sells one half of the horses remaining, and is charged a single horse on the way out as a trading fee.

He then has one horse left on which to ride home with his proceeds.

**HOW MANY HORSES DID HE START OUT WITH?**

*Answers on page 505*

# THE CLIMBING MONKEY

A rope is passed over a frictionless pulley, which is suspended from the ceiling. From one end of the rope there is suspended a 15-pound weight that exactly balances a monkey who is holding on to the other end of the rope.

**IF THE MONKEY CLIMBS THE ROPE, WILL HE RISE ABOVE OR SINK BELOW THE HEIGHT OF THE WEIGHT?**

*Answers on page 505*

# HUMOROUS SIGNS

*In a New York restaurant:*
Customers who consider our waitresses uncivil ought to see the manager.

☗

*In the window of a Kentucky dealer in washing machines:*
Don't kill your wife. Let our washing machines do the dirty work.

☗

*In an Arkansas shoe repair shop:*
If your shoes aren't ready, don't blame us. Two of our employees have gone after a heel to save your soles.

☗

*On a Connecticut road:*
Drive like hell, and you'll get there.

☗

*In a Montreal restaurant:*
The Early Bird Gets the Worm! Special Shoppers' Luncheon before 11 a.m.

☗

*In a cemetery at South Bethlehem, Pa.:*
Persons are prohibited from picking flowers from any but their own graves.

*On a New York loft building:*
Wanted—Woman to sew buttons on the fourth floor.

*On a farm-gate in Ohio:*
Peddlers beware! We shoot every tenth peddler. The ninth one just left.

☖

*In a restaurant in Cleveland, Ohio, which featured a 50-cent hang-over breakfast:*
One jumbo orange juice, toast, coffee, two aspirins and our sympathy.

*On a Tennessee highway:*
Take Notice: When this sign is under water, this road is impassable.

☖

*On the card of a Hollywood jewelry store:*
We hire out wedding rings.

☖

*Above the coffee percolator of a roadside dining car east of Lancaster, Pa.:*
Use less sugar and stir like the devil. We don't mind the noise.

☖

*On a blackboard outside a London church, during the blitz:*
If your knees are knocking, kneel on them.

☖

*In Pennsylvania, surmounted on a large reproduction of a match:*
This is the forest prime evil.

*In a Kingston, Ont. repair shop:*
Closed July 1 to July 15.
Open July 21 for sure.

*In clinic waiting room:*
Ladies in the Waiting Room Will Please Not Exchange Symptoms. It Gets the Doctors Hopelessly Confused.

*In a Rochester plumber's window:*
Do it yourself—then call us before it's too late.

*In a Shreveport realtor's window:*
Get lots while you're young.

*On a church bulletin board:*
This church is prayer-conditioned.

*In the window of a Boston necktie emporium:*
Come in and tie one on.

*On a convalescent home in New York:*
For the sick and tired of the Episcopal Church.

*In a Pittsburgh bakery window:*
CREAM PUFFS—6 FOR 29¢
The flakiest, puffiest of puffs crammed full of creamy mustard.

*In a yard near Lake Arrowhead, Cal.:*
Worms with Fish Appeal.

♔

*Across a blasted wine shop window in Birmingham, England:*
We are carrying on with unbroken spirits.

♔

*In a Tacoma men's clothing store window:*
FIFTEEN MEN'S WOOL SUITS—$3.00
*They won't last an hour!*

♔

*On a dairy:*
You can't beat our milk, but you can whip our cream.

♔

*Billboard near North Augusta, S.C.:*
Try Our Easy Payment Plan. 100% Down. No Future Worries About Payment.

♔

*On Bing Crosby's front lawn:*
Keep off the grass. Remember when you, too, were struggling for recognition.

*In a Chicago restaurant:*
Dreaded Veal Cutlets

*In a brassiere shoppe:*
We fix Flats.

*Warning posted in an office at a southern air base:*
CAUTION—Make sure brain is engaged before putting mouth into gear.

*In a garage in Albuquerque, N.M.:*
Don't smoke around the gasoline tank. If your life isn't worth anything, gasoline is!

*In the maternity department of a St. Louis hospital:*
Ladies Ready to Bear Department.

*On a movie theatre:*
Children's Matinee Today. Adults Not Admitted Unless With Child.

*On a Los Angeles dance hall:*
Good Clean Dancing Every Night but Sunday.

*In a New York restaurant:*
Pies like mother used to make before she took to bridge and cigarettes.

*In a restaurant near an Army camp:*
Watch your coat, hat, and girl friend.

♔

*On a Los Angeles movie marquee:*
GO FOR BROKE
LAS VEGAS STORY

♔

*In front of an Oshkosh mortuary chapel:*
The fact that those we have served once return again, and recommend us to their friends, is a high endorsement of the service we render.

♔

*Outside London striptease theatre:*
HERE THE BELLES PEEL

♔

*On a newly seeded lawn at Wellesley College:*
Don't Ruin the Gay Young Blades!

*Flashed on the screen of an Albany, N.Y. motion picture theatre:*
A $5.00 bill has been found in the aisle. Will the owner please form a line outside the box-office.

♔

*In the lobby of a hotel in Rochester, Minn., home of the Mayo Clinic:*
Please do not discuss your operation in the lobby.

# MIXED BAG

Below, you will find 45 questions, each of which is guaranteed to bear no relation to any other—or to anything else, for that matter. Four choices are given for each question. Check the one you believe is correct.

A score of 30 is fair; 35 is good; and if you score over 40, you're a trivia expert to be reckoned with!

*Answers on page 505*

1. The busiest airport in the world is:
   Chicago (O'Hare)        New York (J.F. Kennedy)
   Los Angeles             London (Heathrow)

2. William Shakespeare was born in:
   1450      1540      1564      1605

3. La Scala in Milan is a (n):
   Museum      Opera House      Church      Palace

4. Of the following, the city that is *not* on the Mississippi River is:
   Kansas City      Minneapolis      St. Louis      Memphis

5. An oxymoron is a (n):
   Coughing fit      Idiot      Chemical compound      Figure of speech

6. "Big Six" was the nickname of:
   Walter Johnson        Christy Mathewson
   Ty Cobb               Mel Ott

7. Of the following, the only word that is *not* an acronym—a word formed by joining together the first letters of a phrase—is:
   Laser      Photon      Radar      Scuba

8. The opera *Carmen* was composed by:
   Verdi      Wagner      Bizet      Offenbach

9. The Bull of Demarcation was a:
   Noted matador         Hindu hero
   Papal document        Treaty

10. A griffin is a fabulous animal resembling a cross between a (n):
    Hawk and goat         Eagle and lion
    Man and goat          Horse and lion

11. The former colony of the Belgian Congo is now the nation of:
    Botswana      Zaire      Zambia      Tanzania

12. Little Jack Horner pulled out of his pie a(n):
    Peach      Plum      Apple      Cherry

**378**

13. The nickname "Seward's Folly" was applied to:
   Oregon    Hawaii    Alaska    Cuba

14. The words "*Veni, vidi, vici*" were spoken by:
   Caesar Augustus              Julius Caesar
   Cato                         Cicero

15. Newfoundland became part of Canada in:
   1790    1812    1865    1949

16. Of the following, the city which is closest by air to New York is:
   Lima    Rio de Janeiro    Amsterdam    Buenos Aires

17. The first President to throw out the first ball of the baseball season was:
   McKinley    Taft    Wilson    Harding

18. Tapioca is made from:
   Rice    Bread    Cassava root    Whey

19. The heaviest organ in the human body is the:
   Heart    Liver    Pancreas    Kidney

20. A sirocco is a(n):
   Rug    Camel    Wind    Oasis

21. A violin has this many strings:
   Three    Four    Five    Six

22. Bessarabia is now part of:
   Turkey    U.S.S.R.    Egypt    Iran

23. The hero of *The Iliad* is:
   Hector    Achilles    Ulysses    Ilium

24. A philippic is a:
   Tirade    Drug    Humanitarian    Disaster

25. The giant panda is a native of:
   Australia    China    Japan    India

26. Tacitus was a Roman:
   Emperor    Historian    General    Architect

27. The poem "Kublai Khan" was written by:
   Wordsworth    Blake    Shelley    Coleridge

28. Indonesia was once a colony of:
   England    The Netherlands    France    Germany

29. A cedilla is a(n):
   Insect    Diacritical mark    Spanish dance    Cigar

30. The locale of the novel *The Good Earth* is:

    Egypt    China    Iowa    Ireland

31. An object made of 18-carat gold contains this proportion of pure gold:

    One quarter    One half    Three quarters    Two thirds

32. The Rialto is the name of a Venetian:

    Canal    Bridge    Theater    Palace

33. The ancient city of Troy was located in what is now:

    Greece    Bulgaria    Turkey    Cyprus

34. The name James Oglethorpe is connected with the state of:

    Delaware    Rhode Island    Virginia    Georgia

35. A jetty is a(n):

    Airport    Pier    Servant    Dish

36. The winner of the first Super Bowl was the:

    Kansas City Chiefs            Green Bay Packers
    New York Jets                 Baltimore Colts

37. The capital of Colombia is:

    Caracas    Cartagena    Bogota    Quito

38. The Rand in South Africa is noted for the mining of:

    Diamonds    Gold    Silver    Uranium

39. The Roman numeral MCDLXVI in Arabic numerals is:

    1666    1466    1716    1186

40. Captain Ahab is a character in the novel:

    *Mutiny on the Bounty*        *Two Years Before the Mast*
    *Moby Dick*                   *Lord Jim*

41. Of the following, the musical instrument which is *not* a reed instrument is the:

    English horn    French horn    Oboe    Bassoon

42. A bivalve is a(n):

    Mollusk    Tool    Machine    Artery

43. Of the following, the only river which does *not* run through Germany is the:

    Danube    Rhine    Rhone    Oder

44. A travois is a:

    Vehicle    Dwelling    Dog    Pantry

45. The headquarters of the League of Nations was in:

    New York    Paris    Rome    Geneva

**380**

# LANDMARKS

This quiz will test your knowledge of the world's most famous structures. The seasoned traveler will have an edge here, but even if you're only an armchair globe-trotter, you're sure to have heard of most of these landmarks.

Below, you will find 40 questions. There are four choices listed for each. Check the one you believe is correct.

A score of 22 is passing; 30 is good; and 35 marks you as an expert.

*Answers on page 505*

1. The largest office building in the world, in floor area, is the:
   World Trade Center          Empire State Building
   Pentagon                    Sears Tower

2. The Kremlin in Moscow is a:
   Fortress      Plaza.      Building      Street

3. The Great Pyramid of Cheops is approximately this many years old:
   50,000      20,000      5,000      2,500

4. The Alhambra in Granada, Spain, was built by:
   Turks      Spaniards      Portuguese      Moors

5. The largest religious structure in the world is:
   St. Peter's Church (Rome)          Angkor Wat
   Notre Dame Cathedral (Paris)       Mohammed's Tomb

6. The "Forbidden City" of the Tibetan Buddhists is:
   Katmandu      Lhasa      Shangri-La      Sikkim

7. The first domed stadium was built in:
   New Orleans      Houston      Pontiac      Los Angeles

8. The longest man-made object in the world—the fuel pipeline—is approximately this many miles long:
   25,000      10,000      2,000      750

9. The palace at Versailles was built by:
   Napoleon      Louis XIV      Louis XI      Cardinal Richelieu

10. The first subway in the world was built in:
    Boston      Paris      London      New York

11. The ruins at Chichen Itza, Mexico, are the remains of this Indian civilization:
    Aztec      Mayan      Inca      Toltec

12. The Statue of Liberty in New York was paid for by donations from:
    American citizens          French citizens
    The French government      The American government

13. The Mount Rushmore Memorial contains the busts of Washington, Jefferson, Lincoln, and:
    Jackson      T. Roosevelt      Wilson      F. D. Roosevelt

14. The longest big-ship canal in the world is the:
    Suez      Panama      Welland      Volga-Baltic

15. The Hoover Dam lies on this river:
    Missouri      Colorado      Mississippi      Rio Grande

16. The Parthenon is located in:
    Rome      Jerusalem      Athens      Alexandria

17. The Shwe Dagon pagoda in Rangoon, Burma, is a shrine of this religion:
    Hinduism      Shintoism      Buddhism      Taoism

18. The step pyramid common in ancient Mesopotamia is often called a:
    Campanile      Ziggurat      Stupa      Pharos

19. At Stonehenge, the stones are arranged basically in the form of a(n):
    Cross      Circle      Square      Oval

20. The longest single span bridge in the world is the:
    Verrazano-Narrows             Golden Gate
    Chesapeake Bay Bridge-Tunnel  Mackinac Straits

21. The longest deep-water bridge in the world is the:
    Verrazano-Narrows             Golden Gate
    Chesapeake Bay Bridge-Tunnel  Mackinac Straits

22. The village of Mont-St.-Michel lies off the coast of:
    Normandy      Picardy      Gascogny      Flanders

23. The largest tomb ever built is the:
    Tomb of Lenin        Great Pyramid of Cheops
    Ruwanweli Pagoda     Mausoleum of Halicarnassus

24. Excluding water tunnels, the longest tunnel in the world is the:
    Brooklyn-Battery     Simplon
    Gotthard             Hampton Roads

25. From end to end, the Great Wall of China stretches approximately this number of miles:
    1,500      1,000      500      250

26. The Dome of the Rock, or Mosque of Omar, is located in:
    Mecca      Medina      Damascus      Jerusalem

27. Of the following, the only man who did *not* have a part in the construction of St. Peter's Church in Rome is:

    Michelangelo     Raphael     Bramante     DaVinci

28. The Taj Mahal was built as a:

    Palace     Fortress     Tomb     Treasury

29. The Coliseum in Rome was originally known as the:

    Circus Maximus              Flavian Amphitheater
    Theater of Dionysus         Forum Romanum

30. The tallest monument in the world is the:

    Statue of Liberty           Gateway Arch
    Washington Monument         San Jacinto Column

31. The Brandenburg Gate is located in:

    Nuremberg     Hamburg     Berlin     Potsdam

32. The Golden Gate Bridge connects San Francisco with:

    Oakland     Berkeley     Marin County     San Mateo County

33. The geodesic dome was designed by:

    Marshall McLuhan            R. Buckminster Fuller
    Thomas Huxley               Wernher von Braun

34. The Temple of the Emerald Buddha is located in:

    Saigon     Bangkok     Angkor Wat     Mandalay

35. The largest covered stadium in the world is (the):

    Astrodome                   New Orleans Superdome
    Wembly Stadium              Soldier's Field

36. The scientist who performed experiments using the Leaning Tower of Pisa was:

    Copernicus     Galileo     Bacon     DaVinci

37. The tallest structure in Europe is the:

    Spasskaya Tower             Eiffel Tower
    Cathedral of Chartres       KLM building

38. Of the following, the only structure located in Istanbul is the church of:

    Saint Basil                 Santa Sophia
    Saint Constantine           Santa Maria

39. The longest steel arch bridge in the world is the:

    Sydney Harbor               Bayonne
    Tappan Zee                  Glen Canyon

40. Big Ben is the name of a London:

    Building     Bell     Tower     Clock

# WHEN IN ROME...

When in Rome, do as the Romans do—speak Italian. The question is, what language would you speak if you were in each of the localities listed below.

The box contains a list of 20 languages. Next to each place name, write the name of the one language from the box which is predominantly spoken in that locality. Each language may be used only once.

In some of the places listed, more than one language is spoken. Choose only the language which, among those in the box, is most widely spoken in that locality.

A score of 8 is good; 13 is excellent; and 17 is the mark of an able linguist.

*Answers on page 506*

| | |
|---|---|
| ARABIC | DUTCH |
| SPANISH | FRENCH |
| DANISH | AFRIKAANS |
| KHMER | PORTUGUESE |
| BRETON | GERMAN |
| PERSIAN | MANX |
| HAUSA | GREEK |
| CATALAN | SINHALESE |
| BENGALI | ALEUT |
| SERBO-CROATIAN | ITALIAN |

1. Brazil _____
2. Haiti _____
3. South Africa _____
4. Austria _____
5. Colombia _____
6. Aruba _____
7. Sicily _____
8. Yugoslavia _____
9. India _____
10. Alaska _____
11. Jordan _____
12. Brittany _____
13. Isle of Man _____
14. Iran _____
15. Nigeria _____
16. Andorra _____
17. Cambodia _____
18. Greenland _____
19. Sri Lanka _____
20. Crete _____

# SUPERLATIVES

Below, you will find 23 questions on our planet's superlative waterways, land masses, etc. For each, your job is to fill in the blank on the right with the place name which deserves the superlative on the left.

A score of 12 is good; 17 is superior; and if you score 20 you're the greatest!

*Answers on page 506*

1.  Largest continent         _____

2.  Largest nation (area)      _____

3.  Largest nation (population) _____

4.  Smallest nation (area)    _____

5.  Largest city (population)   _____

6.  Most densely populated nation _____

7.  Largest ocean            _____

8.  Largest lake             _____

9.  Deepest lake            _____

10. Highest lake             _____

11. Longest river           _____

12. Highest waterfall       _____

13. Greatest mountain range _____

14. Highest mountain      _____

15. Deepest depression     _____

16. Largest desert          _____

17. Largest island          _____

18. Longest archipelago     _____

19. Largest peninsula       _____

20. Largest gulf             _____

21. Greatest tides          _____

22. Biggest meteor crater    _____

23. Largest gorge           _____

# LEADING LADIES

Here's one for movie buffs. Below, you will find the titles of 50 well-known films, each followed by the name of its leading man. Your job is to fill in the name of the leading lady who played opposite him in that film.

A score of 25 is fair; 35 is good; 40 is excellent; and 45 marks you as a first-class cinemaphile.

*Answers on page 506*

1. *Gone with the Wind:* Clark Gable and _____

2. *Casablanca:* Humphrey Bogart and _____

3. *On the Waterfront:* Marlon Brando and _____

4. *Rebecca:* Laurence Olivier and _____

5. *Camille:* Robert Taylor and _____

6. *The Blue Angel:* Emil Jannings and _____

7. *Queen Bess:* Errol Flynn and _____

8. *Rosemarie:* Nelson Eddy and _____

9. *Top Hat:* Fred Astaire and _____

10. *Algiers:* Charles Boyer and _____

11. *The Way We Were:* Robert Redford and _____

12. *Cat on a Hot Tin Roof:* Paul Newman and _____

13. *Love Story:* Ryan O'Neal and _____

14. *Bonnie and Clyde:* Warren Beatty and _____

15. *Romeo and Juliet:* Leslie Howard and _____

16. *South Pacific:* Rossano Brazzi and _____

17. *The Apartment:* Jack Lemmon and _____

18. *A Star Is Born:* James Mason and _____

19. *Random Harvest:* Ronald Colman and _____

20. *West Side Story:* Richard Beymer and _____

21. *Hurricane:* Jon Hall and _____

22. *Of Human Bondage:*
Laurence Harvey and _____

23. *My Fair Lady:* Rex Harrison and _____

24. *Johnny Belinda:* Lew Ayres and   _____

25. *Tarzan:* Johnny Weissmuller and   _____

26. *Gigi:* Louis Jourdan and   _____

27. *Manhunt:* Walter Pidgeon and   _____

28. *Woman of the Year:* Spencer Tracy and   _____

29. *Doctor Zhivago:* Omar Sharif and   _____

30. *The King and I:* Yul Brynner and   _____

31. *The Merry Widow:* Fernando Lamas and   _____

32. *Singing in the Rain:* Gene Kelly and   _____

33. *The Blue Dolphin:* Alan Ladd and   _____

34. *The Thin Man:* William Powell and   _____

35. *East of Eden:* James Dean and   _____

36. *Lenny:* Dustin Hoffman and   _____

37. *Pillow Talk:* Rock Hudson and   _____

38. *The Solid Gold Cadillac:* Paul Douglas and _____

39. *Bus Stop:* Don Murray and   _____

40. *Mary Poppins:* Dick Van Dyke and   _____

41. *The African Queen:* Humphrey Bogart and   _____

42. *A Touch of Class:* George Segal and   _____

43. *Cabaret:* Michael York and   _____

44. *It Happened One Night:* Clark Gable and   _____

45. *The Sound of Music:* Christopher Plummer and   _____

46. *Mrs. Miniver:* Walter Pidgeon and   _____

47. *They Shoot Horses, Don't They?:* Michael Sarrazin and   _____

48. *Who's Afraid of Virginia Woolf?:* Richard Burton and   _____

49. *Mr. Deeds Goes to Town:* Gary Cooper and   _____

50. *Scenes from a Marriage:* Erland Josephson and   _____

# ARE YOU A GOOD WITNESS?

Do you *observe* or do you merely *look*? When your eye takes in a scene, does it register detail or does it just gather a vague, fleeting impression? The following test is designed to see how well you can report the facts.

Examine the picture on the opposite page for *two minutes*. Try to remember as much as you can. Then, cover the picture with a piece of paper. Answer the questions about details depicted in the picture.

Be careful to observe the time limit. You have *two minutes* to examine the picture and *two minutes* to answer the questions.

*Answers on page 507*

TIME LIMIT: 4 MINUTES

1. On what floor was someone looking out the window? _____

2. On what street was the Bakery Shop? _____

3. What time of day did the accident take place? _____

4. Was the person who was hit a male? _____

5. Was there a traffic light on the corner? _____

6. What was the license number of the parked car? _____

7. Was the driver a female? _____

8. Which storekeeper was standing on the street? _____

9. How many policemen were at the scene? _____

10. Were there more than 10 people in the crowd? _____

11. Was the butcher's first name Max? _____

12. Were there any children in the crowd? _____

13. From what state was the car that hit the bicycle? _____

14. Was it a four-door car? _____

15. How many trees were in the picture? _____

16. Were there any animals on the street? _____

17. Was the butcher's address 23 State Street? _____

18. Was the ad on the wall for cigarettes? _____

19. Was the weather mild? _____

20. Was the driver of the car alone? _____

# HOW MUCH DO YOU KNOW ABOUT THE AMERICAN REVOLUTION?

Below, you will find 25 questions that will test your knowledge of events that occurred before, during, or immediately after the American Revolution. There are four choices given for each. Check the one you believe is correct.

A score of 16 is good; 19 is very good; and 22 marks you as a patriot and historian.

*Answers on page 507*

1. The king of England during the American Revolution was:
   George II        George III        George IV        George V

2. The first shots of the American Revolution were fired at:
   Lexington        Concord        Bunker Hill        Yorktown

3. In 1775, Ethan Allen and his Green Mountain Boys seized:
   Fort Tyler        Bennington        Fort Ticonderoga        Champlain

4. The influential pamphlet *Common Sense* was written by:
   Nathan Hale    Samuel Adams    Thomas Paine    Benjamin Franklin

5. The Declaration of Independence was signed in:
   New York        Boston        Philadelphia        Washington, D.C.

6. George Washington crossed the Delaware River to attack a British force stationed at:
   Chester        Phillipsburg        Trenton        Wilmington

7. The battle that is generally regarded as the most important of the American Revolution was:
   Saratoga        White Plains        Concord        Germantown

8. The last battle of the American Revolution was:
   Monmouth        Yorktown        Long Island        Saratoga

9. The American guerrilla leader known as the "Swamp Fox" was:
   John Barry                    Horatio Gater
   Francis Marion                Thomas Sumter

10. John Paul Jones's ship was named the:
    *Serapis*        *Bon Homme Richard*        *Drake*        *Lexington*

11. The treaty that formally recognized the new nation of the United States was the Treaty of:
    Versailles        Paris        Quebec        Yorktown

12. The American Revolution began in 1775; it ended in:
    1776        1778        1779        1781

13. The British commander at the battle of Yorktown was:
    Howe        Cornwallis        Leger        Burgoyne

14. Of the following, the only state that was one of the original 13 states was:
    Vermont        Maine        South Carolina        West Virginia

15. The first person to sign the Declaration of Independence was:
    John Hancock                Benjamin Franklin
    Thomas Jefferson            Thomas Pinckney

16. The first capital of the United States was:
    Philadelphia        Boston        New York        Washington, D.C.

17. Betsy Ross's first flag contained this many stars:
    One        Six        Thirteen        Fifty

18. At the battles of Lexington and Concord, the total number of British casualties was closest to:
    20        200        2000        20,000

19. "Give me liberty or give me death." These words were spoken by:
    Patrick Henry                Nathan Hale
    Johnny Tremain               Benjamin Franklin

20. The battle of Bunker Hill was fought closest to the city of:
    Boston        Providence        Concord        Hartford

21. The first Vice-President of the United States was:
    John Quincy Adams            John Adams
    Samuel Adams                 John Hancock

22. Valley Forge is located in the state of:
    New York        Pennsylvania        New Jersey        Virginia

23. The first Secretary of Treasury of the United States was:
    Thomas Jefferson             Alexander Hamilton
    Henry Knox                   James Madison

24. The first state to ratify the Constitution was:
    Pennsylvania        Delaware        Rhode Island        Massachusetts

25. The chief authors of *The Federalist Papers* were James Madison, Alexander Hamilton, and:
    James Monroe                 Thomas Pinckney
    John Jay                     George Washington

# WHO SAID IT?

Below are listed 48 famous quotations, from the recent or distant past. Each phrase is associated with one particular person. You have the job of figuring out who used which of these famous statements. You have heard or read them all, at one time or another. Can you properly identify the sponsors?

Below each statement is a list of four names, one of which is the correct source for that phrase. Circle the letter in front of your choice.

A score of 26 is good; 33 is excellent; and 40 makes you a true historian.

*Answers on page 507*

Answers on page 507

1. *To thine own self be true.*
   - a) Wordsworth
   - b) Bible
   - c) Shakespeare
   - d) Plato

2. *Man proposes, but God disposes.*
   - a) Daniel Webster
   - b) Thoreau
   - c) Thomas A. Kempis
   - d) John Wycliffe

3. *Love is blind.*
   - a) Chaucer
   - b) Shakespeare
   - c) Keats
   - d) Aristotle

4. *We will bury you.*
   - a) Fidel Castro
   - b) Idi Amin
   - c) Adolf Hitler
   - d) Nikita Krushchev

5. *A foolish consistency is the hobgoblin of little minds.*
   - a) Thoreau
   - b) Nathaniel Hawthorne
   - c) Wordsworth
   - d) Ralph Waldo Emerson

6. *Good-night, Mrs. Calabash, wherever you are.*
   - a) Jimmy Durante
   - b) Noel Coward
   - c) Al Jolson
   - d) Eddie Cantor

7. *We have nothing to fear but fear itself.*
   - a) Winston Churchill
   - b) Dwight Eisenhower
   - c) Franklin Roosevelt
   - d) Charles de Gaulle

8. *One small step for man; one giant leap for mankind.*
   - a) John Glenn
   - b) Neil Armstrong
   - c) Virgil Grissom
   - d) Frank Borman

9. *Look before you leap.*
   - a) John Milton
   - b) John Heywood
   - c) Sir Thomas More
   - d) Maimonides

10. *Honor thy father and thy mother.*
    a) Aeschylus  c) Confucius
    b) Shakespeare  d) Exodus, Old Testament

11. *The public be damned.*
    a) John D. Rockefeller  c) William Vanderbilt
    b) Marie Antoinette  d) Richard Nixon

12. *From each according to his ability, to each according to his needs.*
    a) Charles Darwin  c) Leo Tolstoy
    b) Karl Marx  d) Henry David Thoreau

13. *Am I my brother's keeper?*
    a) Isaac  c) Cain
    b) Jacob  d) Abel

14. *Something is rotten in the state of Denmark.*
    a) Hamlet  c) King Lear
    b) Macbeth  d) Othello

15. *To err is human.*
    a) Jesus Christ  c) Victor Hugo
    b) William Shakespeare  d) Jean Jacques Rousseau

16. *Don't count your chickens before they are hatched.*
    a) Sophocles  c) Hans Christian Anderson
    b) Aesop  d) The Brothers Grimm

17. *It is a riddle wrapped in a mystery inside an enigma.*
    a) Benjamin Disraeli  c) Jonathan Swift
    b) Henry Fielding  d) Winston Churchill

18. *How do I love thee? Let me count the ways.*
    a) John Keats  c) Elizabeth Barrett Browning
    b) Ralph Waldo Emerson  d) Robert Browning

19. *I am not a crook.*
    a) John Dillinger  c) Richard Nixon
    b) "Pretty Boy" Floyd  d) John Dean

20. *Rope a dope.*
    a) Joe Frazier  c) Henny Youngman
    b) Jonathan Swift  d) Mohammed Ali

21. *Religion is the opium of the people.*
    a) Karl Marx  c) Leon Trotsky
    b) Charles Darwin  d) Nikita Krushchev

22. *The buck stops here.*
    a) Theodore Roosevelt  c) Lyndon Johnson
    b) Harry Truman  d) John F. Kennedy

23. *Bah, humbug!*
    a) Charlie McCarthy        c) The Cowardly Lion
    b) Ebineezer Scrooge       d) Captain Hook

24. *It is a tale told by an idiot, full of sound and fury, signifying nothing.*
    a) William Faulkner        c) William Shakespeare
    b) Paul Simon              d) Aesop

25. *Damn the torpedoes! Go ahead!*
    a) Admiral Farragut        c) Douglas MacArhur
    b) Winston Churchill       d) Robert E. Lee

26. *I have been a stranger in a strange land.*
    a) Robert A. Heinlein      c) William Shakespeare
    b) Exodus, Old Testament   d) Gospel of John, New Testament

27. *Frankly, my dear, I don't give a damn.*
    a) Rhett Butler            c) Charles Bovary
    b) Prof. Henry Higgins     d) Philip Marlowe

28. *The times they are a-changin'.*
    a) Pete Seeger             c) Arlo Guthrie
    b) Woody Guthrie           d) Bob Dylan

29. *A rose is a rose is a rose.*
    a) Dorothy Parker          c) Alice B. Toklas
    b) Gertrude Stein          d) Phyllis Diller

30. *Ask not what your country can do for you; ask what you can do for your country.*
    a) Franklin D. Roosevelt   c) John F. Kennedy
    b) Robert F. Kennedy       d) Edward Kennedy

31. *Let them eat cake.*
    a) Mary, Queen of Scots    c) Marie Antoinette
    b) Josephine               d) Alexandra, Empress of Russia

32. *Take my wife—please!*
    a) Jimmy Durante           c) Noel Coward
    b) Henny Youngman          d) David Steinberg

33. *We are not amused.*
    a) Marie Antoinette        c) Queen Victoria
    b) Queen Elizabeth I       d) Richard III

34. *I hear America singing.*
    a) Robert Frost            c) Lawrence Welk
    b) Allan Ginsburg          d) Walt Whitman

35. *Death, be not proud.*
    a) John Donne              c) William Shakespeare
    b) John Keats              d) William Wordsworth

36. *Carry on, and dread nought.*
    - a) Admiral Farragut
    - b) Abraham Lincoln
    - c) Ralph Waldo Emerson
    - d) Winston Churchill

37. *Give me liberty, or give me death!*
    - a) Nathan Hale
    - b) Patrick Henry
    - c) George Washington
    - d) Thomas Paine

38. *Out, out, damned spot!*
    - a) Lady Macbeth
    - b) Ophelia
    - c) Desdemona
    - d) Scarlet O'Hara

39. *I want to be alone.*
    - a) Sarah Bernhardt
    - b) Greta Garbo
    - c) Ellen Terry
    - d) Grace Kelly

40. *And she brings you tea and oranges that come all the way from China.*
    - a) Paul Simon
    - b) Art Garfunkel
    - c) Leonard Cohen
    - d) Bob Dylan

41. *Hope springs eternal in the human breast.*
    - a) Alexander Pope
    - b) John Dryden
    - c) Ben Jonson
    - d) Jonathan Swift

42. *Call me Ishmael.*
    - a) Theodore Dreiser
    - b) William Faulkner
    - c) Edgar Allan Poe
    - d) Herman Melville

43. *I never met a man I didn't like.*
    - a) Roy Rogers
    - b) Will Rogers
    - c) W.C. Fields
    - d) P.T. Barnum

44. *For dust thou art, and unto dust thou shalt return.*
    - a) William Shakespeare
    - b) William Wordsworth
    - c) Genesis, Old Testament
    - d) Matthew, New Testament

45. *May you live all the days of your life.*
    - a) Jonathan Swift
    - b) Dorothy Parker
    - c) Johnny Carson
    - d) Christopher Morley

46. *Remember the Alamo!*
    - a) Daniel Boone
    - b) Col. Sidney Sherman
    - c) Daniel Webster
    - d) Davy Crockett

47. *I had a dream.*
    - a) Robert F. Kennedy
    - b) Winston Churchill
    - c) Franklin D. Roosevelt
    - d) Martin Luther King

48. *This land is your land, this land is my land.*
    - a) Joan Baez
    - b) Woody Guthrie
    - c) Phil Ochs
    - d) Pete Seeger

# PASSIONATE PAIRS

Below, you will find listed the names of 50 people, whose love affairs, in fiction, myth, and history, have become legendary. These romantics lived in many countries, and during many periods of history, from Biblical times to the present.

Each name listed below is associated with one particular person, but that person's name has been left blank. Can you fill in the blanks and reunite the passionate pairs?

A score of 26 is fair; 34 is great; and 42 is top-notch.

*Answers on page 507*

1. Marc Antony and      ————————————

2. Boaz and      ————————————

3. Penelope and      ————————————

4. Romeo and      ————————————

5. William Randolph Hearst and      ————————————

6. Tristram and      ————————————

7. Rhett Butler and      ————————————

8. Madame Pompadour and      ————————————

9. Heloise and      ————————————

10. Paris and      ————————————

11. Lillian Hellman and      ————————————

12. Robin Hood and      ————————————

13. Dante and      ————————————

14. Eurydice and      ————————————

15. The Duke of Windsor and      ————————————

16. Sir Lancelot and      ————————————

17. Isis and      ————————————

18. Simone de Beauvoir and      ————————————

19. Pygmalion and      ————————————

20. Robert Browning and      ————————————

21. Ingrid Bergman and      ————————————

22. Carole Lombard and _____

23. Napoleon and _____

24. Humphrey Bogart and _____

25. George Bernard Shaw and _____

26. Nell Gwynne and _____

27. Heathcliff (*Wuthering Heights*) and _____

28. John Alden and _____

29. Emma Hamilton and _____

30. Woodrow Wilson and _____

31. Katherine Hepburn and _____

32. F. Scott Fitzgerald and _____

33. Yoko Ono and _____

34. Prince Albert and _____

35. Pip (*Great Expectations*) and _____

36. Liv Ullmann and _____

37. Beatrice (*Much Ado About Nothing*) and _____

38. George Eliot and _____

39. Richard Burton and _____

40. L'il Abner and _____

41. Henry Miller and _____

42. Blanche DuBois (*A Streetcar Named Desire*) and _____

43. Carlo Ponti and _____

44. Popeye and _____

45. Mick Jagger and _____

46. Katherine (*The Taming of the Shrew*) and _____

47. Pyramus and _____

48. Jay Gatsby (*The Great Gatsby*) and _____

49. Justinian and _____

50. Jacob and _____

# HOW TO BREAK A PENCIL WITH A DOLLAR BILL

This is a great trick which baffles everyone. It is extremely easy to perform.

All you need is a pencil and a dollar bill. Take a dollar bill and fold it in half lengthwise. You smooth down the crease with great deliberation. Make a point of it to indicate that you are sharpening the dollar bill.

Now fold over the bill once more in the same direction to put the paper into four thicknesses. Once again, you press down the edge of the paper very firmly, making a show so that it seems you are trying to get the paper to have a razor-sharp edge. You might use a knife to press the edge of the paper.

When you are quite satisfied that the bill is sharp, ask someone in your audience to hold the pencil for you at arm's length.

The pencil, of course, should be a full-length pencil—not a stub. Emphasize that the pencil should be held firmly.

Now you take the folded dollar bill and you lift the paper high above your head.

With one sharp, swift stroke you bring the bill down against the middle of the pencil, and the pencil will break in two under the stroke.

How is this feat accomplished? Was it really due to the sharpness of the bill?

Of course not. The answer is that as you swing down the bill—and you swing the bill down with great swiftness—you extend your pointing finger, the finger next to your thumb, along the edge of the bill.

Your movement is so fast that no one can detect your finger. It's the finger that smashes against the pencil and breaks it sharply into two.

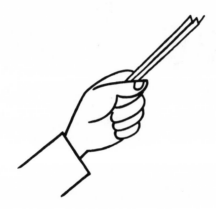

With any ordinary pencil, this trick won't fail. All this goes to show that the human mind is gullible, and the hand is quicker than the eye. You will either receive great rounds of applause, or querulous looks of amazement at how you accomplished your feat.

Some other people in the audience might even try to sharpen dollar bills for the next 15 minutes. And if you are merciful, you might tell them, after they've failed, how the trick was done.

# HANDS UP!

You are going to prove to your friends that you possess telepathic powers.

Start off by casually telling your audience that you can tell exactly what is going on behind you without looking. Of course, your friends will not believe you. You offer to prove it.

Turn your back to your friends. Direct one of them to hold up one hand high over his head. Tell him he must leave it there until you tell him to put it down.

Then ask him to lift the corresponding leg (i.e., the left leg if he is holding up the left hand) and cross it over the other leg.

Wait until you are sure that he has done so. Then tell him that he may uncross his legs. Tell him to put his upraised hand down next to his other hand, with the palm facing up.

Now you can turn around and tell your friends exactly which leg was crossed over which. And if your friends think you just took a lucky guess, you can do it over and over, and get the right answer every time.

What is your secret? Well, the key to this stunt lies in the fact that when you hold your hand up high in the air, the blood will rush out of it. When you put that hand down again, it will be noticeably paler than your other one.

Of course, once you see which hand is paler, you can also tell which leg was crossed, since you told your friend to cross the leg which corresponds to the hand that was raised.

# FIVE AGAINST ONE

With this trick, you can impress your friends with your unbelievable strength.

All you need is a broomstick. Hold the broom off the ground, with both hands grasping the base.

Now have five friends grab the broom with both their hands, and have them try to push it down so that the bristles of the broom touch the floor.

How can five people push against one and lose? By moving the broom slightly either to the right or to the left, you can deflect the downward pressure of those five pairs of hands, so that in effect, they will be pushing sideways, not down. They will never be able to get that broom to touch the floor.

# ENOUGH ROPE

A nice way to amuse the crowd is to get a fine young fellow and tie a cord to his wrists. Then, loop another string through *this* and tie both ends to the wrists of a young lady—the prettier the better.

You challenge this couple to extricate themselves without tearing or breaking the string. You explain that they can't lose. . . . If they get free, they are winners. . . . If they don't, the whole thing results in a tie!

Trying to get out of this mess is quite a bit of fun for the two players and the spectators. The funny part of it is, *it can be done!*

Let the young couple frolic around a bit, but if they should happen to feel that they've been roped in, give the young fellow the following instructions: Take your partner's rope and slip a loop of it underneath the rope tied to your own wrist.

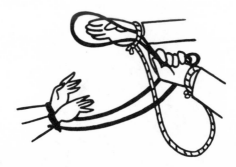

When that has been done, all you have to do is place your hand through the loop and, believe it or not, you're free!

# READING ASHES

Here's one way of winning a reputation without risk. You publicly announce that you have the faculty of reading ashes. When the inevitable challenge ensues, you ask each guest to choose the name of some celebrity.

As the names are called out, you write them down on separate slips of paper. You then fold the slips so that the writing is covered, shuffle them in a hat and ask any one of your guests to pull out and retain a single slip. Then, with much dramatic ado and hocus-pocus, you place the remaining slips on a plate, light them with a match, and watch them burn.

When the last bit of paper has gone up in smoke, you ponder over the ashes and then gravely call out the name on the slip which has been drawn and retained. And lo! To the astonishment of all, you have called out the *right* name. You mysteriously explain this performance by insisting that you read the ashes, and thus eliminated all names but the one which was drawn.

Now this trick is charlatanry of the first water. The colossal deceit is accomplished by writing down the first name called on each and every one of the slips, paying no attention to the other names called.

# GUESSING CITIES

As in most mind-reading games, you need a partner to help you accomplish this trick. Take your girl friend, or your wife—if your wife won't play, take someone else's wife—and tell the crowd that you and your partner are going to mystify them by guessing the name of any city which the company decides upon.

While your partner is out of the room, the group picks a city. Your partner is then invited back into the parlor. You seat her with her back turned toward you, so that nobody can reasonably suppose that there is any possibility of your transmitting signals to her by motion or act.

Let us suppose that the city chosen is Denver. The performance might run as follows:

You call out "Washington." Your partner answers "No." "Chicago?" "No." "Toledo?" "No." "Des Moines?" "No." "Boston?" "No." "Denver?" "Yes."

You and your partner continue to baffle the audience by *always* guessing the correct city, even though the correct city happens to be the seventh city called, the eighth city called, the twelfth city called, or the third city called. Apparently it is not a matter of order. . . . Clearly it is not a matter of intonation, since you call *all* names in the same even voice.

The key to the mystery lies in the fact that certain cities are composed of two words. In the given case, it was Des Moines. Your partner knows that the correct answer is *the second city after the two-word city!* On the next trial, it would be the *third* city after the two-word city; on the third trial, the *fourth* city; and so on according to the following formula: 2, 3, 4, 5, 4, 3, 2, 1. In other words, the *fifth* time you present the trick, your partner knows that it is the *fourth* city after the two-word city.

# IN CAHOOTS

In order to do this trick, you will need a partner. Remember that you both must understand the signals and must be attuned to each other, or the trick will not work.

What you are attempting to do is to have one of you pick out the name of the person that the other one is pointing out, without seeing the pointer or seeing the designated person.

You and your partner begin by claiming to your audience that, aided by telepathic waves, your partner can see without using his eyes. To demonstrate this psychic phenomenon, have your partner turn his chair around so that his back is to the audience. Ask everyone to be as quiet as they possibly can.

While you are setting up, explain to your audience that your partner, in order to prove that he is really psychic, is going to identify the names of the people that you will point to, even though he will not be able to see either you or anyone else in the audience. To enhance the effect of this feat, be as dramatic as you can be.

When you have set up the chairs in such a way that it is impossible for your partner to see what you are doing, you shout theatrically, "*Are we in cahoots?*" In a voice that sounds like it comes from beyond the grave, your partner should croak, "Yes."

Now you begin to whirl around the room like a dervish, gesturing excitedly. You spin from one person to another, faster and faster, pointing to each person in turn with an outstretched arm.

As you point to the first person, you shout, "*I point to the East!*" When you point to the next person, you exclaim, "*I point to the West!*" You continue to whirl, shouting at the next two people in succession, "*I point to the North! I point to the South!*"

You may go around the room and point to as many people as you want, always shouting the same incantation in the same order. Finally, you reach a crescendo of drama and noise as you point to someone and ask, "*To whom do I point?*"

And then your partner, in as scary a voice as he can muster, answers you with a name. And mysteriously, it is the *right* name. You may do this trick again and again, and somehow he will always get it right. How does he do it?

Actually, the only special ability your partner needs to do this trick is a good ear and an ability to listen carefully. While you are setting up for this trick, you will be talking continuously about your partner's special powers and the need for quiet and cooperation. Your running commentary will be sure to bring some response from your audience. All your partner need do is identify the voices of the people speaking. The last person who spoke before you shout the words "*Are we in cahoots?*" is the person to whom you will point.

If your partner cannot identify the voice which spoke last, he must answer "No" to the question "*Are we in cahoots?*" That is your signal to carry on for a few minutes longer, insisting on more quiet, or more cooperation, or something on that order, until you have elicited the response you need. Then you can ask the question again. If you get a *Yes* answer, you are ready to go.

Remember that even though all your whirling and shouting have absolutely nothing to do with how the trick is done, they add immeasurably to the interest and excitement.

# MIND OVER MATTER

For this, as for other mind-reading tricks, you'll need a confederate. Your claim is that your partner can guess any object in the room the audience names.

Have your partner leave the room for a moment while your audience settles on a particular object. Then summon him back into the room.

You then proceed to ask him questions, like "Is it a chair?" "Is it a couch?" "Is it a rug?" To each of these questions, your confederate will answer NO, until you come to the chosen object. His answer to that question will be YES!

During the question-and-answer part of this trick, you'll be sitting perfectly still, giving no hint of whether the answer to each question is YES or NO. As you ask your questions, don't change the inflection of your voice. And don't change the form of the question—even one bit. Your audience must believe that your partner is completely on his own.

How does he do it? Unlike other mind-reading tricks, your partner knows when the selected object is being named because of a signal which *he* gives to *you*, instead of the other way around.

Of course, you and your partner will have arranged the signals beforehand. The signal can be anything at all—he might scratch his head, or cross his legs, or put a hand on his hip. In fact, the two of you can use all of these signals in sequence to utterly confound your audience.

You, as the questioner, must carefully watch your partner for the chosen signal. Don't worry about your audience, for they will be so busy examining *your* actions they will never concentrate on watching your partner.

When the mind-reader wishes you to feed him the chosen object, he will show you the prearranged signal. Then, when you ask the key question, he will answer YES.

The more signals you use in this trick, the more confused your audience will be, even if they *are* watching the mind-reader as well as you.

This trick can be performed hundreds of times before anyone catches on.

# I SEE A GHOST

In order to put this stunt across in a big way, first plant a background. Get the company started on psychology, discussing powers of observation, or anything else along that line. This all leads up to your challenge that very, very few people indeed can observe and follow directions.

You insist that there is *always* a slip somewhere. To prove your point, you offer to conduct an experiment. You challenge a number of the guests to follow some simple directions. You ask the other half to act as judges. Have them note the errors made by the participants.

Accordingly, line up six, eight or ten people in a row. Stand at the head of it. Your group faces front, toward the judges. Then you explain that you are going to say certain things and do certain things. You expect the second man in line to copy to the letter your speech and to mimic your acts without flaw. You expect the third man in line to copy *his* speech and *his* acts *with exactitude*, and so on right down the line.

You then tell the participants that you are going to say "I see a ghost!" The second man is to ask "Where?" Then you make answer and assume a pose.

He, in turn, must copy *your* performance with the *third* person in line.

You then call out "I see a ghost!" The second man in line loudly queries "Where?" You shout "There!" and *you stretch your right hand forward clear across your chest!*

Second man calls out "I see a ghost!" Third man says "Where?" Second man says "There!" and stretches out his hand in like manner. This goes on until the end of the line is reached. When the last man says "I see a ghost!" you answer "Where?" acting as *his* partner.

You follow up this business by again shouting "I see a ghost!" Second man asks "Where?" As you shout "There!" *you stretch forth your left arm, crossing it over the right!*

Meanwhile the judges are sitting, making notes, observing errors. Since some errors there *will* be, it will appear that there is some merit to your contention.

You have previously explained that you will issue four sets of commands. On the third round, as you exclaim "I see a ghost!" and the second man asks "Where?", you shout, "On one knee!". . . . Whereupon you drop down on your right knee, keeping your arms outstretched all the while.

This manoeuvre is copied all down the line until all participants have dropped down to the floor.

As the fourth round commences, you once more call out "I see a ghost!" The second man says "Where?" and then, *Surprise of Surprises!* you give him a good hard shove!

The whole line sprawls all over the floor, bowled over like a set of tenpins! It's a beautiful sight for the judges to watch!

Hooray for psychology!

# PRIZE INSULTS

You have a bad habit . . . *you breathe!*

♔

Don't go away mad . . . *just go away!*

♔

THINK! *It may be a new experience!*

♔

You can't be two-faced. . .*or you wouldn't be wearing the one you've got!*

♔

Don't think it hasn't been pleasant to meet you . . . *because it hasn't!*

♔

Why be difficult, when with just a little more effort you can be impossible!

♔

What's on your mind? *If you will forgive the overstatement!*

♔

You're certainly trying . . . *very* trying!

♔

The sooner I never see your face again, the better it will be for both of us when we meet.

♔

You should go a long way . . . *and the sooner the better.*

♔

**408**   I could grow to dislike you intensely . . . *but I'm not even going to bother.*

If you have a minute to spare, tell me all you know.

When I think of you I know it's not the heat . . . *it's the stupidity!*

Go jump into the ocean and pull a wave over your head.

If a horse had your brains, he'd still be a horse.

Your visit has climaxed an already dull day.

Why don't you come over and have dinner . . . *if you don't mind imposing!*

You've got a brain . . . *but it hasn't reached your head.*

I'm not in the habit of forgetting faces, but in your case I will make an exception.

I'm really pleased to see you're back, particularly after seeing your face.

**409**

# HOW TO SOLVE FIVE-LETTER ALFABITS

The idea is to try to form as many words as you can out of the letters which compose the given title.

The answers are governed by the following rules:

1. Words must be composed of five-letter roots. Pluralized four-letter words such as HOURS, TARTS, etc., and inflected verb forms such as TRIES, MAKES, etc. are barred.

2. Only one form or tense of a word may be used—either WORTH or WORTHY, START or STARTED, TASTY or TASTELESS, GROWING or GROWN, etc. In other words, you may use either the noun form or the verb form, either the noun form or the adjective form, but not both.

3. Foreign, obsolete, or archaic words are taboo. Reformed spellings are out.

# CONGLOMERATION

There are at least 51 words, each of five letters or more, that can be made out of the letters in the word CONGLOMERATION.

If you can find 25 of them, you're doing fine; 35 is tremendous; and 45 words is absolutely outrageous!

*Answers on page 508*

| 1. _____ | 18. _____ | 35. _____ |
| 2. _____ | 19. _____ | 36. _____ |
| 3. _____ | 20. _____ | 37. _____ |
| 4. _____ | 21. _____ | 38. _____ |
| 5. _____ | 22. _____ | 39. _____ |
| 6. _____ | 23. _____ | 40. _____ |
| 7. _____ | 24. _____ | 41. _____ |
| 8. _____ | 25. _____ | 42. _____ |
| 9. _____ | 26. _____ | 43. _____ |
| 10. _____ | 27. _____ | 44. _____ |
| 11. _____ | 28. _____ | 45. _____ |
| 12. _____ | 29. _____ | 46. _____ |
| 13. _____ | 30. _____ | 47. _____ |
| 14. _____ | 31. _____ | 48. _____ |
| 15. _____ | 32. _____ | 49. _____ |
| 16. _____ | 33. _____ | 50. _____ |
| 17. _____ | 34. _____ | 51. _____ |

# INCANTATIONS

There are at least 22 words, each of five letters or more, that can be made out of the letters in the word INCANTATIONS.

    If you can find 12 of them, you're pretty good; 15 is even better; and 18 puts you with the experts.

*Answers on page 508*

| | | |
|---|---|---|
| 1. _____ | 8. _____ | 16. _____ |
| 2. _____ | 9. _____ | 17. _____ |
| 3. _____ | 10. _____ | 18. _____ |
| 4. _____ | 11. _____ | 19. _____ |
| 5. _____ | 12. _____ | 20. _____ |
| 6. _____ | 13. _____ | 21. _____ |
| 7. _____ | 14. _____ | 22. _____ |
| | 15. _____ | |

# OPERATIONAL

There are at least 40 words, each of five letters or more, that can be made out of the letters in the word OPERATIONAL.

    If you can find 22 of them, that's fine; 30 words is wonderful; and 35 is quite remarkable.

*Answers on page 508*

| | | |
|---|---|---|
| 1. _____ | 14. _____ | 28. _____ |
| 2. _____ | 15. _____ | 29. _____ |
| 3. _____ | 16. _____ | 30. _____ |
| 4. _____ | 17. _____ | 31. _____ |
| 5. _____ | 18. _____ | 32. _____ |
| 6. _____ | 19. _____ | 33. _____ |
| 7. _____ | 20. _____ | 34. _____ |
| 8. _____ | 21. _____ | 35. _____ |
| 9. _____ | 22. _____ | 36. _____ |
| 10. _____ | 23. _____ | 37. _____ |
| 11. _____ | 24. _____ | 38. _____ |
| 12. _____ | 25. _____ | 39. _____ |
| 13. _____ | 26. _____ | 40. _____ |
| | 27. _____ | |

# CONSOLIDATED

There are at least 17 words, each of five letters or more, that can be made out of the letters in the word CONSOLIDATED.

A score of 10 is very good; and 14 is terrific.

*Answers on page 508*

1. _____  7. _____  12. _____
2. _____  8. _____  13. _____
3. _____  9. _____  14. _____
4. _____  10. _____  15. _____
5. _____  11. _____  16. _____
6. _____  17. _____

# SCHOLARSHIP

There are at least 13 words, each of five letters or more, that can be made out of the letters in the word SCHOLARSHIP.

A score of 7 is dandy; 10 is just magnificent.

*Answers on page 508*

1. _____  5. _____  10. _____
2. _____  6. _____  11. _____
3. _____  7. _____  12. _____
4. _____  8. _____  13. _____
9. _____

# PHILODENDRON

There are at least 12 words, each of five letters or more, that can be made out of the letters in the word PHILODENDRON.

A score of 7 words is pretty good; 10 is outstanding.

*Answers on page 508*

1. _____  5. _____  9. _____
2. _____  6. _____  10. _____
3. _____  7. _____  11. _____
4. _____  8. _____  12. _____

**412**

(DIRECTIONS FOR SOLVING FIVE-LETTER ALFABITS ARE ON PAGE 410)

# DISCRETIONARY

Out of the letters in the word DISCRETIONARY, one can theoretically make 41 words of five or more letters.

    If you come up with 20, you are performing excellently. If you deliver 28, you're performing incredibly. And if you can fill in the spaces with 36 words, you can really puff up your chest.

*Answers on page 508*

1. _____
2. _____
3. _____
4. _____
5. _____
6. _____
7. _____
8. _____
9. _____
10. _____
11. _____
12. _____
13. _____
14. _____

15. _____
16. _____
17. _____
18. _____
19. _____
20. _____
21. _____
22. _____
23. _____
24. _____
25. _____
26. _____
27. _____

28. _____
29. _____
30. _____
31. _____
32. _____
33. _____
34. _____
35. _____
36. _____
37. _____
38. _____
39. _____
40. _____
41. _____

# DERISIVELY

There are at least 16 words, each of five letters or more, that can be made out of the letters in the word DERISIVELY.

    If you can fill in the spaces below with at least 10 words, that's very good; 12 words is first-rate; and 14 words gets you a blue ribbon.

*Answers on page 509*

1. _____
2. _____
3. _____
4. _____
5. _____

6. _____
7. _____
8. _____
9. _____
10. _____
11. _____

12. _____
13. _____
14. _____
15. _____
16. _____

**413**

(DIRECTIONS FOR SOLVING FIVE-LETTER ALFABITS ARE ON PAGE 410)

# DROP DEAD

This is a swell dice game which can be played by any number of people. You need five dice and a dice cup. *Number Five* and *Number Two* on the dice are anathema.

The first player rolls. If either a *Five* or a *Two* appears, the roll is DEAD, and any die which showed either a *Five* or a *Two* is lost. In other words, if the first roll turns up *One, Two, Three, Five, Six,* the *Two* and the *Five* are eliminated, the player loses two dice, and he scores nothing. He then rolls the *One, Three* and *Six*. He scores only on those throws in which no *Five* and no *Two* shows up.

On any such roll, the total of the pips showing is scored. The score is cumulative: that is, if 15 is scored on the first roll, and the second roll is dead, and the third roll is dead, and 1 is scored on the next roll, then the total score is 16.

The player keeps on rolling till he DROPS DEAD. That is accomplished by rolling *Twos* and *Fives* with the last remaining dice or die. At this point, the player has nothing left to roll with, having lost all five dice.

Highest score wins. There's a lot of fun and excitement in this fast-moving game!

# BLOTTO

BLOTTO, played with five dice, is unlike most dice games inasmuch as it calls for the exercise of judgment. Each player is entitled to three rolls with the five dice during each inning. There are seven innings.

You roll five dice on the first roll and you then make an election mentally. You can roll for *ones, twos, threes, fours, fives, sixes* or for a straight. Suppose you turn up three *fours* and you decide to roll for *fours*. You pick up the other two dice and roll them. If you roll another *four* on your second throw, you attempt to turn up the last *four* on your third and last throw with the fifth and last remaining die. If you fail, your score for that inning is 16 in the *Four Column*.

Your opponent, on his first roll, turns up two *twos*, a *three*, a *four*, and a *five*. He mentally elects to scorn the two *twos* and go for BLOTTO!—a straight! On the second throw, he rolls a *three*. If he doesn't want to take a chance of missing out on the straight on the third and last throw, he may pick up the *two*, the *four* and the *five* and roll these three dice, leaving the two *threes* on the table. . . . If he gets another *three*, his score for that inning is a 9 in the *Three Column*.

The rules provide that you only score once in each column. In other words, your opponent can never again score in the *Three Column* and in the next inning his choice of play is narrowed down. As the game proceeds, the choice gets less and less, until on the seventh and last inning, each player can only throw to fill up his score in the last remaining column.

|  | TOM | DICK | HARRY |
|---|---|---|---|
| *Ones* |  |  |  |
| *Twos* |  |  |  |
| *Threes* |  |  |  |
| *Fours* |  |  |  |
| *Fives* |  |  |  |
| *Sixes* |  |  |  |
| BLOTTO |  |  |  |
| **TOTAL** |  |  |  |

Highest score wins!

A straight or BLOTTO counts as 35.

Each player must declare his choice and score only after the third and last roll in each inning.

To explain more fully how the game operates, let us say that you throw two *sixes* on your first roll. You mentally decide to play *sixes*, so you pick up the other three dice. On your second cast, you get no *sixes*. On your third cast, you throw two *ones*, and a *three*. The dice as they now lie show two *sixes*, two *ones*, and a *three*. At this point, it is up to you to declare your choice and your score. There is no reason in the world why you shouldn't declare your score as 2, counting the two *ones* and leaving the *Six-Column* for a better throw at some future time.

**415**

# PIG

Perhaps this is the most exciting dice game that has ever been invented. It is good for any group of people from 2 to 12, and will intrigue any age group, children as well as adults, or a mixture of adults and children. This is a game we recommend without qualification.

PIG has the unusual quality for a dice game of requiring strategy. Luck, nevertheless, is a predominant factor.

To play PIG you need two dice and a dice cup, a piece of paper, and a pencil. A score card is laid out as shown in the diagram below.

The object of the game is to score 100 points. There is no second place. The one who scores 100 points first wins the entire pot.

To begin, each player places a counter, or chip, in the pot. When adults play, the game takes on much more excitement if each player puts in an agreed upon coin, such as a nickel, a dime, a quarter or a half dollar.

Beginning with any player, each player rolls one die once. The one who has the highest throw begins the game. If two players roll the same number of pips—for example, two players roll 6—then these two players roll again to see who rolls first. There is no particular advantage in being first. As a matter of fact, it is an advantage to be last. The first player—the player who has rolled the highest with one die—then puts the two dice in his cup and rolls. After his turn is finished, the player sitting next to him on his left becomes the second roller, and so on until everybody has had a turn with the dice.

Let us say that the first player now rolls a 5 and a 3. His score is 8. He may, at his option, continue to roll. Let us say that on his next roll, he rolls a 3 and a 4, which together make 7. His score is now 15. He may again, at his option, continue to roll.

Why shouldn't he continue to roll?

Answer: Because if he rolls a 1 on either of two dies he wipes out his entire score *for that round*. In other words, if he takes a chance to increase his score of 15, he may very well lose those 15 points by throwing a 1 on either of the dice. That's how the name of "Pig" was given to the game. When a player has a fairly good score, he might consider stopping and not being a pig, be satisfied with what he has and score it. However, if he continues and hits a 1, he gets zero for the round.

Now there are some very interesting developments. For one thing, if a player hits two 1's, popularly called "Snake Eyes," with his two dice, he gets a score of 25, and may continue to roll if he wants to.

Or if a player scores a double, like two 2's, two 4's, two 5's, or two 6's, he scores double the amount of the throw. Thus a player who throws two 5's, which count up to 10, actually scores 20 for such a throw.

The first player to score 100 presumably wins the game, but this is not quite true, for every player in the game is entitled to the same number of throws. A look at the score card will show the game divided up into innings.

Let us say that Player No. 3 scores 102 in the 4th inning. Player No. 4, Player No. 5, and Player No. 6 are entitled to their turns. If Player No. 4 achieves a score of 105, he is the pesumptive winner. However, Player No. 6 may score 108 on this same round, and then he would be declared the winner and take the entire stake of the pot.

When any player scores 100 in a certain inning, that inning becomes the final inning.

The rules of PIG follow essentially the same rules of all other dice games. If any one dice rolls off the table, the throw is considered void, and the player throws again. During any throw, the dice must be shaken in the cup and rolled out quickly. They may not be manipulated in any way. It is obviously a slight advantage to be last, since one can then see how many points have been scored by the first opponent to reach 100, and therefore knows that he must be exceed that total or else lose. A player who scores 100 may continue to throw at his option. He may elect to do so for fear that another player who rolls after him has, for example, a score of 96, and that even with his 100 points he is likely to be overtaken if he quits. These become exciting decisions in the heat of the game.

# FUNNY EPITAPHS

*In Hatfield, Mass.:*
> Beneath this stone, a lump of clay, lies Arabella Young;
> Who on the 21st of May began to hold her tongue.

♔

*Over the grave of a dentist:*
> Stranger! Approach this spot with gravity!
> John Brown is filling his last cavity.

♔

*In an English cemetery:*
> It was a cough that carried him off,
> It was a coffin they carried him off in.

♔

*In Lost Creek, Colorado:*
> Here lies the clay of Mitchel Coots,
> Whose feet yet occupy his boots.
> His soul has gone—we know not where
> It landed, neither do we care.
> He slipped a joker up his sleeve
> With vile intention to deceive;
> And when detected, tried to jerk
> His gun, but didn't get his work
> In with sufficient swiftness, which
> Explains the presence here of Mitch.

♔

*In Falkirk, England:*
> At rest beneath this slab of stone,
> Lies stingy Jimmy Wyett;
> He died one morning just at ten
> And saved a dinner by it!

♔

*In St. Mary Winston College, Oxford, over Merideth, an organist:*
> Here lies one blown out of breath,
> Who lived a merry life, and died a Merideth.

*On the grave of his wife:*

> Here lies my wife: here let her lie!
> Now she's at rest—and so am I.
>
> *John Dryden*

☦

*Epitaph for a friend:*

> On the twenty-second of June
> Jonathan Fiddle went out of tune.
>
> *Ben Jonson*

☦

*In Oxfordshire, England:*

> Here lies the body of John Eldred
> At least, he will be when he's dead;
> But now at this time he's alive
> The 14th of August, Sixty-five.

☦

*In St. George's Churchyard, Somerset:*

> Here lies Poor Charlotte,
> Who died no harlot,
> But in her virginity,
> Though just turned nineteen
> Which within this vicinity
> Is hard to be found and seen.

*In Enosburg, Vermont:*

> Here lies the body of our Anna
> Done to death by a banana;
> It wasn't the fruit that laid her low,
> But the skin of the thing that made her go!

**419**

*In the Cheltenham Churchyard:*
> Here lie I and my two daughters,
> Killed by drinking Cheltenham waters.
> If we had stuck to Epsom Salts
> We wouldn't be lying in these vaults.

*On the tombstone of a pedestrian:*
> This is the grave of Mike O'Day
> Who died maintaining his right of way.
> His right was clear, his will was strong,
> But he's just as dead as if he'd been wrong.

*In Boot Hill Cemetery, Dodge City, Kansas:*
> Played five aces.
> Now playing the harp.

*At Great Torrington, Devon:*
> Here lies a man who was killed by lightning;
> He died when his prospects seemed to be brightening,
> He might have cut a flash in this world of trouble,
> But the flash cut him, and he lies in the stubble.

*On the grave of a fisherman:*
> Here lies the body of Jonathan Stout,
> He fell in the water and never got out,
> And still is supposed to be floating about.

*In Pawtucket, R.I. over Dr. William Rothwell, who always paid the check*
    *at parties:*

               This is on me.

              ♔

*In Pere Lachaise Cemetery, Paris:*

        Here lies Pierre Cobachard, grocer.
        His inconsolable widow dedicates this monument
        to his memory, and continues the same business at
        the old stand, 167 Rue Mouffetard.

              ♔

*In Suffolk, England:*

        Stranger pass by and waste no time
        On bad biography and careless rhyme.
        For what I am, this humble dust encloses;
        And what I was is no affair of yourses.

              ♔

*In Falkirk, England:*

        Here under this sod and under these trees
        Is buried the body of Solomon Pease,
        But here in this hole lies only his pod
        His soul is shelled out and gone to God.

              ♔

*At Selby, Yorkshire:*

        Here lies my wife, a sad slattern and shrew;
        If I said I regretted her, I should lie too!

              ♔

*In Shutesbury, Mass.:*

        Here lies my husbands, I, II, III,
        Dumb as men could ever be.
        As for my IV'th, well, praise be God!
        He bides for a little above the sod.
        Alex, Ben, Sandy were the first three's names,
        And to make things tidy, I'll add his—James.

*In Providence, R.I.:*

> The wedding day decided was,
> The wedding wine provided,
> But ere the day did come along
> He'd drunk it and died, did.
> > *Ah, Sidney! Sidney!*

*On Charles II:*

> Here lies our sovereign lord the king,
> > Whose word no man relies on;
> He never says a foolish thing,
> > Nor ever does a wise one.
> > > *Lord Rochester*

*In Canaan, New Hampshire:*

> Here lies, cut down like unripe fruit,
> The wife of Deacon Amos Shute.
> She died of drinking too much coffee,
> Anno Dominy eighteen forty.

*On the grave of a waiter:*

> By and by
> God caught his eye.

*In Brookfield, Conn.:*

> My wife lies here.
> I am glad of it.

*In Plymouth, Mass.:*

> Here lies the bones of Richard Lawton,
> Whose death, alas! was strangely brought on.
> Trying his corns one day to mow off,
> His razor slipped and cut his toe off.
> His toe, or, rather, what it grew to,
> An inflamation quickly flew to.
> Which took, alas! to mortifying
> And was the cause of Richard's dying.

*In Burlington, Vt.:*

> Beneath this stone our baby lays,
> He neither cries nor hollers,
> He lived just one and twenty days,
> And cost us forty dollars.

*In Kilmurry Churchyard, Ireland:*

> This stone was raised by Sarah's lord,
> Not Sarah's virtues to record—
> For they're well known to all the town—
> But it was *raised* to keep her *down.*

*In Skaneateles, N.Y.:*

> Neuralgia worked on Mrs. Smith
> Till neath the sod it laid her.
> She was a worthy Methodist
> And served as a crusader.

*In Williamsport, Pa., over the grave of a man kicked to death by a colt:*
Peaceable and quiet, a friend to his father and mother, and respected by all who knew him, and went to the world where horses do not kick, where sorrow and weeping is no more.

*In Bath Abbey:*

> Here lies Ann Mann; she lived an old
> Maid and she died an old *Mann.*

# MIND-READING

This is one of the simplest and most baffling card tricks ever created, and can be performed by anyone with literally no practice. This trick is particularly recommended as sure-fire, and never fails to create a sensation!

Place five cards face down on a table, or permit the guests to pick any five cards out of the deck and place them on the table, side by side.

You advise that you are going to leave the room. You ask the guests to lift one card and *only* one, and to make a mental note of what it is. When you are recalled, you study the cards with a show of deep reflection, and then, after a few seconds, with any kind of hocus-pocus that you wish to invent, you pick them up *in the order in which they lie,* moving from right to left, and placing one card on top of another. You then put these five cards in your pocket and make a further show of intense concentration.

In a second or two, you take *four* cards out of your pocket and lay them on the table where the other five were before, face down and in the same position, leaving room for Card 3. You ask, "Was it the middle, missing card you picked?" If the answer is "Yes," you produce it immediately, extracting it from your pocket, and exhibiting it to the startled guests. If the answer is "No," you move Card 4 over to where Card 3 originally was. This now leaves the space originally occupied by Card 4 blank.

You now ask whether the chosen card occupied the space now blank. If the answer is in the affirmative, you immediately produce the card in question. If in the negative, you now move Card 5 over to occupy the blank space. Then, point to the end of the line of cards, indicating the place where Card 5 should be, and ask if the *last* card in the line was chosen. If so, you produce it. If not, you continue to re-position the cards, until you have determined the position of the card that was picked.

As soon as you are told *where* the card was, you produce it.

You continue to perform this miracle of mind-reading again and again, to the utter bewilderment and consternation of the guests, who hopelessly try to fathom the mystery.

Mathematically, your chances of being right are just *one out of five,* but somehow you hit the bull's eye every single time!

This fine trick is performed as follows: You plant four cards of the deck in your pocket. When you pick up the five cards on the table, you place them in the same pocket, holding them separate with your finger from the four strangers. . . . Extract the four cards and place them on the table. . . . After your questions have elicited information as to the *position* of the chosen card, you pull out that card from among the five in your pocket.

For example, suppose the guests chose Card 1. That, of course, would be the top card. Suppose the guests chose Card 3. You count off the top two cards in your pocket, pick out Card 3, and say, "I knew it all the time!"

# SPELLING BEE

Astonish your friends with a deck of cards. Out of a deck, select an entire suit—13 cards.

Hold the 13 cards face downward in your hand. Arrange the cards as follows: *Three, Eight, Seven, Ace, Queen, Six, Four, Two, Jack, King, Ten, Nine, Five*. When you hold them face down, the *Three* should be on top.

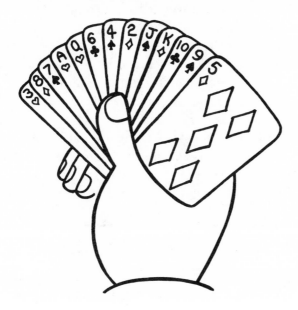

Explain to your guests that you are going to produce particular cards out of the pile you hold—by spelling for them.

Call out the letter *A* and remove the first card from the top of the pile, placing this card at the bottom of the deck. Next you call *C*, and take the second card off the top of the deck, placing it at the bottom. Now call out *E*, and take the third card and place it at the bottom of the deck.

You spelled out *Ace*. You face up the fourth card, and it *is* the *Ace*.

Remove the Ace from the pile. Then continue, spelling out the letters *T W O* by calling out the letters and placing the next three cards at the top, one by one, at the bottom of the deck. After you've spelled out *Two*, turn the next card on the top face up, and it will be the *Deuce*.

Remove the *Deuce* from the deck, and continue in the same way, moving five cards to the bottom to spell out *Three*. The next card exposed will be the *Three*. In this manner, you can spell out the entire pack from *Ace* to *King*.

Always remember to remove the card that you face up from the deck, or you will upset the order of the cards.

As easy as this trick sounds, you can bet your friends will spend lots of time trying to find out how on earth you've done it.

# TELEPATHIC DOCTOR

This trick requires a little bit of preparation beforehand, but it really pays off. It is sure to absolutely stun your audience, and even keep them awake nights wondering how you pulled it off.

Tell the group that you know a doctor who has telepathic powers. Even from miles away, he can see what's going on in this very room!

Naturally, your audience will ridicule your assertion. To prove it, you get out a deck of cards, and ask someone to pick one card out of the deck.

When someone has chosen a card (let us assume, for example, that it is the *Eight of Clubs*), show it to everyone in your audience.

Then select one of your guests, and give him the doctor's telephone number. Have him dial the number, and ask for Doctor Block. He is to explain the purpose of his call to Doctor Block, and ask him to identify the chosen card. Hopefully, Doctor Block will be at home.

When your guest reaches the doctor and explains to him the nature of the phone call, the telepathic physician will promptly identify the *Eight of Clubs*. And your friends will fall right out of their chairs.

|  | Clubs | Diamonds | Hearts | Spades |
|---|---|---|---|---|
| **Ace** | SMITH | LEININGER | HUDSON | GINSBERG |
| **Two** | LEWIS | SCARLATTI | JONES | ROBERTS |
| **Three** | WINTZ | PAUL | CANNON | BARODI |
| **Four** | MULLER | SKULL | FEIGENBAUM | PAPPAS |
| **Five** | SANDERSON | HOFFMAN | ROOT | WHITE |
| **Six** | GIRARD | SHAND | MACK | STRAUSS |
| **Seven** | MAROOTIAN | COUSINS | MARSH | FENTON |
| **Eight** | BLOCK | ROAN | COOPER | ANSON |
| **Nine** | GOLDBERG | SCHEER | MARTIN | LANDER |
| **Ten** | BARROW | SPEARS | HOWARD | PAYNE |
| **Jack** | LESLIE | CARTER | CLAUS | MILAN |
| **Queen** | HAMMOND | GORDON | RAND | BELL |
| **King** | BURNS | SCOTT | BERGER | VINCENT |

But how did you manage this remarkable feat, without even speaking to the doctor yourself? The answer lies in the preparations you and your partner have made at some earlier date.

You and your accomplice must both have, in a convenient place, a copy of the list shown on the opposite page.

Each card in the deck, as you can see, has been assigned a name. Therefore, when the *Eight of Clubs* was chosen, you knew that by calling your friend and asking for *Dr. Block*, you were signalling your friend that the chosen card was the *Eight of Clubs*. Asking for *Doctor Fenton* would have signified the *Seven of Spades; Doctor Berger* would have meant the *King of Hearts*.

As soon as a card is chosen, you must find an opportunity to consult your chart. You might do this by pretending to look up the doctor's telephone number in your notebook.

Once you know the code word for that card, you can instruct your guest to call the doctor and explain the situation to him. Your accomplice, who will be expecting some strange phone calls every now and then, should quickly consult his own chart while your guest is explaining what is going on. By the time the explanation has been made, your partner should be able to name the correct card promptly and with no hesitation.

If your friends want another demonstration, you must, of course, refuse, on the grounds that you can't keep wasting the doctor's time.

What makes this trick so extremely effective is that you never speak to your accomplice, and therefore your audience never suspects you are conveying signals to him.

# COPS AND ROBBERS

All you need for this one is a single deck of cards and a good sense of humor.

Begin by holding up four Jacks so that your friends can see them. Place them as shown here.

Explain to your audience that these four Jacks are four robbers, and that the deck, which you have placed face down in front of you, is a house. The four robbers are going to rob the house.

First, put the four Jacks *face down* on top of the deck. Then you begin to narrate this story to your friends.

"The first robber," you say, "goes into the first storey." As you say this, pick up the top card and slide it into the pile somewhere at the bottom.

"The second robber goes into the second storey of the house," you continue. Pick up the next card and place it, face down of course, in the middle of the deck.

"The third robber," you continue, "goes into the third storey."

Now turn up the fourth card so that it is face up on top of the deck. "The fourth robber stands look-out," you say.

"Suddenly, the look-out spots the cops, and he yells, 'Let's get out of here! The cops are coming.' As a warning signal, he bangs three times on the roof of the house." You now tap three times on top of the deck. Then take the exposed Jack off the top of the pile, and without a moment's hesitation peel off the next three cards one by one, tossing them face up for your audience to see, as you intone, "Here comes the second robber! Here comes the third robber! Here comes the fourth robber!" Each of the three cards you expose will be a Jack.

How was this done? Let's go back for a moment to the first step, when you held the four Jacks in your hand and showed them to your audience. What you *don't* show to your audience is the three other cards that you are hiding behind the last Jack. Make sure that these three cards are hidden carefully, so that no one but you can see them. Actually you are holding *seven* cards—not four.

When you put the cards face down on top of the pile, the cards on top of the pile will, of course, be the three cards you were hiding. It is these three cards that you now proceed to place, one by one, into the middle of the deck.

**428**

When you have completed this step, you are left with the four Jacks you pretended to put in the middle of the deck all in a row right at the top of the pile!

# HEART-BREAK

For this trick, all you need are a deck of cards and a dramatic touch.

Hold three *Aces* in your hand so that your friends can see them. Be sure to hold them exactly as shown in the illustration. Ask your friends to look at the cards in your hand and verify that these cards are the *Ace of Clubs*, and *Ace of Spades*, and the *Ace of Diamonds*. They may not touch the cards, nor rearrange them.

When everyone has had a chance to look, place the three cards face down in front of you. Announce that, by saying the magic words, you are going to make the *Ace of Diamonds* disappear, and the *Ace of Hearts* take its place.

Say the words *Hocus Pocus,* or *Abra Cadabra,* or *Afghanistan Bananistan,* or any other silly words you can think of, while you mysteriously wave your hands over the cards. After a few seconds, have one of your friends pick up the cards and examine them. Sure enough, he will find that the *Ace of Diamonds* has disappeared, and the *Ace of Hearts* has taken its place.

How did you do it? Well, as you see from the diagram, the red *Ace* was positioned behind the two black *Aces*. This positioning enabled you to hide most of the *Ace of Hearts*—the card which you were really holding all along—behind the two black *Aces*. By showing only the bottom portion of the heart, you gave your friends the false impression that it was the *Ace of Diamonds*.

# PHOTOGRAPHIC MEMORY

Once you know how to do this simple trick you can really dazzle everyone with your incredible memory.

All you need is a deck of cards, and a little acting. First, you casually turn your conversation toward the subject of memory. When everyone is interested, you mention that your memory is really so good that you can remember every card in a deck simply by looking at the deck once. Of course, nobody believes you, so you offer to prove it.

Get out a deck of cards, and hand it to someone. Tell him to remove one card from the deck, without showing you what it is. Then take back the deck, and explain that by looking through the deck you will be able to recall which card is missing.

Insist on absolute silence, so that nothing will interfere with your concentration. Then slowly go through the deck, pausing here and there for effect, until you have seen each and every card.

Actually, you will not be pausing only for effect. The key to this trick is to add the cards together, by assigning each card a number, to get a total for the entire deck. The cards should be counted in this way:

| | | | |
|---|---|---|---|
| Ace—1 | Five—5 | Eight—8 | Jack—11 |
| Deuce—2 | Six—6 | Nine—9 | Queen—12 |
| Three—3 | Seven—7 | Ten—10 | King—13 |
| Four—4 | | | |

If you add each card in this way, you will reach a total of 91 for each suit, or 364 for the whole deck.

Now when one card is removed, you will reach a total that is less than 364 when you add the cards together. By subtracting your total from 364, you will reach the number of your card. For example, if a Jack had been removed from the deck, your count would add up to 353. By subtracting 353 from 364, you reach 11, the number assigned to the Jacks.

But how do you know *which* Jack has been removed? It could be the Jack of Diamonds, the Jack of Clubs, the Jack of Spades, or the Jack of Hearts. In order to find out which, it is necessary to make up an excuse to look through the cards one more time. This is where your dramatic talent comes in. You might say something like, "I think I remember which one is missing, but I'm not absolutely positive. Let me take one more quick look, just to see if it's there, and then I'll tell you."

Since this feat of memory seems so impossible, no one will forbid you to look through the cards one more time before you settle on an answer. And you only need a brief half-minute to leaf through the deck and note the Jacks.

Should you spot the Jack of Hearts, the Jack of Clubs, and the Jack of Diamonds, you know for sure that the missing card is the Jack of Spades.

It is important to remember that if you add incorrectly, you will come out with the wrong final total and thus the wrong card. So be sure to insist on complete silence from your audience, for you will need to concentrate severely to keep track of the numbers you are adding in your head.

# SEEING THROUGH THE DECK

Your object is to pick out of an entire deck of cards the one card someone in your audience has chosen. Your materials are a deck of cards and a pencil.

To prepare for this trick, spread a full deck of cards out fan-wise on a table, face down. Ask one person in your audience to slide one card out of the pack and look at it. Have him show it to two or three other people.

Meanwhile, pick up the remaining cards in the deck and stack them. When a few of your friends have seen the card that was chosen, have one of them slide the card back into the stacked deck, anywhere at all.

Now pick up the deck, turn around for a moment to look at it, and Alamazoo! You pull the chosen card out of the deck. Marvellous!

How do you do it? Sometime before you spread the cards out on the table, you take a pencil and draw three or four lines down one side of the deck. Do not let anyone see you do this.

When you spread the cards on the table, no one will be able to see your pencil marks. When someone slides the chosen card out of the pile to look at it, simply gather the cards together again, and turn the deck around. If the side of the deck with the pencil marks was on your right when you fanned the deck out on the table, it should be on your left when the chosen card is placed back in the pack.

You then turn around so that your back is to your audience and examine the sides of the deck. The pencil lines on the marked side of the deck have a tiny white break in them. On the other side of the deck, if you look closely, you will see a card with three or four tiny pencil dots on it. That's the card!

# HOW TO SOLVE A REBUS

Rebus games are fun; they are fun for everyone in the family. You will find solving the rebus puzzle a delight.

Using pictures to indicate words is as old as ancient Egypt. The Indians of the United States, too, used pictographs (sometimes carved on trees) to indicate words.

As an entertainment idea the rebus has been employed for centuries; but never before has the rebus been presented in book form in the particular way in which it is found here.

## SAMPLE REBUS

## SOLUTION

Perhaps the best way to explain the rebus game is to start with a simple example. Let's work it together:

(1)  HAND — AND = H.

(2) Cross out the A, the N, and the D, and what you have left is one H.

(3) Add the word C H A I N. Now you have H C H A I N.

(4)  The next picture shows a CAN. So you cross out C A N from H C H A I N and you are now left with H H I.

(5) Now add a T, and you now have H H I T.

(6) Take away one H, and what is left is the three letter word HIT.

**432**

Let's check this out with what the cartoons say. The first cartoon figure says "What a batter dreams about." Well, of course, a batter dreams about a hit.

The second cartoon character says that the word means "A great performance." You'll agree that a great performance is a hit.

To make sure you completely understand the procedure, let's work out still another example:

(1) B A T H T U B — H A T leaves B U T B.

(2) B T U B — B B leaves T U.

(3) T U + G = T U G

The first cartoon character says that the word is a kind of boat. Of course, you've heard of a tug boat.

The second cartoon character slyly says to the politician: "You could call it pull." The stevedore is correct. If you pull something, you tug it, or tug at it.

Now you're ready to start. Take a pencil and paper, and put down the names of the pictures, plus the names of all the letters you see. Be sure that you note correctly whether the picture or letter is a plus or a minus. Then work your addition and subtraction, and you will come up with the answer.

You can always check your answer in two ways:

(1) The answer should fit exactly into the boxes provided.
(2) The answer should coincide with what the characters say.

Check with the answers given in the back of the book.

Here's wishing you lots of fun.

# REBUS GAME NUMBER 1

*Answers on page 509*

# REBUS GAME NUMBER 2

*Answers on page 509*

**434**

(DIRECTIONS FOR SOLVING REBUS GAMES ARE ON PAGE 432)

# REBUS GAME NUMBER 3

*Answers on page 509*

# REBUS GAME NUMBER 4

*Answers on page 509*

(DIRECTIONS FOR SOLVING REBUS GAMES ARE ON PAGE 432)

# REBUS GAME NUMBER 5

*Answers on page 509*

# REBUS GAME NUMBER 8

*Answers on page 509*

**436**

(DIRECTIONS FOR SOLVING REBUS GAMES ARE ON PAGE 432)

# REBUS GAME NUMBER 7

*Answers on page 509*

# REBUS GAME NUMBER 6

*Answers on page 509*

(DIRECTIONS FOR SOLVING REBUS GAMES ARE ON PAGE 432)

# REBUS GAME NUMBER 9

*Answers on page 509*

# REBUS GAME NUMBER 10

*Answers on page 509*

(DIRECTIONS FOR SOLVING REBUS GAMES ARE ON PAGE 432)

# REBUS GAME NUMBER 11

*Answers on page 509*

# REBUS GAME NUMBER 12

*Answers on page 509*

(DIRECTIONS FOR SOLVING REBUS GAMES ARE ON PAGE 432)

# REBUS GAME NUMBER 13

*Answers on page 509*

# REBUS GAME NUMBER 14

*Answers on page 509*

440

# REBUS GAME NUMBER 15

*Answers on page 509*

# REBUS GAME NUMBER 16

*Answers on page 509*

(DIRECTIONS FOR SOLVING REBUS GAMES ARE ON PAGE 432)

# REBUS GAME NUMBER 17

*Answers on page 510*

# REBUS GAME NUMBER 18

*Answers on page 510*

(DIRECTIONS FOR SOLVING REBUS GAMES ARE ON PAGE 432)

# REBUS GAME NUMBER 19

*Answers on page 510*

# REBUS GAME NUMBER 20

*Answers on page 510*

(DIRECTIONS FOR SOLVING REBUS GAMES ARE ON PAGE 432)

# HILARIOUS HEADLINES

*From a Heraldsburg, Cal. paper:*
CAR LEAVES ROAD, SUFFERS BROKEN NOSE

♕

*From a Burlingame, Cal. paper:*
SANTA ROSA MAN DENIES HE COMMITTED SUICIDE IN SAN FRANCISCO

♕

*From the Spokane Chronicle:*
GRILL SUSPECT OVER BIG BLAZE

♕

*From the Boise, Idaho Statesman, announcing birth of triplets:*
THREE OF A KIND GIVES PAIR FULL HOUSE

♕

*From an Oakland, Cal. paper:*
HAMM FAILS TO IDENTIFY YEGGS

♕

*From a Dallas paper:*
THUGS EAT THEN ROB PROPIETOR

♕

*From the Toledo Times:*
SCENT FOUL PLAY IN DEATH OF MAN FOUND BOUND AND HANGED

♕

*From a San Francisco paper:*
DEAD OFFICER ON S.F. FORCE FOR 18 YEARS

♕

*From the San Antonio, Tex. Express:*
"LEONORE" ONLY OPERA BEETHOVEN WROTE ON MONDAY EVENING

*From an Oshkosh, Wis. paper:*

PEACE OR WAR DEEMED NEAR

*From the La Grange, Ga. News:*

REV. KEY RESIGNS; ATTENDANCE DOUBLES

*From the Wheeling, W. Va. Intelligencer:*

WILD WIFE LEAGUE WILL MEET TO-NIGHT

*From a Walla Walla, Wash. paper:*

ONION PROSPECTS REPORTED STRONG

*From the Springfield Republican:*

40 MEN ESCAPE WATERY GRAVES WHEN VESSEL FLOUNDERS IN ALE

*From a Los Angeles paper:*

COUNTY OFFICIALS TO TALK RUBBISH

*From the Greensboro, N.C. News:*

SAM M—,80, HELD FOR SHOOTING GRANDMOTHER'S HUSBAND

*From the Chicago Tribune:*

WIFE GIVES BIRTH TO A BOY; HE ASKS OLD AGE PENSION

*From the Halifax, Canada Herald:*
JUNE BABIES FLOOD OTTAWA HOSPITAL

*From a New York paper, reporting on a rape by a group of soldiers:*
COMMISSION TO EXAMINE PRIVATES—WILL LEAVE NO STONE UNTURNED

*From the Oakland, Cal. Tribune:*
TWO CONVICTS EVADE NOOSE; JURY HUNG

*From the New York Journal-American:*
STEALS CLOCK, FACES TIME

*From an Austin, Tex. paper:*
JURY GETS DRUNK DRIVING CASE HERE

*From a Texas paper:*
NEBRASKA OFFICERS BEST BANK BANDITS

*From the Boston Transcript:*
HOTEL BURNS; TWO HUNDRED GUESTS ESCAPE HALF GLAD

*From a Bridgeport, Conn. paper:*
INFANT MORALITY SHOWS DROP HERE

*From the Cleveland Plain Dealer:*
GYPSY ROSE HAS A 5½ -POUND STRIPLING

*From an Alhambra, Cal. paper:*
DRIVER OF DEATH CAR HELD ON NEGLIGIBLE HOMICIDE

*From a Los Cruces, N.M. paper:*
MAN IS FATALLY SLAIN

*From the Lansing State Journal:*
SENATE PASSES DEATH PENALTY—Measure Provides for Electrocution for All Persons Over 17.

*From a New York paper:*
FATHER OF TEN SHOT—MISTAKEN FOR RABBIT

*From the Wichita Falls, Tex. Record News:*
ENRAGED COW INJURES FARMER WITH AX

*From the Redondo Beach, Cal. South Bay Daily Breeze:*
MANY ANTIQUES AT D.A.R. MEETING

# HUMOROUS CROSSWORD NO. 1

*Answers on page 510*

## ACROSS

1. Younger siblings and ants
5. Water, water, everywhere and very good to drink
8. Generally goes with rack
9. Lest you forget the wound
10. That Greek thing Keats immortalized
11. Generally speaking, generally speaking
12. Fellers like the girl who won't say this
13. What you toast besides bread
15. Sine qua non of a fencer
17. When it comes to dough, we all _____it.
19. Describes many a purse and many a head
21. Colloquial negative
23. A critic will go places to_____ things
24. Happy, sad, or dead, it's final
25. One wager
27. Look at it backwards or forwards, it's an exploit
28. Starts to pay off old scores, and ends in new debts
29. Something you can count on

## DOWN

1. A plum that has seen better days
2. Haven for expatriate Americans
3. This is original
4. Insert "E" between these letters to make "X"
5. It can be seen
6. He starts by selling a bill of goods, turns floorwalker, and winds up paymaster
7. Traditionally, the law has a long one
9. All it takes is a little polish
11. What junior will be some day
13. Here's where you get off!
14. Where you are when you're in the dog house
16. Proves that there's no fuel like an old fuel
18. Works his son's way through college
20. Top it off with a "P"
22. Many a gag writer takes an old one and puts new teeth in it
24. Head it up with an "H" and it's a rotter, with an "R" it's companion to a rod
26. This degree guarantees the holder has mastered the first two letters of the alphabet
27. Say it once and it's pop; say it twice and it's another kind of art

# HUMOROUS CROSSWORD NO. 2

*Answers on page 510*

## ACROSS

1. Good for preserving everything but your liver
8. What chickens and certain apartment dwellers have in common
9. The bean that sustains the army
11. The last resort of the unimaginative
13. What you never do at Vegas
14. When you're all wet a towel might help, but a martini's_____
16. Strike an egocentric note
18. What you throw in when you're all wet
20. Hurrah for the sun god
22. When cows give beer
24. It's only human to
26. A candle that's all dolled up
28. In, out, up, or down, it's foot-wise
30. The kind of motive that gets people going
31. He'd sell the grapes of wrath for profit

## DOWN

1. It makes work for a lawyer, and play for a performer
2. The English have a houseful of them
3. To do this to a lady might win you a disaster
4. It's a choice that's not binding
5. Two-thirds of one
6. Like glass, it's often broken
7. He suffers from sceptic poisoning
10. Vigor's twin
12. The female in the middle of this is rather sheepish
15. The spirit of '76
17. Apparel once popular with women
19. Squeeze this on a cat and get a sourpuss
21. Begin this crafty word with a "C", you ride in it; begin it with a "D", you throw it
23. It's what makes humans run
25. Music of Hell's Angels
27. Neither's mate
29. Mathematician's dessert

# HUMOROUS CROSSWORD NO. 3

*Answers on page 510*

## ACROSS

1. One of those little things that count, if you ask any golfer
5. Water over the dam—with Uncle Sam's help
8. Two-thirds of an orange
9. You'll get the two middle letters of this word with ease
10. The woman in every man's life
11. The lot on which King Arthur built his court
12. 999
13. A vehicle on which passengers play hide and sick
14. Friend of the walrus
18. The end of London and lower side of New York that are slums
19. Add "G", and throw it on the fire; and "X", and enjoy it with a bagel
20. If you can't get it all, settle for this
22. You shouldn't take this standing up
23. What any gangster might take you for
24. A nicely named French city
25. The quintessential hole
26. A pastime in which your number is up unless your numbers are up

## DOWN

1. One who originates old jokes
2. Holds you smell bound
3. If it breaks, you'll curse
4. With an "E" in the middle, it's cosy; with an "I", it's noisy
5. Begin it with "AT", it's a try; begin it with "CON", and be scornful
6. For victory
7. What generally follows *you* down South
9. The kind of praise that means damnation
11. Display rack for medals
13. Not quite a strike
15. Cash on hand
16. Choose, don't settle
17. Where you will find the greatest collection of bullthrowers in the country
20. Floating zoo
21. Most folks could find this in piety
22. A morsel in any mouth except that of the horse
24. Men prefer girls who don't _____ too much

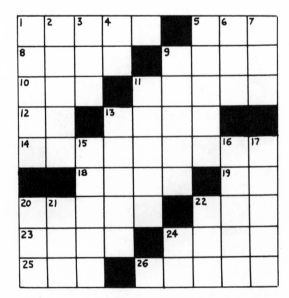

# HUMOROUS CROSSWORD NO. 4

*Answers on page 510*

## ACROSS

1. You can draw this from a bank, but it tastes better from a keg
5. With poor relatives, it's usually touch and _____
6. Uncle Sam's favorite son
7. Hail and farewell in the land of the lei
9. A husband's last word
11. The kind of head on an intellectual
13. Something that's a sum thing
16. He who can lose and laugh
17. What you'll become if you eat like a bird—one peck at a time
18. Wet or dry, it gives a clean sweep
20. Easy to stub
22. All that's left at the end
25. Top it off with "G" for a good growl
26. A man who suffers from good health in his community
27. What you do most while working a crossword

## DOWN

1. No good citizen of California would even _____ in Florida
2. Million dollar rating
3. A man who peddles soft-soap made mostly of lye
4. You can't have an infinitive without it
5. *Prize insult:* Your photo will do, but where's the _____ that's supposed to go under it?
6. A mineral that sounds like what a cheat does to his victim
8. Sometimes this bullet-stopper is used to top a cop
10. You'll find them in front of many city dwellings
12. If it suits the goose, it's good enough for him, too
14. Round and heavenly
15. Begin it with a "B", it's a fish; begin it with an "M", it's a bulk. (If you don't get this one, you'll feel like one.)
19. Feather it and avoid a splash!
21. You'll have to dig for this
23. Add an "M", it's a border; add an "N", it's a fowl; add an "X", it's a jinx
24. Abbreviated sex appeal

# HUMOROUS CROSSWORD NO. 5

*Answers on page 510*

## ACROSS

1. The only thing the critics haven't panned
5. The only time a husband and wife get a thrill out of holding hands is when they're holding this kind
9. The way to kill it is to get a committee to go to work on it
10. A feline that will make you cry for its last syllable
11. McCoy's trait
12. Two-thirds of America's beginning
13. The Greek Annie Oakley
15. This one commands attention
16. He gives it to 15 across
17. What your eyes do to save your face
21. A real pain in the neck
23. Round at the ends and high in the middle
25. According to critics, this garment should be found in its first three letters
26. The artist and the experimenter go out on this
27. An exasperating toy with a variable belly band
28. A fancy way to see

## DOWN

1. Two words: according to some men, one leads to the other
2. Pindar is responsible for this form
3. What a salesman looks for, a journalist composes, and an actress dreams about
4. An ultra-modernist who put his imagination in the mixing bowl
5. Add "K" and you'll have courage
6. Affects the tide and the untied
7. A French pal
8. A romance in which the hero dies in the first chapter
14. The only thing in England that's higher than the King
17. Hailing at sea
18. Presidential toe that does the kicking
19. A small one is better than a big loaf, if you ask any actor
20. This is this, and that's that
22. The only pleasant thing associated with the word *bill*
24. Primary in importance

# HUMOROUS CROSSWORD NO. 6

*Answers on page 511*

## ACROSS

1. The sweetest notes in the whole world
8. N - M - E
9. Municipal underworld
10. The kind of Fall we have every year
12. What every woman takes of what every woman wears
14. Put an "L" in front of this and you'll have something to go on
15. Generally precedes "G"
16. Ingredient in I-strain
19. The four letters most commonly seen before Q
21. Like the old bucket
23. Four-fifths of this is worth a penny
24. What women are to men, and vice versa

## DOWN

1. Not a real show—just a take-off
2. The kind of egg that gets better with storage
3. Not a bad joint at all
4. Modern antique
5. What old maids exclaim when they see males
6. What the champ terms a challenger
7. A type of ball that always bounces into trouble
11. Cap it with garb and it smells
13. Underwear for a feather frock
17. One man's _____ is another man's umbrella
18. Be it ever so humble, there's none like your own
19. When you follow this, you're inclined to be happy
20. The guy who's agin it
22. Add *to* and it's worth a subway ride

# PICK THE LAST COIN

How'd you like to play a game you can almost always win? You'll need five pennies, four nickels, and three dimes.

Set up the coins on a table as shown:

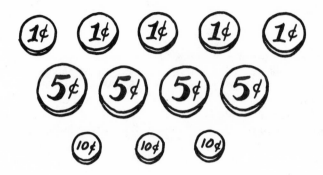

The rules of the game are:

The players take alternate turns.

At each turn, a player is allowed to pick up as many coins as he wants to—as long as the coins are of the same denomination. For example, on his turn, a player may pick up one, two, three, or four nickels from the middle row, but no dimes and no pennies. Or he may pick up as many pennies as he wants to, or as many dimes as he wants to.

The object of the game is to force the opposing player to pick up the last coin on the table.

If you go first, you remove two dimes. With this move, you always win. Nothing your opponent can do will help him.

There are five losing positions:

LOSING POSITION I: Two coins on each of two lines.

If your opponent takes one coin, you remove a row of two coins, leaving him with the last coin.

If he takes two coins, you take one of the remaining two coins, again leaving him with the last coin.

LOSING POSITION II: Three coins on each of two lines.

If your opponent takes three coins, you take two coins on the remaining line.

If he takes two coins from one of the rows, you take the whole row.

If your opponent takes just one coin, you follow suit and take one coin from the other row. This leaves the coins in LOSING POSITION I, described above.

LOSING POSITION III: Four coins on each two lines. You can easily maneuver the coins from this position into LOSING POSITION I or LOSING POSITION II, no matter what moves the other player makes.

LOSING POSITION IV: One coin on each of the three lines. In this position, your opponent can only take one coin. In your turn, you also take one coin, leaving the last coin for him.

LOSING POSITION V: A combination of three, two, and one coin on three lines. From this position, you can maneuver your opponent into one of the four LOSING POSITIONS described above.

For example, if your opponent goes first and takes a penny from the top row, you then take all three dimes, leaving him in LOSING POSITION III.

If he takes two pennies, you take all the nickels, leaving him in LOSING POSITION II.

You will find you can always make a countermove for any move your opponent makes, leaving him in one of the LOSING POSITIONS, provided you go first.

However, if your opponent goes first and makes this move, he will win—if he knows how to follow up.

Your second best move as the starting player is to move one dime. If your opponent does not follow up by removing just one dime, you're a sure winner.

When you play this game, try to use as many alternative moves as you can, so that your opponent does not catch on to the winning move. If you vary your first moves, you will find you can go on winning almost every single game you play!

# COIN ROWS

All you need for this simple trick is six coins of the same size.
    Arrange the coins on a table, as shown.

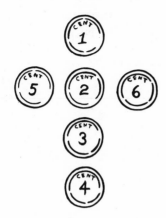

    Your object is to arrange the six coins so that they form two even rows made up of four coins each. You may only move one coin in order to accomplish this task.
    First, let your friends try it. When they are thoroughly bewildered, show them how to do it.
    Simply pick up the bottom coin in the vertical row, and place it directly on top of the center coin, the one that belongs to both rows.

    You will see that each row now contains four coins.

# THE IMPRISONED DIME

You can make a dime move all by itself almost like magic. You only need a cloth-covered table, a glass, a dime, and two nickels.

Put a dime on the cloth-covered table. Place one nickel on either side of the dime. Now cover the dime with an upside down glass, in such a way that the glass is resting on the two nickels.

Your object is to remove the dime from underneath the glass without touching the glass or touching any of the coins.

To do this, use your fingernail to scratch the table-cloth with short, fast strokes. For best results, scratch the cloth as close to the glass as possible. As you keep scratching the cloth, the dime will begin to move. Slowly, a bit at a time, it will creep toward the edge of the glass, and then out from beneath it.

# THE NICKEL TRICK

This stunt may take a little bit of practice before you can do it perfectly, but you will really astound your friends. All you need is a business card, or a playing card, and a nickel.

Hold out your left hand in front of you, with your palm facing up and your fingers slightly separated. Balance the card on your index finger.

Now place the nickel on top of the card. Be sure to place the nickel directly on top of the first joint of that finger, so that it is properly balanced.

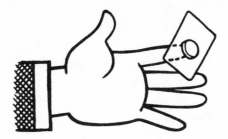

The challenge is to remove the card without touching that nickel.

Snap your fingers briskly against one edge of the card, using the thumb and index fingers of your other hand. This is the part of the trick which may require a little bit of practice: you must be careful not to strike the underside of the card, or you will knock the nickel off of the card. Be sure to hit only the edge of the card.

If you have hit the card correctly, with a brisk and sharp motion, the card will fly out, leaving the nickel undisturbed on your finger.

# ALLITERATIVE RHYMES

Here is a selection of *tours de force* concocted by some of our wilier versifiers.

Cardinal Wolsey was the son of a butcher. With his rapid rise to political eminence, he managed to draw an unhealthy quota of jealous antagonists. William Pitt made capital of Wolsey's humble origin by lampooning him in these lines:

> *Begot by butchers, but by butchers bred,*
> *How high His Highness holds his haughty head.*

A couple of centuries ago, the medical profession was not held in high repute—perhaps with good cause. Here are some anonymous lines that reflect the temper of the day:

> *Medical men my mood mistaking,*
> *Most mawkish, monstrous messes making,*
> *Molest me much.*
> *More manfully my mind might meet my malady.*
> *Medicine's mere mockery murders me.*

Addressed to the same group, here are some playful lines:

> *I need not your needles,*
>     *They're needless to me;*
> *For kneading of needles*
>     *Were needless you see.*
> *But did my neat trousers*
>     *But need to be kneed—*
> *I then should have need*
>     *Of your needles, indeed!*

David Garrick, likely the most famous English actor of the 18th century, patronized an apothecary and physician by the name of Dr. John Hill. When Hill died, Garrick penned his obituary in the following lines:

> *For physic and farces*
> *His equal there scarce is;*
> *His farces are physic,*
> *His physic a farce is!*

But it took one Mr. Poulter, a resident of Winchester, England, to top all previous efforts. He composed what is probably the longest alliterative poem on record. Poulter ran the full gamut from A to Z, as witness the following:

An Austrian army, awfully arrayed,
Boldly by battery, besieged Belgrade.
Cossack commanders cannonading come
Dealing destruction's devastating doom.
Every endeavor engineers essay
For fame, for fortune, forming furious fray.
Gaunt gunners grapple, giving gashes good,
Heaves high his head, heroic hardihood.
Ibraham, Islam, imps in ill,
Jostle John Jarovlitz, Jem, Joe, Jack, Jill;
Kick kindling Kutosoff, king's kinsmen kill.
Labor low levels loftiest, longest lines.
Men march mid moles, mid mounds, mid murd'rous mines,

Now nightfall's near; now needful nature nods,
Opposed, opposing, overcoming odds,
Poor peasants, partly purchased, partly pressed,
Quite quaking, quarter, quarter quickly quest.
Reason returns, recalls redundant rage,
Saves sinking soldiers, softens Signiors sage.
Truce, Turkey, truce, treacherous Tartar train,
Unwise, unjust unmerciful Ukraine,
Vanish vile vengeance, vanish victory vain.
Wisdom wails war, wails warring words.
Xerxes, Xanthippus, Ximines, Xavier,
Yet Yassey's youth ye yield your youthful yest,
Zealously, zanes, zealously, zeals zest.

# STORIES FOR A LAUGH

Two WOMEN MET again after many years and began exchanging histories. "Whatever happened to your son?" asked one woman.

"Oh, what a tragedy!" moaned the other. "My son married a no-good who doesn't lift a finger around the house. She can't cook, she can't sew a button on a shirt, all she does is sleep. My poor boy brings her breakfast in bed, and all day long she stays there, loafing, reading, eating candy!"

"That's terrible," sympathized the first woman. "And what about your daughter?"

"Oh, she's got a good life. She married a man who's a living doll! He won't let her set foot in the kitchen. He gives her breakfast in bed, and makes her stay there all day, resting, reading, and eating chocolates."

A RABBI, A PRIEST, and a minister were playing poker. Suddenly, the police burst into the room. "Sorry, gents, but gambling's illegal," said one of the officers, and he hustled the religious trio down to the court.

"I'm sorry about this," said the judge, "but now that you're here there's only one thing to do. Since you're all men of the cloth, I think I can trust your word. So I'll ask you if you were gambling, and whatever you answer, I'll believe you. We'll start with you, Father."

"Your Honor, surely it is important to be certain that we define what we mean by gambling. In a narrow, but entirely valid sense, what we describe as gambling is only truly so if there is a desire to win money, rather than merely to enjoy the suspense of the fall of cards. In addition, we might confine gambling to situations where the loss of money would be harmful, as—"

"Okay, Father," the judge interrupted. "I see that in the manner in which you define the word, you were not gambling. Now how about you, Reverend?"

The minister said, "I entirely agree with my learned colleague."

"Fine," said the judge. "And now you, rabbi. Were you gambling?"

The rabbi looked at his two friends, and then back at the judge, and asked, "With whom, Your Honor?"

A CRUISING SHIP was sailing near Iceland when the captain spied an iceberg right in his ship's path. He tried to steer around it, but found to his horror that something was wrong with the rudder. The ship wouldn't turn.

Maintaining his calm, the captain immediately wired for help, and ships and helicopters were dispatched. In the meantime, the captain tried to think of some way to keep the passengers from noticing the fearful peril ahead.

Then he remembered that there was a magician aboard. So he called the man in and explained the situation. "Please do a show for the passengers to keep them occupied," said the captain. "If it becomes unavoidable for us to hit the iceberg, I'll signal you. When you see me signal, just tell the audience that for your final act, you'll split the ship in two. By the time they realize you weren't fooling, help should arrive."

So the magician did as he was told, and put on a lively and entertaining show, pulling rabbits out of his hat and making things mysteriously disappear. Then he noticed the captain frantically signaling to him. Obediently, the magician announced: "Ladies and gentlemen, for my final illusion, I shall split this ship in two."

At that moment, the iceberg was reached. The ship rocked with the impact and listed dangerously to one side. The passengers fell into a state of panic. Half of them were thrown into the sea.

Amidst all the brouhaha Mr. Finkelstein, clinging to an upside-down railing, bumped into the magician. Shaking his head disapprovingly, Finkelstein snarled, "Wise guy!"

ABE SELTZER WAS PASSING a golf course when he was struck in the head by a golf ball.

Seething, Abe picked up the ball and gestured wildly at the player running anxiously toward him. "I'll sue you in court for five hundred dollars!" Abe shouted angrily.

The golfer tried to excuse himself. "I hollered 'Fore!'" he said.

"All right!" answered Abe, "I'll take it."

# THE ANSWERS

## EAT, DRINK, AND BE MERRY.................... Page 12

| | |
|---|---|
| 1. Corn | 27. Lemon |
| 2. Milk | 28. Beet |
| 3. Bananas | 29. Bass |
| 4. Tarts | 30. Peanuts |
| 5. Blueberry | 31. Pea |
| 6. Tea | 32. Chestnut |
| 7. Cabbages | 33. Grapes |
| 8. Honey, Vinegar | 34. Shrimp |
| 9. Turkey | 35. Plum |
| 10. Fish | 36. Peach |
| 11. Lollipops or wine | 37. Chicken |
| 12. Molasses | 38. Coffee |
| 13. Pike | 39. Wine, Bread |
| 14. Pear | 40. Cheese |
| 15. Apple | 41. Candy |
| 16. Chowder | 42. Soda Water |
| 17. Beer | 43. Potato, Potato |
| 18. Eggs | 44. Ham |
| 19. Mustard | 45. Porridge |
| 20. Cream | 46. Gingerbread |
| 21. Sugar, Spice | 47. Liquor |
| 22. Beef | 48. Nuts |
| 23. Pie | 49. Fig |
| 24. Stew | 50. Orange |
| 25. Cherries | 51. Bacon |
| 26. Bean | 52. Pudding |

## IT'S THE LITTLE THINGS THAT COUNT.............. Page 14

| | |
|---|---|
| 1. Muffet | 26. New York |
| 2. Tenderness | 27. Lamb |
| 3. The world | 28. Snips, snails |
| 4. Heaven | 29. Cat feet |
| 5. A lot | 30. Girls |
| 6. You cry | 31. Beast |
| 7. Hurts | 32. Near shore |
| 8. Dangerous thing | 33. Your horn |
| 9. Dog (or girl) | 34. Jack Horner |
| 10. Rooney | 35. Lamb |
| 11. Friends | 36. Pot |
| 12. Buttercup | 37. Know |
| 13. Its own | 38. Pasadena |
| 14. Prayer | 39. Bo Peep |
| 15. Girl | 40. Slave |
| 16. Lies | 41. House |
| 17. Children | 42. Two-shoes |
| 18. Horn | 43. Engine |
| 19. Acorns | 44. Birdie |
| 20. Jug | 45. Pond |
| 21. Lead | 46. Faith |
| 22. Curl | 47. Orphan |
| 23. Bethlehem | 48. Music |
| 24. Oaks | 49. Margie |
| 25. Pitchers | 50. Acre |

## AROUND THE HOUSE....... Page 16

| | |
|---|---|
| 1. Rocking chair | 13. Plate |
| 2. Broom | 14. Tub |
| 3. Tables | 15. Shades |
| 4. Closet | 16. Bureau |
| 5. Telephone | 17. Dish |
| 6. Range | 18. Iron |
| 7. Kitchen sink | 19. Lamps |
| 8. Davenport | 20. Curtain |
| 9. Kettle | 21. Bowl |
| 10. Pitchers | 22. Shower |
| 11. Mirror | 23. Pillow |
| 12. Frying pan | 24. Cupboard |

## FANFARE .................. Page 17

| | |
|---|---|
| 1. Fandango | 11. Fanny Brice |
| 2. Fancy-free | 12. Infantry |
| 3. *White Fang* | 13. Fan-tan |
| 4. Faneuil Hall | 14. Fan the flame |
| 5. Fan mail | 15. Profane |
| 6. Infant | 16. Fancy Dan |
| 7. *Fanny Hill* | 17. *Fantasia* |
| 8. Trip the light fantastic | 18. *Fantine* |
| 9. Fantasy | 19. *Fantastic Voyage* |
| 10. Fanatic | 20. Fanback |

## BODY ENGLISH............. Page 18

| | |
|---|---|
| 1. Hands | 13. Elbow |
| 2. Heart | 14. Face |
| 3. Fingers, toes | 15. Tongue |
| 4. Skin | 16. Throat |
| 5. Eyes | 17. Thumb |
| 6. Teeth | 18. Belly |
| 7. Ears | 19. Arches |
| 8. Liver | 20. Legs |
| 9. Feet | 21. Arm |
| 10. Chin | 22. Chest |
| 11. Ankle | 23. Calf |
| 12. Neck | 24. Shoulder |

## THE NIGHT GAME ......... Page 19

1. Fly-by-night
2. *In the Heat of the Night*
3. Nightgown
4. Night life
5. "Day and Night"
6. Florence Nightingale
7. *Hard Day's Night*
8. One-night stand
9. *Long Day's Journey into Night*
10. *Twelfth Night*

464

465

13. Gain
14. Gale
15. Gang
16. Gear
17. General
18. Ginger
19. Girl
20. Glare
21. Glean
22. Glee
23. Grail
24. Grain
25. Grange
26. Green
27. Grin
28. Lager
29. Lain
30. Lair
31. Lane
32. Large
33. Lean
34. Learn
35. Leer
36. Liar
37. Liege
38. Lien
39. Line
40. Linear
41. Linger
42. Nail
43. Near
44. Niggle
45. Rage
46. Rail
47. Rain
48. Range
49. Real
50. Reel
51. Regain
52. Regal
53. Regale
54. Reign
55. Rein
56. Rile
57. Ring

## SHEEPISHLY .............. Page 42

1. Heel
2. Heil
3. Help
4. Hiss
5. Less
6. Lisp
7. Peel
8. Plies
9. Seep
10. Sheep
11. Ship
12. Sleep
13. Slip
14. Spiel
15. Sylph

## IMPLAUSIBLE .............. Page 42

1. Able
2. Aisle
3. Ample
4. Apse
5. Bail
6. Bale
7. Ball
8. Base
9. Basil
10. Bell
11. Bile
12. Bill
13. Blimp
14. Isle
15. Label
16. Lamb
17. Lamp
18. Lapel
19. Lapse
20. Liable
21. Libel
22. Limb
23. Lime
24. Limp
25. Lisle
26. Male
27. Mall
28. Meal
29. Mile
30. Pail
31. Pale
32. Pall
33. Pause
34. Pile
35. Pill
36. Plausible
37. Plea
38. Pliable
39. Pull
40. Sable
41. Sail
42. Sale
43. Sample
44. Sell
45. Simple
46. Slab
47. Slam
48. Slap
49. Slime
50. Slip
51. Small
52. Smell
53. Smile
54. Spell
55. Spiel
56. Spill

## SINGULARLY .............. Page 43

1. Airy
2. Ally
3. Gain
4. Gill
5. Glans
6. Gnarl
7. Grail
8. Grain
9. Gray
10. Grill
11. Grin
12. Gull
13. Gully
14. Lain
15. Lair
16. Lung
17. Nary
18. Rail
19. Rain
20. Rally
21. Ring
22. Ruin
23. Rung
24. Sally
25. Sang
26. Silly
27. Sing
28. Slang
29. Slay
30. Sling
31. Slug
32. Snag
33. Snarl
34. Sully
35. Yarn

## MARGARINE .............. Page 43

1. Again
2. Anger
3. Area
4. Aria
5. Gain
6. Game
7. Gear
8. Grain
9. Gram
10. Grim
11. Grime
12. Grin
13. Image
14. Main
15. Mane
16. Mania
17. Mare
18. Mean
19. Mine
20. Name
21. Near
22. Rage
23. Rain
24. Range
25. Ream
26. Rear
27. Rein
28. Ring

## PUNCTILIOUS .............. Page 44

1. Clout
2. Coin
3. Cost
4. Count
5. Input
6. Lint
7. List
8. Loin
9. Lost
10. Lout
11. Lust
12. Opus
13. Pint
14. Pious
15. Plot
16. Post
17. Pout
18. Punt
19. Scup
20. Silt
21. Slip
22. Slit
23. Slop
24. Slot
25. Snip
26. Soil
27. Soul
28. Soup
29. Spin
30. Spit
31. Spoil
32. Spot
33. Spout
34. Stop
35. Stun
36. Toil
37. Tulip
38. Upon

## STATUTORY .............. Page 44

1. Arty
2. Auto
3. Ratty
4. Roast
5. Roust
6. Rout
7. Rust
8. Rutty
9. Sort
10. Sour
11. Star
12. Start
13. Stay
14. Stoat
15. Story
16. Stout
17. Stray
18. Strut
19. Tart
20. Tasty
21. Taut
22. Toast
23. Tort
24. Tour
25. Tout
26. Tray
27. Trot
28. Trout
29. Trust
30. Tryst
31. Tutor

## NOTHINGNESS .............. Page 45

1. Eight
2. Ensign
3. Ethos
4. Ghost
5. Gist
6. Goes
7. Gone
8. Gosh
9. Hinge
10. Hint
11. Hiss
12. Hoist
13. Hone
14. Hose
15. Host
16. Inset
17. Into
18. Nest
19. Night
20. Nine
21. Ninth
22. Noise
23. None
24. Nose
25. Nosh
26. Note
27. Nothing
28. Onset
29. Sent
30. Shin
31. Shine
32. Shoe
33. Shot
34. Sight
35. Sign
36. Signet
37. Sine
38. Sing
39. Singe
40. Site
41. Snot
42. Sonnet
43. Stein
44. Sting
45. Stone
46. Tennis
47. Then
48. Thin

## EUPHONIOUS............. Page 45

| 1. Heinous | 7. Pious | 13. Spin |
| 2. Hone | 8. Poise | 14. Spine |
| 3. Hoop | 9. Ponies | 15. Spoon |
| 4. Hose | 10. Shin | 16. Spun |
| 5. House | 11. Ship | 17. Supine |
| 6. Noise | 12. Shun | |

## CAPRICIOUS.............. Page 46

| 1. Acor | 9. Pour | 16. Scrip |
| 2. Carp | 10. Proa | 17. Soar |
| 3. Coup | 11. Rasp | 18. Soup |
| 4. Crap | 12. Scar | 19. Sour |
| 5. Crisp | 13. Scarp | 20. Spar |
| 6. Crop | 14. Scour | 21. Spur |
| 7. Croup | 15. Scrap | 22. Upar |
| 8. Pious | | |

## STOPPAGE ............... Page 46

| 1. Apse | 10. Peat | 19. Spot |
| 2. Estop | 11. Pest | 20. Stag |
| 3. Gape | 12. Poet | 21. Stage |
| 4. Gate | 13. Pope | 22. Step |
| 5. Goat | 14. Post | 23. Stop |
| 6. Page | 15. Sage | 24. Tape |
| 7. Past | 16. Soap | 25. Toga |
| 8. Paste | 17. Spat | 26. Tope |
| 9. Pate | 18. Spate | |

## TEST YOUR SPATIAL
## REASONING ............... Page 58

*Part One:*

| | 8. 6 | 4. No |
| 1. 6 | 9. 8 | 5. Yes |
| 2. 5 | 10. 5 | |
| 3. 8 | | *Part Three:* |
| 4. 7 | *Part Two:* | A. 3 |
| 5. 5 | | B. 4 |
| 6. 11 | 1. No | C. 4 |
| 7. 6 | 2. Yes | D. None |
| | 3. No | E. 3 |

Give yourself two points for each correct answer in *Part One.* Give yourself five points for each correct answer in *Part Two,* but first subtract from this sum one point for each incorrect answer in *Part Two.* Give yourself three points for each correct answer in *Part Three.*

| PERFECT: | 60 |
| SUPERIOR: | Over 48 |
| GOOD: | 41-48 |
| FAIR: | 34-40 |
| POOR: | Below 34 |

## ARE YOU THOROUGH?..... Page 62

| *Part One:* | *Part Two:* |
| 1. 15 | 1. 30 |
| 2. 12 | 2. 46 |
| 3. 18 | 3. 33 |
| 4. 6 | 4. 18 |
| 5. 2 | 5. 9 |
| 6. 5 | 6. 9 |
| 7. 5 | 7. 5 |
| 8. 4 | 8. 8 |
| 9. 4 | 9. 13 |
| 10. 1 | 10. 0 |

Give yourself one point for each correct answer.

| PERFECT: | 20 |
| SUPERIOR: | Above 18 |
| GOOD: | 15-18 |
| FAIR: | 11-14 |
| POOR: | Below 11 |

## TEST YOUR LOGIC NO. 1 ... Page 65

| 1. 2 | 21. 4 | 41. 4 |
| 2. 1 | 22. 2 | 42. 21 |
| 3. 27 | 23. K | 43. 54 |
| 4. 3 | 24. 8 | 44. 5 |
| 5. 12 | 25. I | 45. 1 |
| 6. F | 26. Q | 46. 5 |
| 7. F | 27. F | 47. 90 |
| 8. 9 | 28. 9 | 48. 7 |
| 9. T | 29. D | 49. 10 |
| 10. 1 | 30. T | 50. 4 |
| 11. 2 | 31. 17 | 51. 2 |
| 12. 4 | 32. O | 52. 11 |
| 13. 3 | 33. 6 | 53. 2 |
| 14. 4 | 34. 3 | 54. 2 |
| 15. 3 | 35. 7 | 55. 3 |
| 16. 4 | 36. 4 | 56. False |
| 17. 15 | 37. I | 57. Northwest |
| 18. 77 | 38. 9 | 58. 30 minutes |
| 19. 3 | 39. 3 | 59. T |
| 20. 4 | 40. 27 | 60. 3 |

Give yourself one point for each correct answer.

| PERFECT: | 60 |
| SUPERIOR: | Over 55 |
| GOOD: | 45-55 |
| FAIR: | 30-44 |
| POOR: | Below 30 |

## COUNT THE CUBES ........ Page 70

| 1. 2 | 6. 15 | 11. 19 |
| 2. 4 | 7. 27 | 12. 22 |
| 3. 6 | 8. 18 | 13. 14 |
| 4. 8 | 9. 15 | 14. 20 |
| 5. 12 | 10. 10 | 15. 40 |

For questions 1 through 9, give yourself one point for each correct answer. For questions

10 through 15, give yourself three points for each correct answer.

| | |
|---|---|
| PERFECT: | 27 |
| SUPERIOR: | Over 24 |
| GOOD: | 21-24 |
| FAIR: | 15-20 |
| POOR: | Below 15 |

### HOW SHARP IS YOUR MEMORY? .................. Page 72

The numbers below the following designs should be circled: 1, 3, 4, 5, 7, 12, 13, 14, 15, 17, 19. All other designs should be marked with an X.

Give yourself two points for each design correctly marked. From this sum subtract one point for each design incorrectly marked. Score zero for any unmarked design.

| | |
|---|---|
| PERFECT: | 42 |
| SUPERIOR: | Over 30 |
| GOOD: | 25-30 |
| FAIR: | 19-24 |
| POOR: | Below 19 |

### DO YOU HAVE A HEAD FOR FIGURES? ................... Page 76

| | | | |
|---|---|---|---|
| 1. | 8 | 18. | 24 |
| 2. | 16 | 19. | 55 |
| 3. | 55 | 20. | |
| 4. | 80¢ | | |
| 5. | 8 | | |
| 6. | 43 | | |
| 7. | 1¼ minutes | | |
| 8. | 63 | | |
| 9. | 465 | 21. | |
| 10. | 20 | | |
| 11. | 2/3 | | |
| 12. | $14 | | |
| 13. | 10½ days | | |
| 14. | Yes | | |
| 15. | Yes | | |
| 16. | 10 | 22. | B = 7; C = 6; D = 4; |
| 17. | 3:00 | | E = 3; F = 2 |

20.
```
    5 C 4
  x C 5
  2 F A Y
A 1 F 6
A C 4 8 Y
```

21.
```
    7 9 5 4
  x   6 9
  7 1 5 8 6
4 7 7 2 4
5 4 8 8 2 6
```

For questions 1 through 19, give yourself one point for each correct answer. For questions 20 through 22, give yourself three points for each *entirely* correct answer.

| | |
|---|---|
| PERFECT: | 28 |
| SUPERIOR: | Over 23 |
| GOOD: | 18-23 |
| FAIR: | 11-17 |
| POOR: | Below 11 |

### TEST YOUR LOGIC NO. 2 ... Page 79

| | | | |
|---|---|---|---|
| 1. | 3 | 3. | 2 |
| 2. | 30 | 4. | 3 |

| | | | |
|---|---|---|---|
| 5. | 1 | 33. | 2/5 |
| 6. | 3 | 34. | 5 |
| 7. | 4 | 35. | F |
| 8. | 4 | 36. | 3 |
| 9. | 1 | 37. | 4 |
| 10. | 4 | 38. | 3 |
| 11. | 3 | 39. | 13 |
| 12. | 8½ | 40. | 10 |
| 13. | 3 | 41. | 2 |
| 14. | 1140 | 42. | 3 |
| 15. | 2 | 43. | F |
| 16. | 5 | 44. | 18 |
| 17. | 5 | 45. | 2 |
| 18. | 4 | 46. | 4 |
| 19. | 30 | 47. | 47 |
| 20. | SRQ | 48. | 2 |
| 21. | 4-10-2-8-10-8 | 49. | 1 |
| 22. | 200 | 50. | 4 |
| 23. | 2 | 51. | 3 |
| 24. | 3 | 52. | 10 |
| 25. | 550 | 53. | 2 |
| 26. | 41 | 54. | 3 |
| 27. | 4 | 55. | 1 ounce |
| 28. | 6 | 56. | 3 |
| 29. | 12 | 57. | 10 |
| 30. | 2 | 58. | 1 |
| 31. | 2 | 59. | P |
| 32. | 15 | 60. | 1 |

Give yourself one point for each correct answer.

| | |
|---|---|
| PERFECT: | 60 |
| SUPERIOR: | Over 55 |
| GOOD: | 45-55 |
| FAIR: | 30-44 |
| POOR: | Below 30 |

### DO YOU THINK STRAIGHT?. Page 84

| | | | | | |
|---|---|---|---|---|---|
| 1. | T | 13. | F, F, T | 25. | T |
| 2. | F | 14. | F, T, F | 26. | F |
| 3. | F, T | 15. | T, F, F | 27. | F |
| 4. | F | 16. | T, F, F | 28. | T |
| 5. | F, T | 17. | F, F, T | 29. | T |
| 6. | F, F, T | 18. | T, F | 30. | F |
| 7. | F | 19. | F, T, F | 31. | F |
| 8. | T, F | 20. | F, F, T | 32. | T |
| 9. | F, F, T | 21. | F | 33. | F |
| 10. | F, T, F | 22. | F | 34. | F |
| 11. | F, F, T | 23. | T | 35. | T |
| 12. | F, F, T | 24. | F | | |

Give yourself one point for each correct answer to each conclusion. (You may therefore score up to three points on some questions.)

| | |
|---|---|
| PERFECT: | 63 |
| SUPERIOR: | Over 60 |
| GOOD: | 50-60 |
| FAIR: | 35-49 |
| POOR: | Below 35 |

*Part One:*

1. Substitute the previous letter of the alphabet for each letter in the message. Thus, in the word SEND, S becomes R, E becomes D, N becomes M, and D becomes C. In this code, "Bring Help" is AQHMF.GDKO.

2. For every letter in the message, substitute the preceding and following letters of the alphabet. In this code, "Bring Help" is AC QS HJ MO FH GI DF KM OQ.

3. For every letter in the message, substitute the third letter in the alphabet that follows it. Thus, in the word ENEMY, E becomes H, N becomes Q, E becomes H, M becomes P, and Y becomes B. In this code, "Bring Help" is EULQJ KHOS.

4. In this code, numbers are substituted for each letter in the alphabet. Each letter gets a number equivalent to its position in the alphabet. For example, A equals 1, B equals 2, C equals 3, etc. In this code, "Bring Help" is 2 18 9 14 7 8 5 12 16.

5. In this code, the alphabet has been reversed. Z becomes A, Y becomes B, etc. In this code, "Bring Help" is YIRMT SVOK.

*Part Two:*

1. Duck
2. Gull
3. Robin
4. Crow
5. Hen
6. Pigeon
7. Hawk
8. Owl
9. Parrot
10. Sparrow
11. Eagle
12. Chicken
13. Bluebird
14. Blackbird
15. Stork

*Part Three:*

1. Cow
2. Tiger
3. Horse
4. Monkey
5. Rabbit
6. Squirrel
7. Sheep
8. Cat
9. Mouse
10. Buffalo
11. Camel
12. Skunk
13. Donkey
14. Gorilla
15. Elephant
16. Bear
17. Lion
18. Panther
19. Llama
20. Mule
21. Antelope
22. Baboon
23. Goat
24. Rhinoceros
25. Zebra

Give yourself four points for each correct answer in Part One. Give yourself one point for each correct answer in Parts Two and Three.

| | |
|---|---|
| PERFECT: | 60 |
| SUPERIOR: | Over 53 |
| GOOD: | 42-53 |
| FAIR: | 27-41 |
| POOR: | Below 27 |

**DO YOU HAVE A MECHANICAL BENT?** . . . . . . . **Page 92**

| | | | |
|---|---|---|---|
| 1. | b | 6. | b |
| 2. | a | 7. | c |
| 3. | b | 8. | c |
| 4. | a | 9. | d |
| 5. | b | | |

10. c (The nut can be turned by striking its edge with the hammer.)
11. c
12. b (The next step would be to build another mound of stones or dirt under the rear axle. You can then kick the spare tire free, and the flat will be high enough from the ground for you to remove it.)
13. c
14. c

Give yourself one point for each correct answer.

| | |
|---|---|
| PERFECT: | 14 |
| SUPERIOR: | Over 11 |
| GOOD: | 9-11 |
| FAIR: | 6-8 |
| POOR: | Below 6 |

**DO YOU HAVE PATTERN SKILL?** . . . . . . . . . . . . . . . . . . . . . **Page 96**

Give yourself one point for each x-mark you placed correctly.

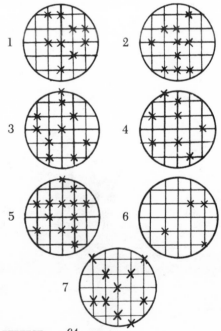

| | |
|---|---|
| PERFECT: | 64 |
| SUPERIOR: | Over 55 |
| GOOD: | 45-55 |
| FAIR: | 33-44 |
| POOR: | Below 33 |

## TEST YOUR LOGIC NO. 3 ...    Page 99

| | |
|---|---|
| 1. 2 | 31. 11 |
| 2. 16 | 32. 80 |
| 3. 3 | 33. 8 |
| 4. 3 | 34. 3 |
| 5. 4 | 35. 3 |
| 6. T | 36. 4 |
| 7. 4 | 37. 1 |
| 8. 63 | 38. 4 |
| 9. K | 39. 6 |
| 10. 2 | 40. 21475 |
| 11. John | 41. 5 |
| 12. 32 | 42. T |
| 13. 5 | 43. 2 |
| 14. 5 | 44. 1 |
| 15. T | 45. 100 |
| 16. 2 | 46. 48 |
| 17. 27 | 47. 12 |
| 18. 26 | 48. F |
| 19. 4 | 49. 2 |
| 20. 4 | 50. G |
| 21. 4 | 51. 16 |
| 22. 4 | 52. 11 miles |
| 23. U | 53. S |
| 24. 40 | 54. 3 |
| 25. 3 | 55. 1 |
| 26. 1 | 56. 2 |
| 27. F | 57. 8 |
| 28. 15 minutes | 58. F |
| 29. 80¢ | 59. 840 |
| 30. 3 | 60. 3 |

Give yourself one point for each correct answer.

| | |
|---|---|
| PERFECT: | 60 |
| SUPERIOR: | Over 55 |
| GOOD: | 45-55 |
| FAIR: | 30-44 |
| POOR: | Below 30 |

## CROSSWORD PUZZLE
## NO.  1 ..................... Page 124

## CROSSWORD PUZZLE
## NO.  2 ..................... Page 125

## CROSSWORD PUZZLE
## NO.  3 ..................... Page 126

## CROSSWORD PUZZLE
## NO.  4 ..................... Page 127

**CROSSWORD PUZZLE**
NO. 5 . . . . . . . . . . . . . . . . . . . . . **Page 128**

**CROSSWORD PUZZLE**
NO. 8 . . . . . . . . . . . . . . . . . . . . . **Page 131**

**CROSSWORD PUZZLE**
NO. 6 . . . . . . . . . . . . . . . . . . . . . **Page 129**

**CROSSWORD PUZZLE**
NO. 9 . . . . . . . . . . . . . . . . . . . . . **Page 132**

**CROSSWORD PUZZLE**
NO. 7 . . . . . . . . . . . . . . . . . . . . . **Page 130**

**CROSSWORD PUZZLE**
NO. 10 . . . . . . . . . . . . . . . . . . . . . **Page 133**

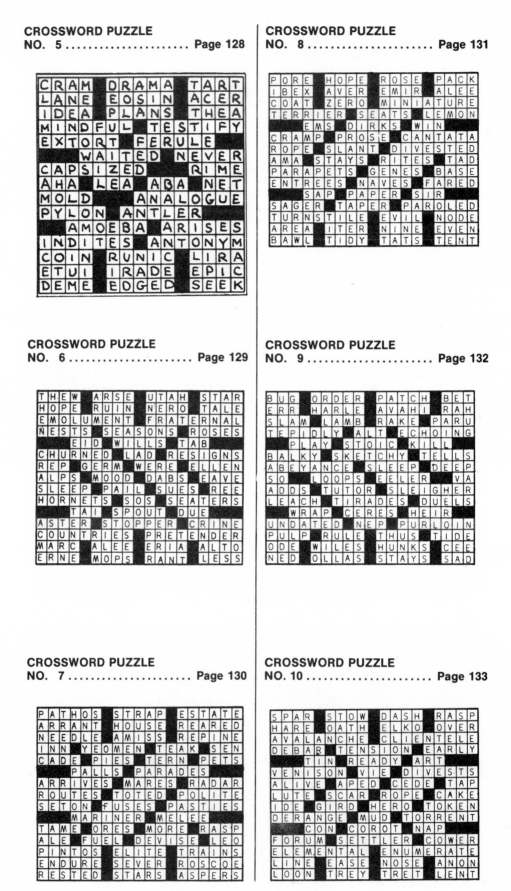

**CROSSWORD PUZZLE NO. 11** .................... Page 134

```
ARMS ASS STAINS
SEAT PET LINNET
PALE EAR ENTREE
SLEEP PARDS ODE
RETONES CALL
BAG WARDS DUDES
ALAS ITS MAR
DESIGNS BUBBLES
ROT CUR SAVE
HATED CANAL DEW
IRAN HUDDLED
ART REPEL GOOSE
TATTER NEE OGLE
UNLOAD CRY MEAL
STEEPS ESE SETS
```

**CROSSWORD PUZZLE NO. 14** .................... Page 137

```
GLAD ASTER COLD
LIMA STAGE AMIE
IRON SILOS NICE
BASEBALL HEATER
OIL LAID
TONSIL DEPRAVES
ORIEL LEVEE ILA
ADEN SATED MAIN
SEC AIMER MONTE
TREMBLER LEADER
ALES TIE
BARREN LANDINGS
ERIC TRACE ROLE
NICE LENIN ANON
TAEL YEATS NEWS
```

**CROSSWORD PUZZLE NO. 12** .................... Page 135

```
WANT PLEAS BEST
ICER RANGE ACHE
TRAY ODDER GOON
HEROIC SNIP NOD
USED TEAPOTS
RUSTLERS SLAM
ENE EDITH STIFF
ADAM SPOOF SCAR
LOSES SPOOL ARE
ONES STROLLED
CANDLES SAVE
ASA LACK GENTLE
RIBS RAISE DRAW
IDLE CLEAR EIRE
BEET HELPS RODS
```

**CROSSWORD PUZZLE NO. 15** .................... Page 138

```
CRIB ASTOR DEMI
LATE SPADE EVEN
ACED SANDS LEAK
DEMOTICS OVERLY
URGE SUIT
DARIEN CONCEDED
AGONY PRUDE OAR
RAMS FOILS SIRE
EVA SLUMS RANTS
DENATURE ROUGHS
RUTS COON
PLIANT SHUTTLES
ROOM ECLAT EARL
ANTI ROUSE RIGA
YEAS STEED SNOB
```

**CROSSWORD PUZZLE NO. 13** .................... Page 136

```
SHOT CATER TOSS
PAVE AROMA ALOE
ELAN RIPER TEAR
DELAYED RESTORE
NET AGREE
PACTS LIE DRANK
ARES PAD HASTEN
PEN RAP RUN OWE
ENTAIL SOT SNEE
RASPS COW VEERS
PETAL FIN
CHOOSER CREATOR
HOPI SNORE TIDE
AMEN TACIT OMEN
PENT SLABS REST
```

**CROSSWORD PUZZLE NO. 16** .................... Page 139

```
SPAR SCOFF ONCE
TORE PEDAL ROLL
IRKS ADDLE DOOM
RESTORE CEMENTS
INK LOSER
SHOVE BAN DEALT
WIFE DUB BADGER
ELF REMOVAL RAE
ELEVEN RAT MESS
TYROS PET DIETS
LIVED 50D
PARTNER LUGGAGE
AREA RIGID ELLA
STAG SLUMS TEES
TYPE ESSAY SENT
```

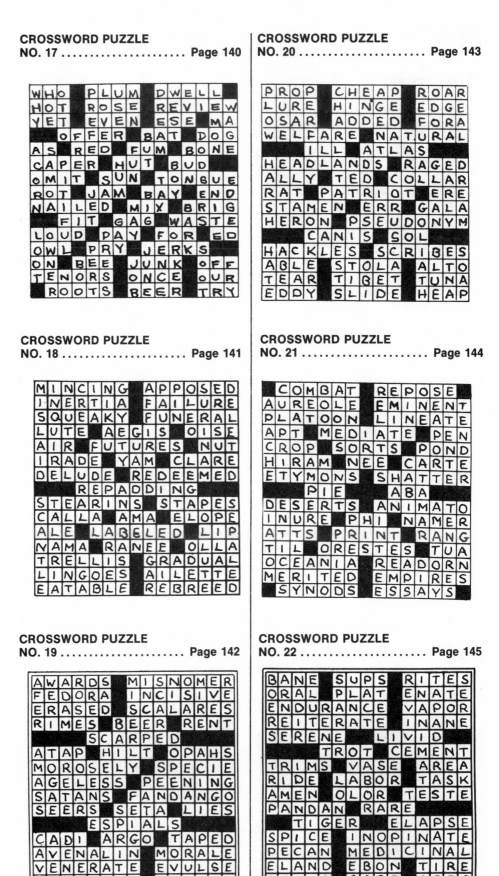

**474**

## MURDER IN THE LIBRARY .. Page 154

If the night watchman, in passing Mr. Parker's house, had seen Mr. Parker commit suicide in his library at 7:30 P.M. on January 2, the light in that room must have been burning; yet, the watchman stated that he had turned it on when he entered the room.

## THE STYMIED SAVAGE ..... Page 155

The missionary said, "I will die by fire." If the medicine man judged the statement to be true, he would be forced to have him shot. This would make the statement false. For a false statement, the missionary would indeed be burned to death. But this would make the statement true, and then he would have to be shot instead. The only way out of this vicious circle was to let the clever missionary go free.

## THE RIDDLE OF THE RED WINE ..................... Page 156

The same quantity of wine was transferred from the bottle as water was taken from the jug. Let us assume that the glass would hold a quarter of a pint. After the first manipulation the bottle contains three-quarters of a pint of wine, and the jug one pint of water mixed with a quarter of a pint of wine. Now, the second transaction consists in taking away a fifth of the contents of the jug, that is, one-fifth of a pint of water mixed with one-fifth of a quarter of a pint of wine. We thus leave behind in the jug four-fifths of a quarter of a pint of wine (one-fifth of a pint) while we transfer from the jug to the bottle an equal quantity (one-fifth of a pint) of water.

## RELATIVELY SIMPLE........ Page 156

Ann is Joan's daughter.

## SUBURBS.................. Page 157

Set out the data as follows, using $x$, $y$, and $z$ to represent the unknowns.

| Name | Resides at | Works at |
|---|---|---|
| $x$ | S | R |
| R | — | B |
| $y$ | B | $x$ |
| E | — | $y$ |
| $z$ | — | — |

In any line down or across, each capital letter may appear only once. Then clearly $x$ = T. Therefore, $y$ = S, and $z$ = B. Mr. Blackheath must work at Ealing.

## KILLED IN ACTION......... Page 157

Young. Since Mrs. Lewis had never had a niece or nephew, and since Mrs. Smith had once had a daughter, Mrs. Smith could not have been the sister of Mrs. Lewis. Therefore, the slain man could not have been Mr. Smith.

Stacey returned alive to this country and hence is eliminated.

Because the slain man was married, Jones could not have been he.

It is obvious from the statement (2) that the victim could not have been Lewis.

Therefore, by elimination, the slain man must have been Young.

### THE OHIO LIMITED . . . . . . . . Page 158

Brown is the engineer.

The guard lives halfway between Cleveland and New York. He cannot earn one-third of Mr. Jones's salary, because that sum cannot be divided into three equal parts. Mr. Robinson lives in Cleveland. Therefore, Mr. Brown must be the guard's neighbor.

Since Mr. Jones must therefore live in New York, the guard is Jones. Brown cannot be the fireman, so he must be the engineer.

### THE SIMPLE-MINDED MAID . Page 158

It was not necessary for the maid, having discovered that the fourth letter was *I*, to ascertain what *I* stood for.

### THE CHECKERBOARD . . . . . . Page 159

The diagram below shows the solution to the problem.

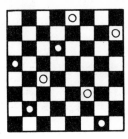

### THE STOLEN CAMEO . . . . . . Page 160

Geoffrey Warren was considered the foremost appraiser in London. His sales were based on the reputation of his firm for both integrity and knowledge. While polishing the cameo to which he had given such unstinted praise, he discovered that it was a forgery. He had to prevent the terrible discovery from being made by anyone else. A firm like Warren and Company couldn't afford to be mistaken. They were highly reputable and were expected to know what was genuine and what was bogus. Geoffrey Warren stole the cameo to destroy it. His reputation was worth more than £5,000.

### THE SIX AUTHORS . . . . . . . . . Page 161

White, essayist
Brown, poet
Green, humorist
Pink, historian
Gray, playwright
Black, novelist

### IN COLD BLOOD . . . . . . . . . . . Page 162

The answer to this perplexing problem is to be found in the fact that it is a tenet of the law in all civilized countries that the innocent may not be made to suffer with the guilty. The sisters were Siamese twins.

### DIRTY FACES . . . . . . . . . . . . . . Page 163

The two boys had seen each other's face. Each naturally assumed that his own resembled the other's.

### THE FIVE PEDAGOGUES . . . . Page 163

This is a very simple problem if one works it out diagrammatically. The subjects taught by the five pedagogues are shown in the chart below:

| INSTRUCTORS | SUBJECTS | | | | |
|---|---|---|---|---|---|
| Mr. Botany | | G | | H | |
| Mr. Geometry | B | | | | S |
| Mr. French | B | G | | | |
| Mr. History | | | F | | S |
| Mr. Syntax | | | F | H | |

### THE LEGIONNAIRES . . . . . . . Page 164

Frank lives in Bangor; Tom lives in Miami; Sam lives in Los Angeles; John lives in Reno; Paul lives in Buffalo.

Frank says, "The state I come from borders on only one other state." There is one state in the Union that borders on only one other state: the state of Maine. Therefore, Frank comes from Bangor.

Paul drove to the Convention in a car that has a license plate that begins with N. Only two of the four cities under consideration are in states beginning with the letter N. Therefore, Paul lives either in New York or Nevada. If we assume that Paul lives in Nevada, then Tom's statement, "I live west of Paul," becomes false because Reno is the farthest west of all five cities. It is therefore established that Paul lives in Buffalo.

Sam says, "I live east of John and north of Tom." Since Reno is farthest west, Sam must live in either Miami or Los Angeles. But Sam cannot live in Miami since that is the farthest city south, in which case he couldn't live north of anyone. Therefore, Sam lives in Los Angeles.

### AT CENTRAL STATION . . . . . . Page 164

Dan is going to Greenfields.
If he were going to Kemp, Midvale, or

476

Deane, he would have purchased a $3 ticket. If he were going to Banstock, he would have gotten on the Midvale train. If he were bound for Fogwell, any train would do. So, Dan must be going to Greenfields.

## THE MAILBOX

No. Contango was just as much to blame as his secretary. His key was delivered in the locked mailbox.

## THE DIFFICULT CROSSING

Four trips. First he takes the duck over, leaving the dog alone with the corn. Then he takes the dog over and brings back the duck. Then he brings the corn over and leaves the corn with the dog. Then he comes back for the duck.

## THE FRATERNITY CONVENTION

Mr. Grocer is the Baker.

Mr. Butcher is the Lawyer.

Mr. Doctor is the Artist.

Mr. Artist is the Butcher.

Mr. Baker is the Doctor.

Mr. Lawyer is the Grocer.

Mr. Butcher, addressing Mr. Grocer, says that he heard that Mr. Grocer mashed his finger at his store under a tub of butter. Now, Mr. Grocer, having a store, is either a baker, a butcher, or a grocer. He cannot be a grocer because no man bears the name of his trade. A tub of butter would be found in a bakery but not in a butcher shop. *Therefore, Mr. Grocer is a baker.*

Mr. Artist cannot be either the doctor or the grocer because he would not refer to them in the third person, and Mr. Artist cannot be the baker because we have already established that Mr. Grocer is the baker. Mr. Artist cannot be the artist, because no man bears the name of his profession. Therefore, Mr. Artist must either be the lawyer or the butcher. We can be sure that he is not the lawyer because Mr. Doctor, while talking to him mentions the lawyer, as if he were some other person. *Therefore, Mr. Artist must be the butcher.*

Mr. Doctor states that he goes deep-sea fishing with the lawyer every week. Mr. Doctor cannot be the butcher or the baker because Mr. Grocer has already been established as the baker and Mr. Artist has been established as the butcher. Again, the man who goes deep-sea fishing with the lawyer cannot be the doctor because it is Mr. Doctor who is talking and Mr. Doctor is not a doctor. Therefore, the lawyer goes deep-sea fishing with either the grocer or the artist.

But the lawyer does not go deep-sea fishing each week-end with the grocer who lives in Milwaukee. This fact becomes evident when it is realized that Milwaukee is situated inland more than 1,000 miles from either the East Coast or the West Coast of the United States and from the Gulf of Mexico. It would be impossible for a resident of Milwaukee to take a weekend trip each week to do deep-sea fishing. Therefore, by elimination, the lawyer goes deep-sea fishing with the artist. *This establishes Mr. Doctor as the artist.*

We still must determine who is the doctor, who is the lawyer, and who is the grocer. We can infer, however, that two of these men live in the same town.

The doctor lives in Milwaukee; the grocer lives in Milwaukee. The lawyer lives on the seacoast. Mr. Baker, talking to Mr. Lawyer, mentions that he got in a new interesting case at the office. He says that he will tell him about it during next week. This argues very strongly that Mr. Baker lives in the same city as Mr. Lawyer. It must be remembered that the Convention has been in session for a full week at St. Louis. Therefore, the lawyer presumably would leave for either the East Coast or the West Coast or the Gulf at the close of the Convention. In any event, his route home could not possibly take him through Milwaukee. Moreover, he has just seen his friends and has already taken a week's vacation and there is no reason to believe that he is going off another few hundred miles simply to visit. This reasoning points to the fact that the man who says so casually that he will drop in to tell Mr. Baker about his new interesting case during the week must be the doctor who lives with the grocer in Milwaukee. *This establishes the doctor as Mr. Baker, and the grocer as Mr. Lawyer.*

*Of course, then, Mr. Butcher is the lawyer.* His interest in the baker's mashed finger could have been actuated by other than professional motives. He could simply have been interested in determining how serious an accident his fraternity brother, the baker, had sustained. Moreover, since he has asked the baker to play golf with him during the week, it is very likely that they, too, live near each other. There is nothing to indicate that the baker does not actually live in the same town with the lawyer.

**477**

### THE HORSE RACE ......... Page 167

Regent; Mr. Lewis.

Mr. Smith's horse could not have won, because the horse that won was black.

Mr. Bailey's horse did not win.

Therefore, Mr. Lewis's horse must have won.

Tally-ho could not have won, because he broke his ankle at the start, and so could not have been Mr. Lewis's horse.

Sonny Boy could not have been Mr. Lewis's horse because he had previously run.

Therefore, Regent must have been Mr. Lewis's horse, and the winner of the race.

### THE STOLEN ANTIQUE ..... Page 168

Mrs. Black.

Mr. Brown won money at cards; therefore, from the first statement, we know that Mrs. Brown was not the thief.

Since Mrs. Brown played cards, the other female guest referred to in the third statement must have been Mrs. White.

Since Mrs. Black and Mrs. White did not play cards, neither of their husbands could have been the thief.

If Mr. Brown had paralysis of the hands and arms, he could not have played golf with Mr. Black; therefore, Mr. Brown could not have been the thief.

This eliminates all but Mrs. Black and Mrs. White.

Since Mr. Black had not previously met Mrs. White, Mrs. White could not have been the one with whom Mr. Black had played golf that day; therefore, Mrs. White could not have been the thief. By elimination, Mrs. Black must have been the thief.

### FIVE MASTERS............. Page 168

Each girl got two artists right, the five in order being:
(1) Degas; (2) Matisse; (3) Renoir; (4) Picasso; (5) Klee.

### FIGHT TO THE FINISH ...... Page 169

Dan is Tim's cousin. Bill is wearing colored trunks. Mike says his son is the fighter.

### IT REALLY HAPPENED ONE NIGHT .................... Page 170

On close consideration of the facts, it is apparent that Winston's objective was to waken Malcolm solely for the purpose of *awakening him.* He never intended to communicate with him. Nor did he.

The only reason that Winston could have for wishing to accomplish his apparent mischief was that Malcolm, by sleeping, was doing *him* a mischief. You see, Winston and Malcolm were both tenants in the same apartment house, and Winston's bedroom adjoined Malcolm's. Malcolm was snoring so loudly that Winston couldn't fall asleep. The victim's only chance, which he cleverly saw, was to disturb the disturber and beat him to the snooze.

### THE MURDERED CARD PLAYER.................... Page 171

Rudolph murdered Robert.

The first statement makes it plain that Robert's brother is the murderer, and Robert then is innocent.

Ralph cannot be Robert's brother because he has met Robert's father only once. Therefore, Ralph is not guilty.

Since Ronald, the host, is about to give evidence against the murderer, he cannot be the murderer.

Therefore, Rudolph must be the murderer.

Since the host, Ronald, is about to give evidence, he must still be alive; and Rudolph, the murderer, obviously cannot be the victim.

This leaves as the murdered man either Robert or Ralph.

Since Ralph is a cripple and Rudolph has known Ronald for only five days, Ralph and Rudolph are the men with whom Ronald did not customarily bowl; so one of them must have eaten with the murdered man on the night previous to the murder. Rudolph was in jail and so it was not he. Then Ralph must have eaten with the victim.

Ralph then is not the victim, and since Rudolph and Ronald have both been previously eliminated, Robert is obviously the murdered man.

### THE FIRED WATCHMAN..... Page 171

Casey said that he had *dreamt* the night before that Peabody would be killed. Casey was the night watchman and must have been sleeping *on the job.*

### THE MUNICIPAL RAILWAYS. Page 172

The illustration shows the required direc-

**478**

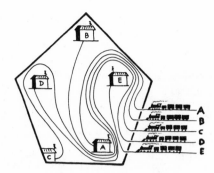

tions for the five lines, so that no line shall ever cross another.

## THE DEAD TOURIST ....... Page 172

Seeing Mrs. Elkins' picture in the Boston society column, and reading the details of the tragic death of her husband, Mr. Harper remembered that Mrs. Elkins had been to his travel bureau to purchase tickets for a European trip. Examining the files, he discovered that she had bought one round-trip ticket and one one-way ticket. This led him to believe that she never expected Mr. Elkins to return.

## A NARROW ESCAPE ....... Page 173

The fallacy is that Mr. Drake, who must have been looking out the window on the right side of his car to see any possible damage, could not have seen the sun on that side while he was traveling north.

## THE LOST COIN ........... Page 174

Paul is the rightful owner of the coin. While a person does not lose his right of ownership merely because he drops something on another person's land, Bill's statement that he dropped this same coin on this same spot four months ago is not convincing. Both he and Dan agree that the coin glitters. But a coin buried beneath the sand for so long would lose its sparkle. Therefore, we may conclude that Bill is lying. As for Sam and Brad, they are mistaken about the law. Seeing or finding something does not in itself confer ownership. Paul is right. He owns the land; therefore, he owns everything on it.

## THE ISLAND OF KO ........ Page 174

If the inhabitant questioned were Red, his second response would have to be "Red." If he were Green, his second response would have to be a lie, "Red." Therefore, he must be a Half-Breed. His second response is therefore a lie, so his first response is true. Tom is the name of the Half Breed.

Tom's third response must be true. Therefore, Dick is the Red. Obviously, Harry must be the Green.

## THE CARETAKER .......... Page 175

The man could not have hanged himself without something by which to climb to the high chandelier, but it is specified that the room was vacant. Therefore, he must have been hanged by someone else, who had later removed the evidence that would readily suggest a murder.

## THE MARINERS ............. Page 176

The *Hispaniola;* Cherbourg.

Brine is Captain of the *Albatross* because he was host to Tarr on that ship.

It is obvious from the statement about Mrs. Salt that her husband's ship has not been in dry dock just previous to this trip, because she was taken off his ship eight days ago when it landed.

Therefore, Salt's ship cannot be the *Hispaniola,* which has been in dry dock for seven weeks, and must be the *Americus.*

Tarr's ship then is the *Hispaniola.*

The last statement shows that the *Americus* is headed for Liverpool.

The *Albatross* must be headed for New York because the fact that it shipped a stowaway back by the *Americus* proves that it was going in the opposite direction to the *Americus.*

Therefore, the *Hispaniola* must be bound for Cherbourg.

## THE VANISHED COIN ....... Page 176

The coin which had been inadvertently mislaid was a great rarity. The stranger, being a collector of antiques and coins, happened to have in his vest pocket the only other specimen extant of the coin which Lewis had brought from the Continent. If the stranger submitted to a search of his person, the prize coin would have been found upon him and he would have been accused of stealing it. If he resisted the accusation of theft, his own coin would have been taken from him, since all would have avowed that the coin belonged to Lewis. The stranger did not wish to lose his own valuable coin. The reason that the stranger did not exhibit his own coin to the assembled guests in the first instance was that since he was an invited guest it would have been a breach of propriety to steal the show from Lewis, who was a member and inordinately proud of his prize find.

### THREE SONS .............. Page 178

Brown, Jr., could not have been the politician (statement 2).

Since Smith, Sr., because of being a paralytic, could not have played golf (statement 4), and since the politician's father played golf (statement 3), Smith, Jr., could not have been the politician.

If neither Brown, Jr., nor Smith, Jr., was the politician, Jones, Jr., must have been he.

Statement 1 tells us that the lawyer frequently played tennis with his father. Because Smith, Sr., could not have played tennis (statement 4), Smith, Jr., could not have been the lawyer. We have previously discovered that he was not the politician. He must, then, have been the banker.

Since Jones, Jr., was the politician and Smith, Jr., was the banker, Brown, Jr., must have been the lawyer.

### THE MARKED FOREHEADS . Page 178

Alex reasoned to himself as follows: Either the cross on my forehead is blue or it is green. I see a green cross on the forehead of Tom, and I see a green cross on the forehead of Joe. Each of us has his hand up because each of us sees at least one green cross. If my forehead were labeled with a blue cross, Joe would be putting his hand up solely because he sees a green cross on the forehead of Tom, while Tom would be putting his hand up solely because he sees a green cross on the forehead of Joe. But each one, seeing that my cross was a blue cross, would realize very soon that they were raising their hands because they saw a green cross on the forehead of each other. Being intelligent boys, either of them would have folded his arms by this time in the realization that his cross must have been marked green. For if the cross on Tom's forehead were blue, Tom would realize that Joe would not be raising his hand at all, and if the cross on Joe's forehead were blue, Joe would realize that Tom would not be raising his hand at all.

Therefore, it appears that both Tom and Joe are a bit confused and cannot make the foregoing deduction. The only reason that they cannot arrive at this conclusion must be that I am *not* marked with a blue cross.

### THE BLIND BUTLER........ Page 179

Three socks.

### TRACKS IN THE SNOW ..... Page 180

The tracks were made by a peg-legged man wheeling a wheelbarrow. Between the footprint and the impression made by the butt end of a wooden stump, lies the track of the wheel of the wheelbarrow. At one point, toward the middle of the trail, there is evidence that the man paused to rest. The prints left by the two wheelbarrow butts are there to show this. They are wider apart and larger than the tracks left by the man. While the man rested, he brought his foot and wooden leg parallel. Then he lifted the wheelbarrow and started off again.

### AN EXERCISE IN LOGIC..... Page 180

Only statements (3) and (5) are necessarily true.

### THE SIX HOODLUMS........ Page 181

Slud was the murderer. The judge reasoned as follows:

A) Dan is innocent because he couldn't be the murderer if either of his statements is true.

B) Mat is innocent for the same reason.

C) Red is innocent because if we assume that he is guilty the following statements become true:

> *Red:* Me and Mike were together from 10 to 12 away from the rest of the gang.
> *Mike:* I never saw a gun in my life.
> *Jim:* All of us except Dan were in Chi when it happened.

In view of this true statement by Jim, Spud's second sentence becomes false, rendering his first one true:

> *Spud:* Only one of us witnessed the murder. Now since the murder was witnessed, and since Red and Mike were together at the time, Mike must have been the witness. But this leads to a contradiction in view of Mike's true statement.

D) Jim is innocent because if we assume that he is guilty the following statments become true:

> *Jim:* All of us except Dan were in Chi when it happened.
> *Spud:* Only one of us witnessed the murder.
> *Dan:* I was in Philly when it happened.
> *Mat:* I was at the neighborhood movies, at the time, with some other one of the boys.
> *Red:* Me and Mike were together

from 10 to 12 away from the rest of the gang.

These statements are contradictory because Mat's statement above can't possibly be true in view of the above facts. With whom did Mat go to the movies? Not with Red, Mike, or Dan, according to the foregoing. Obviously, it couldn't have been with the murderer, Jim. And Mat specifically excluded Spud as his companion. He said "Spud's the murderer. I was at the neighborhood movies, at the time, with *some other one* of the boys." If this last statement is held true, then the assumption of Jim's guilt must be dropped.

E) Mike is innocent because if we assume that he is guilty then the following statements become true:

> *Dan:* I was in Philly when it happened.
>
> *Mat:* I was at the neighborhood movies, at the time, with some other one of the boys.
>
> *Red:* Me and Mike were together from 10 to 12 away from the rest of the gang.

If Mike was the murderer and Mike and Red were alone when the woman was shot, then Red must have been the sole witness. This makes Spud's statement: "Only one of us witnessed the murder," a true statement. Spud, then, must have made a false statement when he said: "I was not even in town on the night of the killing." Of course, then, Spud *was in Chicago* on the night of the murder. So was Mat. He went to the neighborhood movies with "some other one of the boys." With whom? His statement specifically excluded Spud as his companion; Dan was in Philly; Red and Mike were at the scene of the crime; therefore, the only one of the boys that could have been at the movies with Mat would have been Jim. This analysis places all the men in Chicago on the night of the murder, with the exception of Dan. If this is so, then Jim's statement: "All of us except Dan were in Chi when it happened" must be true, rendering Jim's first statement "Mike pulled the trigger" false.

F) Spud is the guilty man. He is so proved through a process of elimination. Although he cannot be directly proved to be guilty, no statement or fact conflicts with the theory of his guilt. Since one of the men is guilty by hypothesis, it must be he. Assuming Spud guilty, the following statements become true:

> *Dan:* I was in Philly when it happened.
>
> *Jim:* All of us except Dan were in Chi when it happened.
>
> *Spud:* Only one of us witnessed the murder.
>
> *Red:* Me and Mike were away from the rest of the gang when it happened.

Who was the witness? Well, either Mat or Jim. For if Spud is guilty, Mat's statement: "I was at the movies, at the time, with some other one of the boys," becomes false.

## DR. LIMEJUICE ............. Page 182

Sniggersby held the lantern, and Wallop painted the doctor's nose.

Call the three boys A, B, and C (in order of interrogation), and their answers A1, A2, A3, and so on.

Then B3 and C3 are lies. Of the remaining statements two only are lies.

If B1 is a lie, A1 and C1 are both lies also; therefore B1 is true.

Then A1 or C1 must be true. It follows that A2 is true.

Now consider A1. If A1 is true, C1 is a lie. And since C3 is a lie, it follows that C is Wallop. In that case A3 is true as well as A1 and A2, which cannot be the case. Therefore A1 is a lie, and C1 is true.

Wallop cannot be A (for if he is, A1 and A3 are both lies) nor C (because C1 is true and if C is Wallop A3 is true also).

Therefore Wallop is B, and B2 is a lie.

Therefore Sniggersby held the lantern, and Wallop did the painting.

A is Sniggersby and C is Tittering.

## THE STOLEN NECKLACE ... Page 183

Bill is telling the whole truth. Hank says that he upset the inkwell. But there is no stain of any kind on the blotter, so his statement is obviously false. Clark says that he walked to the phone and *quickly* dialed Police Headquarters, in the dark. If one is very familiar with a dial telephone, it is entirely possible to dial a number in the dark—but it is not possible to do so *quickly*. Sid's misstatement consists of saying that it was pitch black and he could see the cat's eyes gleaming in the dark. Cat's eyes do not gleam in total darkness. It is true that they are able to reflect even the smallest ray of light, which is usually present even at night, but if it were pitch black, the cat's eyes could not gleam. By the process of elimination, only Bill remains; and indeed there is nothing he says that is contradicted by fact, so we may assume he is telling the whole truth.

## THE NOBLES AND THE SLAVES ................... Page 184

Ugu and Tuga are nobles. Bugu is a slave. Tugu, whose answer Sir Wilfred did not hear, must have said, "I am a noble." If he were a slave he would lie and say that he was a noble. If he were a noble he would tell the truth and say, "I am a noble." Therefore, we can be sure that Ugu is telling the truth when he says, "Tugu says he is a noble." Therefore, the whole of his statement is true, and Ugu is also a noble. This automatically makes Bugu's statement false, proving that he is a slave.

## A SQUARE IN LINDLAND.... Page 184

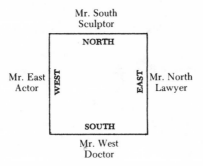

It is at once deducible that the sculptor is Mr. South. The rest follows.

## THE FOUR COEDS......... Page 185

Joan is the oldest, then Jane, Jean, and June.

## THE CLEVER BLIND MAN ... Page 186

The blind man reasoned thus: If there were a black hat on my head and a black hat on the head of the second speaker, then the first man addressed would have seen two black hats. He would have then drawn the inescapable conclusion that his own hat was white.

Similarly, if there were a black hat on my head and a black hat on the head of the first man addressed, then the second speaker would have known that his own hat was white. Since neither of these men were able to draw any conclusion, it is clear that I do not wear a black hat *in combination with someone else wearing a black hat.*

The only question left then for me is: Do I *alone* wear a black hat? If I were, the second speaker would see it and would have been able to definitely conclude the color of his own hat. The second speaker would have said to himself, "My hat is not black, for if it were, the first speaker would have seen two black hats and would have known that *his* hat was white. Therefore, my hat cannot be black."

But the second speaker was not able to draw this conclusion. He could only have failed to do this because he did not see a

black hat on my head. Therefore, since I and another do not wear black hats and since I do not wear a black hat all by myself, there must be a white hat on my head.

## THE FOOTBALL
TOURNAMENT............. Page 186

From statement (1), we know that Albie's team made its only score in the final game by a touchdown; from statement (4), the purple team scored only a field goal in this game. Therefore, Albie's team beat the purple team 6-3 in the play-off.

Statement (3) shows that Ben's team survived the first round by defeating Tulane, and must therefore have been the purple team that was defeated by Albie's team in the play-off.

Knowing the above facts, and statements (3) and (6), we can now bracket the teams thus:

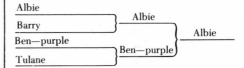

It is now obvious that Bill must have been captain of Tulane.

We see that Tulane was the only team that Albie's team did not meet. Statement (7) proves that Tulane was the brown team.

From statement (2), it is apparent that the red team must have been Barry's and that Albie's team was Tufts.

Since we have found that the red, purple, and brown teams were Barry's, Ben's, and Bill's respectively, Albie's team must have been blue.

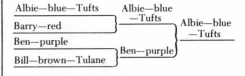

As Trinity did not play Ben's team, the brackets show us that Trinity was Barry's team.

Therefore, Ben's team must have been Temple, and the complete brackets look like this:

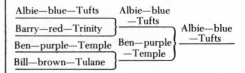

482

**THE RAILROAD SIDING . . . . . Page 187**

E pushes B into C. E returns to the main line, then pushes A and couples it to B. E then draws A and B out into the right siding. E uncouples, goes into segment C, and pushes A out on to the main line, leaving B in the right siding. E comes around and picks up A and pushes it up into left siding, then returns to the main line.

**LUM . . . . . . . . . . . . . . . . . . . . . . Page 218**

| | |
|---|---|
| 1. Alum | 17. Lump |
| 2. Aluminum | 18. Lumpen |
| 3. Alumnus | 19. Lumpkin |
| 4. Antebellum | 20. Pendulum |
| 5. Asylum | 21. Plum |
| 6. Clump | 22. Plumber |
| 7. Columbine | 23. Plume |
| 8. Flummery | 24. Plummet |
| 9. Glum | 25. Plump |
| 10. Illuminate | 26. Postbellum |
| 11. Lumbago | 27. Slum |
| 12. Lumber | 28. Slumber |
| 13. Lumen | 29. Slump |
| 14. Luminary | 30. Vellum |
| 15. Luminous | 31. Volume |
| 16. Lummox | 32. Voluminous |

**LTI . . . . . . . . . . . . . . . . . . . . . . . Page 219**

| | |
|---|---|
| 1. Altimeter | 6. Multiply |
| 2. Altitude | 7. Saltine |
| 3. Cultivate | 8. Stultify |
| 4. Ill-timed | 9. Ultimate |
| 5. Kiltie | 10. Ultimatum |

**ECH . . . . . . . . . . . . . . . . . . . . . . Page 219**

| | |
|---|---|
| 1. Beech | 8. Rechannel |
| 2. Beseech | 9. Recharge |
| 3. Echelon | 10. Recheck |
| 4. Echo | 11. Screech |
| 5. Lecher | 12. Speech |
| 6. Leech | 13. Technical |
| 7. Mechanic | 14. Technique |

**HOU . . . . . . . . . . . . . . . . . . . . . . Page 219**

| | |
|---|---|
| 1. Although | 7. Shout |
| 2. Hour | 8. Silhouette |
| 3. Houri | 9. Thou |
| 4. House | 10. Though |
| 5. Should | 11. Thought |
| 6. Shoulder | 12. Without |

**CLE . . . . . . . . . . . . . . . . . . . . . . Page 220**

| | |
|---|---|
| 1. Article | 2. Barnacle |

| | |
|---|---|
| 3. Clean | 9. Clench |
| 4. Clear | 10. Clergy |
| 5. Cleat | 11. Clerk |
| 6. Cleavage | 12. Clever |
| 7. Cleaver | 13. Inclement |
| 8. Cleft | 14. Particle |

**ORS . . . . . . . . . . . . . . . . . . . . . . Page 220**

| | |
|---|---|
| 1. Borscht | 11. Horse |
| 2. Corset | 12. Morse |
| 3. Corso | 13. Morsel |
| 4. Doorstep | 14. Remorse |
| 5. Dorsal | 15. Torsion |
| 6. Endorse | 16. Torso |
| 7. Floorshow | 17. Worse |
| 8. Gorse | 18. Worship |
| 9. Hors de combat | 19. Worst |
| 10. Hors d'oeuvres | 20. Worsted |

**OCH . . . . . . . . . . . . . . . . . . . . . . Page 220**

| | |
|---|---|
| 1. Brooch | 7. Ochlophobia |
| 2. Epoch | 8. Ochre |
| 3. Hooch | 9. Parochial |
| 4. Loch | 10. Pooch |
| 5. Mocha | 11. Smooch |
| 6. Mooch | 12. Trochee |

**NDA . . . . . . . . . . . . . . . . . . . . . . Page 221**

| | |
|---|---|
| 1. Agenda | 13. Mandate |
| 2. Appendage | 14. Mandatory |
| 3. Bandage | 15. Mendacious |
| 4. Bandanna | 16. Mundane |
| 5. Bondage | 17. Panda |
| 6. Commendation | 18. Quandary |
| 7. Fandango | 19. Recommendation |
| 8. Foundation | 20. Sandal |
| 9. Fundamental | 21. Sandalwood |
| 10. Grandad | 22. Spondaic |
| 11. Mandamus | 23. Sundance |
| 12. Mandarin | |

**ARD . . . . . . . . . . . . . . . . . . . . . . Page 221**

| | |
|---|---|
| 1. Ardent | 16. Hard |
| 2. Ardor | 17. Hardly |
| 3. Arduous | 18. Heard |
| 4. Backward | 19. Hoard |
| 5. Bard | 20. Inward |
| 6. Beard | 21. Lard |
| 7. Board | 22. Leeward |
| 8. Card | 23. Nard |
| 9. Cardinal | 24. Outward |
| 10. Cardoon | 25. Pardner |
| 11. Downward | 26. Pardon |
| 12. Eardrum | 27. Poniard |
| 13. Fardel | 28. Reward |
| 14. Forward | 29. Shard |
| 15. Guard | 30. Sideward |

11. Emotion
12. Hegemony
13. Hemoglobin
14. Hemophilia
15. Lemon
16. Lemonade
17. Memorandum
18. Memoir
19. Memorabilia
20. Memorial
21. Memory
22. Premonition
23. Remonstrate
24. Remorse
25. Remote
26. Remove
27. Semolina
28. Tremor

## EPT . . . . . . . . . . . . . . . . . . . . . . . Page 225

1. Accept
2. Adept
3. Concept
4. Crept
5. Deceptive
6. Except
7. Inception
8. Inept
9. Kleptomania
10. Misconception
11. Peptic
12. Peptone
13. Perception
14. Receptacle
15. Reception
16. Receptive
17. Reptile
18. Sceptre
19. Septennial
20. Septic
21. Septuagenarian
22. Septum
23. Skeptical
24. Slept
25. Streptococcus
26. Swept
27. Transept
28. Wept

## LVE . . . . . . . . . . . . . . . . . . . . . . . Page 226

1. Calves
2. Culvert
3. Delve
4. Dissolve
5. Elves
6. Evolve
7. Involve
8. Ourselves
9. Resolve
10. Revolve
11. Salve
12. Shelves
13. Silver
14. Solve
15. Valve

## OMI . . . . . . . . . . . . . . . . . . . . . . . Page 226

1. Abdominal
2. Abominate
3. Atomic
4. Atomizer
5. Blooming
6. Bromide
7. Chromium
8. Comic
9. Coming
10. Domicile
11. Dominate
12. Dominican
13. Domino
14. Dominion
15. Gnomish
16. Grooming
17. Homicide
18. Homily
19. Indomitable
20. Ominous
21. Omit
22. Prominent
23. Promiscuous
24. Promise
25. Vomit

## API . . . . . . . . . . . . . . . . . . . . . . . Page 226

1. Apiary
2. Aping
3. Capillary
4. Capillose
5. Capital
6. Capitol
7. Capitulate
8. Draping
9. Gaping
10. Lapidary

11. Papillon
12. Rapid
13. Rapier
14. Rapine
15. Rapist
16. Scraping
17. Taping
18. Tapir
19. Vapid

## EVE . . . . . . . . . . . . . . . . . . . . . . . Page 227

1. Achieve
2. Believe
3. Bevel
4. Beverage
5. Eleven
6. Even
7. Evening
8. Event
9. Eventually
10. Ever
11. Every
12. Fever
13. Level
14. Lever
15. Never
16. Peeved
17. Reprieve
18. Retrieve
19. Revel
20. Revenge
21. Seven
22. Sever
23. Several
24. Stevedore
25. Thieves

## LEM . . . . . . . . . . . . . . . . . . . . . . . Page 227

1. Blemish
2. Clemency
3. Dilemma
4. Element
5. Elementary
6. Golem
7. Inclement
8. Lemming
9. Lemon
10. Lemur
11. Polemic
12. Problem
13. Solemn

## AWB . . . . . . . . . . . . . . . . . . . . . . . Page 227

1. Catawba
2. Drawback
3. Drawbridge
4. Jawbone
5. Jawbreaker
6. Lawbook
7. Lawbreaker
8. Sawbones
9. Strawberry
10. Strawboard

## OLE . . . . . . . . . . . . . . . . . . . . . . . Page 228

1. Bolero
2. Cabriolet
3. Cajole
4. Choler
5. Cholera
6. Creole
7. Dole
8. Drooler
9. Golem
10. Hole
11. Hyperbole
12. Indolent
13. Manhole
14. Mole
15. Molest
16. Oleo
17. Pole
18. Polecat
19. Redolent
20. Role
21. Sole
22. Stole
23. Tole
24. Tolerate
25. Whole

## MPO . . . . . . . . . . . . . . . . . . . . . . . Page 228

1. Comport
2. Compose
3. Compost
4. Contemporary

## RAILROAD FLATS . . . . . . . . . . . . . . . . . . . . Page 232

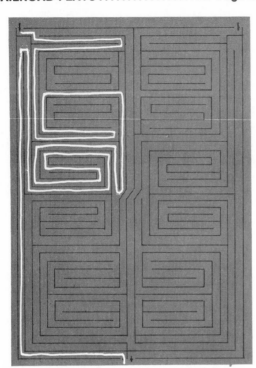

## SECRET GARDEN . . . . . . . . . . . . . . . . . . . Page 234

## INCA STINKER . . . . . . . . . . . . . . . . . . . . . . Page 233

## THE EYES HAVE IT! . . . . . . . . . . . . . . . . . . Page 235

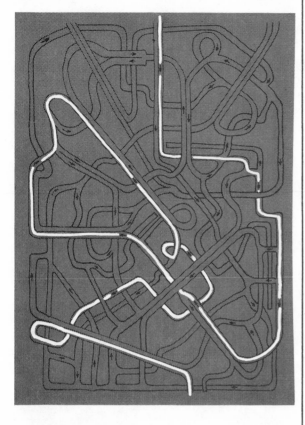

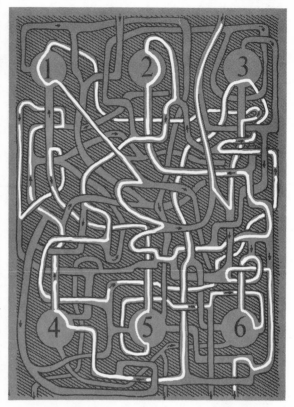

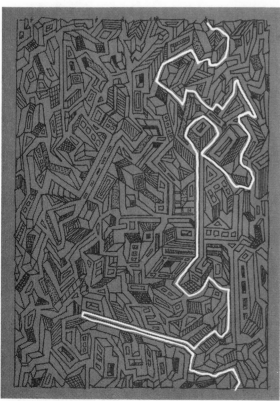

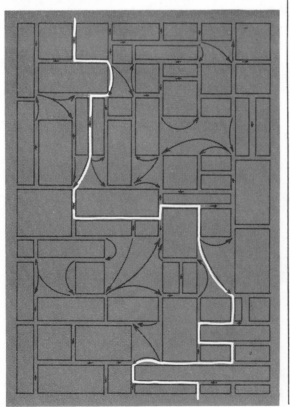

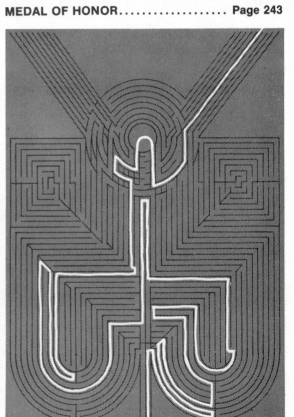

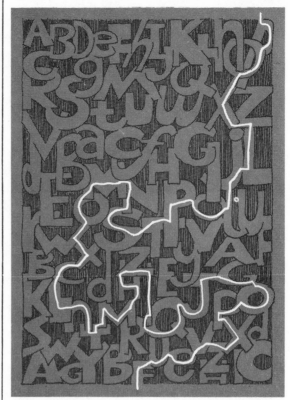

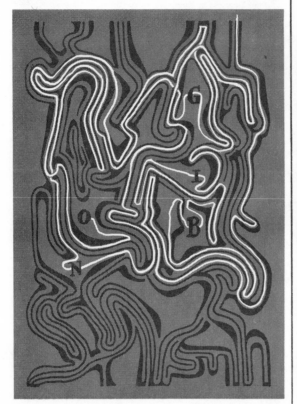

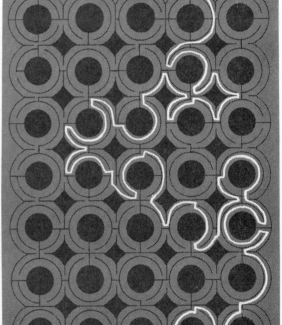

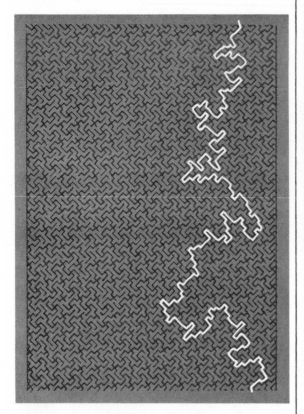

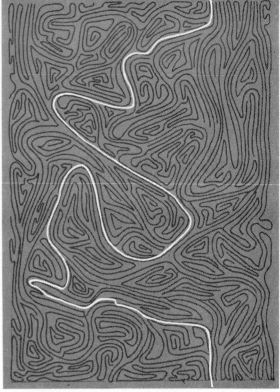

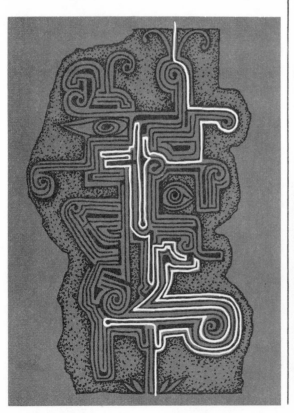

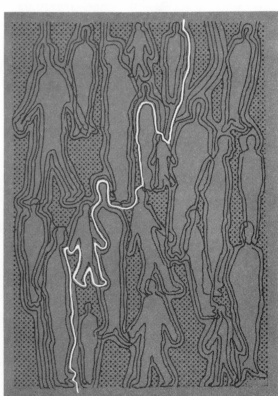

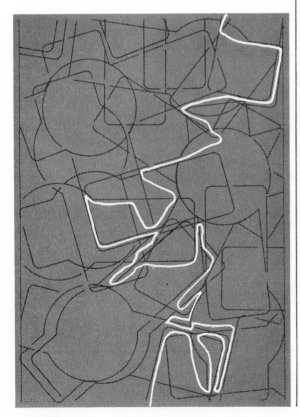

1. Takes, stake, skate, steak
2. Early, layer, relay
3. Chain, China, achin'
4. Owls, lows, slow
5. Throne, not her, hornet
6. Tales, slate, stale, steal, least
7. Dream, armed, madre
8. Tables, ablest, stable, bleats
9. Filer, rifle, flier, lifer
10. Serpent, present, repents
11. Badger, barged, garbed, bag Red
12. Large, lager, glare, regal
13. Grande, ranged, garden, gander, danger
14. Astute, statue, as "Es tu"
15. Chalets, latches, satchel
16. Stripe, priest, ripest
17. Pat, PTA, tap, apt
18. Huts, shut, thus
19. Team, tame, mate, meat
20. Hatred, dearth, thread, red hat
21. Post, tops, pots, opts, stop

(DAVID) VISCOTT
THE LANGUAGE OF FEELINGS

A free person accepts responsibility for the good and. . . . bad in his life. A free person doesn't waste time and energy getting involved in things that can't be changed, but instead focuses on the areas he can affect. . . . He simply defines what his goals are.

| | |
|---|---|
| A | VEDIC |
| B | ISSUS |
| C | SHELLEY WINTERS |
| D | CHACO CANYON |
| E | OPHIDIAN |
| F | THE BAND WAGON |
| G | TARGHEE |
| H | TACONITE |
| I | HAGGARD |
| J | ESTATES |
| K | LEVEE |
| L | APPOSITE |
| M | NORMAND |
| N | GIFFORD PINCHOT |
| O | UNHITCHED |
| P | AMBIT |
| Q | GRIFTER |
| R | EDDA |
| S | OSPREY |
| T | FALSTAFF |
| U | FIFE |
| V | ETHANES |
| W | ERSE |
| X | LASSEN |
| Y | INTENT |
| Z | NONES |
| Z¹ | GIBBET |
| Z² | SENSE |

## ACROSS-TIC NO. 2......... Page 280

ARTHUR MARX
GOLDWYN: A BIOGRAPHY

The Goldwyn touch was not. . . . sheer brilliance or even good box office. . . . It was an ineffable something that had to do with quality, good taste, and honest and intelligent workmanship. It could be compared to a suit. . . . fashioned from an expensive bolt of material.

A  ALICE ADAMS
B  RAFFISH
C  TAFFETA
D  HOOFED
E  ULITHI
F  ROWED
G  MISPRISION
H  ADAMANT
I  RIBBED
J  XENON
K  GAVOTTE
L  OBEAH
M  LEXICON
N  DAS RHEINGOLD
O  WHITLOW
P  YEVTUSHENKO
Q  NETTED
R  ACCENTING
S  BALLOTTEMENT
T  INQUEST
U  OFFSHOOT
V  GATLING
W  REHOBOAM
X  ATTUNE
Y  PONTOON
Z  HIS COWARD LIPS
Z¹ YOWLED

## ACROSS-TIC NO. 3......... Page 282

MICHI WEGLYN
YEARS OF INFAMY

I believed, as did most Japanese Americans, that somehow the stain of dishonor we collectively felt for. . . . Pearl Harbor must be eradicated, however great the sacrifice, however little we were responsible for it. In our immaturity, . . . . many of us believed this was the only way.

A  MARY MARTIN
B  INCISIVE
C  CORDED
D  HORSE FEATHERS
E  IMPERATIVE
F  WHITE WITH SNOW
G  ETHER
H  GIBBOUS
I  LEAVE IT TO ME
J  YEDO

K  NOOSE
L  YESHIVA
M  ERECHTHEUM
N  ALLOCATE
O  RUMORED
P  SWALLOWWORT
Q  OBJECTED
R  FEDERALIST
S  INFILTRATE
T  NACELLE
U  FROSTS AND FASTS
V  APPREHENSIVE
W  MOBILE BAY
X  YOUR WIFE WITHAL

## ACROSS-TIC NO. 4......... Page 284

BOB CONSIDINE
IT'S ALL NEWS TO ME

China was America's problem child, exasperating but tolerated, expensive but endured. If any American, in or out of public office at that time, suspected that one day China would be considered a major menace to the welfare of the United States, he held his tongue.

A  BATTEN
B  OTTER
C  BALL OF FIRE
D  CACODEMON
E  OUT OF FAULTS
F  NIDE
G  STADIA
H  I VIEW IN THEE
I  DIFFUSE
J  IMPART
K  NOLAN RYAN
L  ECCRINE
M  IMPEDED
N  THE HAPPY TIME
O  SEXTET
P  ADJUNCT
Q  LOUISE BROUGH
R  LEXINGTON
S  NESTED
T  ECBATANA
U  WHEELHOUSE
V  SACCHARIDE
W  TEETER
X  OPHIUCHUS
Y  MACABRE
Z  EDWARD THOMAS

## ACROSS-TIC NO. 5......... Page 286

IVAN ILLICH
MEDICAL NEMESIS

By joining together, consumers do have power to get more for their money; changes in licensing and in modes of financing can protect the population not only against non-professional quacks but also, in some cases, against professional abuse. . . .

A   IATRIC
B   VAGRANT
C   ANYTHING GOES
D   NEPENTHE
E   INTRO
F   LOFOTENS
G   LOOKOUT
H   INJUNCTION
I   CONSONANT
J   HIPPOGRIFF
K   MACCABEES
L   EAGER
M   DON BUDGE
N   ICHTHYOSIS
O   COCONINO
P   AFFORDS NO LAW
Q   LINGUINE
R   NOISELESS TENOR
S   EPERGNE
T   MARSALA
U   EMBASSY
V   SQUAMATE
W   IMPOST
X   SPONSON

## ACROSS-TIC NO. 6......... Page 288

(PHILLIP) KNIGHTLEY
THE FIRST CASUALTY

Censors were overworked men in a desperate war. They could find themselves in a lot of difficulty by letting material pass that should have been censored. Their interests and those of the war correspondents were diametrically opposed.

A   KESTREL
B   NIFTY
C   INBREED
D   GIACOMO ROSSI
E   HELLION
F   TREWS
G   LETT
H   EDNA FERBER
I   YPRES
J   TOUSLED
K   HAWSER
L   EVERT
M   FROWN FOR FROWN
N   INTENSE
O   REDHEAD
P   SADDUCEES
Q   THE LADY EVE
R   CONCAVE
S   AMPHIPOD
T   SOPRANO SHAWM
U   UPSET
V   ATTIRED
W   LITHIASIS
X   TENTACLE
Y   YET HOLD ME NOT

## ACROSS-TIC NO. 7......... Page 290

(RAY) OVINGTON
FRESHWATER FISHING

When you are able to cast a dainty dry fly over a mountain stream and entice a trout into leaping at it, there is a sensation that will be long remembered. The bass that bursts out of a crop of lily pads to pounce on your plug will make you jump in response.

A   OKLAHOMA
B   VISTA
C   INANIMATE
D   NABOB
E   GUTTURAL
F   TONED
G   OPPRESSOR
H   NEMESIS
I   FLANNELETTE
J   ROMEO
K   EASTER PARADE
L   SUPPOSITION
M   HITTITE
N   WYCHERLEY
O   ATTENUATE
P   TOSSPOT
Q   EDWY
R   RUTABAGA
S   FOLLOW THE FOLD
T   INJURIOUS
U   SUBURBAN
V   HARMONY
W   IMPLANTED
X   NULLITY
Y   GYNECOCRACY

## ACROSS-TIC NO. 8......... Page 292

SHEPARD GINANDES
COMING HOME

If you are jealous, admit it; it only means you are human. Many parents, unable to admit jealousy, think up reasons for objecting to their childrens' projects. Such reasons are usually detected for what they are. The child feels you are deceiving him and finds ways of retaliating.

A   SOULFUL
B   HEBE
C   ELLIPSE
D   PAAVO NURMI
E   AFFRANCHISE
F   RETIRE
G   DYSTROPHY
H   GARRY TRUDEAU
I   INLY RUMINATE
J   NANTHALA
K   ARMORY
L   NESTOR
M   DEAREST ENEMY
N   ETHELWULF

**495**

O  SACCATE
P  CODDLE
Q  OF JOYS THAT FADED
R  MONKEY BUSINESS
S  INJUDICIOUS
T  NANNIES
U  GYNECOID
V  HAJJI
W  ORTHOSTATIC
X  METHOUGHT I SAW
Y  ETIOLATE


## ACROSS-TIC NO. 9 . . . . . . . . . Page 294

(GREGORY) HEMINGWAY
PAPA: A PERSONAL MEMOIR

That my father would tell me the truth about his mental illness was unthinkable. . . . His act of deception was as much one of love as it was of pride. . . . Nobody ever dreamed of, or longed for, or experienced less, peace than he. He wrote of that longing all his life . . .

A  HUGH CAPET
B  ETHANE
C  MILTON CANIFF
D  INHERE
E  NOT SO DUMB
F  GHERKIN
G  WHITLOW WYATT
H  ADUNC
I  YEDDO
J  POET HIDDEN
K  AMFORTAS
L  PALLID BUST
M  AXLETREE
N  ALCESTE
O  PROWESS
P  EARTHSHINE
Q  ROLLO
R  SCOTTS BLUFF
S  OFFER
T  NOHOW
U  ALGAE
V  LOVE LIFE
W  MAHLER
X  ELATED
Y  MOOSE
Z  OATEN
Z¹  IVES
Z²  RHENISH


## ACROSS-TIC NO. 10 . . . . . . . Page 296

IRVING HOWE
WORLD OF OUR FATHERS

By the turn of the century there was also a scattering of social workers, reformers, teachers, all those do-gooders . . . They taught immigrant fathers the value of knowing how to read and write a few lines of English. They taught immigrant mothers the sacredness of hygiene.

A  IMAM
B  RAMIES
C  VERY WARM FOR MAY
D  INFAMY
E  NORRIS
F  GEOTECTONIC
G  HEIDEGGER
H  ORTHOSTICHY
I  WHELK
J  EFFECTS
K  WITHAL
L  OUBLIETTE
M  RATTAN
N  LEGHORN
O  DEATH TO HIDE
P  OSHKOSH
Q  FANNY
R  OTTAWA
S  UNGUENT
T  REWORDS
U  FEARFUL CHANGE
V  AGGREGATION
W  TRESTLES
X  HOWRAH
Y  ESTHETES
Z  RUTHLESS
Z¹  SONS OF THE DESERT


## ACROSS-TIC NO. 11 . . . . . . . Page 298

(WILLIAM C.) WESTMORELAND
A SOLDIER REPORTS

A commander must learn to live with frustration, interference . . . and criticism as long as he can be sure they do not contribute to failure. I suffered my problems in Vietnam because I believed that success would eventually be ours despite them.

A  WORSTED
B  EVINCIVE
C  SPATE
D  TOMMYROT
E  MUST THOU CHAR
F  OBDURATE
G  RUMINANT
H  ETHICIST
I  LEE TREVINO
J  ABOMASUM
K  NEWLEY
L  DIFFIDENT
M  ALICE MARBLE
N  SAFFRON
O  ONSET
P  LUTES
Q  DEFINE
R  ISOLDE
S  EURUS
T  RECLUSE
U  RAVEN
V  EMEND

W PANAY
X OCCULT
Y RIBBING
Z THESE BUTCHERS
Z¹ SILICATE

## ACROSS-TIC NO. 12 ........ Page 300

ROGER ANGELL
THE SUMMER GAME

Candlestick Park is no supermarket, with its raw concrete ramps and walkways, and its high, curving grandstand. It looks from the outside like an outbuilding of Alcatraz, but it was a festive prison yard during the first two series games here.

A RASKOLNIKOV
B OPRY
C GLOATING
D ESTIVATED
E RUDDIGORE
F AWKWARD
G NOW IS THE WINTER
H GAFFS
I ESPLANADE
J LOST IN THE STARS
K LUFFED
L TRINIDAD
M HEURISTIC
N ERRATA
O SCHWYZ
P ULAN BATOR
Q MOSSBACK
R MITOSIS
S ESPIED
T RUCKSACK
U GHAT
V ATWITCH
W MURMURING PINES
X ENTERTAIN

## ACROSS-TIC NO. 13 ........ Page 302

EDWIN BLISS
GETTING THINGS DONE

Of all the time-saving techniques ever developed, perhaps the most effective is the frequent use of the word "No." The tendency of many time-pressured people is to accept grudgingly new social obligations, new chores at the office, . . . without realistically weighing the cost in time.

A EPIPHYTE
B DEVILS POSTPILE
C WHIRLAWAY
D IMPEDE
E NOSTOLOGY
F BEWITCHED
G LIFE WITH FATHER
H INVECTIVE

I SEETHE
J SQUALENE
K GIFFORD PINCHOT
L ECLECTIC
M THIS OTHER EDEN
N TORQUATE
O ISTHMUS
P NICTATE
Q GUFFAW
R TOFFEES
S HOTTENTOT
T ISOMER
U NAGGINGLY
V GLUCOSE
W SEAMS
X DECOCT
Y OMPHALE
Z NEURON
Z¹ ERNIE NEVERS

## ACROSS-TIC NO. 14 ........ Page 304

(MICHAEL) BRANDER
(THE) VICTORIAN GENTLEMAN

When children were considered old enough to come downstairs to meals, they were . . . served at a separate table with the nurse in charge. . . . It was the widespread Victorian belief that they should not be overindulged. The evening meal would be in the nursery.

A BEDEW
B RICHARD OUTCAULT
C ABAFT
D NEVER LET ME GO
E DOES AWAY WITH
F EWELL
G RESEED
H VERBOSE
I INDENE
J CONECUH
K TURIDDU
L ORISON
M RETENTIVE
N I GOT RHYTHM
O ARNE ANDERSSON
P NULLAH
Q GREAT WHITE HOPE
R EDDO
S NEVE
T TWILIGHT DEWS
U LOWERS
V ETHYLENE
W MEPHITIC
X AND THE BATHS
Y NERISSA

## ACROSS-TIC NO. 15 ........ Page 306

CORNELIUS RYAN
A BRIDGE TOO FAR

The task was monumental, and there

were few guidelines. Never before had there been an attempt to send a mammoth airborne force, complete with vehicles, artillery and equipment, capable of fighting on its own, deep behind enemy front lines.

A CHEROKEE
B OFFENSE
C RHINE
D NODE
E EMIT
F LOWING HERD
G INDENTED
H UPPERCLASSMEN
I SHALL WE DANCE
J REQUIEM
K YAMAMOTO
L AFTON
M NEWT
N ATTEST
O BETTER HALF
P RIFLEMAN
Q IMPEND
R DABBLE IN
S GIVE IN
T ENTENTE
U TABBY
V OVERWHELM
W OPPEN
X FOURTH ESTATE
Y ANCHORS AWEIGH
Z REMIT

**ACROSS-TIC NO. 16 ........ Page 308**

(DWIGHT D.) EISENHOWER
CRUSADE IN EUROPE

Morale is the greatest single factor in successful war. Endurable comparisons with the enemy in other essential factors - leadership, discipline, technique, numbers, mobility, supply, and maintenance - are prerequisite to the existence of morale.

A EMMIES
B IMPLORED
C SHEATHE
D EMMER
E NULLIFY
F HISTORICITY
G ORISONS
H WHEREWITHAL
I ECCENTRIC
J RABBLE IN ARMS
K CONQUEST
L RATCHET
M UNDULATE
N STACCATO
O ABSTAIN
P DEEPEN
Q ETHAN ALLEN
R INSURANCE
S NOGGIN
T EFFRONTERY

U UPPERMOST
V REQUISITE
W OSSIFIES
X PLEIADES
Y EXPELS

**GOING TO THE DOGS ...... Page 320**

1. English setter
2. Mexican hairless
3. Scottish deerhound
4. Skye terrier
5. Clumber spaniel
6. Cocker spaniel
7. Collie
8. Pug
9. Saint Bernard
10. Greyhound
11. Water spaniel
12. Newfoundland
13. Pointer
14. Dachshund
15. Great Dane
16. Fox terrier
17. Irish setter
18. Poodle

**FAMOUS WOMEN .......... Page 325**

1. Florence Nightingale
2. Queen Elizabeth
3. Harriet Beecher Stowe
4. Sarah Bernhardt
5. Anne Sullivan
6. George Sand
7. Queen Isabella
8. Jane Austen
9. Joan of Arc
10. Josephine
11. Elizabeth Barrett Browning
12. Mary Stuart (Mary, Queen of Scots)
13. Louisa May Alcott
14. Marie Antoinette
15. Pocahontas
16. Nell Gwynn
17. Mary Wollstonecraft Shelley
18. Rosa Bonheur

**CORPORATE IDENTITY ..... Page 330**

1. CBS
2. Goodyear
3. Eastern Airlines
4. Mobil
5. Rockwell International
6. Bell Telephone
7. Northwest Orient
8. Olivetti Underwood
9. Chase Manhattan
10. Prudential Life Insurance
11. Pan Am

12. Allstate
13. Am Trak
14. Arm & Hammer
15. General Electric
16. Metropolitan Life
17. National Airlines
18. Cadillac
19. Volkswagon
20. Rolex
21. The Travelers
22. Mercedes Benz
23. Smith-Corona Marchant
24. Westinghouse

**PENMAN'S PUZZLE** ........ **Page 332**

1. Washington Irving
2. Edgar Allan Poe
3. Henry Wadsworth Longfellow
4. Cervantes
5. Homer
6. Rudyard Kipling
7. Henrik Ibsen
8. Daniel Defoe
9. Leo Tolstoy
10. Johann Wolfgang von Goethe
11. Charles Dickens
12. Moliere
13. William Wordsworth
14. Alexander Pushkin
15. Percy Bysshe Shelley
16. Ralph Waldo Emerson
17. Voltaire
18. Dante

**ANIMAL QUIZ** .............. **Page 337**

1. Gibbon
2. Tortoise
3. Lion
4. Hare
5. Rhinoceros
6. Anteater
7. Dolphin
8. Leopard
9. Brown bear
10. Wallaby
11. Wild boar
12. Opossum
13. Chinchilla
14. Koala bear
15. Jackal
16. Llama
17. Armadillo
18. Lynx

**JUGGLING JUGS** .......... **Page 348**

*First step:*
From the biggest jug, which now contains 8 quarts of oil, pour 5 quarts into the 5-quart jug. This leaves 3 quarts in the biggest jug.

*Second step:*
Take the jug that has five quarts in it, and pour 3 quarts into the smallest jug.

*Third step:*
Take the 3 quarts from the smallest jug and pour it into the largest jug. You now have 6 quarts in the largest jug, 2 quarts in the middle-size jug, and nothing in the smallest jug.

*Fourth step:*
Pour the 2 quarts from the middle-size jug into the smallest jug. The middle-size jug is now empty. There are 6 quarts in the largest jug and 2 quarts in the smallest jug.

*Fifth step:*
From the largest jug, fill the middle-size jug. The three jugs now contain the following: the largest jug has 1 quart; the middle-size jug has 5 quarts; and the smallest jug has 2 quarts.

*Sixth step:*
Pour 1 quart from the middle-size jug into the smallest jug. That leaves 1 quart in the largest jug; 4 quarts in the middle-size jug; and 3 quarts in the smallest jug.

*Seventh step:*
Pour the 3 quarts from the smallest jug into the largest jug. You now have 4 quarts in each of the two larger jugs.

**THE SMALL GAME HUNTERS** .................. **Page 348**

Since rabbits have four feet and quail have two feet, the two gentlemen must have shot four rabbits and 13 quail. This would account for 17 heads, 16 rabbit feet, and 26 quail feet. Since four rabbits were shot, and both hunters bagged an equal number, each must have shot two rabbits. Robert claims he shot three times as many quail as rabbits. This means that he shot six quail. Therefore, Gerald shot seven quail.

**LATE FOR TEE** ............. **Page 349**

Mac figured to arrive at eight o'clock. He arrived two hours or 120 minutes later than he would have had he maintained his average speed of 60 miles per hour.

If he had gone along without mishap it would have taken him one minute to traverse each mile. At 15 miles per hour it took him four minutes to traverse each mile. Therefore, he lost three minutes each mile traveled after the trouble started.

Since he lost two hours or 120 minutes,

his car must have been in distress the last 40 miles of the trip. This means, then, that he had traveled 80 miles before his engine started to kick up a fuss.

At 60 miles per hour, it must have taken him 80 minutes to do 80 miles. Since he left at six in the morning, his car must have developed engine trouble at 7:20.

### THE STEEL BEAM.......... Page 349

The ¾-pound weight is equal to ¼ of a beam. Therefore, the beam must weigh four times ¾ of a pound, or three pounds.

### COUNT THE TRAINS....... Page 350

Thirteen trains. Since it takes six hours to make the trip from Washington to New York, the train which is pulling into New York as Tom's train leaves left Washinton at 5 a.m. Tom will arrive in Washington six hours later, or at 5 p.m. He will therefore pass trains which left or will leave Washington at the following hours: 5 a.m.—6 a.m.—7 a.m.—8 a.m.—9 a.m.—10 a.m.—11 a.m.—12 n.—1 p.m.—2 p.m.—3 p.m.—4 p.m. Of course, at the exact moment his train pulls into the Washington station, a train will be leaving for New York. If he is alert, he will also see this one. The answer then is 13 trains.

### SCALING THE ORCHARD
### WALL...................... Page 351

Twenty-six feet. Let $x$ equal the length of the ladder; let $y$ equal the height of the wall. Then, for the shaded portion of the triangle below, we have the equation:

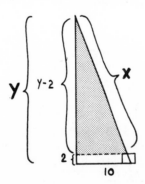

$$x^2 = (y - 2)^2 + 10^2$$

We know that the length of the ladder is equal to the height of the wall. Thus, $x = y$ and the above equation becomes:
$$y^2 = (y - 2)^2 + 10^2$$
$$y = 26 \text{ feet}$$

### THE CYCLISTS AND
### THE FLY .................... Page 351

Fifteen miles. Since the riders are traveling at the same speed, they will meet exactly halfway between their starting points. They begin 20 miles apart; thus, they meet when each rider has traveled 10 miles.

Since they are traveling at the speed of 10 miles per hour, it will take each rider one hour to travel 10 miles. In one hour the fly, traveling at 15 miles per hour, will cover 15 miles, regardless of its path.

### APPOINTMENT
### IN ABILENE................. Page 352

Sixty miles. Let the distance from Poppon's home to Abilene be $d$ and let the time it takes to travel distance $d$ at 15 miles per hour be $t$. Then the time it takes to travel distance $d$ at 10 miles per hour will be $t + 2$.

We now have two equations:

$$d = 15 \text{ mph x } t$$
$$d = 10 \text{ mph x } (t + 2)$$

Clearly, then:

$$15t = 10 (t + 2)$$
$$t = 4 \text{ hours}$$

Traveling four hours at 15 miles per hour, Poppon will cover 60 miles.

### THE STRANDED TEDDY
### BEAR ...................... Page 352

Father arranged the two planks as shown in the accompanying diagram. The shorter plank ran to the concrete island.

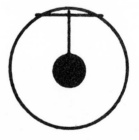

### THE FORTY-TWO BEERS.... Page 353

Who paid for the beers? Why the American, of course! There is no disputing the fact that he paid currency each time he bought a drink. The point is that he increased the value of the currency which he got in return; that is, he increased the 90¢ change he got on each transaction by walking across the border. He added value to the currency by transferring it from one place to another.

**500**

There is nothing more startling about this increase in value than there is about buying an object in China that is worth 10¢ there, and transporting it to America where it is worth 50¢. The American who performed the work of carrying a Guatelavian dollar from Tinto to Guatelavia performed 10¢ worth of work from the viewpoint of economics.

## THE DARING YOUNG MAN.. Page 354

He juggles the balls. This way, one ball is always in midair, and the bridge only has to support 199 pounds at any given moment.

## THE ARTIST'S CANVAS ..... Page 355

The artist's problem can be solved by cutting the canvas into three pieces as shown.

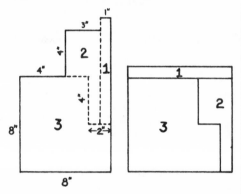

This results in a square nine inches on a side, containing a total of 81 square inches.

## THE EGG MAN............. Page 355

271 eggs.

## THE COMMUTER........... Page 356

The chauffeur, meeting Brown at some point between the residence and the station, saves 20 minutes from his usual trip by not being obliged to proceed from the point where Brown is met to the station and then *make a return trip* to that point. In other words, the chauffeur saves the run of double the distance from the point where Brown is met, to the station. The saving, amounting to 20 minutes in all, means a saving of two 10 minute runs. Therefore, the chauffeur met Brown 10 minutes before he would usually arrive at the station. Since he usually arrived at 5 p.m., he met Brown at 4:50 p.m. Since Brown arrived at the station at 4 p.m. and was met at 4:50 p.m., he walked 50 minutes.

## THE PENSIONER........... Page 356

Ninety years old. Let $x$ equal the man's present age. We can set up the following equation:

$$x = 4\tfrac{1}{2} + 1/6x + 1/5x + 1/4x + 1/3x$$
$$x = 90$$

## THE FRUIT PEDDLERS...... Page 357

The peddlers all had this sign on their pushcarts.

*Apples*
*3 for 10¢*

The first peddler, who had fifteen apples, sold his apples to five customers at three for a dime, thus receiving fifty cents. The second peddler sold nine of his apples to three customers at three for a dime, thus receiving thirty cents, and then sold five customers a single apple each at four cents apiece, thus receiving twenty cents, or a total of fifty cents.

The statement that a sale at four cents each is at a "three-for-ten-cents" rate cannot reasonably be challenged. If you are unconvinced, go to a market and attempt to buy a single item which is marked "three-for-ten" at less than four cents.

The third peddler sold three of his apples to one customer for a dime, and then made ten individual sales at four cents each. He, too, realized the sum of fifty cents.

The same result ensues if we postulate a market sign of "six-for-a-quarter." Here, of course, the individual sale of a single apple would be made at a rate of five cents apiece. The total yield under these conditions for each peddler would be sixty-five cents.

## THE TEACHER'S DILEMMA.. Page 357

Twelve students can be seated in the classroom as shown.

## THE SCHOLARSHIP EXAMINATION ............. Page 358

David won the scholarship with 83 marks. The marks were distributed as set out below.

| | SUBJECTS | | | | | TOTAL MARKS |
| | L | E | S | M | H | |
|---|---|---|---|---|---|---|
| Alfred | 3/12 | 1/27 | 4/10 | 5/1 | 2/13 | 63 |
| Bertram | 1/14 | 5/1 | 2/12 | 4/2 | 3/12 | 41 |
| Cyril | 2/18 | 4/2 | 3/11 | 1/20 | 5/10 | 56 |
| David | 5/10 | 2/26 | 1/18 | 3/18 | 4/11 | 83 |
| Egbert | 4/11 | 3/4 | 5/9 | 2/19 | 1/14 | 57 |

## THE DRY GOODS DEALER .. Page 358

The dry goods dealer takes the piece of material and stretches it along the edge of a piece of paper, marking off five yards on the paper. He then adds the 36-inch width to the five-yard measurement, making a total of six yards marked off on the paper. He folds the paper in half, which gives him a three-yard measure, and then folds this three-yard measure in half, which gives him a yard-and-a-half measure. He then cuts the five-yard piece of material to the point indicated by the yard-and-a-half measure.

## THE SWISS MILKMAIDS ..... Page 359

All the milk cans are manufactured by the same can company, and are of the same size, since all are labeled *No. 10*. But Geraldine's milk can, having a dent in it, obviously holds less milk than the others. Since its cubic content is less, it must weigh less than either of the other two cans.

Molly's milk can weighs most. At the top of the mountain, from where she came, her milk can weighed 11 pounds. On that high location, it weighed exactly the same as Jenny's milk can did in the valley. It is a well-established fact that an object weighs less on a mountain than it does at sea level. Therefore, if Molly's milk can weighed 11 pounds on the mountain, it would weigh more than 11 pounds when she brought it down to the valley. So Molly's milk can weighs the most and Geraldine's weighs the least.

## MRS. ADDEM'S CHILDREN .. Page 359

Let Mrs. Addem's age equal $a$, and let the sum of her children's ages be $s$. We can formulate two equations from the data:

$$a = 3s$$
$$a + 11 = s + 33, \text{ which is the same as:}$$
$$a = s + 22$$
$$\text{Then, } 3s = s + 22$$
$$s = 11$$

The children's ages total 11. Since no two of them were born in the same year, they can only be 6, 3, and 2.

## THE ROPE LADDER ........ Page 360

Five rungs—for as the tide rises, the yacht will, of course, rise with it. The ladder, being attached to the yacht, will rise with the boat.

## BOOTS .................... Page 361

Four dollars and a pair of boots.

## THE LILY POND ............ Page 361

Twenty days. If the lily doubles its area every day, then on the day before it has covered the entire pond it must have covered an area equal to one-half the area of the pond. It covers the entire pond in 21 days; thus it covers half the pond in 20 days.

## THE CAT IN THE WELL ...... Page 362

Thirty-one minutes. In the first two minutes, the cat climbed one foot. In 30 minutes, the cat climbed 15 feet. During the next minute, the cat would have gained the necessary three feet to reach the top. Once at the top of the well, there would be no more sliding back.

## THE PROBLEM OF THE CHAINS .................... Page 362

The cheapest way to make a continuous 30-link chain out of the six five-link pieces is to open up all five links of one piece, then use these five links to join the remaining five pieces. The cost of this chain would be $3.50, 50 cents less than the cost of a brand new continuous chain.

## THE TWO CANOES ......... Page 363

One thousand feet. When the two canoes meet at Point A (*see diagram*) they are 410 feet from one shore. The combined distance the two canoes have traveled is equal to the width of the river.

When they reach their destinations, the combined distance that they have traveled is equal to twice the width of the river.

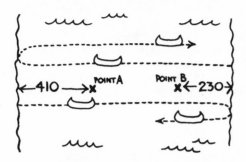

On the return trip, they meet at Point B. Now they have traveled a combined distance of three times the width of the river.

Since at the first meeting the two canoes have traveled a combined distance equal to the width of the river, at the second meeting each canoe has gone three times as far as it had gone when the two canoes first met.

At the first meeting, the slower canoe had gone 410 feet. When that paddler reaches Point B, he must have gone three times that distance, or 1,230 feet. As the diagram shows, this distance is 230 feet more than the width of the river. So we subtract 230 from 1,230 to find the width of the river, which is 1,000 feet.

The amount of time each canoe spends on shore between trips does not affect the problem.

## THE FOUR GOATS......... Page 363

One hundred feet. Before the farmer sells three goats, the area grazed by one goat is equal to one-quarter of a circle with a radius of 50 feet. The area of such a circle is $50^2 \pi$ square feet. One goat, then, grazes over $2,500 \pi \div 4$ square feet, and all four goats graze over a combined area of $2,500 \pi$ square feet.

The remaining goat grazes over an area equal to one-quarter of a circle whose area is $r^2 \pi$, where $r$ equals the length of the tether as well as the radius of this circle.

$$\text{Thus, } \tfrac{1}{4}r^2 \pi = 2,500$$
$$r = 100 \text{ feet}$$

## THE BLIND ABBOT......... Page 364

18 monks

| 1 | 0 | 8 |
|---|---|---|
| 0 |   | 0 |
| 8 | 0 | 1 |

20 monks

| 4 | 1 | 4 |
|---|---|---|
| 1 |   | 1 |
| 4 | 1 | 4 |

24 monks

| 3 | 3 | 3 |
|---|---|---|
| 3 |   | 3 |
| 3 | 3 | 3 |

32 monks

| 1 | 7 | 1 |
|---|---|---|
| 7 |   | 7 |
| 1 | 7 | 1 |

36 monks

| 0 | 9 | 0 |
|---|---|---|
| 9 |   | 9 |
| 0 | 9 | 0 |

## THE COUNTERFEIT COIN... Page 365

Two. The wise man divided the nine coins into three groups of three. First he weighed Group A against Group B. If they balanced, then he knew that each of the coins in these groups were of the same weight, and therefore each of these six coins were made of pure gold.

The counterfeit would then be found in the last group of three. He then took any two of the last three remaining coins, and put one of these two coins on each side of the scale. If these two coins balanced, then the counterfeit coin would have to be the last unweighed coin. If the two coins did not balance, then of course, the lighter coin—the one on the scale that went up—would be the counterfeit coin.

Now suppose that in the first instance, when weighing the two groups of three, one side of the scale went up. It would then be clear that the lighter coin was among this group of three. The sage would then proceed, as stated above, with the three coins among which the lightest one was to be found.

## THE WIFFLEBIRD .......... Page 366

Astounding as it may be, half the foliage was gone no earlier than the thirtieth or last day. Since each day twice as many leaves were eaten as on the previous day, on the thirtieth day twice as many leaves were eaten as were consumed on the twenty-ninth day.

Now the total number of leaves eaten on the thirtieth day was greater by one than the total number of leaves consumed on the first 29 days. This can be demonstrated by merely accounting for (let us say) five days. On the first day, one leaf was eaten. On the second day, two. On the third day, four. On the fourth day, eight; and on the fifth day, 16. The total number of leaves eaten during the first four days equalled 15 leaves, while on the fifth day the number was 16, or one more than all the others combined.

This mathematical relationship will hold true no matter how many days are reckoned. There will always be one more in the last number than there will be found in the total of all the previous numbers combined.

The question is, when was half the foliage consumed? If we were dealing with only five days, 15½ leaves would constitute half of the total of 31 leaves. But since only a total of 15 leaves would be eaten in four days, we would have to wait until the fifth day to account for that extra half leaf which would bring the figure up to 50%. Similarly, in the given problem, half the foliage was not consumed until the thirtieth day.

### THE FISHERMEN . . . . . . . . . . . Page 367

Sixty-seven and one half pounds. When the two fishermen are balanced, the weight of one man multiplied by his distance from the fulcrum equals the weight of the second man multiplied by his distance from the fulcrum. Let these two distances be represented by $x$ and $y$.

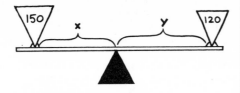

Then $150x = 120y$.

Let $x = 2$ (we need find only the proportion between the two distances, so for now we can let $x$ be any number we choose). Then, $y = 2½$.

When the men switch places, the arrangement looks like this:

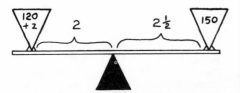

where $z$ equals the weight of the fish.

So, $(120 + z) \times 2 = 150 \times 2½$.
$$z = 67½ \text{ lbs.}$$

### THE VICTORY COLUMN . . . . . Page 367

Two hundred and fifty feet. If you take a sheet of paper and mark it with a diagonal line, as in figure A, you will find that when you roll it into a cylindrical form, with the line outside, it will appear as in figure B. It will be seen that the spiral (in one complete turn) is merely the hypotenuse of a right triangle, of which the length and width of the paper are the other two sides.

In the puzzle presented, the lengths of the two sides of the triangle are 40 feet (one-fifth of 200 feet) and 30 feet. Therefore the hypotenuse is 50 feet. The length of the garland is therefore five times as long, or 250 feet.

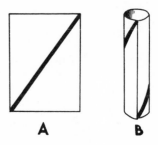

### THE ESCAPING PRISONER . . Page 368

When the guards catch up to the prisoner, they will have traveled the same distance, $d$, as the prisoner. If the time it takes for the guards to travel distance $d$ is represented by $t$, then the time it takes the prisoner to travel distance $d$ is $t + ½$ (because the prisoner had a half hour's head start).

So, we have two equations:

4 mph (guards' speed) X $t = d$
3 mph (prisoner's speed) X $(t + ½) = d$

Clearly, 4 mph X $t$ = 3 mph X $(t + ½)$
$$t = 1½ \text{ hours}$$

In one and a half hours, the dog, traveling at 12 mph, will cover 18 miles.

### THE SAHARA EXPEDITION . . Page 368

The car, of course, has four wheels, so that for a 27,000-mile journey it uses up 108,000 tire miles. Each tire is good for 12,000 miles, and mathematically *nine* tires will suffice.

The real problem is: How can the explorer get through the trip with this minimum number? The first four tires will be used up and discarded after 12,000 miles; one of the five remaining will have to be changed each 3,000 miles as follows: first 3,000 miles—Tires 1, 2, 3, 4; second 3,000 miles—Tires 2, 3, 4, 5; third 3,000 miles—Tires 3, 4, 5, 1; fourth 3,000 miles—Tires 4, 5, 1, 2; fifth 3,000 miles—Tires 5, 1, 2, 3.

Thus each of the nine tires will be used no more than 12,000 miles.

## A CASE OF ORANGES ...... Page 369

Let $m$ equal the number of oranges Mary has. Let $j$ equal the number Jane has, $k$ the number Kate has, and $e$ the number Eliza has. We can then formulate four equations:

(1) $m = j + 20$, and therefore $j = m - 20$
(2) $m = k + 53$, and therefore $k = m - 53$
(3) $m = e + 71$, and therefore $e = m - 71$
(4) $m + j + k + e = 233$

Substituting for $j$, $k$, and $e$ in equation (4), we find that $m = 94\frac{1}{4}$ oranges.

So, the remaining oranges are divided thus: Jane has $74\frac{1}{4}$, Kate has $41\frac{1}{4}$, and Eliza has $23\frac{1}{4}$.

## SMOKE GETS IN YOUR EYES. ..................... Page 369

Six cigarettes. Five cigarettes can be made from the 25 butts. After these are smoked, there will be five more butts. From these five butts, a sixth cigarette can be made.

## NAME THE CARDS......... Page 370

Ace of Spades; Queen of Hearts; Six of Clubs.

## THE HORSE TRADER ....... Page 371

Twenty-nine horses. This problem is very easy if you work it backwards. The trader had one horse on which to ride home. He disposed of the next to the last horse as a trading fee when he exited from the third fair. This makes a total of two. Since he sold half of his remaining string at the fair, he must have had four in order to have had two left. He paid one to get in. So he must have arrived at the last fair with *five* horses.

It's a simple matter to follow through in reverse and figure out that he started business with 29 horses.

## THE CLIMBING MONKEY.... Page 371

The monkey and the weight always remain opposite. The monkey cannot rise above or sink below the height of the weight, for the two are perfectly balanced.

## MIXED BAG ................. Page 378

1. Chicago (O'Hare)
2. 1564
3. Opera house
4. Kansas City
5. Figure of speech
6. Christy Mathewson
7. Photon
8. Bizet
9. Papal document
10. Eagle and lion
11. Zaire
12. Plum
13. Alaska
14. Julius Caesar
15. 1949
16. Amsterdam
17. Taft
18. Cassava root
19. Liver
20. Wind
21. Four
22. U.S.S.R.
23. Achilles
24. Tirade
25. China
26. Historian
27. Coleridge
28. The Netherlands
29. Diacritical mark
30. China
31. Three quarters
32. Bridge
33. Turkey
34. Georgia
35. Pier
36. Green Bay Packers
37. Bogota
38. Gold
39. 1466
40. *Moby Dick*
41. French horn
42. Mollusk
43. Rhone
44. Vehicle
45. Geneva

## LANDMARKS............... Page 381

1. Pentagon
2. Fortress
3. 5,000
4. Moors
5. Angkor Wat
6. Lhasa
7. Houston
8. 2,000
9. Louis XIV
10. London
11. Mayan
12. French citizens
13. T. Roosevelt
14. Suez
15. Colorado
16. Athens
17. Buddhism
18. Ziggurat
19. Circle

20. Verrazano-Narrows
21. Chesapeake Bay Bridge-Tunnel
22. Normandy
23. Great Pyramid of Cheops
24. Simplon
25. 1,500
26. Jerusalem
27. DaVinci
28. Tomb
29. Flavian Amphitheater
30. Gateway Arch
31. Berlin
32. Marin County
33. R. Buckminster Fuller
34. Bangkok
35. Wembley Stadium
36. Galileo
37. Eiffel Tower
38. Santa Sophia
39. Bayonne
40. Bell


**WHEN IN ROME . . . . . . . . . . . . Page 384**

1. Portuguese
2. French
3. Africaans
4. German
5. Spanish
6. Dutch
7. Italian
8. Serbo-Croatian
9. Bengali
10. Aleut
11. Arabic
12. Breton
13. Manx
14. Persian
15. Hausa
16. Catalan
17. Khmer
18. Danish
19. Sinhalese
20. Greek


**SUPERLATIVES . . . . . . . . . . . . Page 385**

1. Asia
2. U.S.S.R.
3. China (Mainland)
4. Vatican City
5. Shanghai
6. Monaco
7. Pacific Ocean
8. Caspian Sea
9. Lake Baykal
10. Lake Titicaca
11. Nile River
12. Angel Falls
13. Himalayas

14. Mt. Everest
15. Dead Sea
16. Sahara
17. Greenland
18. Indonesia
19. Arabia
20. Gulf of Mexico
21. Bay of Fundy, Nova Scotia
22. New Quebec, Canada
23. Grand Canyon


**LEADING LADIES . . . . . . . . . . . Page 386**

1. Vivien Leigh
2. Ingrid Bergman
3. Eva Marie Saint
4. Joan Fontaine
5. Greta Garbo
6. Marlene Dietrich
7. Bette Davis
8. Jeanette MacDonald
9. Ginger Rogers
10. Hedy Lamarr
11. Barbra Streisand
12. Elizabeth Taylor
13. Ali McGraw
14. Faye Dunaway
15. Norma Shearer
16. Mitzi Gaynor
17. Shirley MacLaine
18. Judy Garland
19. Greer Garson
20. Natalie Wood
21. Dorothy Lamour
22. Kim Novak
23. Audrey Hepburn
24. Jane Wyman
25. Maureen O'Sullivan
26. Leslie Caron
27. Joan Bennett
28. Katharine Hepburn
29. Julie Christie
30. Deborah Kerr
31. Lana Turner
32. Debbie Reynolds
33. Sophia Loren
34. Myrna Loy
35. Julie Harris
36. Valerie Perrine
37. Doris Day
38. Judy Holliday
39. Marilyn Monroe
40. Julie Andrews
41. Katherine Hepburn
42. Glenda Jackson
43. Liza Minnelli
44. Claudette Colbert
45. Julie Andrews
46. Greer Garson
47. Jane Fonda
48. Elizabeth Taylor
49. Jean Arthur
50. Liv Ullmann

## ARE YOU A GOOD WITNESS?

1. Second floor
2. Fourth Street
3. At 3 o'clock
4. No
5. No
6. 364
7. Yes
8. The butcher
9. Three
10. No
11. No
12. Yes
13. Ohio
14. No
15. Two
16. Yes
17. Yes
18. No
19. Yes
20. No

## HOW MUCH DO YOU KNOW ABOUT THE AMERICAN REVOLUTION?

1. George III
2. Lexington
3. Fort Ticonderoga
4. Thomas Paine
5. Philadelphia
6. Trenton
7. Saratoga
8. Yorktown
9. Francis Marion
10. *Bon Homme Richard*
11. Paris
12. 1781
13. Cornwallis
14. South Carolina
15. John Hancock
16. New York
17. Thirteen
18. 200
19. Patrick Henry
20. Boston
21. John Adams
22. Pennsylvania
23. Alexander Hamilton
24. Delaware
25. John Jay

## WHO SAID IT?

1. c) Shakespeare
2. c) Thomas A. Kempis
3. a) Chaucer
4. d) Nikita Krushchev
5. d) Ralph Waldo Emerson
6. a) Jimmy Durante
7. c) Franklin Roosevelt
8. b) Neil Armstrong
9. b) John Heywood
10. d) Leviticus
11. c) William Vanderbilt
12. b) Karl Marx
13. c) Cain
14. a) Hamlet
15. c) Victor Hugo
16. b) Aesop
17. d) Winston Churchill
18. c) Elizabeth Barrett Browning
19. c) Richard Nixon
20. d) Mohammed Ali
21. a) Karl Marx
22. b) Harry Truman
23. b) Ebineezer Scrooge
24. c) William Shakespeare
25. a) David Glascow Farragut
26. b) Exodus
27. a) Rhett Butler
28. d) Bob Dylan
29. b) Gertrude Stein
30. c) John F. Kennedy
31. c) Marie Antoinette
32. b) Henny Youngman
33. c) Queen Victoria
34. d) Walt Whitman
35. a) John Donne
36. d) Winston Churchill
37. b) Patrick Henry
38. a) Lady Macbeth
39. b) Greta Garbo
40. c) Leonard Cohen
41. a) Alexander Pope
42. d) Herman Melville
43. b) Will Rogers
44. c) Genesis
45. a) Jonathan Swift
46. b) Colonel Sidney Sherman
47. d) Martin Luther King
48. b) Woody Guthrie

## PASSIONATE PAIRS

1. Cleopatra
2. Ruth
3. Odysseus
4. Juliet
5. Marion Davies
6. Isolde
7. Scarlet O'Hara
8. Louis XV
9. Abelard
10. Helen of Troy
11. Dashiell Hammett
12. Maid Marion
13. Beatrice
14. Orpheus
15. Wally Simpson
16. Guinevere
17. Osiris
18. Jean Paul Sartre
19. Galatea
20. Elizabeth Barrett
21. Roberto Rossellini
22. Clark Gable
23. Josephine
24. Lauren Bacall
25. Ellen Terry
26. Charles II
27. Cathy Linton
28. Priscilla
29. Lord Nelson

30. Edith Bolling
31. Spencer Tracy
32. Zelda Fitzgerald
33. John Lennon
34. Queen Victoria
35. Estella
36. Ingmar Bergman
37. Benedick
38. George Henry Lewes
39. Elizabeth Taylor
40. Daisy Mae
41. Anais Nin
42. Stanley Kowalski
43. Sophia Loren
44. Olive Oil
45. Bianca Jagger
46. Petruchio
47. Thisbe
48. Daisy Buchanan
49. Theodora
50. Rebecca

## CONGLOMERATION ........ Page 410

1. Action
2. Anger
3. Angle
4. Article
5. Camel
6. Canter
7. Cantor
8. Carton
9. Claret
10. Crane
11. Crime
12. Crone
13. Croon
14. Glance
15. Glare
16. Gloat
17. Gloom
18. Goner
19. Grain
20. Granite
21. Grant
22. Grate
23. Grime
24. Groan
25. Groom
26. Lance
27. Linger
28. Mailer
29. Manger
30. Mangle
31. Manor
32. Margin
33. Marten
34. Merit
35. Mingle
36. Moaner
37. Molar
38. Nation
39. Nonce
40. Oiler
41. Onager
42. Orange
43. Ration
44. React
45. Tangle
46. Tiger
47. Tingle
48. Toiler
49. Trail
50. Train
51. Trance

## INCANTATIONS............ Page 411

1. Anoint
2. Cannon
3. Cannot
4. Canon
5. Canto
6. Canton
7. Coast
8. Intact
9. Nation
10. Satin
11. Scant
12. Stain
13. Station
14. Stint
15. Stoic
16. Tacit
17. Taint
18. Tannic
19. Titan
20. Toast
21. Tocsin
22. Tonic

## OPERATIONAL.............. Page 411

1. Aileron
2. Alone
3. Elation
4. Later
5. Linear
6. Liner
7. Loner
8. Looter
9. Lotion
10. Opera
11. Option
12. Paint
13. Painter
14. Parole
15. Patrol
16. Penal
17. Pertain
18. Petal
19. Plain
20. Plane
21. Planet
22. Plant
23. Plate
24. Polar
25. Porno
26. Portal
27. Portion
28. Potion
29. Ration
30. Rational
31. Rationale
32. Renal
33. Retail
34. Tailor
35. Tarpon
36. Tonal
37. Trail
38. Train
39. Trial
40. Troop

## CONSOLIDATED ........... Page 412

1. Canoe
2. Dance
3. Decant
4. Inset
5. Insole
6. Laden
7. Lance
8. Ocean
9. Onset
10. Scone
11. Slant
12. Slate
13. Stale
14. Stool
15. Talon
16. Tocsin
17. Tonsil

## SCHOLARSHIP............. Page 412

1. Chair
2. Chirp
3. Harsh
4. Larch
5. Parch
6. Parish
7. Poach
8. Polar
9. Roach
10. Scarp
11. Scholar
12. Sharp
13. Spoil

## PHILODENDRON........... Page 412

1. Drool
2. Droop
3. Ephod
4. Helio
5. Hinder
6. Hooper
7. Liner
8. Loner
9. Ponder
10. Ridden
11. Ripen
12. Rodeo

## DISCRETIONARY........... Page 413

1. Action
2. Actor

**REBUS GAME NO. 17........ Page 442**

MN + BASKET - MASK -
B = NET

**REBUS GAME NO. 18........ Page 442**

CORN - RN + HAT -
H = COAT

**REBUS GAME NO. 19........ Page 443**

B + RADIATOR - RADIO -
R = BAT

**REBUS GAME NO. 20........ Page 443**

FLAG - L + CLIP + E -
CAGE = FLIP

**HUMOROUS CROSSWORD
NO. 1 ..................... Page 448**

**HUMOROUS CROSSWORD
NO. 2 ..................... Page 449**

**HUMOROUS CROSSWORD
NO. 3 ..................... Page 450**

**HUMOROUS CROSSWORD
NO. 4 ..................... Page 451**

**HUMOROUS CROSSWORD
NO. 5 ..................... Page 452**

**510**

| B | A | N | K | N | O | T | E | S |
| U |   | E | N | E | M | Y |   | C |
| R |   | S | E | W | E | R |   | R |
| L | A | T | E |   | N | O | T | E |
| E | G |   |   |   |   | A |   | W |
| S | E | L | F |   | B | A | R | B |
| Q |   | O | A | K | E | N |   | A |
| U |   | S | C | E | N | T |   | L |
| E | S | S | E | N | T | I | A | L |

511